LOVE AND MARRIAGE IN THE AGE OF JANE AUSTEN

LOVE AND MARRIAGE IN THE AGE OF JANE AUSTEN

RORY MUIR

YALE UNIVERSITY PRESS
NEW HAVEN AND LONDON

Published with assistance from the Annie Burr Lewis Fund.

For information about this and other Yale University Press publications, please contact:
U.S. Office: sales.press@yale.edu   yalebooks.com
Europe Office: sales@yaleup.co.uk   yalebooks.co.uk

Set in Van Dijck MT by IDSUK (DataConnection) Ltd
Printed in Great Britain by TJ Books, Padstow, Cornwall

Library of Congress Control Number: 2023946239

ISBN 978-0-300-26960-4

A catalogue record for this book is available from the British Library.

10 9 8 7 6 5 4 3 2 1

For Robin,
without whom I could never have written this book,
and for so much more . . .

CONTENTS

CONTENTS

ILLUSTRATIONS

1. *Mrs Harriet Quentin*, after François Hüet Villiers, print by William Blake (1820). © The Trustees of the British Museum (1867,1214.710).
2. *A Receipt for Courtship*, by Thomas Rowlandson (1805). First published by Laurie & Whittle. Library of Congress Prints and Photographs.
3. *The Comforts of Matrimony: A Good Toast*, by Thomas Rowlandson (1809). © The Trustees of the British Museum (1871,0812.4497).
4. *Fillial* [sic] *Affection, or a Trip to Gretna Green*, by Thomas Rowlandson (1785). The Elisha Whittelsey Collection, The Elisha Whittelsey Fund, 1959.
5. *Reconciliation or the Return from Scotland*, by Thomas Rowlandson (1793). Yale Center for British Art, Paul Mellon Collection.
6. *The Weddings*, by Thomas Rowlandson (1817). An illustration for Oliver Goldsmith's novel *The Vicar of Wakefield*. The Elisha Whittelsey Collection, The Elisha Whittelsey Fund, 1959.
7. *The Four Seasons of Love*, by Thomas Rowlandson (1814). The Elisha Whittelsey Collection, The Elisha Whittelsey Fund, 1959.
8. *The Arrival of Country Relations*, by Alexander Carse (*c*. 1812). The Buccleuch Collections / Bridgeman Images.
9. *John Thomas Stanley, 1st Baron Stanley of Alderley*, by Isaac Wane Slater, printed by Charles Joseph Hullmandel (*c*. 1828–36). © National Portrait Gallery, London.

PREFACE

A FEW MONTHS AFTER *Pride and Prejudice* was published Jane Austen visited her brother Henry in London. It was the spring of 1813 and among other pleasures of the capital the Austens went to an art exhibition at Spring Gardens, where Jane discovered a portrait that was 'excessively like' Jane Bennet, or rather, Jane Bingley as she had become. 'Mrs Bingley's is exactly herself, size, shaped face, features & sweetness; there was never a greater likeness. She is dressed in a white gown, with green ornaments, which convinces me of what I always supposed, that green was a favourite colour with her.' The author resolved to look for a portrait of Elizabeth, Mrs Darcy, at the next exhibition they went to – 'I dare say Mrs D. will be in Yellow.' However, she was disappointed: nothing resembling a portrait of Mrs Darcy was to be found. Reflecting upon this, she was not really surprised: 'I can only imagine that Mr D. prizes any Picture of her too much to like it should be exposed to the public eye. – I can imagine he wd. have that sort [of] feeling – that mixture of Love, Pride & Delicacy.'[1] It is a rare glimpse of how she imagined the married life of any of her heroines.

Austen's novels always end with the marriage of their principal protagonists, while the married couples whose lives they describe are more often comic than heroic. This was not uncommon for novels of the period, many of which tell the story of a young woman's entrance into the world, her courtship by rival suitors and culminate in her marriage to the right man. In this book I want to examine the excitements and disappointments of courtship, but to continue the story beyond the wedding to include the pains and pleasures of marriage. In doing so I draw principally on the records left by real people – including members of Jane Austen's own family – and supplement them with material from the fiction of the time, which sometimes makes clear the secret thoughts and unspoken assumptions that people left out of their diaries and letters.

Like Austen's novels my concern is with English men and women who were born in the second half of the eighteenth century and who reached adulthood just before or during the long wars against Revolutionary and Napoleonic France (1793–1815). This was the generation of Austen and her siblings, of Scott and Wordsworth, Wellington and Castlereagh; but generations overlap, and I include some members of an older generation, such as James Boswell and Emily, Duchess of Leinster, and some from a younger generation, including Lord and Lady Belgrave and Austen's niece Fanny Knight. As this suggests, my examples come from the whole of the upper layers of society, from dukes to curates, anyone who might be plausibly regarded as a lady or a gentleman. And, like the upper classes as a whole, they were overwhelmingly white and Protestant, usually members of the Church of England, although some were Presbyterians and some were Catholics, and searching through family trees would probably reveal the occasional ancestor who came from India, Africa or the West Indies.

It is not my purpose to advance a single thesis or central argument, to claim that there were more or fewer happy marriages in this period than in any other or that marriage in the early nineteenth century was simpler or more complicated than it is today. It will come as a revelation to nobody to say that relations between husbands and wives at this time were unequal, or that eighteenth- and nineteenth-century Britain was a patriarchal society. Rather, I aim to give a richly textured account of what courtship and marriage felt like for people of this class and time in all its variety, and with an emphasis on the ordinary rather than the extraordinary, and to allow readers to make their own comparisons and draw their own conclusions. And, because marriage cannot be seen in isolation, I will also pay some attention to those people who did not marry, and to those whose marriage had ended with the death of their spouse, although these are large subjects which deserve full-length studies of their own.

This is primarily a study of heterosexual relationships and of love as it was felt between courting couples and husbands and wives. Homosexual relationships and heterosexual relationships outside marriage are touched upon but they are not the main focus, and our sources are too limited for me to discuss them in the depth that I would like. Equally, there are many other forms of love that fall largely or completely beyond the scope of this book: the love of parents for their children and children for their parents; of grandparents and grandchildren; aunts, uncles and other family members; the love between old friends; the love of God, of pets and even of favourite houses and estates – these were often as important, sometimes even more important, as the love for a spouse, but to include them here would make this work impractically long and too diffuse.

The history of courtship and marriage is not a new subject and it has been explored, both in fiction and non-fiction, ever since Austen's day and, indeed, long before. Academic historians have taken a serious interest in it since at least the 1970s when the works of Lawrence Stone and others reached a wide audience and sparked a new excitement with social history broadly, and the history of the family in particular. However, most of these works covered a wide historical sweep (Stone's first work in the field looked at England from 1500 to 1800, and this was not the most ambitious periodisation) and attempted to look at all classes and gradations of society. Too often the outlook and emotions of individuals either disappeared from sight or were roughly manhandled to fit an over-arching argument, while some of the author's own assumptions now appear surprisingly dated.

Research by subsequent historians, including Amanda Vickery, A.P.W. Malcomson, Katie Barclay, Sally Holloway and Leanne Calvert, has significantly advanced our understanding of courtship and marriage in the upper layers of British and Irish society in the eighteenth century, greatly modifying the arguments proposed by Stone. Meanwhile Hazel Jones has brought Jane Austen and her novels into the picture in her excellent and entertaining book *Jane Austen and Marriage*. I have learnt a great deal from all these works, but I approach the subject from a somewhat different angle, and I hope that this book will add to the picture they have drawn, raising fresh questions and contributing illumination rather than conflicting shadows. I have discussed these works and those of other historians in the field, as well as the primary sources that I have used, in the bibliographical essay at the end of the volume.

Because many individuals and couples appear repeatedly in different chapters of the book I have included a *dramatis personae* of the most frequently mentioned figures at the back to remind readers who was who, while previous references can be traced through the index.

The origins of this book go back to my early and continuing love of Jane Austen's novels and my interest in the society of her time, which coincided with my parallel interest in the military and political history of the wars against Napoleon. After spending more than thirty years studying the life of the Duke of Wellington and the role of the British government in the defeat of Napoleon, I turned my attention to the opportunities and difficulties facing younger sons of 'good families' who needed to pursue a career in this period, resulting in *Gentlemen of Uncertain Fortune: How Younger Sons Made Their Way in Jane Austen's England*, which was published by Yale University Press in 2019. The present volume, which is similar in style, scope and method, is intended to complement *Gentlemen of Uncertain Fortune* while giving equal weight to both male and female perspectives. Certainly working on the younger sons has made me acutely aware of the financial difficulties facing many young men from professional, gentry and even aristocratic families, which often made it unwise for them to embark on matrimony until the first flush of youth was a distant memory. Some were prudent and abstained; some were rash and married anyway, and, as we will see, each course could end well or badly. But that is just one thread among many, just as money is only one of the many possible ingredients that make or mar any relationship.

In writing this book I have greatly benefited from all the assistance I have been given over many years working on previous projects, and I would like to thank again all the archivists and librarians, historians and editors, who have so generously helped my research in the past. Some material deployed in these pages was collected many years ago when I came across it incidentally and felt that it was too interesting to ignore, while my understanding of many aspects of the period has been enriched by half-forgotten conversations with other historians sometimes long ago.

Throughout the period I spent working on this book I have been Visiting Research Fellow in the School of Humanities at the University of Adelaide, and I should express my gratitude to the University and in particular to the Barr Smith Library which has – as ever – greatly facilitated my research.

No one doing research into subjects related to Jane Austen need feel isolated, for there is a strong and enthusiastic community of scholars active in the field with the Jane Austen Societies of the UK, North America and Australia producing excellent journals and websites. I would particularly like to thank Gillian Dow, Emma Clery and Devoney Looser for their help and use this opportunity to acknowledge the extraordinary work of the late Deirdre Le Faye who uncovered so much new information about the lives of the Austen family and their associates through many generations. In October 2022 I was privileged to give a talk on 'Those who did not marry: Spinsters and bachelors in Jane Austen's England' (based on chapter 8 of this book) to the Jane Austen Society of Adelaide, and I am most grateful to Barbara Baldock for organising this enjoyable and stimulating event.

I have always been struck by how friendly and generous the great majority of people undertaking serious historical research are, how willing to talk about their subject and assist others by answering queries. In recent years this has frequently been manifested on Twitter, which is often the site for lively but courteous discussions of historical questions, for example the responses I received to a query about the presence of older spinsters in British high society, which I posted in May 2021. I would like to thank everyone who took part in this, and many other such discussions, over the last few years. Of course, there is a darker side to Twitter, and social media in general, and not everyone behaves well, but it would be unfortunate if such behaviour came to be regarded as typical.

I would also like to thank a number of archivists and others who answered my queries while I was working on this book. Elizabeth Finn and Lara Joffe of the Kent Archives supplied me with a copy of Fanny Knight's letter to Miss Chapman, describing her coming out. John Coffey of the Wilberforce Diaries Project sent me a copy of Wilberforce's diary entry describing his wedding. Professor Arthur Burns of the Georgian Papers Programme pointed me in the right direction to follow up a query about Sydney Smith, which in turn led me to the Sydney Smith Society and a helpful response from the Hon. Sec. Sydie Bones. My thanks are also due to Simone Baddeley of the Lincolnshire Archives for helping me chase up a reference to Fane family papers. Pamela Hunter, of Hoare's Bank, sent me images of Cassandra Austen's account ledger, and I had a most enjoyable and informative correspondence with Sharon Lefroy about Anna (Austen) Lefroy and her later life, which was rather less impoverished than I had supposed.

Many people are involved in the publication of a book, and my thanks are due to my agent, Bill Hamilton at A. M. Heath, and to all the staff at Yale University Press, particularly Julian Loose, Frazer Martin, Rachael Lonsdale, and Meg Pettit. Thanks also to Cecile Berbesi who proofread the text.

My old friend Ron McGuigan helped track down obscure information on a number of points, including the history of the 53rd Regiment, which confirmed Mrs Sherwood's account of some of her adventures at sea; while another old friend, Tom Holmberg, alerted me to the story of Mary and William Buckland. Sheila Johnson Kindred (biographer of Jane Austen's sister-in-law, Fanny Palmer Austen), Jennifer Topham (Chairman of the Biggleswade History Society) and Mark Andrew Pardoe all helped in an ultimately unsuccessful attempt to trace the story of Sir John Warren's impulsive proposal back to its original source. Nicholas Blake admirably answered my queries about pensions for the widows of naval officers. Rachel Bynoth shared some of her fascinating research into the Canning family papers, and Louise Carter kindly sent me an advanced copy of her essay on 'Brothers in Arms?'

I would like to thank my old friends who have provided much general encouragement and support for this and for my previous books, notably Charles Esdaile, Christopher Woolgar, Howie Muir, Bob Burnham, Andrew Bamford and Zack White. Elaine Chalus has not only provided me with copies of her articles and much information about Betsey and Thomas Fremantle, but was also kind enough to read the script of the book and make some very useful comments drawing on her great expertise in the social history of eighteenth-and early-nineteenth-century Britain.

Another good friend, Jacqueline Reiter, provided me with a copy of her unpublished paper on the Countess of Chatham and her struggles with mental illness, while also reading this script and providing many shrewd and perceptive comments as well as much encouragement along the way.

I am, as always, immensely grateful for the love and support provided by my sister, Kathie Muir, and her partner, Anthony Psarros, and for their interest in my work.

And finally, fittingly, I wish to thank my deeply beloved and very talented wife Robin, without whose love and support I could not have written this book, and whose comments on reading various drafts have done so much to enhance it. Having spent the last few years reading and writing about marriages of Jane Austen's time, I am more aware than ever how fortunate I am in my own.

CHAPTER ONE

MEETING

LIKE MANY YOUNG WOMEN of her time Jane Austen received very little formal education. At the age of seven she accompanied her older sister Cassandra and their cousin Jane Cooper to board with a teacher, Mrs Cawley, in Oxford, with whom they remained for just six months before both the Austen girls fell seriously ill and were brought home. Almost two years later they went to a proper boarding school at Reading where they remained for eighteen months. When Jane was about to turn eleven and Cassandra was not quite fourteen they returned home for good, receiving the remainder of their education from their parents along with their brothers. This home schooling was rich in literature, history and drama, together with French and music, along with more specifically female accomplishments such as sewing and drawing, rather than the Latin and Greek that their brothers studied. Many girls and younger boys would be taught by a governess, such as Miss Taylor in *Emma*, and although it was more common for boys than girls to be sent away to school, many still received their entire education at home.[1]

Girls generally left the schoolroom in their mid-teens – fourteen or fifteen seems to have been common – although they might continue some studies as well as acquiring accomplishments over the next couple of years under the supervision of their mother, often assisted by a dancing or music master. Boys commonly left school or home and proceeded to university when they were seventeen or eighteen, or began

1

their training for a profession at a younger age: those destined to become naval officers were generally sent to sea at thirteen and fourteen, while budding attorneys and apothecary-surgeons were commonly apprenticed between the ages of twelve and fifteen. The Horse Guards required that an officer be at least sixteen years old when he purchased or was given his first commission as an officer in the army, although this rule had only been introduced in 1802 and even then was bent on occasion. Young men with less need to earn an income might spend a year or more on a grand tour of the Continent, or possibly study at Edinburgh rather than Oxford or Cambridge, which were the only universities then existing in England.

The quality of the education which both girls and boys received varied enormously: in some cases it was extremely superficial with an undue emphasis on social accomplishments for the girls and field sports such as hunting and horsemanship for the boys; while in other families intellectual pursuits were relished, and younger children absorbed both information and an appetite for learning as much from the conversation around them as from their formal studies. Both modern literature and the classics were expected to instil an understanding of the world and of the way people behaved. This, combined with the generally accepted tenets of the Anglican faith in which most children of Austen's background were brought up, would, it was hoped, provide them with a moral core and code of values which would guide their behaviour throughout their lives. Looking back on her childhood, Frances, Lady Shelley, was grateful to the governess who had a passion for the stage and encouraged her to read and absorb many plays. 'I have often since found the knowledge of men and manners thus acquired most useful. . . . Had I not then acquired some knowledge of the world, and of mankind, how could I have steered unharmed through the trying scenes and difficulties of my early married life!'[2]

Nonetheless some young women envied their brothers, either for their instruction in Latin and Greek or for the freedom and independence they would be granted at university or travelling on the Continent. Although she was essentially quite conservative, the twenty-two-year-old Lady Sarah Spencer went further in writing to her younger brother in 1810:

I wish it was the fashion for young ladies to go and travel in the Mediterranean. Why shouldn't I? I am sure most of the young gentlemen who do are much more helpless than any girl, and I am convinced we should manage quite as well, and perhaps *n'en déplaise à vos hautes puissances* [no offence to your high powers], ye lords of the creation, we might derive something more of knowledge and advantage from the journey than is common to the said young gentlemen.[3]

For young women the transition from child to adult was marked by several important rites of passage which we can trace in the experiences of Jane Austen's niece, Fanny Knight. In June 1806, when Fanny was thirteen and a half years old, she was confirmed at Canterbury Cathedral in a ceremony with some 500 other young people. At the age of fourteen she ceased to have lessons with her governess and began to pay morning calls on neighbours with her mother and to join her parents for dessert when they had company: something which she disliked at first, feeling painfully self-conscious. She also began to receive an allowance, which presumably was meant to cover at least part of the cost of her clothes. In October 1808, when Fanny was a little short of sixteen years old, her mother died unexpectedly a fortnight after giving birth to her eleventh child. Fanny then, as the eldest daughter, assumed some responsibilities for managing the household. She 'came out' in 1811, when she was eighteen, along with her cousin Fanny Cage and two friends, Miss Plumptre and Miss Oxenden. They all went to the Ashford ball on 2 October, which Fanny enjoyed 'very much – almost as much as the Races, which were indeed quite delightful'. They then moved on to Canterbury, where they stayed with Fanny's uncle and aunt, George and Harriet Moore (he was a wealthy clergyman, the son of the Archbishop of Canterbury, so he and his wife were perfectly placed to introduce the girls into Kentish society). The four girls dressed alike.

We wore white Crape Dresses trimmed with sattin ribbon & the Bodies [bodice] & sleeves spotted with white Beads, over Sattin Petticoats, the Thursday night, Pearl combs, necklaces, earrings & Broches. We had a hairdresser from Town for the Week, and were all four alike every night. Tuesday even[in]g we had sprigged muslin trimmed with Broad lace over sattin Slips, gold ornaments & flowers in our heads, & Friday we wore yellow gauze Dresses over Sattin, Beads in our heads and Pearl ornaments.[4]

Having been launched into society Fanny was free to dance and flirt, to take an interest in young men and even to receive proposals of marriage. For the daughters of the aristocracy, and young women who aspired to mix in the top flights of London society, there was a further step to take before they had completed their debut: their presentation at court. This was usually the subject of intense anxiety beforehand – both they and their mother, or other female patron, would be dressed in great finery – while the presentation itself often involved hours of waiting in stuffy crowded rooms before a brief and perfunctory introduction to the King, Queen, Princesses and possibly some of the Royal Dukes. However, neither Fanny nor her father had much taste for London or grand society, and she avoided the ordeal until 1835, when her husband's acceptance of office in Peel's short-lived government made it a necessity.[5]

It was not always clear whether a young woman had come out. Early in *Mansfield Park* Mary Crawford puzzles Edmund Bertram by asking him whether Fanny Price had come out yet or not? Fanny certainly dined with the family at home and with the Grants, but she had never been to a ball and her behaviour was conspicuously quiet and modest. Put on the spot, Edmund replied that 'My cousin is grown up. She has the age and sense of a woman, but the outs and not outs are beyond me.' While this testifies to Edmund's esteem and affection for his cousin, his uncertainty – and that of an outsider like Mary Crawford – is surely meant to imply some criticism of the Bertrams for neglecting to make such an important point clear, and, more broadly, for not giving Fanny's position more thought and consideration. However, Sir Thomas ultimately makes amends by organising a ball at Mansfield to mark Fanny's formal debut, something which he has not done even for his own daughters.[6]

For Fanny Price as, no doubt, for many young women facing their first ball, 'she had too many agitations and fears to have half the enjoyment in anticipation which she ought to have had'. Her clothes, her dress and no doubt her appearance generally were the subject of much anxious contemplation, and she would have been much more alarmed had she realised that the ball was being given in her honour. Austen goes on to give a detailed account of the ball: the initial awkwardness as the early arrivals are greeted by Sir Thomas whose grandeur rather freezes the atmosphere; the immediate improvement when the Grants and Crawfords arrive with their ready ease and confidence; Fanny's consternation when she is told by Sir Thomas that she must open the ball by leading the first dance, and how she is capably steered through it by Henry Crawford's polished assurance; her growing enjoyment as she finds that she is gener- ally admired and her hand sought after, and that she still has her two dances with Edmund to come as the crowning pleasure of the evening. 'When her two dances with him were over, her inclination and strength for more were pretty well at an end; and Sir Thomas having seen her rather walk than dance down the shortening set, breathless and with her hand at her side, gave his orders for her sitting down entirely.' By this point it is three o'clock in the morning, and soon afterwards Sir Thomas sends her to bed and she goes, not unwillingly, 'creeping slowly up the principal staircase, pursued by the ceaseless country-dance, feverish with hopes and fears, soup and negus, sore-footed and fatigued, restless and agitated, yet feeling, in spite of every thing, that a ball was indeed delightful'.[7]

Fanny's brother William greatly enjoys the ball, both the dancing for its own sake and seeing his sister's success. He is nineteen, a year older than Fanny, still a midshipman but on the verge of being made a lieu- tenant, 'a young man of an open, pleasant countenance, and frank, unstudied, but feeling and respectful manners', who has seen much of the world and talks of what he has seen with intelligence and spirit. Nonetheless he tells Fanny that if he were attending a public ball at Portsmouth: 'I might not get a partner. The Portsmouth girls turn up their noses at any body who has not a commission. One might as well be nothing as a midshipman.'[8] In part the contrast between Fanny, the belle of the ball, and William, the despised midshipman, is due to the social position and patronage of Sir Thomas Bertram, baronet and Member of Parliament: no one slights William at his uncle's ball. But there is more to it than that. Once a young woman made her debut into society she was regarded as a finished article: a year or two of balls and country house visits might give her added assurance and poise, but only with a commensurate loss of freshness and naivety, and she was as likely to marry at eighteen as at twenty-two or any other age. But young men of eighteen were not generally regarded as ready for marriage; while even at twenty-two they were still seen as rather too young. Most young men, including some younger sons of aristocratic families, lacked a private fortune of any significance, and consequently could not responsibly contemplate marriage until they had sufficiently advanced in their profession to have an income that could support a wife and family. They were most unlikely to reach this point until they were in their mid-twenties at the very earliest: they were frequently much older. But even eldest sons, or those otherwise destined to inherit a comfortable fortune, were unlikely to marry until they were five or ten years older than their sisters were when they had done so. In most marriages the husband was some years older than the wife – something which is still true in contemporary western societies, if not to the same extent – although whether this was primarily due to the preferences of men, or of women, or of both, is debatable.[9]

Certainly society in the early nineteenth century expected that a young man embarking on matrimony would have rather greater experience and knowledge of the world than his bride. His education was likely to have lasted longer and included either some time at a university or training for a profession. Not all those who went to Oxford or Cambridge at the time were particularly studious or interested in intellectual pursuits – John Thorpe in *Northanger Abbey* was a well-recognised type – but even those who neglected their books might pick up a good deal about the manners of society. And manners were a very important part of the intangible signs that defined a gentleman, as Sir Walter Scott made clear in describing his hero in *St Ronan's Well*: 'he bore, in his aspect, that ease and composure of manner, equally void of awkwardness and affectation, which is said emphatically to mark the gentleman'. Admiral Peter Rainier, commanding the East India station in 1805, wrote a letter of advice to his twenty-one-year-old nephew, a lieutenant in the navy, urging him to take full advantage of the opportunity to socialise with Lady William Bentinck, the wife of the Governor of Madras, so as to lessen the 'clownish awkwardness . . . [to] which Young Gentlemen of our profession are so particularly liable' on first being introduced into the 'enlivening society' of ladies. And he went on to encourage the young

man to learn to dance, 'never mind from whom. . . . You may both learn
and improve in it by dancing with the young officers on the Quarterdeck',
assuring him that many good dancers had learnt in this fashion.[10]

Young men might also gain sexual experience in these years, whether
from prostitutes, landlady's daughters, shop girls or a regularly established mistress. Not all did so, and for some of those who did it was a
matter of furtive and unsatisfying fumbling in alleyways or squalid
rooms that left them conscience stricken and possibly with a nasty venereal infection. Others spent a few years indulging in drinking, whoring
and gambling to the full extent that their pay or their allowance, their
credit, their friends and their health would permit. When Thomas
Fremantle, a naval officer in his early twenties, spent a year in London
with his brother Jack in 1788, he described his life in letters to their
younger brother William:

> We spend our time much in the same way as when I wrote you last.
> Jack and a party of us gave a Whores ball at the Barracks a few nights
> ago. I was as you may imagine much diverted and entertained, they
> danced better than any Modest Woman I ever saw, we were just 10
> compleat [sic] Couple and kept it up till very late. Jack goes on just as
> he used to do, that is to say *living fast* but I cannot say I am a bit
> better, neither do I think it is possible to live regular in this precious
> town. I confess I feel more for him than for myself as my constitution
> etc. is in so much better repair.

And a little later he reported that, 'I am now in possession of the Girl I
mentioned I was so much in Love with. She is kept in great Stile by a
d——d fool, and I now contrive to have as much pleasant f——g as I can
lay my sides to without it costing me a farthing.' A couple of years later
the recipient of these letters, William Fremantle, together with his
friend Arthur Wesley, the future Duke of Wellington, was fined £10 and
bound over to keep the peace after a brawl in what was probably a Dublin
brothel.[11] Such exploits were hardly regarded as creditable outside the
circle of the young bucks themselves, but they were widely accepted as
a common, if not inevitable, phase that some young men went through,
and which most then put behind them.

Once a young woman had come out there was a variety of settings in which she might meet potential suitors. The most obvious was at home, where she would meet the friends of her parents and their children. The local circle of half-a-dozen gentry and professional families in a rural neighbourhood provided the immediate society for many members of the upper classes, and a very natural source of marriage partners.[12] The position would be similar in market and cathedral towns, and to some extent even in cities, where families would often mix with a regular network of friends and associates. In these cases couples were likely to have known each other since childhood, while the background and character of both parties and their families were well known, minimising the risk of unpleasant surprises. In some cases the prospective groom would be established in the district already, either pursuing a respectable profession, such as clergyman or attorney, or having already inherited the family estate from his father. Otherwise he might have been away for some years, at sea, in the army, or even just at university or travelling, and would return with an air of worldly experience and enough sophistication to impress a naïve seventeen-year-old who might always have rather admired him.

This familiar circle would be enlivened by friends and relatives who visited them. Tom Lefroy, who was Jane Austen's dancing partner in 1796, was the nephew of the Rev. and Mrs Lefroy, close friends of the Austens, and visited them while studying in London. Nothing could be more natural than a romance in such circumstances, and while the individual was not well known, his local connections could testify to his circumstances and – perhaps to a lesser extent – to his character. The friends of siblings and the siblings of friends were also a ready source of potential partners in this way. School or university friends would be invited to pay a visit and might catch the eye of a sibling, or a visit to a friend might lead to an acquaintance with one of their circle. Here, too, the stranger benefited from a personal recommendation, although young people were not always acute judges of such matters, as is suggested by James Morland's misplaced praise of his friend John Thorpe in *Northanger Abbey*.[13]

Strangers might also arrive in a district unconnected to any of the resident families. They might be gentlemen of independent means, such as Mr Bingley or Admiral Croft, renting a country house for a season or two in order to see if they liked that part of the county; or professional men entering in a district to pursue their career: the Rev. Mr Elton's appearance in Highbury, for example. The generation-long war with France at the turn of the century resulted in a steady circulation of young gentlemen around the country as regiments of the regular army and the full-time militia were posted to different counties, and naval officers looked for quarters on land between spells of employment. Mr Wickham and the other officers of the ——shire Militia appear in Meryton in this way in *Pride and Prejudice*, while in *Persuasion* Anne Elliot first makes the acquaintance of Captain Wentworth when he visits his clergyman brother during a spell ashore.

Friends and neighbours met each other through morning calls, private dinners, attendance at church and a variety of other everyday activities, such as a walk in the country, an encounter at the local shops or a meeting of the hunt. If the local town had a circulating library it was an excellent place for an encounter, whether by chance or contrived. The regular routine would be punctuated by rather more exciting but still very local events: a picnic at a nearby beauty spot such as Box Hill, an invitation to view or take part in private theatricals, or a hastily arranged dance at home to which just a few close friends were invited. More memorable occasions included a private ball given on a larger scale, such as that organised by Sir Thomas Bertram for Fanny Price's coming out, while regular public balls were held in many moderate-sized towns such as Ashford and Canterbury. Public balls often coincided with other festivities, including the assizes, a race meeting or a fair which drew in people from around the district as well as many visitors. There were also semi-public events such as the ball held at the Crown Inn at Highbury, where the open-handed distribution of invitations by Mr Weston made it much less exclusive than Emma had anticipated.

Balls were an excellent opportunity for young men and women to meet, widening their circle of acquaintance and so giving them greater choice in prospective marriage partners, while also giving them a standard against which to judge the members of the opposite sex whom they already knew.

But they also brought the risk of making undesirable acquaintances. This was not just the danger of falling in love with an unsuitable person; once social recognition was granted on the dance floor, it might be difficult to revert to more distant behaviour on discovering someone's lack of status, especially if they were determined to pursue the connection. At a private ball such as Sir Thomas Bertram's, there was some hope that the host would not invite anyone too disreputable, and the guests were likely to be drawn from overlapping circles – both geographic and social – so that an anxious parent might easily be able to discover the identity and circumstances of the young man who was dancing with their daughter. Public balls were naturally less select, although the outright hoi polloi could still generally be excluded, except perhaps for the occasional audacious and attractive milliner's assistant. Such public balls usually had stewards, one of whose tasks was to introduce young people, although they sometimes neglected their duties. For example, at the Hertford ball in 1816, Mrs Calvert was incensed when Mr Brand, a steward known personally to her, ignored her and her daughter while introducing partners to everyone else. 'There we sat solitary. Captain Byron whispered to Walter that it was a crying shame to see her, the prettiest girl in the room, sitting by, and did he think she would stand up with him? Walter advised him to try, and accordingly she did. But not in a hurry shall I forgive Mr. Brand or Lord Cranbourne . . . for not asking her, and I came home completely *disgruntled*, and she looked so particularly well.'[14]

In London, during the season – which was not yet as clearly defined and formalised as it became later in the nineteenth century – the calendar was crowded with social events, both public and private, at which a debutante might attract notice. Of course, the size and prestige of London society meant that competition was fierce: to be beautiful, rich, well connected, confident and charming was scarcely enough to secure success, while ordinary mortals might lose heart at being passed over. Yet many young women, and young men too, seem to have taken it in their stride, especially those who, from their family connections, had every reason to feel at home. The role of the London season as a national marriage market for the elite was widely recognised, if also frequently criticised. In 1789 John Byng wrote of the Duchess of Ancaster that 'my Lady D[uche]ss (like other Ladies), fancys that London is the only Place for a Girl to get a Husband in, and her daughter is of the same opinion'. On the other hand, a generation later, Susan Fox-Strangways declared: 'I think a little of the world [i.e. spending time in London] is a good thing for young ladies to see before they make their choice. It corrects romantic ideas, so natural or pleasant in youth, but anything romantic, or even elevated sentiments, are not of the present day.'[15]

The whole system of bringing girls out into society and marrying them off at an early age was often criticised by contemporaries from a variety of perspectives. Mary Wollstonecraft asked rhetorically: 'What can be more indelicate than a girl's *coming out* in the fashionable world? Which, in other words, is to bring to market a marriageable miss, whose person is taken from one public place to another, richly caparisoned.'[16] George Lamb wrote some verses describing the position of young ladies in the London season in 1807 which include the lines:

And every candid female here allows
How hard a Misses life, who seeks a spouse,
At Operas, plays, and routs we never fail,
Put up, alas! to everlasting sale.[17]

And in 1798 a ladies' magazine printed a fictitious letter purportedly from a young lady:

My papa and mamma have been trying for the last three years to match me, and have for that purpose carried me from our country seat to London, from London to Brighton, from Brighton to Bath, and from Bath to Cheltenham, where I now am, backwards and forwards, till the family carriage is almost worn out, and one of the horses is become blind, and another lame, without my having more than a nibble, for I have never yet been able to hook my fish. I begin to be afraid that there is something wrong in their manner of baiting for a husband or in mine of laying in the line to catch him.[18]

However, we should be cautious about accepting such comments at face value: they were written to shock, amuse or make a point, and while some young ladies were all too aware of the importance of using their brief

moment in the sun to make a good marriage, many others were more sceptical or reserved, neither closing their minds to the possibility of marriage,
nor determined to accept the first half-reasonable offer that came their
way. Most people did not go to a ball, or any other social event, with the
hope of falling in love or finding a spouse at the forefront of their mind. For
many, dancing was a pleasure in its own right, as the eager excitement of
sixteen-year-old Eugenia Wynne makes clear: 'Doctor Harness remained
with us for dinner. He told us that General de Burgh is to give a Ball for the
new year day. These words make my heart beat as if it would jump out of
my breast. Beat for anxiety, wish, fear. I wish to go, I fear not to be asked,
and if I am asked to stay at home, then I hope, then I fear again, and can
think of nothing else. God forgive me if it be a sin.' The following day her
journal records an anxious conference with her older sister Betsy 'about
the gown cap sash shoes we want to wear', although the overriding anxiety
remained whether or not they would be invited. Happily these fears were
laid to rest two days later when 'a herald on horseback (Captain Wyndham)'
arrived bearing their invitation. 'How great was my pleasure I cannot
express.' Her anxiety shifted to the state of the weather, prompted by
heavy rain on the evening preceding the longed-for ball. Fortunately all
went well: 'we danced a great deal and amused ourselves very much . . .
The Ball consisted of 300 persons it lasted till three o'clock in the morning,
after which we . . . returned home very tired.'[19]

Twenty-year-old Lady Sarah Spencer was a little more conscious of
matrimonial possibilities, but they still lacked urgency and had yet to
find a particular focus.

Mrs. Robinson's was a large, good ball. I danced four dances, the two
first with Mr. Robinson, Althorp's friend and a very good partner;
and the two last with Lord Percy, who, being to be one day the Duke
of Northumberland, is of course, the best partner in London, by the
unanimous consent of all the young ladies, who agree that he is the
most charming, interesting, bewitching, fascinating youth that ever
trod with the light fantastic toe the chalked floor of any ballroom in
Europe since the days of his ancestor Hotspur, who I dare say was
reckoned just as delightful by the high-minded, long-waisted dames
of Henry the Fourth's Court. Whether I agree with them is another

question; certain it is that I am as yet perfectly heart-whole and quite happy. We ate a very good supper, and then came home about three.[20]

It was only when a young woman had been 'out' for a number of years, and was in her middle or even late twenties, that she might become anxious at a lack of suitors and look to the future with apprehension. Jane Austen gives us two excellent fictional examples of women in this position: Charlotte Lucas in *Pride and Prejudice* and Elizabeth Elliot in *Persuasion*, and it is worth noting that Charlotte was twenty-seven and Elizabeth twenty-nine.

Thirteen years had seen [Elizabeth] mistress of Kellynch Hall, presiding and directing with a self-possession and decision which could never have given the idea of her being younger than she was. For thirteen years had she been doing the honours, and laying down domestic law at home, and leading the way to the chaise and four, and walking immediately after Lady Russell out of all the drawing-rooms and dining-rooms in the country. Thirteen winters' revolving frosts had seen her opening every ball of credit which a scanty neighbourhood afforded; and thirteen springs shewn their blossoms, as she travelled up to London with her father, for a few weeks annual enjoyment of the great world. She had the remembrance of all this; she had the consciousness of being nine-and-twenty, to give her some regrets and some apprehensions. She was fully satisfied of being still quite as handsome as ever; but she felt her approach to the years of danger, and would have rejoiced to be certain of being properly solicited by baronet-blood within the next twelvemonth or two. Then might she again take up the book of books [the *Baronetage*] with as much enjoyment as in her early youth; but now she liked it not. Always to be presented with the date of her own birth, and see no marriage follow but that of a youngest sister, made the book an evil; and more than once, when her father had left it open on the table near her, had she closed it, with averted eyes, and pushed it away.[21]

Outside the bounds of fiction we find that many single women, even those in their late twenties and older, were by no means ready to accept any proposal that was made to them. We know that Jane Austen herself refused an offer from a younger man whom she liked and knew well when she was just a fortnight shy of turning twenty-seven; and the thirty-three-year-old Frances Poole took a great deal of persuading before she would accept Lord Palmerston's proposal, telling him plainly: 'I was fond of my liberty, happy at home and had never met with that sort of character and disposition that could make me the least inclined to give up those advantages I enjoyed and knew the value of, and to marry as an affair of worldly convenience I ever abhorred the thoughts of, and I knew just enough of myself to be sure that would end in certain misery.' For Jane Austen, Frances Poole and many other women, the disadvantages of remaining single paled in comparison to those of an unhappy marriage, and they resisted whatever social and family pressure they felt to marry unless they were convinced that they could trust their prospective husband, and feel for him the mixture of love and respect which they regarded as the foundation of a successful marriage.[22]

Men were under no pressure to marry early, although eldest sons were certainly expected to marry and father an heir whatever their private inclination. But for most men the knife cut the other way: men who were ready and eager to marry, but could not afford to do so, at least until they were well into middle age. Such men often professed to enjoy the pleasures of a single state, with more or less sincerity; however, it is clear that there were many men, relatively successful in their chosen career, who were frustrated that, in their late thirties or early forties, they were still too poor to marry. Their position was different from that of their unmarried sisters, they had a career to enjoy or endure and were less constrained by social rules; they might even set up with a mistress from a humble background; but long years of waiting could be hard for both sexes.[23]

Not all meetings between prospective marriage partners occurred by chance. Friends or family might deliberately bring a couple together thinking that they were well suited. Mrs Calvert noted on her daughter Fan's twenty-third birthday that she had her eye on a young man who she thought would make her an excellent husband, 'but I fear, should he choose her she will not have him, though amiable and excellent'. Rather less benign was Lord and Lady Sefton's plan to set up Frances Winckley, a very wealthy young woman, with their charming but dissolute and almost bankrupt friend, Sir John Shelley. 'These dear people,' Frances wrote years later without irony or sarcasm, 'had made up their minds that I was the wife most likely to suit, and to *steady* their beloved Sir John Shelley.' They invited her to a party of their own fashionable set to judge if she would do, almost regardless of Sir John's view of the matter. Here her youth and naivety (she was fifteen years younger than Shelley, Sefton and most of their circle) amused them, while she herself was delighted by Shelley, 'perhaps the most entertaining . . . man I ever conversed with'. Her brother warned her that Shelley was a notorious rake who had run through his own fortune and now wanted hers, 'But I knew, by intuition, that my money was not Shelley's object in paying me flattering attentions, although my fortune was partly the cause of the Sefton's anxiety that we should marry, for they loved him.'[24]

Nonetheless there were perils in such match-making and not everyone was as forgiving as Lady Shelley. The most famously successful match-maker of the late eighteenth century – at least by one set of criteria – was Jane, Duchess of Gordon, whose five daughters, none of whom would inherit much money, married three dukes (or heirs to dukedoms), one marquess and – the lone failure – a mere baronet, followed, after his death, by a man with no title at all. The fact that both Jane's own marriage and that of her eldest daughter (to Charles Lennox who became the 4th Duke of Richmond) were conspicuously unhappy counted for little, at least in some eyes; but her maternal activity attracted some ridicule, not least from Gillray, whose caricature shows the extent to which private lives could be the subject of public comment. A similar distaste appeared in Maria Edgeworth's novel *Belinda*, where the heroine is mortified to discover that she is viewed with suspicion by an attractive young man because of her aunt's reputation as a match-maker, and later, in an extremely painful scene, overhears a group of young men discussing her aunt's successes with unconcealed distaste and contempt.[25]

The age of arranged marriages, where the consent of the bride and groom was a mere formality, was now all but over, although there were still cases in the late eighteenth century of young women marrying in order to please their parents, and trusting that their parents would judge better than they could. Such orchestrated marriages seem to have been most common in the higher ranks of the aristocracy, and, by and large, they do not appear to have produced much happiness or fidelity.[26] However long before 1800 it was generally accepted that love was essential to a happy marriage, and that loveless marriages were at risk of leading to adultery and scandal. This led most parents to step back from an active role in bringing couples together, although they still felt free to object to an impractical or unsuitable marriage. In 1815 Lady Caroline Capel expressed this view of a parent's role in discussing her daughter's refusal of an offer: 'I think a *Veto* we have a right to, If Unfortunately it ever becomes necessary, but I am afraid of *persuasion* because if the thing did not turn out happily I could never forgive myself.'[27]

There was less certainty as to whether both parties to a marriage had to be in love with the other, or whether it was sufficient for the passion to be on one side, if it was matched by affection and admiration on the other. In *Belinda*, the heroine at one point contemplates marrying a man who is in love with her and whom she likes, respects and is fond of, but nothing more. The author does not endorse this approach, but the proposed marriage falls apart, not because the heroine realises that romantic love is necessary, but because her fiancé proves to be less worthy than he at first appears. This clears the path for her to marry the hero, once they have discovered that they do indeed love each other. Jane Austen's cousin Eliza Hancock made just such a marriage of esteem when she wedded the Comte de Feuillide in 1781: the love was all on his side, while – as her confidant noted – 'she professes a large share of respect, esteem and the highest opinion of his merits, but confesses that Love is not of the number on her side, tho' still very violent on his . . .'. As the eighteenth century drew to a close it became much less fashionable to admit to such an absence of romantic feeling, although it seems likely that there were still many couples in which there was a marked imbalance of fervour, as indeed there are today, although the taboo against acknowledging it remains as strong as ever.[28]

There was also a strong suspicion of wild, romantic passion – head-over-heels love that looked to others like an unreasonable infatuation based on nothing more than sexual attraction that might soon burn itself out. Mrs Calvert objected strongly to Miss Lee's novel, *Life of a Lover*, because 'the heroine gives herself up too suddenly to love, and too violently for a delicate, well brought up young woman, and when she discovers that he is a married man, I cannot conceive that she is not instantly cured of her passion'. And, writing of the marriage of Lydia and Wickham in *Pride and Prejudice*, Jane Austen makes Elizabeth Bennet reflect, 'how little of permanent happiness could belong to a couple who were only brought together because their passions were stronger than their virtue . . .'. Nonetheless there were some marriages of this kind that proved enduringly happy, where intense passion lasted a lifetime.[29]

For both men and women the ideal marriage encompassed both romantic love and affection, together with respect, esteem and companionship. Few people would have disagreed with Addison's description of the ideal in the *Spectator*, written at the beginning of the eighteenth century:

> Marriage [is] . . . an Institution calculated for a constant Scene of as much Delight as our Being is capable of. Two persons who have chosen each other out of all the Species, with Design to be each other's mutual Comfort and Entertainment, have in that Action bound themselves to be good-humour'd, affable, discreet, forgiving, patient, and joyful, with Respect to each other's Frailties and Imperfections, to the End of their Lives.

More prosaically Matthew Flinders, the navigator, told his wife Ann that: 'There is a medium between petticoat government and tyranny on the part of the husband, that, with thee, I think to be very attainable; and which I consider to be the summit of happiness in the marriage state. Thou wilt be to me, not only a beloved wife, but my most dear and most intimate friend; as I hope to be to thee.'[30]

The caveat was always that the marriage was a happy one, as Lord William Russell wrote to his brother John in 1829, 'You are quite right – there is no happiness like that derived from wife & children, it makes one indifferent to all other pleasures – but then "beware" don't tumble headlong into marriage. Remember when once in, you can't get out & if it don't suit – it is "Hell upon Earth".' And John agreed: 'I will not deny that a man who marries happily is much happier than any body else. But the reverse! & the irrevocable nature of the connexion are most alarming.' It was sufficiently alarming to make many people hesitate, and still more to approach it with some anxiety, only to be swept along by their emotions and by the expectations of society. Frances Poole told Lord Palmerston that in marrying, 'A man undoubtedly risks a great deal; but allow me to say a woman risks still more . . .', but nonetheless she went ahead and agreed to marry him. Courtship was a game played for high stakes, and while it brought much excitement, delight and pleasure, there was also an undercurrent of anxiety, doubts to be suppressed and fears for the future.[31]

CHAPTER TWO

≡►◄═

ATTRACTION

EARLY IN 1794 AN exceptionally handsome twenty-four-year-old Irishman, Robert Stewart, eldest son and heir of Lord Londonderry, came to London to see his dying grandfather, Lord Camden. Stewart was a highly eligible bachelor, with polished manners, keen intelligence and excellent political connections. He had been educated at St John's College, Cambridge and travelled on the Continent, including a visit to Paris in 1791 where he had observed the proceedings of the National Assembly. He was already seen as a rising young man in the Irish parliament, where he steered a line independent of both the government and the Whigs, although he was already sympathetic to Pitt's government in London. Soon after his arrival in England, Stewart met Lady Amelia (Emily) Hobart, the half-sister of Lord Buckinghamshire. She was twenty-two years old and, according to one observer, 'a fine, comely, good-humoured, playful (not to say romping) piece of flesh', and it is clear that she was full of life, vivacity and spirits. The connection between the two was immediate: Stewart fell deeply and irrevocably in love, and his feelings were reciprocated. Soon he was writing to her, 'tell me you love me, on that my existence depends, and I never can grow tired of hearing it'. In worldly terms the match was eminently suitable: as the only child of the late Lord Buckinghamshire's second marriage, Lady Emily had inherited a substantial fortune, while her family already had connections in Ireland. However, the bond between them was deeply personal and enduring. Stewart's mother had died when he was just a year old, and while he got on well with his father, stepmother and half-siblings, it is possible that Emily's love assuaged insecurities that were concealed beneath his calm, reserved manner, while her vitality and good nature helped loosen his stiffness. During their courtship he told her, 'You have given repose to all my disquietudes and opened prospects of happiness which give me a new interest in life.' With no obstacles to overcome, their courtship was swift: they were betrothed before Lord Camden died on 18 April and were married at St George's, Hanover Square, on 9 June 1794. Two years later Stewart's father was elevated to an earldom and Stewart was styled by the secondary title Viscount Castlereagh, the name by which he is remembered as one of the leading British statesmen of the first part of the nineteenth century and one of her greatest foreign ministers.[1]

Few people fell in love as precipitately as Robert Stewart, although many couples married after a courtship of six or nine months, untroubled by the misunderstandings and mistakes needed for narrative tension in a novel. The experiences of Maria Josepha Holroyd make falling in love with the right man appear quite simple and easy. In October 1795 she stayed with friends in Brighton and went to a ball there, although not with 'any great Expectations of pleasure'.

> I danced before Supper with Mr. Stanley of whom I think you have heard before. He was here for a couple of days not long ago and I had the Good Fortune to have him as my Supper Partner. His conversation is of such a different sort to that of young men in general, and we conversed upon such a variety of subjects, that I never passed two or three hours at a Ball more pleasantly, and my ci-devant Flirt Mr. Miller with whom I danced afterwards seemed considerably lessened in my eyes by comparison. We returned home at five o'clock.[2]

Among other things, she and John Stanley talked of books and he recommended the *Vie de Madame Roland* in such warm terms that 'I was very near setting off from the Ballroom to get it.' At this he grew alarmed and suggested that she get her father to 'point out the Passages worth reading'. Her father, Lord Sheffield, was an open-minded man of letters, friend and patron of Edward Gibbon, the renowned historian, but more likely to use his daughter as his secretary than to act as her censor. She replied, 'very prettily that Milord had many avocations both public and private, and that Milord instead of reading, particularly as his eyes were not very good, liked to be read to, etc. etc.' This forced Stanley to confess that some people would think the book rather unsuitable reading for an unmarried young woman, and that although 'if I was his sister, he should say, "Read the book and no harm will come to you; but that it would not sound the thing to talk of the work and quote Mr Stanley for the person who recommended it."' Intrigued she soon obtained the volume and devoured it, reporting to her aunt that '[I] do not feel much corrupted' and that there was nothing improper or indelicate in the book, but that the author 'gives a minute account of all her feelings, and the dawning and progress of her opening mind. As she is thoroughly "naïve", her descriptions may be of such a nature as a gentleman would not exactly chuse to put into a Lady's hand, at the same time that the mind and heart will remain as pure as before the perusal. Now do get it if you possibly can . . . .' When she goes on to recommend with fewer reservations 'Mrs Wollstonecroft's [sic] "Vindication of the Rights of Women [sic]"', observing that it contains 'many sensible and just observations', we get a sense that she had grown up in a family where intellectual arguments were not too constrained by the dictates of convention. It is not surprising that she found the average young man she met at a ball, or even her old flirt Mr Miller, rather dull, or that her interest was piqued by Mr Stanley when she met him.[3]

So who was John Stanley? Six months later, when they had become engaged, she told an old friend that:

He is eldest Son to Sir John Stanley, Bart., of Cheshire, has been in Iceland, published an account thereof, has translated a Poem from the German called Leonora – with considerable additions of his own, is, for anything I know to the contrary, an F.R.S. [he was], and what is more, has the most amiable feeling heart I believe a Man can be possessed of, and what is still more, if faith is to be put in Words Actions and Looks – loves me with the most perfect Love.[4]

He was four years older than Maria Holroyd, and a captain in the Cheshire Militia: he was serving with his regiment at Bexhill when he made the acquaintance of Lord Sheffield's family and went to the ball at Brighton where he made such an impression on Maria. He was sufficiently wealthy to have 'a house of his own furnished in Lower Brook Street, which is a very nice part of the Town'.

> As to a description of the outside of the Man you perhaps would not be enchanted with his first appearance. He is very dark, black eyebrows that meet, and very near-sighted, but he has a sensible and good-humoured countenance, at least I think so, because I know he is both, but all that is of so little consequence I should have forgot to mention whether he was fair or dark, if you had not asked among your other enquiries.[5]

Few people were as high-minded as Maria Holroyd claimed to be, and there is no doubt that many young men and women were first attracted to each other by their appearance. Regency fashions were extremely elegant but also unforgiving, accentuating a 'good' figure while doing little to conceal imperfections. According to Hilary Davidson, the leading modern authority on the subject, the ideal male figure of the period was based on ancient Greek and Roman statues, with strong, wide shoulders, a flat stomach and relatively narrow hips forming an inverted triangle. Tailors struggled to make up the deficiencies of nature, and portrait painters such as Lawrence flattered their subjects by accentuating the similarities, although for some figures, including that of the Prince Regent himself, improvement was beyond the power of human skill.[6]

For young women, the most conventional form of beauty was 'Tall, womanly, full-formed and fair, like the fictional Bertram sisters [in *Mansfield Park*]'. Fair skin and colouring was admired in both men and women: Byron was proud of his 'alabaster skin', while a tan suggested exposure to the sun that – in a young women – might signal immodesty and perhaps even licentiousness.[7] Youth was certainly important, again especially for women, although the Prince famously preferred women who were, or were old enough to be, grandmothers, and built on a generous scale. Indeed, the old jibe about mutton dressed as lamb appears to have originated in his remark, when asked to admire a girl at a concert, '"Girl!" answered he, "Girls are not to my taste. I don't like lamb; but mutton dressed like lamb!"'[8]

Men could – and did – comment openly on the appearance of women, sometimes making crude 'jokes' to other men, and sometimes with hardly greater delicacy, to the women themselves. Other remarks were less offensive but still conveyed that it was important that a young woman's appearance should be pleasing. Jane Austen tells us that, as Catherine Morland grew up, she might overhear her father and mother remark to each other that '"Catherine grows quite a good-looking girl, – she is almost pretty today" . . . and how welcome were the sounds! To look *almost* pretty, is an acquisition of higher delight to a girl who has been looking plain the first fifteen years of her life, than a beauty from her cradle can ever receive.'[9]

Women, especially young unmarried women, were generally more restrained. Even Lady Penelope Pennyfeather, in Scott's *St Ronan's Well*, who was neither young nor unmarried, is clear on what she might and might not say with propriety. '"I did not say handsome, Maria," replied her ladyship, "ladies never say men are handsome – I only said he looked genteel and interesting."'[10] It is unlikely that young ladies discussing potential partners at a ball or in society in Bath, Brighton or London were always so proper among themselves, while they could always convey their meaning through less direct language.

There was more, much more, to appearance than physical attributes, of course, and the clothes someone wore, the confidence with which they wore them and held themselves, and their general manner and demeanour must often have counted for more than their natural beauty or lack thereof. Henry Crawford, in *Mansfield Park*, was not handsome; indeed, when the Bertram sisters first saw him they declared him to be absolutely plain, although gentlemanly and with a pleasing address. 'The second meeting proved him not so very plain; he was plain, to be sure, but then he had so much countenance, and his teeth were so good, and he was so well made, that one soon forgot he was plain; and after a third interview, after dining in company at the parsonage, he was no longer allowed to be called so by any body. He was, in fact, the most agreeable young man the sisters had ever known. . . .' In a similar vein Harriet Arbuthnot conceded that her step-daughter Caroline was 'not pretty', 'but she is so lady like & so very amiable, I cannot help hoping she is as likely to do well & marry happily as many girls who may have more personal beauty than she has'. And although Jane Austen remarked that few men were consciously aware of or influenced by the texture of the muslin worn by a young woman, or whether it was sprigged or spotted, she also conceded that a man would expect the object of his attention to be dressed with neatness and propriety. As Davidson remarks, 'the gentry could not be entirely out of fashion. The old paradox is that women must know about fashion to eschew its excesses; men to assess the degree to which the woman they admire keeps up with but is not overtaken by it. . . . Many agreed that it was important to be well and respectably dressed for one's station, standing out neither in excessive originality nor ostentatious neglect of garments.'[11]

Other personal attributes might also make an early, if not quite so immediate, impression. Maria Holroyd was attracted by John Stanley's conversation, and while they were an unusually intellectual couple, it was not uncommon for lively and amusing talk to make people enjoy each other's company. When Catherine Morland was introduced to Henry Tilney by the Master of Ceremonies in the Lower Assembly Rooms in Bath, her first impression was of 'a pleasing countenance, [and] a very intelligent and lively eye', but the real damage was done when: 'He talked with fluency and spirit – and there was an archness and pleasantry in his manner which interested, though it was hardly under-stood by her.' We may presume that Henry Tilney also danced well, and this would certainly be an important recommendation for many young women; while men who danced conspicuously badly would be at a disad-vantage.[12]

But if it was Henry's conversation that enchanted Catherine, it was that very enchantment that made Henry fall in love with her. When they danced or were having supper, Catherine listened 'with sparkling eyes to every thing he said; and, in finding him irresistible, becoming so herself'. Austen makes the point even more explicitly at the end of the novel in characteristic style:

Henry was now sincerely attached to her, though he felt and delighted in all the excellencies of her character, and truly loved her society, I must confess that his affection originated in nothing better than gratitude, or, in other words, that a persuasion of her partiality for him had been the only cause of giving her a serious thought. It is a new circumstance in romance, I acknowledge, and dreadfully derogatory of a heroine's dignity; but if it be as new in common life, the credit of a wild imagination will at least be all my own.[13]

But while most courtships fed on a growing confidence in reciprocal admiration and attraction, young ladies were meant to be very cautious in signalling their interest, and certainly never take the initiative. When, in Maria Edgeworth's novel *Belinda*, the eccentric Mrs Freke asks 'why, when a woman likes a man, does she not go and tell him so honestly', the heroine is too surprised and abashed to answer the outrageous suggestion, and it is left to her wise and virtuous friend Mrs Percival to respond, 'because if she be a woman of sense, she knows that by such a step she would disgust the object of her affection'. And Maria Holroyd's Aunt Serena cautions her niece, 'you should never show feelings you ought not to express. The Man who thinks of a Wife is, believe me, a very strict observer, however he may seem enamoured.'[14] On the other hand, a young woman could not afford to be too reserved. In *Pride and Prejudice* Charlotte Lucas warns Elizabeth that Jane hides her feelings for Mr Bingley all too well:

If a woman conceals her affection with the same skill from the object of it, she may lose the opportunity of fixing him; and it will then be but poor consolation to believe the world equally in the dark. There is so much of gratitude or vanity in almost every attachment, that it is not safe to leave any to itself. We can all *begin* freely – a slight preference is natural enough; but there are very few of us who have heart enough to be really in love without encouragement. In nine cases out of ten, a woman had better shew *more* affection than she feels. Bingley likes your sister undoubtedly; but he may never do more than like her, if she does not help him on.[15]

The reader is not necessarily meant to agree with Charlotte, but the sequel proves that she is right: Mr Darcy is not convinced that Jane is truly in love with Bingley, and Bingley himself is so unsure that he allows his friend to persuade him to abandon the courtship and leave Netherfield. In the world of the novel everything comes right in the end, but readers would have been well aware that reality was seldom as neat or satisfying as fiction.

Yet if a woman responded too openly to the attentions of a potential suitor she risked humiliation if he then backed away without making a proposal. Pride as much a propriety dictated a measured response, whatever the strength of her actual feelings. When Sir John Shelley began courting the young Frances Winckley, her brother and all her friends strongly opposed his suit, knowing his reputation and fearing that he would make her a bad husband. She had, however, fallen in love with him, but concealed her feelings from everyone while discouraging other suitors. 'Quizzing was the fashion of that day, and I had much to endure and to parry, for I would not allow my friends to think that I had the slightest thoughts of marrying Sir John Shelley.' Possibly because of this lack of encouragement, the London season ended and she left town in early June without Sir John declaring himself, and she fully expected that the excitements of the summer and autumn, the race meeting at Newmarket and the shooting that would follow, would drive her out of his mind. So when she left London, 'I never expected to see Sir John Shelley again. My sole consolation was, that I had never given him any cause to suspect the impression which he had made upon me.' It was not easy for a young woman, especially one with little experience of the world, to judge how far to respond to the apparent interest of a man without going so far as to risk humiliation or heartbreak if he backed off. Besides, she would often have been unsure of her own feelings: attracted, but not yet in love, and reluctant to become entangled until she was sure that his interest was something more than a passing fancy.[16]

Personal qualities and mutual attraction were not all that counted in making a marriage: the other party had to be 'suitable'. When a young woman mixed in company it was the responsibility of her parents and chaperones to protect her from adventurers, and also from charming but impoverished young men who, without meaning any harm, might arouse hopes and emotions that could only lead to disappointment and misery. For example, when Catherine Morland was introduced to Henry Tilney, Mr Allen, her chaperone's husband, promptly made enquiries and was satisfied to find that he was a clergyman from a very respectable family in Gloucestershire and so was perfectly suitable at least as a common acquaintance. If the friendship developed Mr Allen might feel the need to investigate a little further, to confirm the information he had received and perhaps to add some further details. The danger of relying on casual intelligence is illustrated by the way Henry's father, General Tilney, was misled, first by John Thorpe's exaggerated account of Catherine's wealth and prospects, and later by his equally exaggerated account of her poverty.[17]

The most obvious criteria for suitability were money and social status. Although these often went in tandem there was no absolute link between them: some lords and many of their daughters and younger sons were poor, and not all rich men had titles or were even well born. And while both qualities were generally thought desirable, they might be weighed differently according to personal views and circumstances: for some people birth and family connections were paramount, for others possession of a good fortune was the priority, but very few people were indifferent to either.

The heroes of all Jane Austen's novels are either country gentlemen of independent fortune, like Mr Darcy and Mr Knightley, or belong to one of the few professions in which a gentleman might work without losing status: the clergy, like Henry Tilney and Edmund Bertram, or the navy, like Captain Wentworth. Other acceptable careers included the army, the law and, with some reservations, medicine, banking and some other branches of commerce, although in all these cases it was desirable that there be a good family in the background, or at least that a young man had the address and manners of a gentleman, together with some degree of professional success. A handsome young lieutenant-colonel in the army with an assured air was a very different thing from a middle-aged captain whose lack of promotion showed that he lacked the money to buy, or the influence to be given, his next step up the hierarchy.

Many families among the gentry and in the gentlemanly professions had a connection with the aristocracy. Jane Austen's mother was the granddaughter of the sister of the 1st Duke of Chandos, and her brother James's first wife was granddaughter of the Duke of Ancaster, but this gave them no special distinction, nor any useful social or professional connections. Austen parodies an attempt to build too much on such tenuous ties in her depiction of the way in which Sir Walter Elliot and his daughter Elizabeth pursued the dowager Viscountess Dalrymple and her daughter the Hon. Miss Carteret in *Persuasion*.[18]

The immediate members of aristocratic families certainly had an added social cachet, but younger sons in particular often lacked the income to marry a woman who did not have a handsome fortune of her own, as Colonel Fitzwilliam, the younger son of a viscount, explained to Elizabeth Darcy in *Pride and Prejudice*. In fact one-third of the younger sons of peers never married, more than twice the proportion of their eldest brothers.[19] And where money was not a bar to marriage, there was a marked tendency for members of aristocratic families to marry each other. A detailed study of the marriage patterns of British aristocracy by Kimberly Schutte shows that in the late eighteenth and early nineteenth century, just over half of all the daughters of peers who married chose as their partner peers or the sons of peers. An unknown, but not insignificant number of the remainder married the nephews or other family connections of a lord, while others (one in eight of all those who married) married knights or baronets. Not surprisingly this tendency was most marked in the highest reaches of the peerage, in the daughters of dukes and marquesses, while there is also evidence that new arrivals to the peerage took several generations to be fully accepted, their daughters being more likely to marry the sons of other new arrivals in the meantime. How much this reflected active snobbery, and how much simply established social and family networks, seems an open question, although overt pride in rank and lineage for their own sake was more likely to attract ridicule than admiration.[20]

Although many younger sons – and eldest sons too, when an estate was poor or encumbered by debt – dreamt of solving their financial problems by marrying an heiress, purely mercenary marriages were generally viewed with disapproval, and almost any marriage where there was a very marked disparity of fortune or social position might be viewed with some scepticism: was the less prosperous partner really marrying for love or to better their circumstances? However, it was just as unwise to ignore financial considerations completely: for a couple to marry, and in all probability to go on to have a large family, without the income to support it, was regarded as reckless and irresponsible. 'Love in a cottage' was all very well for two healthy young people to contemplate in an idealised abstract, but everyone knew that the reality would be very different, and that poverty and pregnancy were a dangerous combination. Nonetheless many young couples made 'foolish' marriages, generally in the hope that their circumstances would soon improve, with inevitably mixed results. The case of Captain Wentworth and Anne Elliot in the backstory to *Persuasion* expresses the dilemma well: should she have accepted his first, ardent proposal or followed the prudent advice of Lady Russell? There was no shortage of passion on either side, nor esteem and mutual respect: the sole question was whether to trust that Wentworth's confidence in his ability to make his fortune in a dangerous and uncertain profession would be fulfilled, or risk losing forever the chance of marrying the man she truly loved. As we know, Anne accepted Lady Russell's advice, but came to believe that the advice itself had been mistaken, but it is easy to understand both points of view. Jane Austen's own brother Charles had been in a very similar position to the young Captain Wentworth when he proposed to Fanny Palmer in Bermuda in 1807. She accepted him and they were married quite happily, but fortune did not shine on Charles as it did on Captain Wentworth, and the young family were forced to live in cramped and unhealthy conditions when they returned to England in 1811, and Fanny died in childbirth three years later.[21]

To be more specific, a couple who married with an assured income of less than £500 a year from all sources (his profession, any private fortune he had, her marriage settlement) were skating on thin ice. However, the half-pay for a post of captain in the navy was much lower than this: between £128 and £220 a year (according to seniority) before 1814, when it was raised to between £190 and £270; figures which had led the

Naval Chronicle to declare in 1805 that the half-pay of a captain 'will not allow him to support his station in life'. And even during the war a great many naval officers were on half-pay, for there were far more captains and admirals than commands available to them. The situation was no better in the army: a lieutenant-colonel's half-pay was only £200 after it had been increased in 1814, and it was determined by regimental not army rank, a distinction which disadvantaged officers who had been promoted on active service. The importance of some private income in making ends meet is obvious.[22]

Country gentlemen with substantial landed estates might have much larger incomes than all but the most fortunate men in the professions. Jane Austen's brother Edward, who was made heir to the Knight estates at Godmersham in Kent and Chawton in Sussex, had an income of about £8,000 a year, while in *Pride and Prejudice* Mr Darcy's income was said to be £10,000, enough for a house in London and many luxuries and comforts in life. A soldier or a sailor might gain such an income only with extreme good fortune: a naval captain who took an exceptionally valuable prize, or the admiral on a station where there were many such prizes. A top London barrister might have an income of £10,000, at least for a time, and the holders of some of the best paid government offices (some of them life-long sinecures) might reap comparable benefits, although such positions tended to be given to those who already had large incomes. Some aristocrats and a few commoners were even richer: Lord Aberdeen had an income of £16,000 or £17,000 and this was dwarfed by John Lambton, Lord Durham, who once remarked that 'he considered £40,000 a year a moderate income – such a one as a man *might jog on with*'. At least a dozen members of the Commons between 1790 and 1820 had incomes of over £50,000 a year, while Sir Robert Peel, the father of the future prime minister, made a fortune estimated at about £1.5 million (suggesting an income of not less than £75,000 a year).[23]

Great wealth certainly had an allure for some, and a very wealthy young man or woman was likely to have many suitors regardless of their personal qualities. But the predominant view was more sensible: poverty caused unhappiness, but the pleasure given by wealth alone was fleeting and unreliable. For example, in 1780 the Dowager Lady Massereene told her son's prospective father-in-law: 'I am equally persuaded that happiness does not depend on affluence, though it does on a competence, nor can the greatest riches purchase it.' And in 1812 Mrs Jackson wrote to her son George, who was contemplating an imprudent marriage, that:

> I hate the idea of it [marrying or not marrying on financial grounds] beyond what *prudence and necessity* dictate. Generally speaking, even as regards fortune, equal matches are perhaps the happiest; yet I believe there are many exceptions, and if there is enough of fortune on one side, it may be immaterial on which. But it is essential to happiness that there should, at least, be a *competency*; and the habits and dispositions of the parties must determine what in each case a competency is, because, what would be *riches* for some, would, be *poverty* for others.[24]

Assuming that prospective partners in a marriage were suitably matched in terms of income and social status, the next question was their age. There was a strong prejudice in favour of the husband being older than the wife, or, at most, not more than marginally younger. When the twenty-seven-year-old Lord Palmerston (father of the future prime minister) fell in love with Frances Poole in 1767, he had great difficulty in persuading her that her seniority by six years was not an insuperable impediment to their marriage; while Lady Anne Lindsay was well aware that in marrying a man twelve years her junior she would be subjected to much malicious comment and mirth. Mrs Calvert thought it a 'monstrous match' when the engagement of Lady Anna Maria Stanhope to Lord Tavistock was announced, for she was '*eight and twenty*' – actually she was only twenty-four – and he 'barely twenty'. And the marriage of Mrs Spencer Perceval, widow of the assassinated prime minister and the mother of a dozen children, to Lieutenant-Colonel Sir Henry Carr, a widower eight years younger than her, provoked a good deal of gossip and some expressions of disgust.[25]

None of these marriages would have caused any concern if the ages of the parties had been reversed. Men were often ten years or more older than their wives, and Esther Acklom was unusual when, aged nineteen, she proclaimed that she would not have any man over thirty. (The fact that she was extremely wealthy may have been critical in giving her the confidence to set out her requirements so decidedly.) On the other hand, there was nothing uncommon in the reaction of Sir Thomas Picton, one of Wellington's generals in the Peninsular War, when he heard that Lowry Cole – another senior officer then in his early forties – was marrying a thirty-two-year-old bride. He declared that 'when I marry . . . I mean to marry the youngest tit I can find!' It was most common for young women from the professional, gentry and upper classes to marry in their late teens or early twenties, while it was rare for men to do so until they were well past twenty and most often in their late twenties or early thirties, while quite a few had to wait until they were even older. It was only when the groom was very much older than the bride – perhaps several times her age, as when a man in his fifties, sixties or even seventies married a woman of eighteen or twenty – that there was much chance of adverse comment.[26]

Young men were not always eager to marry and settle down, even when they could afford to do so. Sir Thomas Bertram praised Henry Crawford for wanting to marry when he was only twenty-four, and regretted that his own eldest son showed no similar inclination. But in his fictional *History of Rasselas*, Dr Johnson had an inconclusive discussion of the benefits of early and late marriages, acknowledging that couples who married too early, before they knew anything of the world, might choose unwisely. Johnson added that young parents might find that their children were grown up and snapping at their heels when they were barely middle-aged: 'the son is eager to enjoy the world before the father is willing to forsake it, and there is hardly room at once for two generations. The daughter begins to bloom before the mother can be content to fade, and neither can forbear to wish for the absence of the other.' On the other hand, couples who married when they were older might find it harder to adjust to each other's ways, and they were less likely to live to see their children happy and successful adults with families of their own. The advantages and disadvantages cancelled each other out: 'Of the blessings set before you make your choice and be content. No man can taste the fruits of autumn while he is delighting his scent with the flowers of the spring: no man can, at the same time, fill his cup from the source and from the mouth of the Nile.'[27]

There was a less equivocal preference for the bride and groom to come from the same part of the country, so that the bride would not be too greatly separated from her family after she was married. In *Pride and Prejudice* Elizabeth Bennet disputes Mr Darcy's assertion that Charlotte Lucas is fortunate to be settled close to her family, for in her view 50 miles was not close. 'Where there is fortune to make the expence of travelling unimportant, distance becomes no evil. But that is not the case *here*. Mr and Mrs Collins have a comfortable income, but not such a one as will allow of frequent journeys – and I am persuaded my friend would not call herself *near* her family under less than *half* the present distance.' On a grander scale, Mrs Calvert regarded the fact that Sir James Stronge – her daughter's suitor – came from Ireland as a greater disadvantage than that his fortune was not as large as they would have liked, because this meant that it would be difficult for her to see her daughter frequently once she was married. Yet proximity was not invariably an advantage: when they were married Elizabeth and Mr Darcy did not regret the miles that separated her mother at Longbourn in Hertfordshire from them at Pemberley in Derbyshire, and even Jane and Mr Bingley found it convenient to move away from Netherfield.[28]

There were strongly held scruples about the marriage between a widower and his deceased wife's sister – there was a risk that such a marriage might be declared void, although the law would not be clarified until 1835 when existing marriages were validated but all future ones made automatically null. The objection to such marriages was founded on the religious belief that in marriage the husband and wife became one flesh, so that a sister-in-law was equated to a sister, and a marriage regarded as incestuous. The ban created considerable hardship, for it was not uncommon for a widower to ask his unmarried sister-in-law to keep house and help bring up his children, and it was not unlikely in such a case that they might become attracted to each other. This is essentially what happened when Jane Austen's brother Charles married Harriet Palmer in 1820, six years after his first wife, her sister Fanny, had died; and many other examples could be cited, including Richard Lovell Edgeworth whose second and third wives were sisters. Surprisingly little attention was paid to the possibility of a widow marrying her deceased husband's brother, although one would have thought that such relationships were equally natural, and must, in principle, have been equally objectionable.[29]

On the other hand, there were few objections to the marriage of first cousins, which were common. Here too the Austen family furnishes an example: when Eliza de Feuillide was widowed, she was courted by Jane's brothers James and Henry and, after some hesitation, married Henry, despite the fact that he was almost ten years her junior as well as her first cousin. Her letter to her godfather Warren Hastings, announcing the news of her engagement, mentions the fact that Henry was her cousin but neutrally, without any defensiveness or apology, and instead concentrates on 'his steady attachment to me, his Affection for my little Boy, and disinterested concurrence in the disposal of my Property'. Fiction mirrored fact, in this respect at least, with the pairing of Edmund Bertram and Fanny Price in *Mansfield Park*, while in *Persuasion* Anne Elliot is attracted by her cousin Walter Elliot.[30]

Poor health might make a prospective marriage partner appear unsuitable, or at least diminish the desirability of a match, while a suggestion of hereditary insanity running in a family was likely to arouse some alarm. For example, in 1799 James Stuart Wortley became engaged to Lady Caroline Creighton, daughter of the 1st Earl Erne. They were much attached and there were no financial impediments; however, a difficulty arose from his father's concern 'about Lord Creighton, her half-brother, who is confined. But Lord Erne, who is in England, cleared it up to the family, as Lord Creighton's illness was owing to cold bathing in a course of mercury, which disordered his head.' With this doubt resolved, the match went ahead. And there is also a story – although it is surely apocryphal – that when the marriage of Lady Louisa Gordon, daughter of the Duke of Gordon, to the son and heir of Marquess Cornwallis was mooted in 1797, the Marquess was concerned by the strain of the hereditary insanity that had dogged the ducal house of Gordon. The Duchess then reassured him by saying that there wasn't a drop of Gordon blood in her daughter![31]

Issues of character and behaviour would also trouble at least some parents or guardians, and indeed the prospective bride or groom. The heroine of *Belinda* breaks off her engagement to the charming Mr Vincent when she discovers that he has a weakness for gambling; while the opposition of Frances Winckley's brother (her closest relative) to Sir John Shelley's suit because of his indebtedness and wild living has already been mentioned. In 1806, Harriet Wynne was being courted by a young man, John Poulett. One day his family called without him and she 'was sorry to find they had *left John* quite *dead* drunk behaving infamously. I am quite vexed with him, for a drunkard in my opinion is the *worst* of all animals. I hope this was only thro *accident* altho' I rather fear that he has indulged rather in *that way* lately. . . . I went to bed not *at all* happy.' The courtship broke down, although other factors were involved.[32]

In some cases the stigma associated with divorce, illegitimacy or scandal might create an obstacle to a courtship, even when it related not to either of the prospective marriage partners but to their connections. Elizabeth Bennet worried that the silliness and vulgarity of her sister Lydia would reflect badly on her and Jane, putting off prospective suitors of taste; while Lydia's later misconduct might be expected to have an even more chilling effect. Similarly, Mrs Delany reflected that where a wife had been divorced for adultery, her daughters would be treated like damaged goods: 'it is injustice, but . . . who will venture on the daughter, when the mother has proved such a wife?' However, these fears appear rather overstated: Mr Darcy was not deterred, and the daughters of divorced mothers often made good marriages. As for illegitimate children, their status depended largely on how they were brought up and what provision was made for them; illegitimacy in itself mattered less than the material disadvantages it often brought with it.[33]

The great majority of the English upper classes were Anglican, while English Catholics tended to marry other Catholics. Religious differences prevented some marriages, but in other cases they do not seem to have figured largely in the minds of either party or their families. When Scottish or Irish Presbyterians married English Anglicans, the geographical separation loomed larger in most minds than the difference between two well-established and respectable strands of Protestantism. There was more potential for difficulty in a marriage between a Protestant and a Catholic, but the prejudice was less than it had been a generation or two earlier, and there are a number of examples where it appears to have caused no difficulty, the couple going through two ceremonies. Jewish people and other non-Christians were yet to be accepted into the upper ranks of British society on any terms, and so the question of inter-marriage seldom arose, and objections would be made on many grounds, social as well as religious. Far more common was a difference in approach not doctrine, where a couple were attracted but one was much more ardent in their religious commitment than the other. Mary Crawford was not the only young lady to hesitate at the prospect of marrying a clergyman, while many a clergyman or evangelical of either sex would hesitate before marrying someone who appeared worldly and treated religion lightly. This was the position of the newly ordained Rev. William Jones, who was greatly attracted to a charming, wealthy woman who gave little thought to religion.

> what am I doing? Am I, as they call it, in love? With what? with my own folly and, it may be, my own misery. I fear there is something very mean and base in my attachment to my present object. She seems to be an utter stranger to God; and yet I fondly think I could be happy with her. But how can two travel together, except they be agreed? Were I (as I now think happy enough) to marry her, what distress might it not occasion? the more I loved her, the more would it pierce my soul to think that I was embracing in my bosom one who, perhaps, must be after this life everlastingly separated from me. With respect to the training of children, if we had any, and the manage-ment of other parts of our family, how distinctly opposite must our sentiments be! . . . Is it not time to awake? . . . Guide me, O my heav-enly Father!

These doubts proved insurmountable and Jones went on to marry another woman, with a more serious view of religion, but whose sharp tongue made his life uncomfortable at times.[34]

These criteria influenced the way couples themselves, and their fami-lies and friends, viewed a prospective marriage, and even before that, an acquaintance that might turn into a courtship. Unmarried men and women incorporated them into their understanding of the world: no one wished to make a 'poor' or discreditable marriage; everyone wanted – in the abstract at least – a spouse of whom they could be proud and who would delight their parents and friends. Of course, faced with a real, flesh and blood suitor, other, less abstract factors came into play, personal attraction counted heavily and the desire to make a good marriage might shrivel before an intense desire to marry a particular person, regardless of their wealth, social status or other qualifications. Equally, an eminently 'suitable' person might be personally objectionable and in this case most people would not hold their nose – literally or figuratively – and marry them simply for the sake of worldly advantages. But an awareness of what constituted suitability acted as a screening mechanism, ensuring that many people swiftly excluded unsuitable candidates from consideration long before their emotions became engaged, just as they excluded someone who they knew was already married. Exceptions catch the eye – the son of a duke who married a dairymaid, or the young lady who ran off with her singing teacher – but they were rare, and most members of the British gentry, professional and upper classes married someone from roughly their own class and background.

CHAPTER THREE

COURTSHIP

THERE IS A STORY about Admiral Sir John Borlase Warren which unfortunately cannot be confirmed. According to the tale, when Warren was twenty-seven years old, already a baronet, a man of fashion and a rising young naval officer, he went to dinner and was much struck by the young woman, Caroline Clavering, who was sitting opposite him and whom he had never met before. He passed her a note across the table, written in French: 'If you find this heart worthy of you and you deign to accept it, you will make me the happiest of men.' With a promptitude and decision that equalled his own, she replied 'Then you shall be happy.' They were married before the end of the year, and the marriage proved a happy one, even if some subordinates felt that the Admiral's wife was inclined to interfere in their duties and find work for them to do.[1]

Even if the story is untrue, or at least exaggerated, naval officers had the reputation for making precipitous marriages. Jane Austen's cousin, Jane Cooper, met Captain Thomas Williams when she was on holiday on the Isle of Wight at the beginning of July 1792. Before the end of the month they were engaged and the date of the wedding was fixed. And the fictional Admiral Croft remarks in *Persuasion*:

'We sailors, Miss Elliot, cannot afford to make long courtships in time of war. How many days was it, my dear, between the first time of my seeing you, and our sitting down together in our lodgings at North Yarmouth?'

'We had better not talk about it, my dear,' replied Mrs Croft, pleasantly; 'for if Miss Elliot were to hear how soon we came to an understanding, she would never be persuaded that we could be happy together. I had known you by character, however, long before.'

'Well, and I had heard of you as a very pretty girl; and what were we to wait for besides?'[2]

However, it was not just naval officers who sometimes leapt after only the briefest of looks. Mr Collins, in *Pride and Prejudice*, arrives at Longbourn knowing no one but searching for a bride; and he leaves Hertfordshire thirteen days later an engaged man, having, in the meantime, contemplated marrying one Bennet sister and been refused by another, before finding his wife next door at the home of Sir William Lucas. While an exact parallel in real life does not suggest itself, we have the case of Miss Lethieullier who met Mr Pinckard at Margate and agreed to marry him after an acquaintance of, it was said, about ten days: she was greatly attracted by his personal appearance and he, unkind friends speculated, was attracted by her fortune of £20,000.[3] And in 1809 Lady Sarah Spencer told her brother a curious story about their nephew, Sir Arscott Molesworth, who was studying at Cambridge. When the vacation arrived Sir Arscott travelled to Scotland for a fortnight with a friend. They stayed for two days in Edinburgh on their way to the Highlands.

The Scotch are jovial and merry, and hospitable to strangers, whom they *take in*, as we are enjoined. They were the second night invited to a ball, where the Baronet danced with a simple, pleasant virgin of about thirty years of age, who was kind enough to make no objection to his being but eighteen [*sic*: he was either nineteen or twenty]. The ball over, he went home, and next day set off for the Highlands; returned thro' Edinburgh, and the morning after, my dear nephew was waked by a message that Miss Brown and the parson waited for him. Up got my dear nephew, followed the man like a goose, and *was married* like an idiot. On the morrow they left Scotland, the friend in ye basket! [i.e. in ignorance] all the while. Not a word had his companion blinked to him of his exploit, nor to anybody else when he got home, till the modest bride wrote to claim her spouse, to the utter surprise, astonishment, and dismay of all friends. Match this if ye can, ye novel-mongers! He says he proposed to her at the ball, but she refused to marry him then, to be sure, unprepared, without witnesses, etc.; but she told him she would give him time to consider while scrambling over the mountains. For nobody should say she had taken him in; they must be sad liars who do.

Although Miss Brown came from a respectable if relatively poor background it is hard not to believe that in this case, as probably in that of Mr Pinckard and Miss Lethieullier, one party was a fortune-hunter and the other their prey.[4]

Even without the risk of falling victim to adventurers, such impulsive marriages were widely regarded as foolish. Marriage was not something to be entered into on a whim, without any real knowledge of the other person. 'Marry in haste, repent at leisure' was already established as a familiar maxim. The *Lady's Magazine* urged the importance of caution in 1811: 'In the choice of a companion for life, no one will be hardy enough to deny that great circumspection, and a proper knowledge of the disposition of each party by the other, is absolutely necessary. Yet how often do we find this unattended to, in the most material concern of life! Hasty matches are formed; and subsequent misery is but too often the result of them.' Or, as Frank Churchill remarked in *Emma*, 'How many a man has committed himself on a short acquaintance, and rued it all the rest of his life!'[5]

So how do we explain these whirlwind romances? Part of the answer, no doubt, is that couples might be swept along by passion and a sense of adventure. Sometimes their inhibitions – or common sense – would be set aside by the enlivening effects of alcohol; while if a gentleman committed himself to a proposal, however hasty and ill-considered, he was expected to honour it if the lady chose to accept. But there were also men who decided that they wanted to get married, but had very little idea how to set about finding a suitable wife, and who were at risk of proposing to the first bright, attractive young woman who caught their eye. Officers in the army and navy were particularly likely to fall into this mistake, especially if they had been serving abroad for some years and so had fallen out of the way of society at home. They might return to Britain, in their mid-thirties or older, rich enough to afford to get married and eager to settle down and have a home, but with little idea how to find a compatible wife. In 1803 the thirty-one-year-old George Murray, a lieutenant-colonel in the Guards, wrote home to his sister from the West Indies, showing the lack of confidence felt by many men in this position.

> What is a poor man to do who is resolved to marry. If he is entirely employed in life he has not time to study the Lady's character, and even if he does it is ten to one but he is mistaken in the opinion he forms. All his tedious courtship therefore with the addition perhaps of a great deal of anxiety, seems in the end but to make his want of discernment the more conspicuous.
>
> For my part I should be inclined to depend more upon the Opinion of a sensible woman, who was my friend, than upon my own, in so far as misguided the character dispositions etc etc.[6]

Such men were particularly likely to marry an old flame, if she was still single (or had been widowed), or an old friend of the family, especially of their sisters. Widowers were also quite often intimidated by the thought of plunging back into the marriage market after many years of abstinence: Jane Austen's brothers James and Francis took Mary and Martha Lloyd — long-standing friends of their sisters — as their second wives, while Charles Austen, as we have seen, married his deceased wife's sister.

The rules of society made it quite difficult for men and women to get to know each other well. At a ball, a woman was not supposed to dance more than twice with the same man, although as he might also take her in to supper, they could contrive a good deal of conversation if the man was sufficiently at ease to take full advantage of his opportunities. In other words, Henry Tilney, in *Northanger Abbey*, could make a much greater impression on Catherine Morland, and learn more about her, in the space of an evening than George Murray was likely to manage. Similarly, a gentleman with easy manners could pay a young woman many socially acceptable attentions: placing a shawl round her shoulders, handing her into a carriage and the like, that one who was more awkward might easily miss. When Sir John Shelley was showing an interest in Frances Winckley he generally failed to gain access to her crowded box at the opera, but 'he invariably was there at the right moment, to take me to the carriage; which was then an affair of passing at least an hour together in the Crush Room'. It was harder for a young woman to signal her interest, although much might be done by smiles, the gentle pressure of a hand in greeting and by encouraging the man's conversation, as Charlotte Lucas 'good-naturedly' diverted Mr Collins's attention from her friend and to herself at the Netherfield ball.[7]

When Henry Tilney was interested in getting to know Catherine Morland better, he was assisted by his sister Eleanor, who befriended Catherine, and who was able to invite her to tea and on country walks, which Henry could not do in his own name without breaching propriety, although it was perfectly proper for him to accompany them, to give them each his arm and the benefit of his opinions on the picturesque. Equally, Catherine's friendship with Isabella Thorpe enabled Isabella's brother John to assume a greater degree of informality with Catherine than would be permissible for a complete stranger (in this case reinforced by the presence of Catherine's own brother, James Morland). Catherine agreed to go for a drive in John Thorpe's gig. The propriety of this was debatable: they were not exactly alone, for her brother and his sister belonged to the same party, although they were not in the same carriage, but they would be seen together in public in a rather marked fashion. Mr Allen, the sensible husband of Catherine's too complaisant chaperone, expressed disquiet but not complete disapproval: 'Now and then it is very well; but going to inns and public places together! It is not right . . .' On the other hand, there was evidently nothing improper in Catherine travelling part of the way to Northanger in Henry Tilney's curricle, while the rest of his family preceded them in the family chaise. And the pleasure of such a journey was considerable.

> Henry drove so well, — so quietly — without making any disturbance, without parading to her, or swearing at them [the horses]; so different from the only gentleman-coachman whom it was in her power to compare him with! — And then his hat sat so well, and the innumerable

capes of his great coat looked so becomingly important! To be driven
by him, next to being dancing with him, was certainly the greatest
happiness in the world.

Even the great Doctor Johnson acknowledged something very similar:
'If . . . I had no duties, and no reference to futurity, I would spend my life
in driving briskly in a post-chaise with a pretty woman; but she should
be one who could understand me, and would add something to the
conversation.'[8]

Many encounters were quite prosaic and only assumed significance in
retrospect. Harriet Fane first met Charles Arbuthnot when she was a
schoolgirl of fourteen and he a widower of forty still mourning his first
wife. Reassuringly she made no impression on him, but she was quite
struck by him, although, by her own account, she was rather in love with
Captain Thomas Capel of the navy at the time. (Capel was only seventeen years her senior, and was probably equally unaware of her.) Years
later she told her husband, 'It is true I liked him but I never loved him as
I do you; still I did like him . . . .' The next time she crossed paths with
Arbuthnot was in the lobby of the Opera House in the summer of 1811,
when she was not quite eighteen. This time Charles noticed her (she had
probably been pointed out to him earlier in the evening or in the season,
for she had presumably just come out), and made a remark to her as they
passed in the crowd, but she did not recognise him and asked her
companion, 'Who is that?' The answer was '*Mr Arbuthnot.*' 'You must
know I am the *stupidest* person at remembering faces in the world,' she
later told him. 'I should forget my own if I did not look in the glass every
day!' Another eighteen months passed, until the winter of 1812–13,
when they were both staying at Lord Westmorland's country house at
Apethorpe. Most of the men had gone hunting and Harriet wanted a
letter franked (the cover signed by a Member of Parliament, which
meant that the recipient did not have to pay postage). Arbuthnot, who
was joint-secretary to the Treasury, an important government minister,
was in the room with her, pacing up and down and paying her no attention. She did not think he liked her, for he had declined to ride with her
the previous day, and he never paid her the 'little attentions' such as
'*picking up my pocket-handkerchief* or fetching me a chair', which she was

accustomed to receiving from gentlemen, and which she took as a measure of their interest in her. One night, as she went to bed, he was standing beside the door 'and *you did not open it for me*. That was a *heinous crime.*' Nonetheless, after half an hour, she screwed up her courage and asked him to frank the letter, and he came up immediately saying, 'With great pleasure.' 'They were the most cordial words I had ever had from you.' Evidently this was enough to break the ice, and that night, 'I was charmed because you were so afraid I should catch cold . . .'. It was not long before Harriet was telling a friend that Charles was the only man in the party whom she liked, and that she thought him 'perfect'.[9]

It is quite possible that Harriet Fane and Charles Arbuthnot would never have got to know each other well if they had met only in London society. But it was much easier to get beyond a superficial acquaintance if you saw someone in the common light of day, at home or staying in a country house, rather than relying on impressions formed in the glitter and excitement of a ballroom. When Eleanor Tilney invited Catherine to stay at Northanger Abbey she was responding both to her brother's strengthening interest and to her father's approval of the prospective match. In a very similar way, Sarah Spencer reported that one of her brother's friends had invited himself to stay with the family at their place on the Isle of Wight in the summer of 1812:

One of our . . . [London] friends, to my utter astonishment and some pleasure, and more curiosity, has announced himself as our visitor. . . . It is a man I have often mentioned to you – Mr Lyttelton. What he is out of a London ball-room I have yet to learn. I know that in one he is the most extraordinary mixture of brilliant wit, childish nonsense, frivolous small-talk, and a universal sort of scrambling information, which seems all to come out, whether he will or not, from an incessant flow of wild spirits. What such a being can be like at a place like Ryde, all day long with one, is so beyond me that I am really curious about it. He is a great friend of [her brother] Althorp's, just his age, and as unlike him as possible, *extérieurement* at least. If I find him unlike throughout, I shall soon be heartily tired of his company. At any rate, I am glad to grow really acquainted with a London *beau*, it is a gratification I never had before. I ought, to finish

Mr Lyttelton's picture, to tell you that he dances out of time, and is remarkably handsome – the two most striking properties of his one hears mentioned in this thinking town.[10]

The visit was a success: at the end of August, as it was drawing to a close, Sarah Spencer reported that Lyttelton's spirits were as high as ever, 'enlivening us in a very pleasant manner', but that he had 'dropped the character of a mere buffoon with a very good grace, which makes him much the more agreeable as a constant companion, and we all begin to think him a very amiable person'. Still, she could not help adding, 'A perfect stranger among one's most private family circle in a small house is, however, on the whole, not entirely a comfortable thing; and I don't think our gay guest will be very much regretted . . . .' Whether this was protesting too much to curb the matrimonial speculation that her account of Mr Lyttelton's visit was bound to provoke, or an honest statement of the genuine strain of living in close proximity to someone who, however attractive, was still unfamiliar, hardly matters: the visit to Ryde had enabled William Lyttelton and Sarah Spencer to go beyond a ballroom acquaintance and to gauge whether they might be compatible. Each was still cautious, uncertain of the other's feelings, and probably not quite sure of their own, but their mutual attraction was growing and the pace of the courtship would accelerate.[11]

At this point in the courtship material factors, such as wealth and social position, sank into the background: they remained important – without them this stage would probably not have been reached – but now they were taken for granted and the question was much more about character and compatibility. Prospective couples had to decide whether this was the person to whom they wished to be married for the rest of their lives. Did they like them? Did they trust them? Were their interests, outlooks and values similar enough to promise a happy marriage? Were they irritable and hard to live with, or cheerful and amusing? Parents and older friends urged young people to look to qualities that would last rather than those which enchanted for an evening. In 1801 Elizabeth Kennedy advised her daughter, 'When you are of an age to think of settling, let your affections be placed on a steady sober, religious man, who will be tender and careful of you at all times . . . Do not marry a very young man, you know not how he may turn out; it is a lottery at best but it is a very just remark that "it is better to be an old man's darling than a young man's scorn." [12] And in 1824 Lady Granville commented that a young man of her acquaintance might be better as a lover than a husband:

> I cannot make him quite out . . . I think him to begin with uncommonly pleasing. He is so refined, has such an accomplished mind. There is such manliness and good sense, such freedom from all the vanities and littlenesses of his kind. On the other hand, I never saw anyone make so little effort to surmount any little cloud of *humeur*, *chagrin* or *ennui* for the benefit of the society he is in, and he never puts his best leg foremost to promote the satisfaction or amusement of those he is with. . . .
>
> As a lover [he] must be captivating, for zest immediately gives him the most delightful spirits, an appearance of unbounded enjoyment, sociability, unreserve — everything that is charming. But excitement is a short thing and marriage a long, and it is the unclouded ray that is wanted even in the happiest to gild inevitable hours of gloom, anxiety and sickness. Yet to refuse [him], for mother or daughter, what a Herculean labour! [13]

As this suggests, compatibility was not simply a matter of virtue: a man and woman might both have many fine qualities but still be the wrong choice for the other. Lady Palmerston commented on a reported match in 1795:

> I think she is a bold girl, though he may think her a *delicious girl* and feel for her most *tender emotions* I should fear after a very short period she may find a very worthy man, a man of strict honour, a man of learning and science and a man of the truest principals [*sic*] a most unpleasant husband. I wish I may be mistaken but as I know we should fight in less than a week I own I am sorry for Caroline, who has everything to make her life comfortable and ought not to exchange that state without she was sure of *bettering herself*. All this however is *entre nous* . . . [14]

Jane Austen gives us an example of a couple who should have recognised that they were incompatible despite being strongly attracted in Edmund Bertram and Mary Crawford. Here the differences were more a matter of outlook and taste than character as such – Mary was much more worldly and fashionable, keen to cut a figure and spend part of the year in London, while Edmund looked ahead to the life of a prosperous rural clergymen with contentment. It is quite possible that if they had married they might have each adjusted to the other and found a degree of happiness, although it is more likely that the marriage would have been permeated with discontent and suppressed irritation as the charm of their mutual attraction wore thin and the underlying differences reasserted themselves.

Austen also makes the case that a happy marriage depended on mutual respect. This is implicit in all her novels, both in the love stories themselves and in the depiction of other marriages, and she makes it explicit in the advice Mr Bennet gives Elizabeth when he fears that she is marrying Darcy for the sake of money and social position:

> I know your disposition, Lizzy. I know that you could be neither happy nor respectable, unless you truly esteemed your husband; unless you looked up to him as a superior. Your lively talents would place you in the greatest danger in an unequal marriage. You could scarcely escape discredit and misery. My child, let me not have the grief of seeing *you* unable to respect your partner in life. You know not what you are about.[15]

In her next novel, *Mansfield Park*, Austen pursues the theme in depicting Maria Bertram's decision to marry Mr Rushworth without loving or respecting him for the sake of his large income and social position. Her father is uneasy at the prospect and gives her the opportunity to withdraw if she wishes, but is much less emphatic in his advice than Mr Bennet and is secretly relieved when she stoutly declares her lack of qualms. The outcome is not simply an unhappy marriage but open disgrace when she leaves Rushworth and runs off with Henry Crawford, who soon discards her.

Other novelists took a similar line: using a broader brush, Sir Walter Scott describes Miss Rachel Bonnyrigg entrapping a foolish young baronet, Sir Bingo Binks, into marriage, and then being miserable: humiliated by the public displays of his folly and disgusted when 'his brutality became intimately connected with herself'. And Maria Edgeworth, in *Belinda*, depicts with some sympathy the plight of Lady Delacour, who admits to the heroine, 'I married my lord Delacour, knowing him to be a fool, and believing that, for this reason, I should find no trouble governing him. – But what a fatal mistake! – a fool, of all animals in the creation, is the most difficult to govern . . . .' Someone had put it into Lord Delacour's head that he was controlled by his wife, and he was so mortified by the idea that he dug in his heels and refused to listen to her advice on anything. Examples from real life are harder to find, but whether this is because people were seldom so clearly labelled and displayed as fools, or because not many women married a man they despised, is a matter for speculation.[16]

Women were taught from childhood to be modest and not to make a display of their ability or learning, and Jane Austen famously discussed the appeal of ignorance in *Northanger Abbey*: '[Catherine] was heartily ashamed of her ignorance. A misplaced shame. Where people wish to attach, they should always be ignorant. To come with a well-informed mind, is to come with an inability of administering to the vanity of others, which a sensible person would always wish to avoid. A woman especially, if she have the misfortune of knowing any thing, should conceal it as well as she can.' Austen then goes on to distinguish between 'ignorance' and 'imbecility', and 'in justice to men' acknowledges that 'there is a portion of them too reasonable and too well informed themselves to desire any thing more in woman than ignorance'. As so often with Austen, irony and honesty are thoroughly mixed: the reader neither takes the remarks at face value, nor treats them as nothing more than a jest.[17]

The suspicion that men, or at least some men, disliked the thought of a highly intelligent, well-educated woman as their wife existed in reality. Nelly Weeton, a clever, largely self-taught governess struggling on the fringes of gentility, bitterly counted herself fortunate not to come across many intelligent men, 'for I should certainly fall in love with some wise man or other, and what a woful [*sic*] thing it would be! For, with all my vanity, I am not so vain as to suppose I should be admired in return; for mere understanding in a woman – even when accompanied by good temper, which is not always the case – is often rather repellent than attractive when unattended by youth, beauty and riches.' And at the other end of the social scale, the Duke of Wellington, who loved the company of articulate, confident women, disapprovingly remarked that his political ally Sir Robert Peel – a man of outstanding intellect and integrity – had not wished to marry a clever woman, and that Peel's wife had no influence over her husband.[18]

Society in the late eighteenth and early nineteenth century regarded it as very desirable that a wife should look up to, admire and respect her husband; but that a husband might do equally well if he loved, cherished and sought to protect his wife. The common difference in age between them – women marrying when still very young, and their husbands some years older than them – encouraged this inequality, which might be justified, if necessary, by appeals to scripture, tradition or the perceived laws of nature. It was an outlook that was constantly reinforced by the conventions of good manners: a gentleman would give a lady his arm, hand her into her carriage and generally treat her as if she was both precious and fragile. Women were taught that they needed protection, and that there was no one better to get it from than a husband. Yet this was also a time in which the importance of mutual respect as the foundation of a successful marriage was being ever more explicitly acknowledged, not least in novels of the day, which helped to shape the assumptions and expectations of a rising generation.

At one level, courtship was a period of mutual scrutiny in which both parties could get to know the other better and coolly consider whether they might be able to find happiness together. But it was also the time when an initial, tentative attraction either flourished, growing into outright love, or dissipated as the first impulse faded on closer acquaintance. Both men and women might be wary of the dangers of falling precipitately in love – would the other party respond in kind, and even if they did, was a marriage practical? – but even the most cautious person might find that their emotions got the better of them if they sensed a warm response from the object of their affection. When all went well the progression was delightful, although even the happiest love affair was likely to contain occasional misunderstandings and moments of doubt and uncertainty. But this was also a period full of potential embarrassment and perplexity, where it was all too easy to mistake your own feelings or those of the other person; to say too much or too little; and to be genuinely uncertain what you wanted, as well as how to achieve it.

All this is illustrated in the story of John Plumptre's courtship of Fanny Knight. She first met him in 1811, the year she turned eighteen and came out. He was the older brother of her close friends Mary and Emma Plumptre, and was two years older than her, studying at Cambridge and destined for the Bar. Two years later her Aunt Jane described him as, 'A handsome young Man certainly, with quiet, gentlemanlike manners. – I set him down as sensible rather than Brilliant.' And, 'I like him very much. – He gives me the idea of a very amiable young Man, only too diffident to be so agreeable as he might be . . . .' Although he figures frequently in Fanny's diary for several years it was only in 1813 or 1814 that his attentions to her became marked. When Fanny was staying with Jane at her uncle Henry's in London in 1814, Plumptre, who was by then studying the law at Lincoln's Inn, secured a box at the theatre for them and dined with them beforehand, 'which I fancy he was very happy to do'. Jane reported that 'Henry sees decided attachment between her & his new acquaintance [i.e. John Plumptre]'.[19]

Fanny's diary shows that she was flattered and delighted by his attentions, and missed him when he was absent, writing of a concert at Canterbury on her return home where she had expected him, 'No Plumptre! so disappointed.' When she missed him again on another visit to London that June she wrote, 'Oh the misery of suspense' – an entry which may indicate that she was anticipating a proposal.[20] However, over the next few months her feelings cooled and that November she wrote to her Aunt Jane asking for advice, explaining that while she had certainly encouraged his advances and appeared to have secured his affection, she now realised that she did not want him. Although Fanny's letter does not survive, its content is pretty clear from Jane's reply:

I was certainly a good deal surprised *at first* – as I had no suspicion of any change in your feelings, and I have no scruple in saying that you cannot be in Love. My dear Fanny, I am ready to laugh at the idea – and yet it is no laughing matter to have had you so mistaken as to your own feelings – And with all my heart I wish I had cautioned you on that point when first you spoke to me; – but tho' I did not think you then so *much* in love as you thought yourself, I did consider you as being attached in a degree – quite sufficiently for happiness, as I had no doubt it would increase with opportunity. – And from the time of our being in London together, I thought you really very much in love – But you certainly are not at all – there is no concealing it. – What strange creatures we are! – It seems as if your being secure of him (as you say yourself) had made you Indifferent.[21]

Apparently Fanny had been startled by some of his remarks at the races, which appear to have indicated that his always serious views on religion were now becoming those of a killjoy – her family tradition claims that he had come to think dancing and other social amusements unsuitable for Christians, although, as he was still dancing with her at this time, it is possible that there is some exaggeration in this account.[22]

But how had Fanny been so mistaken in her feelings? Her aunt was clear: 'Oh! dear Fanny, Your mistake has been one that thousands of women fall into. He was the *first* young Man who attached himself to you. That was the charm, & most powerful it is.' He was also almost excessively suitable, 'His situation in life, family, friends, & above all his Character – his uncommonly amiable mind, strict principles, just notions, good habits – *all* that *you* know so well how to value, *All* that really is of the first importance – everything of this nature pleads his cause most strongly.' He had a first-rate intellect – he had proved that at university – and was 'the eldest son of a Man of Fortune, the Brother of your particular friend, & belonging to your own County'. But, at least in Jane Austen's eyes, all this counted for nothing if Fanny did not love him. 'I . . . entreat you not to commit yourself farther, & not to think of accepting him unless you really do like him. Anything is to be preferred or endured rather than marrying without Affection; and if his deficiencies of Manner &c &c strike you more than all his good qualities, if you continue to think strongly of them, give him up at once.' Having encouraged him to such a point where he had reason to feel almost certain that his feelings were reciprocated, Fanny must now resolve to 'behave with a coldness which may convince him that he has been deceiving himself. – I have no doubt of his suffering a good deal for a time, a great deal, when he feels that he must give you up; – but it is no creed of mine, as you must be well aware, that such sort of Disappointments kill anybody.'[23]

A further exchange of letters adds a good deal. First, Aunt Jane understandably refused to take responsibility for the decision Fanny had to make for herself. But then she indicated that her own opinion had changed somewhat, presumably in response to Fanny's most recent letter. 'I am perfectly convinced that your present feelings, supposing you were to marry *now*, would be sufficient for his happiness; but when I think how very, very far it is from a *Now*, & take everything that *may be*, into consideration, I dare not say, "determine to accept him." The risk is too great for *you*, unless your own Sentiments prompt it.' In other words, 'You like him well enough to marry, but not well enough to wait.' And they would have to wait until he was sufficiently established in his career to be able to afford to marry, which might take as much as six or seven years. Fanny was still so young, and had met so few men, that the risk of shackling herself by such an engagement appeared unwise unless she was very decidedly in love. 'The unpleasantness of appearing fickle is certainly great – but if you think you want Punishment for past Illusions, there it is – and nothing can be compared to the misery of being bound *without* Love, bound to one, & preferring another. *That* is a Punishment which you do *not* deserve.'[24]

Fanny evidently took this advice – although her aunt was probably not the only person she consulted. Not all aunts, parents or friends would have given the same advice: for some Mr Plumptre's prospects, both by inheritance and career, would have seemed too good to pass up; while others might have believed that Fanny's doubts were transitory and should not be taken seriously. Austen herself recognised that it was not a simple question of whether Fanny's feelings were engaged or not, but rather whether they were sufficiently engaged to endure a prolonged wait before she could marry. And Fanny herself remained quite ambivalent, continuing to show a proprietorial interest in Mr Plumptre even after he married four years later. Indeed, it was only her own marriage in 1820 that gave her peace; until then there was always a lingering doubt as to whether she had made the right decision. Her aunt continued to give her clear-headed advice: 'Why should you be living in dread of his marrying somebody else? – (Yet, how natural!) – You did not chuse to have him yourself; why not allow him to take comfort where he can?' 'You are *not* in love with him. You never have been really in love with him.' And, 'Do not be in a hurry; depend upon it, the right Man will come at last; you will in the course of the next two or three years, meet with somebody more generally unexceptionable than anyone you have yet known, who will love you as warmly as ever *He* did, & who will so completely attach you, that you will feel you never really loved before.'[25]

Other romances, such as that of Robert Stewart and Emily Hobart, progressed with hardly a hiccup from first meeting to wedding in a matter of months, or even less if the couple shared Admiral Croft's outlook. However, there was still a crucial step to take to complete the courtship: the gentleman had to summon up all his courage, muster his worldly advantages and propose; while the lady, advised by her family, had to decide if she would accept him. But before we turn to the business of proposing and the engagement that followed, if an agreement was reached, we need to examine some of the hesitations that might affect even a successful courtship, and the heartbreak that was caused by some unfortunate love affairs.

CHAPTER FOUR

HESITATION AND HEARTBREAK

IF SOME MEN PROPOSED precipitately to women they hardly knew, others dithered, unable to commit themselves. Sometimes they were in love, but doubted whether they could afford to marry; sometimes they were unsure of their own feelings; and sometimes they doubted how a declaration would be received. In most of these cases they suffered considerable distress, while the object of their affection either waited anxiously for them to come to the point, or remained largely oblivious to their feelings.

These doubts were not suffered only by men who were irresolute in other aspects of their lives – indeed, it almost seems that strong, decisive men were particularly at risk of such paralysis at this crucial moment in their private lives. In the summer of 1796 Thomas Fremantle was thirty years old, a highly regarded captain in the navy, commanding a fine frigate, HMS *Inconstant*, in the Mediterranean. In late June he took on board an English family, the Wynnes, who were fleeing the advance of French troops on Florence and Leghorn. He was soon very much attracted to their eldest daughter, eighteen-year-old Betsey Wynne. They remained on board his ship and, less than three weeks later, he wrote to his brother, consciously striving not 'to break out in all the transports of a man violently smitten'. To this end he described Betsey in as unromantic a way as he could manage: 'short . . . not particularly handsome, but a little healthy thing', but then could not resist adding that she 'speaks and writes German Italian French & English, plays incomparably well on the harpsichord, draws well, sings a little and is otherwise a very good humoured sensible dolly'. Her family too were, 'all together very pleasant, and much attached to each other'. The one thing stopping him proposing was his doubt whether he could afford to marry. 'Without getting a sufficiency to keep her in the way I think necessary you may depend upon it I never will engage myself, however I may be distressed in the event.' And distressed he was, adding that, 'You may conceive I am made very unhappy in having so accidentaly [*sic*] tumbled into a snare not to be guarded against. God knows how it will end, I have my fears.'[1]

For the moment at least, caution prevailed: he told Betsey's mother that he was very partial to her, but that his fortune was not sufficient for him to marry and support a family and so thought it better for them to part. Far from being offended, Betsey was greatly impressed by his candour and honesty, and, while miserable, hoped that it all might yet work out. When they parted Betsey's father permitted her to correspond with him and to accept a ring as a keepsake. Admiral Jervis despatched Fremantle to cruise off Algiers, and openly encouraged Betsey to hope that he would take enough valuable prizes to feel able to marry her. Months of uncertainty followed; it was not until the end of November that Fremantle returned and even then he remained indecisive. On 10 December he told his brother, 'I feel every minute more and more distressed, but after very serious reflection I think I have determined finaly [*sic*] about it in the negative, not from any alteration in my opinions of the person alluded to in my letter from Ajaccio, but for want of a sufficiency to make the remainder of one[']s life comfortable.' But the attraction remained and this brave naval officer, accustomed to making rapid decisions on which the safety of his ship and crew depended, wavered. On the last day of 1796 he recorded in his journal 'Am amazingly attached to Betsey, but cannot make up my mind to marry. I can't say I have on the whole behaved very well.' He continued to see the family, and ten days later he proposed and was accepted.[2]

Money was the main, but perhaps not the only cause of Fremantle's hesitation. He was accustomed to his life as a single man, accountable to no one in his private life and with few personal, as opposed to professional, responsibilities. The thought of a wife and children, a home to return to, was both appealing and alarming. The wild debauchery of his youth had lost its lustre, and he told himself that he wanted to settle down. 'When I consider [that] my friends are married, and that I certainly shall not live in the same way I have formerly in London I confess I feel great pleasure in thinking a man may live perfectly happy with a sober sort of Dolly in the Country.' But still, he only managed to half convince himself, and told his brother, 'I am ashamed of my weakness.'[3]

Another normally assured man who hesitated and stumbled when faced with the need to stake his happiness on a marriage proposal was twenty-nine-year-old George Canning. In the summer of 1799 he was a rising young politician, a friend and protégé of the prime minister, William Pitt, the head of a group of devoted friends and widely lauded (if also sometimes disliked) for his wit, his brilliance and his self-confidence. Canning seemed to have every advantage except wealth and family: he was poor compared to most other young politicians, and his family background was complicated, his mother having been reduced by family quarrels and misfortune to working as an actress. A good marriage to a well-connected woman with a fortune of her own was exactly what Canning needed.

That August he stayed with a select party, including Pitt and Dundas, at Walmer. Among the other guests was a twenty-two-year-old woman, Joan Scott, an heiress whose parents were both dead and whose sister was married to the Marquess of Titchfield, son of the Duke of Portland, another important political figure. Writing to his friend Lord Granville Leveson Gower, Canning said that, 'Never was any human being less bent upon falling in love than I was when I arrived at Walmer.' He had never met Miss Scott, but had 'always heard her name coupled with some one or other person who was supposed to be going to be married to her, or who had proposed and been refused', which made him resolved 'to avoid all possible danger of any such report being circulated about myself'. He therefore studiously avoided her company. And yet, when it came time for him to leave he could not bear to depart and, making a clumsy excuse, managed to get his invitation extended by another day. Acutely self-conscious, he felt that it was impossible that 'she should not see both why I staid and what a degree of embarrassment I felt all day at the consciousness of having betrayed myself to her'.

I took no advantage, however, of the opportunity which this day would have afforded me to make any distinct declaration of what I felt towards her. The doubt whether I did in fact feel anything more than a transitory liking, the repugnance which one naturally has to putting one's self in a situation to be refused, and the obvious consideration of the apparent sordidness and speculation of a proposal to a *great fortune*, restrained me from doing or saying almost anything that could be construed into attention to her; and I question whether in any of the most populous days at Walmer I had less intercourse with her than on this day, when We were left almost entirely to each other. The next morning, after lingering as long as I decently could – certainly with the hope of seeing her alone for five minutes, but as certainly without any determination to make use of those five minutes if I should find them – I took leave of her and Lady Jane, and when I got to Dover was fool enough to feel proud of a victory which I fancied I had obtained over myself . . .[4]

Granville Leveson Gower's sister had been one of the other guests at Dover, and seeing her that evening Canning could not resist pouring his heart out to her, both in conversation and in a letter, begging her to discover what Miss Scott thought of him, and bravely declaring that if the result was discouraging he would give up all thoughts of her. 'I am pretty sure I am not born to *die* of love and I am quite sure I shall never be a lover, according to the rules, and dangle in anybody's train for a whole season. . . . It is not easy to say how anxiously I shall look for the first line from you. . . . It is a great weight off my mind, to have written this nonsense to you.'[5]

He then hurried off to tell the prime minister all about it. To his surprise, Pitt was completely unsurprised. He had observed what was going on at Walmer, and it is even possible that Pitt or Dundas had arranged for Miss Scott's invitation in the hope that the two would fall in love. However, when Leveson Gower's sister reported back, the news was discouraging. Miss Scott had not been as impressed by Canning as he had by her – and given his pointed avoidance of her and the awkwardness of his behaviour, it would have been amazing if she had been; even worse, she regarded politics as a very uncertain profession and rather expected that her husband, whoever he might be, would have some money, at least a 'competence', of his own. The only crumbs of comfort in all this were that her heart was not devoted to someone else – she had previously been courted by Arthur Paget but that was now over – and that she expressed no personal dislike of Canning.

Canning's initial reaction to this disappointing account was to give up the pursuit, but he soon realised that he was extremely reluctant to do so. Was he in love, or had he simply thought so much and so intensely about Miss Scott over the last few days that he found it hard to relinquish the idea of courting and winning her? And how real is the distinction between the two? At the same time he was full of doubts. Were Miss Scott's objections to a politician for a lover simply based on the uncertainty of the career, or did she prefer a quiet life in the country rather than mixing constantly in London society? That indeed would be an insuperable obstacle. 'My hopes and desires, & taste & turn of mind are bent, I fear, irrecoverably, to public objects,' and he looked for a wife who would be 'a companion & sharer in all the anxieties, which political life, I am afraid, cannot but produce from time to time; for a faithful adviser in all points (& there are many such) for which the most feminine character of mind is not disqualified: & I should wish to be able to treat her not only as the connection most interested in one's success, but as the most confidential of one's friends.' He thought that Miss Scott was capable of being such a companion, but he was unsure if that was the sort of life she wanted.[6]

The disparity of fortune also aroused his pride, actually counting against the match, at least at that moment. He told Leveson Gower, 'I cannot bear the idea of being the creature of my wife's; and though I might, and do, flatter myself that I want not any such accession of fortune to carry me in due time as high as I am ambitious of going; yet there is a danger, which I cannot but see and have not the courage to despise, of being supposed to rise on a foundation not of my own laying.' He thought that he might soon – perhaps in just one more year – have reached a level of political success that would reduce this risk and greatly lessen the appearance of inequality in the match. But that did not make the immediate dilemma any easier, and he continued to agonise over it.[7]

A few days later he realised that he could not bring himself to walk away. He wrote to his trusted relatives telling them that he had fallen in love, 'What the event will be Heaven knows; but such an anxiety I have never felt before.' He then returned to Walmer and, without formally proposing, made his feelings plain to Miss Scott. At first she responded coolly, remarking that the fancy of a fortnight might soon pass away, and expressing the hope that they might simply be friends, but when he persisted she gradually became less reserved and responded more warmly. She confided that he was nothing like she had expected, for his reputation 'had taught her to be afraid of me, and to expect to be wearied and oppressed by constant endeavours at shining in conversation, by unmerciful raillery and I know not what – and that she had never been more surprised etc.' Evidently she found him a much more interesting and appealing figure on this second visit than she had on the first. And so the courtship progressed, and years later, on another visit to Walmer, Canning wrote to Joan, by then his beloved wife, 'Here I am in the very room in which I first touched my own Love's hand – & put my arm round her, & drew her to me – & she was not very angry – not very angry I think – though it was very saucy in me to do what I did.' There were still significant obstacles to be overcome before George and Joan Canning got married, but they had come to an understanding that shaped the rest of their lives.[8]

If dithering sometimes made men appear foolish, boldness was no guarantee of success, and failure might be painfully humiliating. This was what happened to the young Arthur Wesley, the future Duke of Wellington who, in the spring of 1792, fell in love with Kitty Pakenham. On paper they appeared a perfect match: he was twenty-two, the younger brother of an Irish earl; a captain in the army and an aide-de-camp at Dublin Castle. She was the daughter of Lord Longford, with only a modest fortune, and had just turned twenty: intelligent, lively and attractive, although not an obvious beauty. There was no doubt that she reciprocated Wesley's feelings, but it is not hard to see why her father refused his permission, for the young captain could not even support himself on his pay, let alone a wife and family. However, rather than ease the pain of the refusal, the older man took advantage of the occasion to deliver a lecture enumerating all the suitor's many faults – which may have included a reference to wild living, although the family tradition preserves only a comment on his idleness and taste for gaiety and music

– while making it clear that he had been presumptuous in making his proposal. Painful as this must have been, it was not enough to quench Wesley's hopes forever. Over the next two years, with help from his brother and in response to the outbreak of war with France, he was promoted to a lieutenant-colonelcy and command of the 33rd Regiment of Foot and took his soldiering much more seriously. He then proposed again. Lord Longford had died and the proposal was made to Kitty's twenty-year-old brother, who had assumed the position of head of the family, although the answer was probably dictated by her mother. Again it was negative, and this time Lady Longford forbade her daughter having any further communication with Wesley. The decision was final and not open to appeal. Just why the Pakenhams rejected the young man's proposals with such disdain is not clear, but it is not hard to imagine just how painful the experience must have been for Wesley.[9]

These three cases, Thomas Fremantle, George Canning and Arthur Wesley, illustrate just a few of the many things that could prevent a man's courtship from progressing as smoothly as that of Robert Stewart or John Stanley. Wesley never had a sufficient income to make his proposal reasonable – at the very least it would have required a long and open-ended engagement – and while he had won Kitty's heart, he had failed to impress her family or win them over before putting it to the test. Money was also an issue for Thomas Fremantle, but he may also have hesitated to commit himself to the responsibilities of married life. For Canning, Joan's wealth was both desirable and humiliating. He was not entirely confident that she could be persuaded to love him and expected that her sister and brother-in-law would oppose the match, and might even view him as a fortune-hunter. But he does not seem to have had any doubts that he and Joan would make each other happy; and this is equally true of Wesley and Fremantle. Their anxieties and hesitations did not centre on the character or compatibility of the woman they loved, but on less personal considerations, and their energy concentrated on persuading her, and her family, to agree to the match.

Each of these three courtships must have been extremely frustrating for the women involved. Kitty Pakenham certainly wanted to marry Arthur Wesley, although she would not defy her family to do so. It is not clear whether she blamed anyone for the disappointment – Wesley for being poor; her family for expecting too much on her behalf – or whether she simply regarded it as a misfortune for which no one was to blame. Presumably she urged her parents to accept the proposal and was over-ruled, and she may have accepted that their arguments were not unreasonable; but she did not forget Wesley. Betsey Wynne was more fortunate, but even so she was left dangling and uncertain, spending months not knowing if Thomas Fremantle would ever propose; and knowing, moreover, that the affair was the talk of the Fleet. Joan Scott was better placed, but even for her there was the sudden transformation of a young man who initially showed a pointed lack of interest in her into an ardent and impatient lover, and one who, if she countenanced him, would not please her family.

———◆———

Not all men were serious when they courted an unmarried woman: some were merely trifling, amusing themselves for the fun of it, with no intention of proposing. In some cases this was quite innocent: a few dances, some enjoyable conversation, and before either party knew it an attachment might be formed at least on one side. But other men – and women too – were more deliberate and cynical. Jane Austen's cousin, Eliza de Feuillide, was open in declaring 'flirtation's a charming thing, it makes the blood circulate . . .', while a few years later she was reluctant to marry for a second time because she could not 'bring her mind to give up dear Liberty, and yet dearer flirtation . . .'.[10] Austen admired her cousin but she repudiated this philosophy, and a recurring theme in her novels is the dangers of careless flirtation. This is explored most fully in *Mansfield Park*, where it is central to the plot. Mary Crawford introduces her brother to the reader when she tells her sister-in-law Mrs Grant that 'He is the most horrible flirt that can be imagined', and goes on to say that three of her particular friends in London had each in turn wanted to marry him, but he had eluded them all.[11] As the novel progresses we see Henry flirt with both Maria and Julia Bertram, regardless of the fact that the former is already engaged: this certainly makes the blood circulate for the moment, but it also causes both young women great misery. Henry then turns his attentions to Fanny Price, purely from vanity: he is piqued that she treats him coldly and decides to make her fall in love with him, at least a little. He fails, of course, while falling in love with her himself, proposes in all earnestness and is rejected. Later he renews his flirtation with Maria, now married to the dull Mr Rushworth, and neither Henry nor Maria possess the moral principles and self-control to resist temptation. Their affair leads to her being divorced and ostracised from society, while his best hope of happiness and a worthwhile life is destroyed.

Frances Winckley admits in her memoirs to having behaved badly when she was in love with Sir John Shelley, but thought that he had abandoned his interest in her. That autumn she stayed with a friend, Mrs Wilbraham Bootle, afterwards Lady Skelmersdale, at Lathom. 'I fear that I coquetted considerably with her brother, Brook Taylor, afterwards Sir Brook, who accompanied me on the violin; while his brother, afterwards Sir Herbert Taylor, played the violoncello.' Both brothers had thoughts of marriage – remember, she was an heiress – and Brook became seriously attached to her. 'I have often reproached myself for having flirted so much with him, and for the annoyance it caused to Lady Skelmersdale, who never really forgave me, and who ceased to love me as she had previously done.' Further entanglements followed, which greatly annoyed her brother and left her feeling vulnerable to criticism. She then received a proposal from an attractive figure, Tom Cholmondeley, one of Shelley's own set and his occasional rival, but immediately sent 'a civil refusal, as I had an invincible horror of being again called a "flirt"'. When Sir John Shelley heard this, he at once gave up his existing plans for the autumn 'in order to lay siege in earnest to the "inaccessible heiress," as he called me'.[12]

Young women who rejected multiple offers of marriage from different men were always vulnerable to the accusation of being 'flirts' or 'coquettes', and it is not always clear whether they had, like Eliza de Feuillide, consciously enjoyed exciting male admiration, or whether the criticism of them was simply sour grapes. Esther Acklom was a wealthy, intelligent, strong-minded young woman, whose 'speech was apt to be too frank and her determination too unswerving to render her universally popular'.[13] Nonetheless she attracted a great deal of attention from eligible bachelors, and could be decisive in rejecting them. She made her entrée to London society under the patronage of Mrs Calvert, who was initially pleased when her husband's younger brother and her young charge began flirting. But it did not take long for Esther, then nineteen, to disappoint Charles Calvert, and he was soon joined in the doldrums by a succession of other young – and not so young – hopefuls. Mrs Calvert viewed all this with disapproval and concern. 'She has a way of encouraging men, without meaning to have them, and I gave her a good lecture on the subject.' This made little difference, and in the following year Mrs Calvert noted that when she took Esther to an assembly at Lady Somers, 'There was a very great crowd, and I really was tired of my young lady. She is such a flirt, there is no getting by any men, and she shakes hands and is so intimate with all the young men that I think it a most terrible style.' Soon afterwards Mrs Calvert dropped the connection for a time, but Miss Acklom appears in other letters of the period, resisting the advances of General Tilson at Exmouth and getting engaged several times. One of these suitors was a Mr Madocks (or Maddox) whom she accepted, but then cancelled the engagement following the death of her father, scrupulously repaying 'all the expenses Mr Madocks incurred on her account, to the amount of some thousands of pounds'. This proved little consolation to Madocks if an account written by one of his friends, George Jackson, can be relied upon. 'Having been so cruelly handled by Venus, as an *amant*, he is come to try his luck with Mars, as an *amateur* . . . from being a very handsome and lively-tempered young man he has become quite the reverse. The cruel nymph, Miss Acklom, seems to take delight in this sort of trifling, and playing with edge-tools. Maddox is the second swain she has left in the lurch almost at the very moment of marriage.'[14]

In a similar vein, but a generation earlier, Lady Anne Lindsay was besieged with suitors both in her youth in Edinburgh and later in London. As she was far from wealthy and had no obvious prospects her appeal must have been personal. Her refusal to accept any of these proposals excited considerable hostility. Lord Kames, whose son she had disappointed, abused her in public: 'There she sits looking so good humoured and naïve. What a veil she draws over her heart! You witch, you little she-devil. No sooner do you gain a heart I am told than you tear it in pieces.' And she was widely blamed for first accepting and then rejecting Henry Swinton when it turned out that his fortune was less than her family had believed. Anne's sister Margaret was more under-standing, but her defence was partial in every sense: 'You have a great deal [of charm] and no dissimulation, so all the world sees how you are flattered by the admiration you are receiving. . . . Coquetry of this sort is more a weakness than a fault.' But while Anne's behaviour may have been careless and indiscreet, there was something both wise and honour-able in her refusal to marry any of the wealthy men who proposed, for no other reason that she did not love them.[15]

This was one advantage that women had in courtship. They could not take the initiative, but their right of refusal was absolute and they could generally withdraw from an engagement without loss of character – although, as both Esther Acklom and Anne Lindsay found, there were limits to the tolerance of society.[16] Men, on the other hand, might find that they had inadvertently gone further than they intended and were left with little alternative than to propose or excite considerable opprobrium. Thomas Fremantle was either in this position or close to it when he was trying to make up his mind whether or not to propose to Betsey Wynne: his attentions had been very marked and widely noticed, including by Admiral Jervis (who was not a man any naval officer would wish to disap-point), but he had played the poverty card early enough to provide some justification of his conduct if he had ultimately decided not to proceed. Similarly, Captain Wentworth in *Persuasion* discovered that his behaviour towards Louisa Musgrove had led his friends, the Harvilles, to assume that they were already engaged. 'I was startled and shocked. To a degree, I could contradict this instantly; but, when I began to reflect that others might have felt the same – her own family, nay, perhaps herself, I was no longer at my own disposal. I was hers in honour if she wished it.' And in *Cranford* the rector, Mr Hayter, was 'an old bachelor, but as afraid of matri-monial reports getting abroad about him as any girl of eighteen: and he would rush into a shop, or dive down an entry, sooner than encounter any of the Cranford ladies in the street.' Whether social pressure was really sufficiently strong to force as many men into making proposals against their will as the frequency of the device in literature would suggest is, perhaps, doubtful; but men as well as women read novels and would have been familiar with the idea, and it may sometimes have placed a restraint on their enthusiasm when in the company of unmarried women.[17]

The miseries of unrequited love, or requited love that was thwarted by circumstance, are such a cliché that it requires a conscious effort to look at them afresh and acknowledge the pain that everyone risked and many suffered when they fell in love. Yet this was the darker side of courtship, the counterpoint to the exhilaration and joy of finding a soulmate, and ignoring it would give a misleading and overly rosy picture. Brussels in 1815, on the eve of the Waterloo campaign, is an obvious place to look for both tragedy and romance: the Duchess of Richmond's ball, and all the fine young men who were killed and wounded over the days that followed, creates an irresistible source of glamorous heartbreak. Yet it was not the French but the misfortune of falling in love with the wrong person, and the prosaic but inescapable problem of lack of money, that blighted the lives of three of the daughters of the Hon. John Capel and his wife, Lady Caroline Capel, sister of Lord Uxbridge, Wellington's second-in-command at Waterloo. The Capels belonged to the top flight of British society but, like the Richmonds, they were in Brussels to economise: John Capel had a weakness for gambling that brought his family to the edge of ruin and kept them there. It was a large family: the last baby was born in 1815, which took the tally to thirteen, ten girls and three boys. The three eldest were all girls, and in the spring of 1815 Harriet was twenty-two years old, Georgy was twenty, and Muzzy or Maria was eighteen. All three mixed in society in Brussels and especially with the large British community in which the officers of Wellington's army played a prominent part. Among these officers was Major-General Sir Edward Barnes, who had distinguished himself in the Peninsula, and who would serve as Wellington's adjutant-general in the Waterloo campaign. He soon became a devoted friend of the Capels, as Lady Caroline told her mother: '[He is] one of the most amiable & best creatures I ever met with & doubly devoted to every individual of the Family. . . . He is very rich & most liberal minded – He gives us the most excellent Dinners & suppers in the very best taste whenever we choose to call upon him & asks only those we chuse . . . .'[18]

Barnes seems to have been in love with the whole family, but the object of his particular devotion was Muzzy Capel, and early in 1815 he proposed, only to be refused. Writing to her grandmother Muzzy acknowledged 'that it would in a *Worldly Point of view*, have been a desirable thing, Yet with all his *agremens* that I hear *so much* of, he is not indeed the Sort of person, that would ever have made me happy.' She knew that her parents would have warmly approved the marriage, and her sisters abused her from morning till night for her lack of taste. Defending her decision Muzzy claimed that, 'I am not I think very Romantic, for I do not think *violent Love* necessary to one's happy-ness, but I think you will agree with me that a *decided preference* is absolutely so, and that, that preference even, I never could feel. Therefore there was but one way of acting.' However, she then went on to admit that 'General F___son [Ferguson] suited my taste & feelings much much more, but there was one very decided obstacle, in that way, & indeed the *only* one, (which was, *want of that horrid Money*).' Sir Ronald Ferguson had preceded Barnes in the command in Brussels and also been a good friend to the family: he was also five years older than Barnes and would have turned forty-two in February 1815, so that Muzzy's objection to Barnes was not the twenty year age difference.[19]

A few months later, in June 1815, Muzzy's sister Georgy was involved in an equally unhappy romance when she fell in love with Horace Seymour, one of Lord Uxbridge's aides-de-camp. In the middle of May it had seemed that they might marry, although Muzzy reported that it would be '*almost beggary*' they would be so poor. But in the end Georgy's parents would not agree, although her mother was full of sympathy telling Lady Uxbridge, 'Poor little Soul She has been behaving in a most perfect manner on an occasion that it is impossible not to feel for her in, because the person has *every thing* to recommend him but that detestable article *Money*, A little of which, at least, one cannot do without . . .'[20]

But it was the eldest sister, Harriet Capel, who suffered the most from an unhappy love affair at this time. The object of her devotion was Baron Ernst Trip, a forty-year-old officer who had served in the Peninsular War, was a close friend of her uncle and was now aide-de-camp to the Prince of Orange. Baron Trip does not appear to have reciprocated Harriet's feelings, but rather than be deterred she threw herself at him with an abandon that makes painful reading even two hundred years later. Her first surviving letter to him is dated Christmas Eve, 1814.

I without hesitation commit to paper my sentiments & glory in them, – I am under a full & perfect conviction that time will only add strength & fervancy to them – & that every Christmas day I may live to see, will find me equally devoted to the only Being I ever have or ever shall adore – faithful, unalterable, unchangeable devotion I feel & ever shall feel – I exult in being *at the feet of one* who has told me he can never be to me more than friend – Friend! What a cold word for what I feel – No let me be his slave – & I ask from him but pity & compassion . . .[21]

This established a pattern of self-abasement and desperation which runs through all her letters. When he left Brussels for a time in early 1815 (possibly to get away from her) she pleaded to see him alone, if only for a minute before he left, and when he was away wrote that 'every hour you are absent, I feel that I love you more, that you are more interwoven with my very existence! indeed *mine* is *love*, real love – it is, Ernest, & some time or other you will find it out – you will try friends, flirts, & mistresses, & end with *me*, whose every idea, wish & feeling, is contracted into one little point!'[22]

She flattered him, telling him:

I *cannot* tell you what it is, that is so *dangerously* attractive in you. I very often ask myself questions upon the subject but never can I answer them. I say 'is it personal beauty – is it his manners – his conversation – his sentiments?' No, all these of course, *help*, but still, the *danger* does not lie in *any* of these, but in a sort of *nameless indescribable something* that winds *round* and *round* & *round* one, as silk round a silkworm and entangles, irretrievably entangles one before one is aware where one is . . . in everything about you, there is a peculiarity which it is vain to look for in any other Man.[23]

She declared herself unworthy of him, but thought he might give just a little of himself to her. 'It is this feeling which would make me so little *troublesome* a wife – I should never *dream* of expecting the *undivided* affection of such a Being – I should be grateful for what I had, – I should consider the *least* share of such a treat, as a treasure above all price & therefore should never complain at not possessing all!'[24]

A few weeks after this letter was written, in April 1815, Harriet's parents discovered a portrait of Trip, and presumably evidence of her correspondence, among her possessions. Mr Capel confronted the Baron and hard words led to a duel in which the Duke of Richmond acted as Capel's second. Both men fired and missed – Capel apparently narrowly, while there was some discussion whether Trip had deliberately fired wide or not. Lady Caroline warmly approved her husband's conduct, especially his consideration in keeping the whole affair secret even from her until it was over. (Whether she would have been so pleased if he had been killed, or had killed Trip, is another matter.) Although the statement put out by the Duke of Richmond to explain the affair was scrupulous in avoiding any mention of Harriet's name, the cause of the duel was well known in Brussels and reports soon spread back to England. Nonetheless Sir Edward Barnes now made it clear that, as Muzzy would not have him, he would gladly marry Harriet and so silence the voice of scandal. As Lady Caroline remarked, 'He is infatuated with the Family.' 'Think of her having Such a thing in her power, & also that she thinks of him with the admiration that all who know him do & yet would throw herself away upon a Wretch! I almost believe in Witchcraft, Mama.'[25]

At some point, either before or after the duel is not clear, Harriet and the Baron became lovers, when she went to his room and seduced him. Writing some time later when he was with the army she made her way back to his quarters and wrote to him with undiminished devotion.

I am writing this, Ernest, *from* the room *on* the couch where you *once* promised to be *Mine* for ever – I have been here above half an hour – recollecting every circumstance of those moments of bliss. . . . I have touched nothing except a little Vicar of Wakefield & a few old Poems. Your dressing table drawer was open & I looked in hopes of finding a comb or brush which had touched that dear *picturesque* brown head – but only found two old combs of my *own*, one which fell out one night on the Ramparts, the other I left in your room myself on that never to be forgotten night! Oh God, whatever my errors have been surely they are too severely punished! . . . this dear couch where I passed three *such* hours! Where I clasped on a throat whiter than snow the chain which you promised should *never* leave it.[26]

The outbreak of the Waterloo campaign in the middle of June threw Harriet into a frenzy of anxiety for the safety of her beloved Ernest, and she could not resist writing to him despite evidently promising not to do so.

> Don't be angry with me, Ernest – oh for God sake don't I do not know what I am doing – Could you see me even your heart would feel for me . . . you would not know me could you see me – I am so weak, so *gone* – for four days & nights I have neither ate – drank – or slept – I can scarcely hold a pen or walk, without support – Oh Ernest Ernest – *hearing the cannonading* feeling that every shot had perhaps deprived me of all I love – of every prospect of future happiness, not daring to ask a question – never hearing your name mentioned – Oh God Oh God, every wrong thing I ever have done has been sufficiently punished! These are the first tears I have been able to shed – every vein has been burning in my head – my heart, all, all – oh Ernest am I never to be happy?

The letter went on for pages, written in an enormous hand and much stained with tears.[27]

One more piteous letter followed, 'Oh that some kind creature would put me at once out of my agonies. Is such a life as mine worth having?', and then for six months the letters ceased. The lovers were parted: Harriet with her family, Trip with the army in France. But Harriet did not recover. In early September her mother wrote that she was still 'totally engrossed – absorbed – in an object completely unworthy in every sense, devoid of Religion & of every honorable principle! I believe him to be *every thing* that is *villainous*!' And in November 'pity her I must; In spite of her Error. It is a Melancholy sight to see a young & fine Creature losing her best days in misery & regret; she speaks with the warmest gratitude of My kindness to her, but says it is daggers to her, & that she wishes I would hate her.' Her parents, hoping that a change of scene and company would help, arranged for her to stay with family friends at The Hague, but this did little to help alleviate her misery, which was so intense that it suggests a form of mental illness triggered by the affair.[28]

On New Year's Day 1816, Harriet wrote again to Baron Trip, another desperate appeal to be permitted to share her life with him on any terms he chose and claiming that her mother was so distressed by her state that she would agree to anything to save her life. 'My unabated wretchedness has conquered her.' It is unlikely that this was true, but in February Lady Caroline admitted that her daughter's sentiments were unchanged, although she was 'improved in some respects', being able to help teach the younger children music, and looking, 'in spite of herself . . . very handsome'. There is no evidence of any further meeting with the Baron, or that he ever replied to her last letter, but as late as October 1816 she was still far from recovered from her infatuation, telling her grandmother: 'I am a poor wretch, not worth caring for . . . .'[29]

And then, without warning, came devastating news: Baron Trip was dead, and what was worse, he had committed suicide. He had shot himself in the head early in the morning of 3 November having returned from a party. Various explanations were put forward, including money worries and unrequited love for 'that pretty little Mrs Fitzherbert, who was a Miss Chichester'. Her mother broke the news to Harriet as gently as she could, and her father slept in Harriet's room for the following two nights to comfort her if she needed it, and probably to ensure that she did not follow Trip's example. Lady Caroline reported that, 'Want of sleep & horror at the Act have totally subdued the little spirits she had left,' and that she was endeavouring to keep herself busy and declared her intention of devoting herself to making those around her happy. Her mother was not confident, but began to hope that the Baron's death might actually enable Harriet to find a way forward in time. A few weeks later Harriet told her grandmother that although she suffered severe headaches and felt confused at times, she was suffering less than she had before when Trip was alive. 'I *have* felt the worst I *can* feel, & that for future it is out of the power of Man to render me more wretched than I am! I have no more coldness – no more unkindness to fear from *Him*, & He alone could either bestow or withhold happiness!'[30]

Just over a year later, on Boxing Day 1817, Harriet Capel married a forty-three-year-old widower, David Okeden Parry-Okeden of Moor Critchell in Dorset. Had she recovered sufficiently from her despair to be in love with him, or was the love on his side and for her the marriage a chance to make a new beginning and leave the past behind? We don't know, for no letters from this period appear to have survived. Eighteen months after the wedding, on 24 June 1819, Harriet died in childbirth aged twenty-six.[31]

Harriet Capel's suffering was unusual: most disappointed lovers recovered more quickly and without touching the extremes of despair that filled her for eighteen months, but many also concealed or minimised their suffering, knowing that the pangs of hopeless love were more likely to arouse mockery than sympathy. In most cases parents, friends and siblings soon became bored with the sighs and groans of the heartsick and told them to pull themselves together, or at least to present a proud face to society and not let the world know that they had been disappointed. And because most did so, the extent of suffering is minimised in the historical record. But falling in love was a perilous business, and caution and common sense could do no more than reduce the risks of unhappiness and despair.

CHAPTER FIVE

PROPOSALS, ENGAGEMENTS AND MARRIAGE SETTLEMENTS

ONCE A MAN HAD made up his mind, he still had to summon up the courage to propose. Few men were sufficiently arrogant, or had received enough encouragement, to approach this moment without some trepidation. Jane Austen describes Edmund Bertram's feelings when he contemplates proposing to Mary Crawford: he knew that he wanted to marry her, and, looking back over their courtship, he felt assured of her interest in him; but there 'were points on which they did not quite agree', and, contemplating the life he had to offer her, 'he had many anxious feelings, many doubting hours as to the result'. At times his hopes ran strong, but at others 'doubt and alarm intermingled with his hopes'. He was not willing to give up his plan to become a country clergyman for her sake; would she be willing to give up her preference for living in London part of each year and mixing in society to be with him? 'The issue of all depended on one question. Did she love him well enough to forego what had used to be essential points – did she love him well enough to make them no longer essential? And this question, which he was continually repeating to himself, though oftenest answered with a "Yes," had sometimes its "No."'[1]

John Stanley, Member of Parliament, Fellow of the Royal Society and intrepid traveller to Iceland, could not summon up the courage to speak to Maria Holroyd as he intended at Sir J. Coghill's ball, and instead wrote to her stepmother the following morning with his proposal. And John Pitt, Earl of Chatham, poised on the brink of proposing for a full month,

unable to find a moment when opportunity and nerve coincided sufficiently for him to speak. His delay left all concerned, including even his
sister, in a state of exasperation and impatience, while the object of his
addresses, Mary Townshend, was reported to be 'not a little fidgetty
[sic]'. And yet both Stanley and Chatham were eminently suitable bachelors, they required their bride to make no sacrifice of taste or habit
other than leaving her parents' home, and their feelings were already
reciprocated.[2]

When a gentleman finally summoned up his courage to make his
proposal there were few established rules or conventions for him to
follow. There is little evidence of men going down on a bended knee, nor
were engagement rings yet common, although they were not unknown.
Quiet and privacy were obviously desirable, especially if the gentleman
had any doubts of the lady's response, yet they might be hard to achieve,
for an unmarried lady would not often be left alone without a chaperone
unless the man had first spoken to her parents or guardians. Some men
did so – Mr Collins assures Elizabeth Bennet that he has her mother's
blessing for what he is about to say, while it was not uncommon to write
in the first instance to the woman's father, asking permission to court his
daughter, as a preliminary measure. The most convenient situation in
which to make a proposal was either inside when she was at home or, if
the weather was kind, outside while walking in the shrubbery or grounds.
However, Mr Elton proposed to Emma in the carriage taking them both
home from dinner at Mr Weston's, and as we have seen, John Stanley
intended to propose at a ball, although presumably in a quiet corner, not
in the midst of dancing.[3]

Some men also preferred to propose in a letter rather than doing so in
person. Edmund Bertram weighed the advantages and disadvantages of
avoiding seeing Mary's immediate reaction to his declaration. He felt
that he would be able to write much that he could not say and give her
time to reflect before she gave her answer, 'and I am less afraid of the
result of reflection than of an immediate hasty impulse; I think I am.'
But then, Mary was staying with her worldly friends in London, and
Edmund feared that if she consulted them they would not use their
influence in his favour. 'My greatest danger would lie in her consulting
Mrs. Fraser, and I at a distance, unable to help my own cause. A letter

exposes to all the evil of consultation, and where the mind is any thing short of perfect decision, an adviser may, in an unlucky moment, lead it to do what it may afterwards regret. I must think this matter over a little . . .'[4]

Once the proposal was made it was up to the woman to decide to accept, reject or something in between, as when she indicated that she liked the gentleman, but felt that she needed to get to know him better before committing herself. In some cases the man did not ask for more than this – permission to court her and to be accepted as a possible future spouse – while in other cases he might be quite willing to accept this as better than a complete rejection. In this case the man had committed himself and could not easily withdraw his offer, while the woman was free to take him up on it or not as she subsequently chose; although in practice her position was less advantageous than it sounds, and she was unwise to keep a lover dangling for long if she had no intention of accepting him.

Some proposals were absolutely unwelcome. Far from feeling flattered by having attracted the admiration of the man in question the woman might feel mortified, regarding him as not remotely suitable, and fore-seeing the embarrassment of refusing him and perhaps continuing to mix in his society afterwards when he might resent her decision. Emma Woodhouse's irritation at Mr Elton's presumption in proposing to her was of this kind, as was Elizabeth Bennet's at Mr Collins's ponderous proposal, much heightened in the latter case by his refusal to understand that her unqualified negative actually meant no.[5]

Sometimes an unwilling woman might succeed in warning off a lover before he actually committed himself to a proposal. For example, in 1805, Eugenia Wynne felt no enthusiasm for 'Colonel Plaidwell' [probably Pleydell], a younger son whom, she was assured, had good prospects, but who she was convinced 'wants Sense – and some people doubt his *personal courage* which is still worse'. To her 'surprise and annoyance' he paid her 'an immense long Visit' and 'look'd *vastly sweet*, but did not dare say much because I put on my coldest face'. Two days later he came again: 'The poor man was growing very tender and coming near the wind – but I always took care to turn off the conversation or to call in a third person that might prevent his declarations – I wish'd to save him a proposal which I mean to reject.' Meanwhile he discussed his position with the friends with whom she was staying, from which it appeared that his financial position was less promising than Eugenia had been told, something which, not unnaturally, confirmed her intention of rebuffing him: 'to make such a match without any Love on my side, would be dreadful – therefore I did everything to make him comprehend that I do not want him'. Eventually, after more than a week of awkwardness but without any actual proposal, the Colonel took the hint and backed away, leaving Eugenia again feeling relieved. 'Col. Plaidwell has giv'n a proof of good sense and has ris'n in my good graces – he was to have din'd here to day instead of which he sent an excuse stating his regret at being obliged to deprive himself of the honor of coming, but from what he had lately heard he had every reason to suppose that his presence would not be agreable [*sic*] to me – Thus is the whole affair happily at an end.'[6]

Wherever possible the disappointed suitor would take his leave and keep away from the former object of his attachment, at least until time had a chance to lessen the embarrassment, and ease the wounded feelings, that his misdirected proposal and its rejection had aroused. The unpleasantness of having a resentful Mr Collins remaining a guest in the Bennets' home after he had come to understand that Elizabeth genuinely did not want him is all too easy to understand. Some men might react with sorrow rather than anger, and at the height of the romantic era there was always a remote chance that the heartbroken lover might commit suicide, a thought which made most women more careful than ever to frame their rejection in as kind a manner as possible. Yet the most common reaction seems to have been the persistence of admiration and affection, which sometimes renewed itself in a second, or even third proposal if circumstances changed. Mr Darcy was certainly mortified when Elizabeth Bennet refused his first, ungracious, offer; but his reflections upon it did not lead to any lessening of his regard for her, or prevent him proposing a second time when he had some reason to believe that her feelings might have changed. And the Duke of Wellington not only proposed twice to Kitty Pakenham when he was a young man in Dublin; he also renewed his suit twelve years later on his return from India, and this time was rewarded with success – although the obstacle in his case had never been her feelings, but his poverty and her family's doubts, material considerations which his success in India had laid to rest.[7]

Conversely, a woman might initially accept a proposal and then break it off after considering it more carefully. In the autumn of 1802 Jane Austen received a proposal from Harris Bigg-Wither, the younger brother of her close friends Elizabeth, Catherine and Alethea Bigg. She accepted it, only then to withdraw her consent the following morning, hurrying away in some distress and confusion, although the friendship with the sisters survived, and Harris himself married happily several years later. From a worldly point of view the match would have been very advantageous; however, the young man was 'awkward, & even uncouth in manner', and evidently not remotely her intellectual equal, and a night's reflection convinced her that she would be most unwise to marry him. Similarly, the young Frances Winckley accepted a proposal from Mr Randal Wilbraham, a good, worthy man, highly educated and with a strong sense of religion, but much older than her and a widower. He courted her with talk of the good she might do for the poor of his parish and the needs of his three motherless children. 'By these means he excited all that was best in my enthusiastic nature, and, as I had resolved to give up the world, and my early inclinations, I hoped to become a martyr to duty. In an evil hour, I consented to become this unhappy man's wife.' However, when he endeavoured to kiss her, she felt repelled and flew to her room, convinced of her mistake. 'Early next morning I gave Mr. Wilbraham his *congé*, which he received with such fury and indignation as made me realize that I had had a providential escape from wretchedness for life.'[8]

It was also possible for a woman to impose conditions when accepting a proposal. The most common was the approval of her parents, while she might also stipulate that his parents agreed to the match. Other conditions might arise from circumstances. Many prolonged engagements began with an agreement to marry when they could afford to do so, an event which might depend on the success of his career or the death of a relative who would leave one of them enough money to make marriage possible. A woman might even agree to marry a man on condition that he first improved his morals. Richard Lovell Edgeworth (father of the novelist Maria Edgeworth) recalled in his memoirs that Lady Jacob, a wealthy widow much courted by foolish suitors, imposed this requirement when she consented to marry his friend, Sir Francis Delaval, a man of talent and accomplishments, but whose life was irregular. However, this 'was a species of trial not much to the taste of Sir Francis, he therefore abandoned the field to his insipid rivals'. It is hard to believe that Lady Jacob was much disappointed, or perhaps even surprised.[9]

Other proposals had a rather less forbidding reception. In 1806, a year after she dealt so firmly with Colonel Plaidwell, Eugenia Wynne attracted the attention of another younger son, Robert Campbell, whose father was 9th Laird of Skipness and whose family was connected to the Duke of Argyll. On 30 April she noted in her diary that he had accompanied her to the rehearsal of the new opera and 'on our return he seemed much agitated and ask'd me at last to let him come and speak to me tomorrow mor[nin]g – I cannot mistake his meaning'. Clearly he was going to propose, but how should she respond? 'I know him so little, that altho' what little I know *I like*, I am at a loss how to act – He seems to like me, and is extremely clever and agreable [*sic*] – I have consulted my Sisters and Mrs. Bankes – they advise me to become better acquainted with him ere I determine – all this makes me feel very strange, and it makes my heart beat to think of tomorrow –.'[10]

Mr Campbell called the next day and the couple were left alone together. He proposed 'in the handsomest and most honorable manner, and with all the feeling of a Man who is sincere – That sort of agitation is strangely catching and I felt cruelly embarrassed at first, but at last, we grew bolder as our Conversation got into a better strain – He did not at all urge or press me for an answer and only ask'd leave to see me often and give him opportunity of winning my affections – which of course, I did not deny.' He went on to explain his position to her: he was a second son, entirely dependent on his father '(who is very rich and fond of him)'; although he was certain of inheriting an estate worth £1,000 a year which was entailed upon him when his father died. He had been trained as a lawyer, but disliked the profession and hoped to obtain a diplomatic post which he thought would suit him better. Eugenia was impressed: 'He certainly has talents, his family is excellent, and I make no doubt that I shall very shortly think him worthy of my regard.' And it was clear that, without being ready to commit herself, she was strongly inclined to favour his suit: 'Splendor, nor riches, is not what I seek – I am certain that I should be happy with a moderate income, with a Man of whom I have a good opinion, He is very well looking – and I should think about thirty – The Bankes' think I ought not to marry him, unless his father allows him £1000 a year – but I think that I should be satisfied with less . . . .'[11]

When Eugenia gave Robert Campbell reason to hope that his addresses might not be unwelcome, he wrote to his father telling him of his desire to marry her and asking for his blessing – and an income that would allow him to marry. A reply could not be expected for some time (presumably the laird was on his estates in Scotland), and in the meantime the young couple continued to see each other, and Robert introduced Eugenia to his brother William. Eugenia's initial uncertainty did not last long, for less than a week after Robert had made his proposal she was writing in her journal 'the more I see of him, the more I like him' and that she spent the whole evening at a ball talking to him. Her doubts were now focused entirely on whether his father would agree to the match, and they 'really become painful to me now, and I feel but too well that should his Father deny his approbation to our marriage, I never should know again what it is to be happy in this world'. Two days later she acknowledged that 'I cannot sleep of late and I do not feel well.' And when she found that some friends knew of the tentative engagement, their congratulations made her uneasy; 'it made my heart ache to hear them *wish me joy* when perhaps there is sorrow in store for me I cannot make out how the world knows it already – I told them however that it was still very uncertain . . . .'[12]

Reading this, we can see why Mrs Calvert declared that young men should seek their father's approval before proposing to anyone, but equally it is not hard to understand why most suitors would regard this as putting the cart before the horse, as well as opening the door to unwelcome parental advice and interference. Still, a marriage united two families as well as two individuals, and parents, especially those of the woman, had an important part to play, and their blessing could neither be disregarded nor taken for granted. In *Northanger Abbey*, Catherine Morland's parents refused to permit her marriage to Henry Tilney until his father had renounced his outright opposition to the match; while there are several instances of well-born young men being packed off abroad in the hope that they would forget an unwelcome attachment. In the 1830s, Lady Hardy and Lady Jersey met and agreed to combine forces to quash an engagement their children had made without their approval – and succeeded in doing so. At the other extreme, parents might put pressure on their daughter to accept an unwelcome proposal: Mrs Bennet attempted to make Elizabeth accept Mr Collins, and Lady Balcarres told her daughter Anne, 'You must be sensible that you are not very young. You are past 16 and, everyone must allow, a woman to all intents and purposes. You also have to consider very calmly whether you would be contented to find yourself at 50 an old maid like Sophy Johnston, your old friends dead, on a scanty income, which would scarcely afford you a bone of mutton and potatoes.' But despite this Anne Lindsay refused the offer, as she would go on to refuse many more before she finally accepted Andrew Barnard twenty-six years later.[13]

However, most parents were inclined to follow the lead of their children, giving advice where there was doubt or uncertainty, but accepting a fixed determination with real or assumed good grace. Fathers in particular were thought to be susceptible to the persuasion of their daughters, unable or unwilling to withstand tearful pleas and domestic scenes – and perhaps also aware that if they refused their permission, their daughter and her lover might elope to Scotland. As Jane Austen remarked, 'Who can be in doubt of what followed? When any two young people take it into their heads to marry, they are pretty sure by perseverance to carry their point, be they ever so poor, or ever so imprudent, or ever so little likely to be necessary to each other's ultimate comfort. This may be bad morality to conclude with, but I believe it to be truth . . . .'[14]

If the father did prove obdurate in his opposition to an otherwise reasonable match, considerable pressure might be brought to bear upon him to relent. When the politician Lord Hawkesbury refused his blessing to his eldest son's proposed marriage in 1794 – he was intensely ambitious for his son, and did not want him even thinking of marrying until he was at least thirty – Canning, Pitt, Dundas and even King George III were enlisted in the campaign, urging Hawkesbury to change his mind, or advising young Jenkinson on the best way to soften his father. In the end it was only when Jenkinson told his father that he was too lovelorn to attend parliament and would withdraw for a session, perhaps forever, that his father gave way. Not all such tales had a happy ending, but, as this suggests, bystanders generally had a predisposition to favour young love rather than parental prudence.[15]

If the man's proposal was accepted, the couple would announce the news to a few close friends and family, although often with a caution not to spread it more broadly until all the details were settled, especially if one set of parents had yet to give their consent. It was a time when emotions ran high and love burned bright: a mingling of excitement, hope, confusion and anxiety lest it all be too good to be true. On 13 January 1813 Sarah Spencer wrote to her beloved brother Robert, who was serving in the navy:

> I am going to be married – there's the point. And tho' I have written it often and think it *always*, somehow I can hardly believe or understand it yet at all. Althorp [her brother] has written it to you. Clifford [a family connection], who has spent the last few days here, is writing you the result of *his* observations, and I hope that out of these letters you will collect some sense. I despair of putting any into mine, though today, as my future husband (yes, it is really true; come, let me believe it), Mr Lyttelton, is hunting, I am somewhat more calm than is my usual case. . . .
>
> As to describing or expressing the extreme wish I have – for you to be acquainted with him, and to learn to love him, my Bob – it is in vain to attempt it. I shall not attempt either to give you any idea of his character; it is such as to ensure my happiness, if it is not wholly destroyed by my own fault. If I do throw it away, I shall deserve anything bad. You must excuse my incoherent and uncomfortable style, dearest, I am sure you will! You cannot imagine the state of mind into which the certainty of being preferred by the person whom reason and inclination greatly approve, and the prospect of so awful a change of life and accession of duties, throws me. . . . Mind, I shan't for some months certainly, perhaps a year, become a matron. It is near the usual time of a return from hunting, and I am getting into my usual fidget at the prospect of a visit and conversation, which I must, however, learn to be accustomed to soon, or it will be sad work indeed.[16]

A month later the novelty had worn off just enough to make her feel a little more comfortable in William Lyttelton's presence, and to enable her to revel in her position and prospects:

What happiness is mine all round me – slippery, dangerous, blinding happiness! . . . my *intérieur* is so full, so brimful of perfect delight, that it well accords with the cheerfulness of the scene. For the clock is fast wearing away at the minutes to the happy hour of twelve, when a well-known step will sound along the passage, and a well-known voice will be heard at my door, announcing my daily visit from him on whom I do feel my happiness hangs and depends with something of a sensation I won't attempt to describe or express. If I could succeed in giving you an idea of what it is to respect, and admire, and love with one's whole heart, a person whose warm affection one is sure of possessing, and with whom one is assuredly to spend one's future life, in the most intimate, the most sacred of all connections, I should be afraid, my Bob, that you would forthwith look about for some Maltese fair one, or perhaps some Greek damsel, to realize my description.[17]

Maria Holroyd was equally happy in looking forward to spending the rest of her life with John Stanley, telling her aunt, 'as far as I can see, I think I may be a most happy woman – too happy, when the prospect is so good, I cannot check apprehensions. I cannot deserve the happiness I enjoy and have enjoyed at home, with the addition of such expectations as I may indulge.' And to another trusted correspondent she wrote, 'I believe I may say with the most perfect assurance of not being deceived, that the most amiable and feeling heart in the world is entirely mine. . . . You may suppose me agitated; but indeed I am much more so than is rational. However I cannot help it. Sorrow is more easily to be borne with fortitude than joy beyond all the hopes I ever had formed.' A few weeks later she reflected:

How fortunate, how providential every event of late has turned out for me! This dear Woman [her stepmother] who has made us all happy, by making me so for one, has, in some degree, harmonized my temper and disposition, and I am sure I am more equal to being a good Wife now than I should have been two years ago. Alas! if I am not one I have no excuse, which is a melancholy reflection; the sin must all rest on my Shoulders, for this Man would make the Devil love him and behave well to him.[18]

Once a couple were engaged they were free to spend more time together and were less strictly chaperoned. Jane Austen's niece Anna and her fiancé Ben Lefroy wandered happily through the country lanes near Steventon during their engagement, just as Charles Bingley and Jane Bennet took frequent walks in the shrubbery and beyond to have a little time away from her family and visitors. Mrs Calvert noted in her journal that Sir James Stronge made Isabella 'play for him every evening on the pianoforte, and sits over her, admiring her. We have the pianoforte in the ante-room and we talk in the drawing-room *with the door open*. The lovers are at this moment sitting under a tree before the windows reading, "The Lady of the Lake" and I have sat down to write.'[19]

The sight of the couple mooning over each other sometimes amused third parties and sometimes wearied them. After a month, Mrs Calvert grew tired of their incessant delight in each other and commented in her journal that she was 'completely tired of love making, though I suppose Sir James is less trouble than any other young man would be'. And a year before her own engagement Sarah Spencer had acted as chaperone when her cousin met her fiancé:

[T]he first meeting between the two young people [after '*six long weeks* of absence'], as they say, took place; and, to be sure, any gentleman or lady with such pale faces, dry lips, and senseless brains, as they were, I never saw. They neither of them knew what they said or did, and I was of the greatest use in putting in a *water-gruellish* sort of observation every now and then, just to fill up the pauses between the nonsense that came out at first. Soon, however, Lord H. recovered his senses, and we had some good conversation . . .[20]

There are a few, rare, references to engaged couples cuddling and kissing, and it seems plausible that this understates the frequency with which couples began to take liberties and go beyond the bounds of propriety. However, those bounds were deeply ingrained – in the men as well as in the women – and it seems that in the vast majority of cases such transgressions were relatively innocent, where they occurred at all. A few couples certainly went further. In 1773 the *Lady's Magazine* warned its readers of the dangers of pre-marital sex, while many novels touched on the subject, generally with an abhorrence that is focused on the woman who, in at least one case, 'flies to a nunnery to save him [her prospective husband] from her "polluted embraces"'. Not all novelists were so severe: one male writer has a character dismiss such doctrines as unrealistic and confined to fiction; while Jane Austen permits Lydia Bennet to marry Wickham, regarding their marriage as a sufficient punishment for them both. Outside the world of novels we have good reason to believe that Lady Anne Lindsay had sexual affairs with both William Windham and Lord Wentworth, while in 1818 Harriet Spencer, an unmarried niece of the Duke of Devonshire, had an affair with the Marquess of Blandford which resulted in the birth of a daughter. In both these cases the women went on to make respectable marriages, although Harriet Spencer's only took place after the Duke of Devonshire used the full weight of his social *éclat* to ensure that she was received in the top flight of English society, and even then she lived abroad with her husband, a German count. But as far as we can tell these were outliers, and couples of the gentry and upper classes seldom pre-empted their wedding night.[21]

Less alarmingly, Frances Winckley thoroughly enjoyed the months of her engagement to Sir John Shelley, meeting his fashionable friends and delighting in all the excitement of the London season. 'Lady Cowper, who had been lately married, was my favourite chaperone, and took me to the opera, and to balls and routs. She danced as much as I did, and it was not *then* thought strange that an "engaged" young lady should dance with others, besides her affianced husband.' Everyone would by then have known that she was engaged, for once both families had given their approval it was not desirable to keep it secret, and it would be widely announced, sometimes even by a notice in the press.[22]

Engaged couples were also permitted, indeed expected, to write frequently to each other when separated. Such letters were sometimes intended to be circulated widely to family and friends, while in other cases they were more intimate and were not expected to be shared. Men who were absent on active service in the army or navy wrote home describing their experiences and the country in which they were serving: some consciously shielded their fiancée from the grim details of warfare, but others were relatively open. Robert Garrett was a young officer who served under Wellington in the Peninsula from 1811 until late 1813, when he returned home having been wounded. He wrote more than sixty surviving letters to Charlotte Bentinck in which he described his narrow escapes, the fate of his fellow officers and the hardships of campaigning. 'I told you in the beginning of my letter I was very badly off & you will easily conceive it when I tell you all I got [to eat] yesterday, after beginning our march at 3 in the morning & being engaged with the enemy from about 2 till 6, was some coarse barley meal at about 9 at night, which I got out of the haversack of a Frenchman that was killed . . .' And, when he was wounded at the Battle of Sorauren in July 1813, 'the wound I received on the 28th though a severe one is not dangerous. A musket ball entered my left arm at the back of my wrist, & taking a direction upwards was extracted from the inside. The surgeons of the division at first wished to have taken my arm off, but I strongly opposed it. The wound is very painful.' Garrett's letters were not especially intimate – he knew that they were to be read by Charlotte's extended circle, and there was always a risk of them going astray, even being captured at sea and published in the French newspapers, to inhibit any great display of passion, but he ended them by sending his 'very, very best love to you'. Unfortunately Charlotte's letters have not survived, but at one point he tells her '[your] dear letters smell so nice and sweet that I fancy myself at Ramsgate again when I put them to my poor nose'.[23]

Other letters were clearly meant for the recipient alone. Hester Mundy described her fluctuating spirits to Sir Roger Newdigate: at one moment she was calm enough to contemplate writing him 'a very saucy Letter', but then she was suddenly consumed with doubts over the 'utter impossibility of my Ever obtaining any better hold of your affections, than what your blind partiality now gives me & which I much fear will diminish as you become more clear sighted.' Harriet Fane also needed reassurance, writing to Charles Arbuthnot, 'Will you when you speak to me call me yr *very dearest* Harriet?' she asked:

I should never refuse you anything then. . . . Did you kiss your letter while you were writing to me? Our lips have then touched the same paper. How much I wish you were here now. . . . I always receive your letters a little after nine when I come in from walking after dinner, & I come up into my own rooms to read them, & when I go down again Edward sometimes says 'Well Harriet I hope it was very agreeable' & I say 'No business of yours Sir'; but what time do you think I answer them? What o'clock do you think it is now? Very near *three*, it is really very wrong but I don't come up to bed till nr twelve & then I gener-ally read yr letter over *nine or ten* times before I sit down to answer it.[24]

Couples also exchanged gifts: Robert Garrett sent Charlotte Bentinck some sheet music which the regiment's bandmaster had copied out at his request, and 'a little box of trifles', including some buttons, two bottles of jasmine and a ring, although he apologised that the last item was not more elegant as everything he could find for sale in Lisbon was 'so vulgar'. He was also disappointed in being unable to purchase any casta-nets. In return Charlotte sent him violets – a flower associated with faithful love – a hand-worked purse, and her mother sent him a ring, signifying her approval of the engagement. At the other end of the scale, Robert Peel, son of one of the richest men in England, gave Julia Floyd a pearl necklace worth over £1,000. Maria Holroyd noted that John Stanley 'seldom comes empty-handed, and if we do not marry soon, he will ruin himself first by the handsome presents he makes me'. She, and many other young women, also received costly presents from their own fami-lies, generally contributions to their wedding trousseau. A particularly intimate and important present was a miniature portrait, while locks of hair, sometimes made into bracelets, were also common and laden with significance.[25]

Very long or indeterminate engagements were generally recognised to be hard on both parties. If their marriage could not take place until his career had flourished or a relative had died, couples might wait years without ever being entirely sure that their patience would be ultimately rewarded. Jane Austen warned Fanny Knight against accepting John Plumptre when the marriage could not take place for several years, and she had the admirable Mrs Croft deplore the idea of 'an uncertain engagement; an engagement which may be long. To begin without knowing that at such a time there will be means of marrying, I hold to be very unsafe and unwise, and what, I think, all parents should prevent as far as they can.' Yet such cases were not uncommon, especially with younger sons who had to make their fortune, and where the alternative was a marriage without sufficient money on either side to support a family.[26]

But even a short engagement was not always particularly enjoyable. Eugenia Wynne married Robert Campbell less than three months after he proposed to her; but those months were filled by a roller-coaster of volatile emotions which she lovingly recorded in her journal. First, there was the anxiety of whether his father would approve the marriage and provide them with a sufficient income; then she was miserable that he seemed to put his career ahead of marrying her, which led to a quarrel and then to a reconciliation. Each then behaved badly: she flirted furiously with Lord Burghersh, and he abandoned Eugenia to go to a concert with Mrs Sidney, to whom he was paying far too much attention: jealousy, scenes, recriminations and renewed promises left them more intensely in love than ever. Eugenia was then horrified by a story very detrimental to Campbell's character – she does not record the details – which cast the whole marriage in doubt and caused intense distress before his brother, supported by written testimony from Lord Rosslyn, proved that the story was baseless, or at least that if Robert had been foolish, he had not behaved dishonourably. It is hard not to feel some sympathy for the impatience of Eugenia's brother-in-law Captain Fremantle at her constant oscillation between love and despair, but although in one way she evidently revelled in the drama of these crises, her misery at times was real and heartfelt. 'I spent a sleepless night in tears - I never, never, have felt so unhappy! – to think that I love him so much, and he loves me so little! is insupportable to me . . .' It is unlikely that Campbell was enjoying the engagement very much either, although they were both getting to know each other's characters much better.[27]

The length of an engagement was often determined by the negotiations over the settlement that were conducted by lawyers representing both families. Their delays frequently caused great frustration to everyone else. In her novel *The Semi-Attached Couple*, Emily Eden wrote of 'the usual difficulty about settlements which attends all marriages, whether there be any property to settle or not'. And even when both families were being generous the wheels could grind slowly. Less than a fortnight after John Stanley proposed, Maria Holroyd wrote that 'Papa has been more kind than anything you can imagine, and has determined from the first that the affair should not be stopped or delayed by the want of anything in his power to forward it. Mr. Stanley's father is as generous on his side, and the general kindness of everybody is to me very overcoming.' That was in the middle of May 1796, and by the end of that month Maria was hoping that the wedding might be in the second week of July, so that they could have some of the summer together before she accompanied Stanley when he rejoined his militia regiment. However, the lawyers did not finish their work until 11 September, and the documents then had to be sent to Stanley's father for signature, adding at least a further week to the wait. Therefore 'Monday or Tuesday in the week after this must be the day. I think it cannot be longer. I really cannot be Maidenly enough to help being heartily rejoiced things are drawing to a conclusion. It is a very tiresome state to be in, especially expecting for so long past as we have that a fortnight would conclude, and always finding another and another fortnight tacked on.' Even this proved a false dawn, and it was not until 6 October that everything was finally signed and sealed. Maria was almost past exasperation: 'There cannot be anything more ridiculous than the quantity of writing these lawyers chuse to perform on these occasions. There were nearly 100 Skins of Parchment, and as many of the Deeds were triplicates, and others duplicates, you may imagine what a sight of Sheep skins there were.' The all-too-frequently postponed wedding took place five days later at Fletching Church, Sussex, near Sheffield Park, her father's estate.[28]

The level of interest displayed by the families on each side in these negotiations varied considerably. Some fathers were content to leave it largely to the lawyers, especially where they had little discretion because their daughter's marriage portion, or their son's inheritance, was determined by their own marriage settlement. But on other occasions the family could take an active part, especially if they were unenthusiastic about the match. Some engagements broke down at this stage, where one party found that the other was less well off, or less willing to provide for their child, than they had supposed. Both Anne Lindsay and Esther Acklom had engagements broken off through quarrels over marriage settlements, although in both cases there is reason to believe that they were more relieved than disappointed, and that this may have been as much a pretext as a cause of the rupture. Even if the engagement was not broken off, the terms of the settlement might disappoint one side or the other and affect the way that the match was viewed by the wider family, if not the principals. For example, when Charles Paget married Lady Elizabeth Monck in 1805, his mother commented that 'her family have been very shabby, considering that they gave out last year that she was [*sic*] a large fortune, which, they have now frittered down to seven thousand five hundred pounds . . .'. It was not a propitious start for relations between mother-in-law and daughter-in-law.[29]

Most couples tried to detach themselves from these negotiations. Women in particular expressed disinterest bordering on distaste for the haggling that went on, claiming not to understand the points in dispute (and this must often have been true, for nothing in a girl's, and not much in most boys' education prepared them for the intricacies of different hypothetical contingencies dreamt up by the attorneys). Not unnaturally, both the principals wished to concentrate on their approaching wedding and the commencement of their married life with the person they loved, not their rights as widows or widowers, or the disposal of property they would inherit when their parents died in many years' time. This reluctance to engage with the subject may have disadvantaged women more than men, if only because the lawyers who were apparently acting on their behalf were really acting on behalf of their fathers and their fathers' estates, whose interests were not identical to those of their daughters. Yet the emotional toll of close involvement in the negotiations could be high and immediate, while the financial disadvantage was distant and hypothetical, so it is not hard to understand the decision to remain aloof.[30]

Just how bruising such negotiations might be when the couple themselves were involved, or even kept closely informed, is shown by the experiences of Charles Arbuthnot and Harriet Fane. Harriet's family did not like her engagement to Charles: not only was he a widower with four children, who was more than twice her age, his social background was also inferior to hers, and he had no capital or landed property, something which his excellent political connections and senior position in the government did not entirely offset in their eyes. For his part, he naturally resented their disapproval and felt that they were demanding that he give more to Harriet's settlement than he could afford, while being niggardly in their own contribution. Because Harriet loved and trusted her family she was torn, and this resulted in quarrels and ill-feeling between her and Charles, despite the intensity of their love for each other. At one point she wrote to him, 'I have felt most severely all that has lately been passing between us.' She had looked over their earlier letters and 'with bitterness and regret have marked the difference between them and those I now receive'. She was 'so thoro'ly worried and wretched this last week that my spirits are subdued, I have not been able to bear up against the idea that I am your ruin . . . I sat and cried for an hour before I wrote to you, the depression of spirits was such as to make me wish to lie down & die . . . the clock is now striking four, and I feel no inclination to sleep.' This *cri de coeur* produced an affectionate letter from Charles which healed the rift and, after much discussion, a solution was found: Charles would insure his life for £10,000, which would secure Harriet's financial future (and that of any children they might have) in the event of his death.[31]

Marriage settlements did not follow a uniform pattern, varying enormously to reflect the circumstances and wishes of the two families, but there were certain common elements. If the groom was heir to an estate, the marriage settlement was usually the vehicle by which the entail on the estate would be extended to the next generation, that is, his eldest and as-yet-unborn son; which meant that the groom had only a life interest in the estate, so that he could not sell or significantly depreciate it. (Frequently some parcels of land or other property were left out of the entail to provide some financial flexibility.) However, it should be remembered that most men were younger sons and not heirs to estates, and even those who ultimately became very wealthy had usually not made their fortune before they married. The settlement also provided for the bride if she was widowed. The common law 'dower right' to one-third of the income of the estate was extinguished and replaced by a pension or jointure, whose level was usually specified as a fixed sum per annum. This jointure was often calculated as a proportion of her portion (that is, her fortune that she brought to the marriage). In the late eighteenth and early nineteenth centuries the rule of thumb was that the jointure should not be less than one-tenth of the portion, and it was frequently higher, especially if her fortune was small. While the husband was still alive the wife would also commonly receive a smaller sum as 'pin money' to cover some of her private expenses and to give her a degree of financial independence from her husband: this money was protected from the husband and his creditors.[32]

Settlements also contained provisions for the children of the marriage, especially the daughters and younger sons: the boys might receive a certain sum when they came of age and the daughters when they married; or they might have to wait until their mother, or both parents, died. At a minimum, their mother's portion was likely to be divided between them when she died, but it was more common for them to receive a share of the total settlement, including the contribution that came from the paternal estate. Obviously no one knew how many children, if any, the marriage would produce, and while some settlements specified a set sum that each child would receive, others allocated a lump sum to be divided between them. The amount tended to be the same for both the boys and the girls, except for the eldest son who was usually favoured even when there was no paternal estate to be handed down. Sometimes a child's inheritance was conditional: daughters might only inherit if they married with their parent's approval; or parents might be able to divide a lump sum between their children in any way they wished; while in other cases the child's share was guaranteed, giving them a certain independence.[33]

The most important provision of a settlement was that the wife's portion, and the contribution from the groom or his father, should be placed in the hands of trustees who would invest it conservatively. Part of the income from these investments would pay the wife's pin money and the rest would usually be available to the couple – which legally meant the husband. However, not all settlements included this provision: in some cases the whole capital was paid to the groom or his father in return for a legal commitment to pay pin money, jointure and children's fortunes. Such an arrangement was obviously dangerous, providing far less security than having the capital sequestered in the hands of trustees, and the lawyers on the bride's side should have opposed it as strongly as possible. Yet many settlements took this form – including some where there was no social or financial inequality between bride and groom, and where both parties came from wealthy aristocratic families – while others employed trustees. It is not at all clear what determined which model would be followed or whether the use of trustees became more common in the late eighteenth and early nineteenth centuries, although by the later nineteenth century the employment of trustees had become the norm.[34]

The contribution of the two families to the marriage settlement varied greatly, although usually some money came from each side. The bride's portion was often determined, at least in part, by her parents' marriage settlement, which might specify that she was to receive a certain sum or certain property on her marriage. Her father might choose to add to this minimum, although doing so might create an expectation that he would be equally generous to his other daughters and his younger sons, which could stretch the resources of even a wealthy family if several daughters got married in rapid succession. A large contribution to the settlement might also be used to compensate for a degree of social inferiority on either side, so that the son or daughter of a plain gentleman marrying a child of the peerage might literally pay for the privilege; although there are other examples of a socially and financially superior family providing the great bulk of the settlement. Marriage settlements were not restricted to the top flight of society, with cases found even among small shopkeepers and other people of modest means and no social pretensions; they were the norm among the gentry and those in the gentlemanly professions, as well as among substantial land-owners and the aristocracy.[35]

Three examples of settlements put flesh on these generalisations. When Jane Austen's parents married in 1764, her mother brought leasehold property in Oxford and the expectation of £1,000 when *her* mother died; while Mr Austen contributed some freehold properties in Tonbridge and a one-third share of further property, all of which would only become his on the death of his stepmother (which took place four years later). These properties were all placed in trust: the real estate was soon sold and the proceeds used to purchase South Sea annuities, whose dividends contributed to the family income and, many years later, gave Mrs Austen an income of £210 after her husband's death in 1805. Further up the social scale, when Sir Arthur Wellesley finally married Kitty Pakenham in 1806, she brought a portion of £4,000, with a further £2,000 to follow on her mother's death. He contributed £20,000, or half the fortune he had made in India, and these sums were placed in the hands of trustees: her brother Edward Pakenham, his brother Gerald Wellesley and some attorneys to do the actual work. Was the scale of Sir Arthur's contribution – so much larger than that of the Pakenhams – simple generosity or a way of emphasising how far he had come from the humiliation of his repeated rejection by her family a dozen years before? Lord Chatham could not afford to be so open-handed, for the estates he had inherited were heavily mortgaged and his principal asset was a pension granted by parliament in honour of his father, Pitt the Elder. Bank of England 3 per cent annuities with a face value of just over £5,000 were placed in the hands of trustees (as such bills generally traded at a discount their actual value would have been less than £5,000). Mary was promised £400 a year in pin money and, if he died first, she would receive a jointure of £1,000 a year, paid quarterly and drawn, if necessary, from the pension. If she died first, the income from the capital was to be paid to her widower for his lifetime and then divided between their children, excluding the eldest boy (who would inherit his father's title and the bulk of his estate, including the pension). The boys would receive their share when they turned twenty-one; the girls when they married. If the Chathams had gone on to have six children, the girls and younger boys would have stood to inherit no more than the Bennet girls in *Pride and Prejudice* – £1,000 apiece – although their social and political connections might have ensured that they received some further assistance. However, the marriage proved childless.[36]

Marriage settlements were designed to achieve two purposes that were both regarded as important by contemporaries. They aimed to preserve the core of the estate for the next generation, protecting it from an extravagant or wastrel heir; and they provided financial security for the widow and made some provision for the daughters and younger sons of the marriage. They were not completely successful in achieving either objective. Some men still ran up huge debts that ruined their estates and blighted the lives of their successors, while widows and their children sometimes struggled to receive their legal entitlements. However, such failures were relatively unusual. Wives generally received their pin money, widows their jointure and children their inheritance, even when the head of the family was negligent or incompetent. The system was far from perfect, but it gave a financial underpinning to the position of women within marriage that was important both materially and for their self-respect.

——⟐——

CHAPTER SIX

WEDDINGS AND HONEYMOONS

MOST WEDDINGS IN REGENCY England were relatively simple affairs. They were often conducted at short notice, almost as soon as the lawyers had completed the business of preparing the settlements. Most brides were married close to home, with at least some of their family present, but it was not uncommon for the parents and siblings of the groom to be absent or only sparsely represented. Jane Austen's brothers all married in their bride's home parish, and there is no evidence that she attended any of these weddings. As her niece Caroline later remarked, 'Weddings were then usually very quiet. The old fashion of festivity and publicity had quite gone by, and was universally condemned as showing the great bad taste of all former generations.' It has often been noted that Austen never describes the wedding of any of her heroines in detail and ridicules an excessive concern for dress and appearances in her account of Mrs Elton's reaction to the wedding of Emma Woodhouse and Mr Knightley: 'The wedding was very much like other weddings, where the parties have no taste for finery or parade; and Mrs. Elton, from the particulars detailed by her husband, thought it all extremely shabby, and very inferior to her own. – "Very little white satin, very few lace veils; a most pitiful business! – Selina would stare when she heard of it." '[1]

Canon law dictated that weddings in churches had to take place between eight o'clock in the morning and noon, and that the intention to marry had to be publicised by an announcement ('reading the banns') in the church where the ceremony would be held on the three preceding Sundays, to allow for objections to be made or impediments to be revealed. Almost all couples in England were married in an Anglican service: the law made explicit exception for Jewish people and Quakers, but all other non-Anglicans were expected to comply. Catholics, like Eugenia Wynne, not only did so, but were also married by a Catholic priest, if possible on the same day. There was no restriction on marriages in Lent – indeed spring and early summer seem to have been the most popular time for weddings – nor even on Christmas Day. Even so the small population of most parishes meant that weddings were relatively uncommon in most churches – Mr Austen performed only a handful of wedding services in a typical year in his two country parishes – although a busy city church might conduct several in a single day. The extreme example was St George's, Hanover Square, the parish church of fashionable Mayfair, which spewed forth a steady stream of married couples, over one thousand in 1816 alone, with no fewer than nine weddings celebrated on Christmas Day.[2]

The only alternative to a church wedding, short of leaving England, was to be married by special licence, and this could only be issued by the Archbishop of Canterbury, who generally restricted these licences to members of the elite: privy councillors, the aristocracy, judges, baronets, knights and Members of Parliament, and their connections. As a result such private weddings attained a social cachet – Mrs Bennet dreamt that Elizabeth and Mr Darcy might marry by a special licence, although it is not clear whether he would have been able to obtain one if he had wished to do so. Private weddings were very popular among the upper classes in this period, especially among the fashionable trend-setters in high society: the Duchess of Devonshire, her sister Lady Bessborough and her two daughters Georgiana, Countess of Morpeth, and Harriet (Harry-O) Leveson Gower, Lady Granville, (to give them their married titles) were all married in private ceremonies. These private weddings were generally held in the bride's home, usually in the drawing room, with only a few close family present, and they still had to be performed by an Anglican clergyman. However, they might be held at any time of the day, including in the evening: George Canning married Joan Scott at 7.30 p.m. on 8 July 1800, and Harriet Cavendish married Granville

Leveson Gower at Chiswick House at 8 p.m. on Christmas Eve 1809 and they left for their honeymoon an hour later. Even stranger was the timing of Sydney Smith's brother Bobus' wedding to Caroline Vernon, a connection of Lord Lansdowne's, which took place at 5.30 on the morning of 9 December 1797, with the happy couple setting off on their honeymoon soon after 6 a.m. when it must still have been dark.[3]

Some members of the elite were so unfashionable as to prefer the idea of marrying in a church. When Maria Holroyd was finally able to settle the plans for her wedding she remarked that 'it will take place here [Sheffield Place] and at Church, which I like much better than a House, unless there was some good reason for preferring the latter'. And the Duke of Bedford told his son, Lord William Russell, 'I am decidedly of the opinion that the marriage should be in church. Those sort of private marriages which take place in houses never appear to me to carry with them the sanctity and solemnity of the marriage vow.' Yet the final decision was not up to the Duke, nor his son, and the wedding was held in the bride's mother's house in Hertford Street. Similarly, it is reported that, before she was married, Priscilla Wellesley-Pole expressed a wish to be married in church, but was told that this was impossible, 'as people would think it so odd and unlike other people'.[4]

The Duke of Bedford also gave his son some paternal advice in the same letter. He warmly approved his son's choice of a bride and had no doubt of their happiness, but warned his son against the dangers of extravagance, cautioning him to 'Avoid all unnecessary expense in the first instance, and begin with economy. If you get involved in difficulties at the outset, you may never recover them . . .'. Given that the Duke himself was notoriously prodigal, regularly outspending his stupendous income, the homily may have irked Lord William, but at least it was softened by an offer to pay any existing debts to allow the couple to start afresh. The Duke also urged his son to retain his position on the Duke of Wellington's staff and to take his career as a soldier seriously: 'I will candidly own to you that I should feel a severe disappointment if you did not continue your professional views.' And he offered to purchase a lieutenant-colonelcy of a regiment as soon as an opportunity arose as the best way of gaining the practical knowledge Lord William needed.[5]

Such letters were not uncommon. Lady Bessborough's mother, the redoubtable Lady Spencer, gave her daughter a lengthy screed in which she warned her child to avoid giving her husband the slightest grounds for jealousy, whether of any man, woman or even of her own family: he should feel that he was absolutely first in her affections and consideration, and she should be willing to give up anything and anybody to preserve his peace of mind. Lady Spencer also preached the virtues of economy (albeit with less hypocrisy than the Duke of Bedford) and warned her daughter against the evils of gambling. Her daughter should mind her manners, avoid favouring one set of people over another, not chase after fashion and strictly adhere to the tenets of religion, while avoiding all forms of dissipation and worldly temptations. Lady Bessborough would have been a different person – or living in a completely different milieu – if she could have followed this advice; as it was, it almost seems that she spent the rest of her life systematically flouting every one of her mother's injunctions.[6]

After these conventional pieties it is refreshing to read the advice given to Harriet Janvrin by her aunt, who was also the mother of her husband-to-be:

Mutual love is the first step towards (happiness), without which it cannot take root; but it is not all. . . . You doubtless think it easier to please a husband than to please a father. A short time will undeceive you in this respect. . . . The age of tyranny over our sex is nearly at an end . . . but there still exists a stumbling block against which reason will never be fully able to prevail, that is the love of power. . . . Very few men will ever allow that a wife can have reason on her side; it is all one whether she be wise or foolish; if she thinks not as he does, she must be wrong. . . . Our lives are much more sedentary than those of men, and therefore we have much more time for reflexion and thought. . . . You must make yourself acquainted with the exact state of your income, and with that which you can and ought to afford yourselves. . . . I cannot command your love, but I hope to acquire it. Come here when you like, be open with me, and you may do with me what you please.[7]

Although weddings were generally quiet, private affairs, they could still provide the occasion for conspicuous displays of wealth and grandeur, frequently centred around the bride's trousseau and jewellery. For example, when Georgiana Cavendish married Lord Morpeth in 1801, Nunn and Barber, lacemen and haberdashers, presented her family with a bill of £3,368 9s. 6d. for lace, muslin, ribbons and handkerchiefs (although it is possible that this included items for her mother and sister on the occasion). And when Richard Viscount Belgrave, heir to the second Earl Grosvenor, married Lady Elizabeth Leveson Gower, daughter of the Marquess of Stafford, in 1819, Lord Grosvenor spent £3,662 on jewellery for the bride and £373 on a new carriage for his son. In 1797 the *Lady's Magazine* reported that at the wedding of Princess Charlotte, George III's eldest daughter, to the Hereditary Prince of Württemberg that year, she wore 'a nuptial habit of white satin, with a train or pellice of rich crimson velvet with fur trimmings', while the Prince wore a suit of 'silk, shot with gold and silver richly embroidered; gold and silver flaps and cuffs; under his coat the order of St Catherine; over his shoulder the blue watered ribbon insignia of the German Order of the Golden Fleece'. Royalty were, of course, an exception to most rules; however, when the actress Miss Farren married Lord Derby that same year her wedding garments were put on display where 'A great number of simpletons', in Eliza de Feuillide's sharp phrasing, went to see 'thirty Muslin dresses each more beautiful than the other, and all trimmed with the most expensive Laces, Her Wedding Night Cap is the same as the Princess Royal's and costs Eighty Guineas – I have no patience with such extravagances, and especially in such a Woman.' Even at the less exalted level of Miss Grey, the heiress whom Willoughby marries in *Sense and Sensibility*, we are told that her wedding clothes could be seen at the warehouse prior to the event as a form of advertising.[8]

Brides and their mothers were often busy in the months before the wedding selecting the fabric and supervising the making up of her trousseau. This was an entire wardrobe, with the wedding dress itself the most important garment, but only one of many. Most wedding dresses were intended to be used on other occasions. Annabella Milbanke wore 'a muslin gown trimmed with lace at the bottom, with a white muslin curricle jacket, very plain indeed, with nothing on her head', while Mary Elizabeth Lucy was dressed in 'snow-white silk with a wreath of orange blossoms, a "lace veil of texture fine as a spider's web", accompanied by bridesmaids in white cashmere wearing bonnets lined in pink silk'. White was becoming popular but was still a long way from being universal. Mrs Austen, Jane's mother, was married in her travelling clothes, while some women wore riding habits for the service, including Lady Elizabeth Fox-Strangways who 'was dressed in a green riding habit, black hat and feather; a long white veil fell down over her face'.[9]

Grooms generally wore normal morning clothes, not necessarily new for the occasion; what is most noticeable is how seldom anyone comments on them: their appearance, manner and emotions are described far more frequently than their attire, which is taken for granted and felt to be of negligible importance.[10]

Then as now, weddings were a time of heightened emotion for the bride, the groom and for their families. George Canning, not otherwise renowned for his lack of confidence, confided to his aunt a few hours before the ceremony, 'I believe the feeling is something like that of going to be executed. It is strange, and wild, and tumultuous, and though I am happier than ever man was, yet it is an awful feeling and full of serious-ness and deep and quick-succeeding reflections.' William Wilberforce wrote in his diary, 'To Church abt 11½ & married . . . My dearest Barbara, compos'd but inwardly agitated. I suddenly mov'd to tears in Service & much affected . . . .' At the wedding of Marianne Clayton and Colonel Henry Fox in 1786, the bride's sister noted, 'She trembled and had her eyes quite full, but she did not cry . . . *He* had his eyes quite full also, and looked agitated, which was just what I wished . . . .' And Letitia Perceval 'wept bitterly' through the whole of her wedding to Major Powlett, 'and with great difficulty repeated the necessary parts of the Service'.[11]

The service itself was simple and allowed for little innovation, although on at least one occasion the clergyman left 'out all the excep-tionable parts' – although which bits were felt to be exceptionable is not specified. As a result, 'The ceremony appeared to be over in less than ten minutes – which I think made it more tremendous. The idea that so short a time can alter things so strangely, is very formidable.' It is unlikely that the excisions included the need for the bride to commit to 'honour and obey' her husband, although this requirement gave many women pause for thought. Lady Elizabeth Fox-Strangways' 'voice trembled, but she did her best – did not articulate the word "obey", but behaved on the whole very prettily'. However, Maria Holroyd told her friend with some pride that 'I went through the Ceremony very boldly – that is – did not leave out the word "Obey". I pronounced it indeed with as much satisfaction, as much certainty of having a pleasure in Keeping the Vow, as the word Love. And one of us must alter very much before I find it difficult to keep that promise.'[12]

Wedding rings were given by both grooms and brides, varied from plain bands to finely engraved or chased designs and were sometimes inscribed with a short declaration of love or the couple's initials and perhaps the date of the wedding. Women often wore their ring between two other rings – 'keepers' – which might contain jewels. In 1791, as their long-deferred wedding approached, William Harness asked Elizabeth to send him 'the measure of your finger for the pledge of our eternal affection'. Three weeks later he announced with triumph, 'I have bought the ring.' When Fitzroy Somerset's arm was amputated on the evening of Waterloo (without anaesthetic) he called out, 'Hey, bring my arm back. There's a ring my wife gave me on the finger.' And in 1812, before the birth of their first child, Ann Flinders wrote a letter of farewell to her husband Matthew in case she died in giving birth. In this she said: 'My wedding ring is thine, & I should like thee to wear it for my sake, on thy little finger, if it will fit there – remember it was a pledge of union, of faith, of love & of all which renders domestic life happy.'[13]

On 13 March 1813 Lady Sarah Spencer married William Lyttelton, an event which is vividly described in a letter from his sister who accompanied him to the ceremony:

We left Davies Street *tête-à-tête* in a chaise and four about two o'clock. He appeared in very good spirits – talked on indifferent matters till we reached the Lodge at Wimbledon. This said Wimbledon is quite a country seat, and there is at least half a mile's drive through a pretty park before you reach the house. This gave time for the gentleman to grow rather nervous; he said, 'When she hears the carriage how her heart will beat!' from whence I inferred that his was not at that moment very peaceably resting within him. I gave him my hand; he said: 'Do not make me shed tears before the time.' We drove up to the door, were shown into a handsome drawing-room. Lady Spencer said we were a quarter of an hour before the appointment. I answered that was all right. He was soon sent for, and in about ten minutes we were summoned to march in procession to the church. Lady Sarah being extremely anxious to have it as private as possible, the party consisted merely of her sister and two brothers and I myself.

The church stands within about 200 yards from the house through a little shrubbery. She walked slowly between her father and William, seeming as if she could hardly support herself, well dressed, but not finely. The church is so small that it gave me the idea of a private chapel, just room for us to kneel round the Communion Table. The service was extremely well performed by Mr Allen, Lord Althorp's former tutor, a man much attached to the family. The parties concerned said their lessons very audibly, though with much feeling on both sides. When William signed his name to the register Mr Allen shook him by the hand and said, 'God bless you, Sir.' I never shall forget the look with which he returned the benediction. Lord and Lady Spencer then embraced him and seemed to accept him as a very dear son. We then walked back rather more briskly than we went, and found a *collation* with all the delicacies of the marriage season, of course, including an enormous plumb [*sic*] cake. . . .

. . . He talked to me of his Sarah the night before he was married in terms of rapturous admiration; he said ever since she had consented to be his, he had felt quite another man, that he hoped he was already a better, as he was certain he was a more religious, one from the force of her example; the conformity in their ideas and principles on every subject was something wonderful, and such as must make their union only increase in felicity as it was strengthened by time.

I left them soon after four o'clock, one munching a hunch of dry bread, the other relishing a piece of hard biscuit, side by side on a sofa, looks beaming with love and joy. Lord and Lady Spencer were to leave the coast clear immediately after dinner, and Wimbledon is to be their headquarters during the compleat honeymoon. They both said they wished their solitude to be occasionally interrupted, and made me almost promise that I *would dine and sleep there, before it was long.*[14]

Parents and other family members could also find weddings emotionally draining. Caroline Lybbe Powys's mother did not attend her daughter's wedding in 1793 because she could not bear the distress of losing a daughter 'who till latterly I had never parted with for even one night'. At Elizabeth Fox-Strangways' marriage her father and aunt were both in tears, thinking of the bride's mother who had died several years before. And when George Canning got married, the prime minister, William Pitt, was so nervous and emotional that he could not sign as a witness, and one of Canning's friends signed in his place. Not everyone was so affected, of course. When Maria Bertram of Mansfield Park married James Rushworth of Sotherton Court, 'her mother stood with salts in her hand, expecting to be agitated – her aunt tried to cry' but neither was actually moved, unlike her father, who 'was indeed experiencing much of the agitation which his wife had been apprehensive of for herself'.[15]

After the service was completed the bride and groom sometimes left immediately on their honeymoon and sometimes stayed for the wedding breakfast. This might be very simple, as when Jane Austen's niece Anna married Ben Lefroy in 1814, 'The breakfast was such as best breakfasts then were: some variety of bread, hot rolls, buttered toast, tongue or ham and eggs. The addition of chocolate at one end of the table, and the wedding cake in the middle, marked the speciality of the day. . . . The servants had cake and punch in the evening . . . .' Or it might be rather more elaborate: 'There was a splendid breakfast of course. The Cake was cut in due form, over the Bride's head, by Aunt Fanny and me – and we performed all the ceremonies of garters and squeezing cake through the ring etc.' Sometimes the celebrations took on a rather modern air, as Mary Russell Mitford noted with some relish:

The bride and her second sister set off to Brighton [on the honeymoon with the groom], and I and the youngest remained to do the honours of the wedding-dinner. Of course, we all got tipsy – those who were used to it comfortably enough, and those who were not, rather awkwardly – some were top-heavy and wanted tying up like overblown carnations, some reeled, some staggered – and one fell, and catching at a harp for a prop, came down with his supporter and a salver of coffee which he knocked out of the servant's hands; such a crash, vocal and instrumental I never heard in my life![16]

Some couples did not have a honeymoon, with the bride moving straight into her new home, which she might have to share with her husband's mother or other relatives. In other cases, where the husband was an army or navy officer, the couple might spend the first weeks of their marriage in lodgings in a port town, enjoying a brief interlude together before he sailed on active service. Some naval wives even accompanied their husbands on board and spent their honeymoon at sea, as Eugenia Wynne's sister Betsey did when she married Captain Fremantle. In 1786, Captain George Palmer took his new wife and two of her friends on a month-long honeymoon cruise in the Irish Sea, including the Isle of Man and the Scottish coast, in a twenty-gun sloop, whose accommodation might have made even Mrs Croft flinch, although it is clear that they spent some nights ashore. And Matthew Flinders, the explorer, hoped to take his newly married wife Ann with him on the *Investigator* (a ship little if any larger than Palmer's) all the way to Australia soon after their marriage, but the Lords of the Admiralty discovered the scheme and expressed their disapproval, so that Ann was forced to return to her father's house, and they parted not to be reunited for nine years due to his detention by the French at Mauritius on his homeward voyage.[17]

If stories such as this suggest an almost excessive determination not to be apart, Sir Arthur Wellesley veered in the other direction. Having returned from India in September 1805 he proposed to Kitty Pakenham by letter, not having seen her for twelve years. She accepted him with some hesitation (not unreasonably wishing that they could renew their acquaintance first and perhaps even that he might spend some time courting her). He was then almost brutally efficient, arriving in Dublin with his clergyman brother Gerald on 8 April 1806, getting married on the 10th, and heading back to London by express on the 13th, leaving Kitty to follow, escorted by Gerald. He was genuinely busy, but his refusal to give his wife priority over official business was all too symptomatic of the pattern of their married life.[18]

However, most couples set aside a few weeks or a month for the honeymoon, which could take a variety of forms. When Francis Austen, Jane's brother, married Mary Gibson in 1806 they spent their honeymoon in a lengthy stay with his wealthy brother Edward, whose house at Godmersham provided a level of comfort and even luxury that was otherwise beyond their means. But even wealthy couples sometimes spent their honeymoons on a series of visits to relatives in different parts of the country, while Robert Stewart (later Lord Castlereagh) and his wife Emily stayed with Lord Ancram, while exploring the Scottish border country on foot. In *Mansfield Park* the newly married Rushworths spent the first few days of their marriage at Sotherton and then proceeded to Brighton where there was plenty of society and amusement even in winter, reserving the greater delights of London for later.[19]

Most couples retreated a little from society for their honeymoon, looking to concentrate on each other for a time, and frequently retired to a borrowed house, belonging to friends or family, for a few weeks. Assuming they were wealthy, they would probably bring their own valet and lady's maid with them, but otherwise the staff would come with the house, and the couple would not need to supervise them or have any domestic duties. Sometimes they were alone, but it was equally common for them to be accompanied by one or two family members or friends, or for them to be joined by visitors after a week or two by themselves. It might be a formidable test of a still new and possibly fragile relationship for the couple to have no one at all to turn to for amusement, or to express their feelings, other than each other. Brides in particular were often thought to need a female companion, a sister, close friend or even mother, for part at least of the honeymoon; but the adjustment to married life could be hard for both parties. As one novelist put it, 'many a fondly devoted bride has . . . during the very first week, often wished for her usual occupations, as much as her lover has for his gun and pointers.' Too much leisure could lead to boredom and even irritation, especially for young women used to living in large, bustling families or for young men accustomed to constantly mixing among a coterie of other young men. As the historian Hazel Jones comments, 'A familiar presence eased the transition from the single to the married state for any couple unused to long hours in each other's company and viewed in this light, the inclusion of a third, fourth or even fifth party on a wedding journey appears eminently desirable.'[20]

The presence of a familiar face also softened the blow which most brides felt at parting from their family – leaving home permanently in a way which few had done before, even if they had been sent to school or gone on long stays with relatives and friends. Men, by contrast, were more likely to have already taken this step, especially if they were pursuing a career, while others would bring their bride back to the family home, which might even be vacated for them. Many women, even if happy with their new husband, felt the pain of separating from their family sharply. Mrs Calvert was accompanied on the first part of her honeymoon by her mother, but the time came for her mother to leave the young couple and return to Ireland. Years later, in an account written for her children, she recalled: 'Never shall I forget the sensation I experienced when, early in the morning as I lay in bed, I heard the step of her carriage put up, and the carriage drive from the door. I felt, as it were, abandoned among strangers, and I believe should have been long in recovering my spirits, but for the kindness of your dear father, who fully understood my feelings.'[21]

Sex was, inevitably, an important element in the honeymoon, often colouring the couple's relations for the rest of their lives. Although it is impossible to prove, it seems reasonable to assume that most brides, except widows, were virgins when they married and that most grooms were not; but we have very little direct evidence for the experiences of the wedding night. As far as we know, no bride or groom kept a sexually explicit diary recording her or his experiences in the manner of the coded passages in Anne Lister's journal (see below, chapter 8, pp. 151–2), so that we are left with the inferences drawn from other material. These give an overwhelmingly positive impression – indeed the letters of newly married wives became renowned for the enthusiasm and excitement they exuded. For example, Julia Peel told her mother, 'My Robert says truly that I am well but he does not add what I do, which is that I believe myself to be the very happiest of all human beings. I am thank God united to a thoroughly amiable Man and one *whom I adore, for whom I would willing risk existence itself.*' While Queen Victoria wrote in her journal soon after her marriage, 'MY DEAREST DEAREST DEAR Albert sat on a footstool by my side, and his excessive love and affection gave me feelings of heavenly love and happiness I never could have hoped to have felt before! He clasped me in his arms, and we kissed each other again and again! His beauty, his sweetness and gentleness – really how can I ever be thankful enough to have such a *Husband*!' Of course, these examples do not show that other brides did not have a miserable time, coupled with selfish or inept men who had little interest in giving them pleasure, and it is plausible to imagine that disappointment was less likely to be recorded and then to survive in the sources than delight. But we should not imagine that most young ladies in Regency England went to their wedding bed with the feelings of a martyr, although Miss Brownlow of Bath was probably unusual in ordering ' "transparent night chemises of the thinnest muslin and *gauze* – some striped some spotted – with bows of white satin and other absurdities" for her honeymoon attire'.[22]

If the couple were staying with family and friends during their honeymoon, they might expect that their behaviour would be observed and even commented upon, often without much delicacy. A relatively innocent example comes in the comment of George Selwyn in 1768 that the newly married Lord Beauchamp 'is seen out so early in a morning that it does not look as if much business was doing'. And Mrs Arbuthnot delighted in the story that when Lord Barham got into bed on his wedding night 'he told his bride he wd read her a chapter in the Bible to tranquillize her mind! Upon which she blew out the candle . . .'. Servants, of course, might also gossip, overhear conversations and arguments, inspect the bed when they were making it and draw their own conclusions, so that the privacy of a newly married couple – or anyone else – was relative, not absolute.[23]

In most cases couples seem to have been eager to please each other – and to be pleased – in the early weeks of their marriage, and not just in bed. Two days after her wedding, Eugenia Campbell (née Wynne) 'had a little fever in the night which alarmed Robert who flew for the Doctor and wanted to send for Sir Walter Farquhar [the leading London physician of the day] – how much his agitation, and the affection he showed me endeared him to me . . .'. After all the uncertainty of her engagement, she felt relief at having made the right choice after all:

> every instant makes me more sensible of my happiness in being united to a Being, I so dearly love, and who has such a heart and so much feeling with which he amply repays my affection – after all the uneasiness, the fears, my love for him has cost me it is impossible for me to describe with what gratitude I look towards my God for having now placed me in a situation which sanctions all my tenderness and even makes it a duty – I spent half the day in bed and by following the prescriptions of Doctor Beauchamp I soon was much better, tho' I felt very weak – Robert would not leave me for an instant the whole day – He is the kindest and best Nurse.[24]

Maria Holroyd, now Maria Stanley, was equally happy, telling her Aunt Serena:

> Your prophecies and wishes will all come to pass. They must; and, barring unforeseen misfortunes, such as human beings must inevitably meet with, we shall be one of the happiest pairs in England. As to the degree of happiness which I am now feeling continuing, I should be very sorry if it could, for it is certain 'Joy goes but to a certain bound, beyond 'tis agony,' since we are both at this moment the most uncomfortably happy people you can imagine. . . . I only feel it is not a dream when he is out of the house, which is a difficult matter to get him to be. . . . Indeed, you none of you know half the value of his inestimable heart, much as you love him.[25]

And Lady Sarah Lyttelton, as she now was, felt much the same even after five months of married life, writing to her parents from Stockholm, which she was visiting with her husband as part of a tour that would go on to include Russia, 'I cannot too often assure you, from the bottom of my heart, of my entire and indescribable happiness in my wanderings, as far as it depends (and you know best how very far that is) upon incessant, undeservable, and, if possible, still increasing kindness and attention shown me by him whom you saw me tied to for life five happy months ago . . . .'[26]

Yet married life, even in its earliest days, could not be unalloyed bliss, and Eugenia Campbell was distressed to discover that her kind husband had a temper and could be irritated by the inconveniences of travel. Arriving in Liverpool *en route* for Scotland, 'We were much disappointed in finding our things not yet arrived from Swanbourne – Robert was a little out of humor about it, and with some cause – yet – I saw him so for the first time – and I am so spoilt by his indulgence – that altho' he said nothing cross or unkind to me – I chose to cry for an hour about it, and felt ashamed of myself – he recovered his usual good temper even before I had recovered my Spirits.'[27]

Eugenia's sister Betsey was very happy with Captain Fremantle on her honeymoon, noting that 'I daily think more and more that I have ensured my future felicity by marrying one who so well deserves my love and regard[;] nothing on my part will be wanting for us both to be happy.' But inevitably there were the odd ruffles and tiffs: 'Fremantle attacked me for some nonsense or other I am too *inanimate*, but we were very friends at last, I see that very little is required to make him uneasy and must be still more on my guard.' And, a week later, 'I behaved very foolishly towards Fremantle[,] caused him much uneasiness and made myself very unhappy, certainly not intentionally[.] I was very angry with myself afterwards but it was too late, all for a trifle and nonsense.' Fortunately the next morning brought a reconciliation, 'Was unhappy all the morning as I saw I had given F. real cause to be angry with me however it was better explained and we were friends again.' Two days later she added, 'The honeymoon is over but it finished almost better than it began, I flatter myself that the months that are *to come* will all be *honeymoons* for me.'[28]

And so couples gradually got to know each other rather better than they had done amidst the heady excitement of falling in love and being engaged. The Rubicon of sex had been crossed, but they had yet to discover how they would get on living in the same house amidst all the distractions, amusements and petty annoyances of everyday life. Whether the future would bring a deepening of their affection or creeping disillusionment remained to be seen: for better or worse they were married, and whatever happened their lives would be intimately entwined.

CHAPTER SEVEN

ELOPEMENTS, ABDUCTIONS, MISTRESSES AND *MÉSALLIANCES*

A COACH RATTLES AT high speed along a country road, the postillions wielding their whips to spur the horses on. Close behind an angry gentleman of middle years shakes his whip furiously as he pursues them, supported by three followers, one of whom has lost his hat and wig as his horse bounds forward. Leaning out of each side of the coach a young man and a young woman, both fashionably dressed, point pistols at the pursuing man. A signpost points to Gretna Green. The scene is a print by Thomas Rowlandson, titled with heavy irony *Fillial [sic] Affection, or a Trip to Gretna Green,* and it was published just in time for Christmas 1785 (see plate 4).[1] It is easy to suppose that scenes like this were largely fictional, belonging to the province of romantic literature and to the imaginary world of 'Regency' novels. But elopements were actually quite common in the eighteenth and early nineteenth centuries, and Rowlandson's scene was echoed, at least occasionally, in reality. Only three years before, John Fane, 10th Earl of Westmorland, aged twenty-three, had eloped with Sarah Anne Child, the seventeen-year-old daughter of Robert Child of Osterley Park. Child was a wealthy banker and Sarah his only child and heir. It is said that Westmorland had proposed but been refused by the father, who believed that his great wealth counted for more than the young man's aristocratic lineage and considerable landed estates. Once he discovered that his daughter had left, Child set off in furious pursuit and eventually caught up with the couple between Penrith and Carlisle, not far from the Scottish border. Reaching them, Child shot the leading horse of Westmorland's carriage, but in the ensuing confrontation one of the Earl's servants cut the leathers suspending the body of the older man's carriage to the springs, while the others pulled the dying horse from the traces. The young couple then resumed their journey and were married at Gretna Green on 20 May, and later repeated the ceremony at Westmorland's estate of Apethorpe on 7 June. The outraged father consoled himself by entailing his property on his heirs female: so that while his daughter would inherit a life interest in his fortune, it would then pass on to her daughter and not to her son, the next Earl of Westmorland.[2]

On another occasion, in 1814, the eloping couple's chaise broke down before they were half-way to Scotland. They hid in a nearby copse and the postboys – well paid to assist them in their hour of need – turned the chaise around so that it appeared to be heading in the opposite direction. The pursuing father appeared on the scene, but accepted the word of the postboys that the chaise belonged to two sportsmen who had gone off shooting while waiting for it to be repaired. He therefore continued on the road to Scotland, while the young couple followed slowly and cautiously in his wake, once the chaise had been repaired. Beyond Penrith the father learnt that another chaise was on the road a little ahead of him, travelling at speed to the border. Not doubting that it contained his daughter he hurried on, accompanied by the brother or friend who had travelled with him all the way from London. Eventually they overtook the chaise at the little posting station at Hesket. The father leapt down, ripped open the door of the chaise and pulled its occupant from his seat, demanding the return of his daughter. A brawl followed with both gentlemen rolling in the dust before the father realised that this was the wrong chaise and that its occupants were two respectable young men *en route* to stay with Lord Elcho! Profuse apologies and the inherent interest of the story made amends, and the father continued on to Gretna Green where he was relieved to find that his daughter had yet to appear. He and his supporter entertained the Gretna minister, and were unstinting in their provision of whisky to everyone at the inn, but the landlady had a soft spot for young lovers (who had provided her with much good business over the years) and sent one of her servants to warn them to take another road if they approached. The message was heeded: the young couple proceed on a tour of Scotland for several months, and the father eventually tired of his wait at Gretna and went home after a fortnight. When the couple eventually appeared at Gretna there was no obstacle to their marriage, which had become the more necessary as the lady was now pregnant. Whether the father ever forgave them remains unknown.[3]

At the time the word elopement had a broader range of meanings than it does today. It might refer to a young couple running away together in order to get married without the consent of one or both sets of parents; but it might also refer to a married woman going off with a lover and even, although less commonly, to a debtor escaping his creditors or an apprentice leaving his master.[4] Couples headed for Gretna Green, just over the border from England, because there they could be married under Scottish law, which allowed girls as young as twelve and boys as young as fourteen to be married without the consent of their parents, unlike in England where both sexes had to be twenty-one before they could defy parental objections. They could also be married immediately in Scotland, not needing to apply for a special licence or to wait while the banns were read on three successive Sundays. Most couples who eloped did so in order to circumvent parental objections: frequently the bride was still some years short of her majority and her parents might think that she was too young to marry; or they might regard the prospective groom as lacking in fortune or social status to be a suitable match; or they might have some other objection, either to him personally (perhaps he had a reputation which did not fill them with confidence) or to his profession. In other cases couples felt impelled to elope when the young woman discovered that she was pregnant.

Not all couples went to Scotland: some crossed the Channel to France or Belgium, and others managed the whole business so quietly that it can be difficult to know whether it really was an elopement or not. An example of this was the marriage in 1790 of Spencer Perceval, a thirty-year-old barrister, to Jane Wilson, the daughter of a Member of Parliament and old soldier, Sir Thomas Wilson. Spencer and Jane had been in love for several years, and his elder brother, Lord Arden, had married her sister with her father's blessing in 1787. But Perceval's prospects were not especially encouraging – he had yet to make his mark at the bar – and Sir

Thomas refused his consent to their marriage. In 1790 Jane turned twenty-one, and five weeks later she and Spencer were quietly married at East Grinstead when she was apparently visiting friends or relatives (presumably the banns had been read, but no one attending this particular church recognised the names of the couple). Soon afterwards Perceval wrote to a friend, reporting that everything had ended happily: 'You, I am sure, will be pleased to hear, that Mrs P. and myself have been to Charlton, on Sir T[homas]'s invitation, and were received with all the kindness and warmth that a very affectionate parent (as he certainly is) could bestow on his daughter. He also has told me that he will make up her fortune, just what it would have been had she married with his consent, and was not satisfied till he made us repeatedly assure him that we were convinced we had his full forgiveness.' It is impossible to know how many other couples were equally adroit in circumventing parental opposition without needing to leave England.[5]

Spencer Perceval went on to become prime minister in 1809, and it is remarkable how many other leading politicians of the period had also eloped. Westmorland served in successive Pittite cabinets for almost thirty years from 1798, having previously been Lord Lieutenant of Ireland. And Lord Eldon, the famous Tory Lord Chancellor, had run off with Elizabeth Surtees and been married by the Presbyterian minister at Blackshiels – the most convenient point in Scotland to Newcastle where they lived. Nor was Eldon the only Lord Chancellor of the period who had eloped: Thomas, Lord Erskine, the Lord Chancellor in the Ministry of All the Talents, had eloped in 1770 with Frances Moore, the daughter of a Member of Parliament, and married her at Gretna Green. More remarkably, he eloped a second time in 1818, thirteen years after his first wife's death, when he was in his late sixties and a peer of the realm. According to the story that was widely circulated, he left London disguised in women's clothing, including 'a large Leghorn bonnet and veil', in order to escape detection by his eldest son. At Gretna Green he married Sarah Buck, a blacksmith's daughter, who had been his mistress for many years. This second marriage was unhappy: she was reported to be both violent and unfaithful to him, and he unsuccessfully attempted to divorce her in 1820, although it is possible that his primary purpose in marrying her was to legitimate their existing children, and in this he succeeded.[6]

There are no comprehensive records of the number of couples who eloped, or even of those who were married at Gretna Green, but in his memoirs Robert Elliott one of the several successors of Joseph Paisley, the most famous of the Gretna Green ministers, states that he married a total of 3,872 couples between 1811 and 1839, an average of 138 a year. Other ministers at Gretna, such as David Lang and John Linton, probably married at least as many, although some of these couples may have been locals or from other parts of Scotland who were not eloping. Still, it is clear that elopements were far from rare and that many a parent in England would have been conscious that if they pushed their opposition to their daughter's attachment too far they might find that their parental authority had its limits. In 1805 Mrs Calvert commented on the news that Lord Petre's daughter had eloped with her drawing master, 'What a disgraceful thing! Oh, my dear girls! May you never do a thing of that sort! I believe it would break my poor heart.'[7]

When a couple arrived at Gretna they usually proceeded to the inn, where the staff were well accustomed to such visitors and were adept at making all the necessary arrangements and at judging how much the couple could afford to pay. Until 1811 they were most likely to be married by Joseph Paisley, 'the blacksmith parson' (although Elliott, who married his granddaughter, says that he had never been a blacksmith, but a farmer and a fisherman, before discovering that the marriage trade was much more profitable). The actual service was simple. The minister asked the couple their names and places of abode; they were then asked to stand up and if they were single.

Each is next asked: – 'Did you come here of your own free will and accord?' Upon receiving an affirmative answer the priest commences filling in the printed form of the certificate.

The man is then asked 'Do you take this woman to be your lawful wedded wife, forsaking all other, keep to her as long as you both shall live?' He answers 'I will' The woman is asked the same question, which being answered the same, the woman then produces a ring which she gives to the man, who hands it to the priest; the priest then returns it to the man, and orders him to put it on the fourth finger of the woman's left hand [and] repeat these words, with this ring I thee wed, with my body I thee worship, with all my worldly goods I thee endow in the name of the Father, Son, and Holy Ghost, Amen. They then take hold of each other's right hands, and the woman says 'what God joins together let no man put asunder.' Then the priest says 'forasmuch as this man and this woman have consented to go together by giving and receiving a ring, I, therefore, declare them to be man and wife before God and these witnesses in the name of the Father, Son, and Holy Ghost, Amen.'[8]

The couple often left Gretna almost immediately after the ceremony was completed, sometimes returning to Penrith or even further back on their route that same day. When John Scott, later Lord Eldon, eloped with Elizabeth Surtees, they returned as far as Morpeth after their hasty marriage. Unfortunately the inn was full and it was only by the kindness of Mr and Mrs Nelson, the innkeeper and his wife, who gave up their own bed, that the exhausted young couple found any accommodation for their wedding night. They remained at Morpeth for several days, having written to their parents, waiting for a reply and uncertain whether or not they would be forgiven. Elizabeth later told her niece that this was the most miserable part of the business: 'Their funds were exhausted, they had not a home to go to, and they knew not what their friends would say.' But then John's brother Henry appeared, bringing an invitation from his father for the couple to come to the family home, which was gladly accepted.[9]

Most parents appear to have accepted the marriage when it was too late to prevent it and to have forgiven their child rather than risk permanently alienating them. Rowlandson depicted the scene in a companion piece to *Fillial Affection* entitled *Reconciliation or the Return from Scotland* in which the young couple are shown in, the servants wreathed with smiles, the young woman's mother on her feet and her father full of forgiveness rather than anger while the young woman is overcome by emotion at the reunion (see plate 5). But not everyone could overcome their outrage. Sir Edward Knatchbull, who had married Jane Austen's niece Fanny Knight in 1820, could not forgive Mary-Dorothea, his daughter by his first marriage, who, in 1826, eloped with Fanny's brother Edward. The reason for his opposition to the match is not clear – there was no social or legal obstacle, despite the tangle of relationships which it would produce (Edward would become Sir Edward's son-in-law as well as his brother-in-law), although the same reasoning which barred marriage to a deceased wife's sister would find such a connection unpalatable. However, it is possible that he objected to Edward Knight on personal grounds or that he could not forgive the defiance of his wishes. Whatever the reason the elopement caused both Sir Edward and Fanny intense misery, and although in time she was inclined to accept it, he refused to do so. Sir Edward did not see his daughter again for more than ten years after the elopement, and then, in the following year, she died in childbirth, plunging him into fresh grief.[10]

While elopements were relatively common, abductions were not. When they did occur in England they typically involved deception rather than violence. A man would induce a young woman or girl into his carriage and then carry her off, persuading her to marry him in Scotland by arguing that after several days alone in his company her reputation would be ruined if she refused, and that no one would believe that she had not gone with him voluntarily. Almost invariably the motive was financial: she had a substantial fortune or was an heiress. The most famous and brazen example of such an abduction occurred in 1826, when Edward Gibbon Wakefield, a widower of gentlemanly manners, great charm and self-confidence, engineered an elaborate plot involving his brother and servants, which succeeded first in securing the person of Ellen Turner, a school girl who had just turned fifteen, whom he had never met, and then in inducing her to agree to marry him, through a series of increasingly elaborate stories: first that her mother was ill and needed her at home; then that her father was going to meet them; and finally that her father's business was ruined and could only be saved by her agreeing to marry Wakefield. Remarkably, Miss Turner appeared to thoroughly enjoy the escapade, with countless witnesses subsequently reporting her to have been in high spirits and laughing merrily. For his part, Wakefield seems to have fallen at least half in love with her and, either from delicacy or caution, did not consummate the marriage. He made no resistance when her uncles and her father's lawyer, supported by two Bow Street officers, finally caught up with the couple in Calais and demanded her surrender. Once Ellen realised that all his stories were lies and that she had been played for a fool rather than heroically sacrificed herself for the sake of her father, she forsook Wakefield completely. Amidst immense publicity a trial followed – Wakefield voluntarily returning to England, although it is hard to imagine how he hoped to escape conviction once Ellen's father was determined that he should be prosecuted. He was sentenced to five years in prison and went on to become a famous campaigner in liberal and radical causes, including prison reform and the colonisation – without the use of convicts – of South Australia and New Zealand. The marriage was annulled, and Miss Turner's reputation suffered surprisingly little: in January 1828 she married Thomas Legh of Lyme Park, the grandest house in the district, and three years later she died in childbirth, still only nineteen.[11]

The abduction of Ellen Turner was clear cut, but in other cases there was much more ambiguity. In 1791 Clementina Clerke was a fourteen-year-old boarder at a school in Bristol and – since the recent death of her maternal uncle – the heir to several slave plantations in Jamaica. Richard Vining Perry, a local surgeon apothecary, cultivated her acquaintance and they were soon on good terms. One day he sent a carriage for her to the school, purporting to come from her guardian inviting her to take tea. She left in this, but Perry then carried her off to Gretna Green, and thence to the Continent, where he kept constantly on the move until her family and friends gave up the pursuit and accepted the *fait accompli*. However, her school mistress remained outraged, and Richard Perry was prosecuted in 1794 after the couple returned to England. The case was decided when Clementina gave evidence that far from being abducted she had accompanied Perry willingly, and that it was an elopement not an abduction. By this time she had already had one child with Perry and was pregnant with twins and so it is equally possible that she was telling the truth, or that she had come to accept her marriage, and was willing to lie in order to save the father of her children from a conviction on what was then still a capital offence. Public opinion was sympathetic to Perry, although a generation later it would be very hostile to Wakefield.[12]

Some eloping couples were aware of the risk that their action might be mistaken for an abduction, and that this would encourage the woman's family to pursue them. The easiest way to avoid this danger was for her to leave a note declaring her intention before she climbed through the bedroom window and down the ladder into her lover's arms, but in 1771 one 'young lady of fortune' went further, 'and to avoid the imputation of his stealing her, she rode the first on the horse and stole him'. On the other hand, a young lady – with the help of her mother and servants – also took the initiative in what appears to be a clear case of abduction in Ireland in 1827, where they kidnapped John Hely Hutchinson Grady, a sixteen-year-old schoolboy, who is described as being immature and of weak intellect, and carried him off to Gretna Green where the young woman, Helen (or Ellen) Richards, and he were married. The motive in this case appears to have been that Miss Richards was pregnant and that her lover had either abandoned her or was unable to support her. Grady's father, a successful barrister, protested, leading to an inconclusive trial in 1828, although the final upshot of the story is unknown.[13]

Abductions were always more common in Ireland than in England and more often accompanied by violence or the threat of violence. But here, as in England, there was a sharp decline in the second half of the eighteenth century which continued into the nineteenth, with cases becoming rare and highly publicised. However, the true number of abductions was probably always rather larger than appears on the record, with successful cases, where the woman's family decided to make the best of a bad lot by treating the abduction as a voluntary elopement, being concealed. In many of these instances it is likely that the 'husband' was paid off with a pension and the couple did not live together, although neither was able to marry again while the other was still alive.[14]

Not all elopements ended in marriage. When Lydia Bennet ran off with George Wickham they proceeded no further than London, and it appears that Wickham never had any intention of marrying her. She was not greatly troubled by her position: 'She was sure they should be married some time or other, and it did not much signify when.' This was not only morally wrong, according to the standards of the day, but also foolish; for if Wickham abandoned her, as he surely would as soon as he grew tired of her or she got pregnant, she had no legal claim upon him, and her only recourse would be to return in disgrace to her family, if they would have her, or join the countless thousands of 'fallen women' who worked the streets of London and other cities of the period. Such a fate was unusual for a girl from Lydia's background. As her uncle, Mr Gardiner, remarked, Wickham risked retaliation from her family and friends by ruining her and losing the support of the colonel of his militia regiment (Lydia had been staying with the colonel's wife): 'His temptation is not adequate to the risk.' It turned out that he was forced to flee in any case, having run up large debts that he could neither pay nor ignore, and took Lydia with him with little thought to the consequences. In the end he did quite well out of the adventure, being bribed and coerced into marrying Lydia in exchange for the payment of his debts, an increase in her settlement, including an immediate annual allowance of £100 a year, and a commission in the regulars, although it is unlikely that he found marriage to Lydia either economical or especially comfortable.[15]

But, as Mr Gardiner's comments suggest, girls from less privileged backgrounds – the daughters of poor clergymen, teachers, half-pay officers, widows and such like – were much more vulnerable to being seduced and then abandoned, often without even enough money to make their way home. Their families lacked the resources, and often the knowledge, needed to pursue them, or the means needed to pressure a reluctant seducer into matrimony. The same was obviously true, to an even greater extent, of families further down the social scale: dairymaids, shopgirls and servants were all vulnerable to the sexual advances of their social 'superiors', although their employer might offer them some protection if only to protect his or her claims to respectability. Nor should it be assumed that young women were without feelings or agency of their own, and while some were pitiful victims of cynical seduction or even rape, others, like Lydia, were motivated by love and passion, heedless of the consequences.[16]

Some men went to extraordinary lengths to seduce a young woman who had caught their eye. In early 1817 the twenty-three-year-old Marquess of Blandford, son and heir of the 5th Duke of Marlborough, met the sixteen-year-old Susannah Adelaide Law, the daughter of a Dublin provision merchant who was then living in London. He wooed her ardently and asked her to marry him, while stating that for family reasons the ceremony had to be performed privately and kept secret. They were accordingly married on 6 March in her parents' house, with her mother and sister present, and the Marquess's brother officiating. Mrs Law entered the marriage on the flyleaf of the family Prayer Book, and Blandford settled £400 a year on Susannah. They then went to live in his house in Manchester Street, but called themselves Captain and Mrs Lawson. In fact the marriage was a complete sham: the man who performed it was indeed the Marquess's brother, but he was an army officer not a clergyman. Blandford's friends all knew about his latest love, one of them remarking that he was 'in raptures about a mistress he has got, & to whom he has given a settlement'. Were Susannah and her family deceived? It is hard to believe that they had no suspicions of the legitimacy of the marriage, and it is at least possible that they deliberately pushed their doubts to one side, while hoping for the best. Yet Susannah herself appears to have believed that she was indeed married, and she may have felt the service had been legitimate in the eyes of God, even if it was not legally binding. After all, a generation earlier, the Prince of Wales had performed a similar trick to overcome Mrs Fitzherbert's scruples, but had not let this stop him marrying Caroline of Brunswick a decade later in return for parliament settling his debts, and there are other stories of young lords going through dubious ceremonies with women who were, nonetheless, always regarded as their mistresses, not their wives.[17]

When Susannah discovered the deception she protested vehemently, and in order to pacify her Blandford agreed to take her to Scotland and marry her there. By this time Susannah was pregnant and a Scottish wedding would also legitimise her baby. In March 1818 she gave birth to a daughter, and that August 'Captain and Mrs Lawson', together with their baby daughter, servants and several of his friends, headed north. However, no wedding took place, and Blandford took care that they were never introduced in society as a married couple. When she returned to London, Susannah went back to live with her parents. Soon afterwards Blandford sent word by one of his friends that the affair was over and that he was about to marry the daughter of the Marquess of Breadalbane. Susannah collapsed on receiving this message and remained ill for several weeks. The financial settlement Blandford had promised proved insecure, although his mother took over the obligation and paid Susannah the full £400 a year for nine years. For reasons which are unclear, it was then halved to only £200 a year and Susannah was required to give up Blandford's letters to her, some of which he had signed 'Your affectionate husband'. It does not appear that Susannah ever remarried, although it is said that her daughter married 'a man of fortune'. The whole story became public in 1838, when a newspaper claimed that Blandford's subsequent marriage was bigamous; that his children by it were illegitimate; and that Susannah's daughter was the rightful heir to the Duchy of Marlborough (a title which could descend through the female line). The case went to court, but with no evidence of a legitimate marriage taking place either in England or Scotland, the decision maintained the status quo, effectively declaring that Susannah had been Blandford's mistress and nothing more.[18]

Relatively few men were in a position to give their mistress £400 a year for life, although some may have been more extravagant than this when an affair was at its height. The financial side of such relationships is usually obscure, but we have some evidence for the unusually formal arrangements made by the 1st Lord Conyngham in the 1760s and 1770s. Conyngham instructed his attorney to draw up legal agreements with several women: Elizabeth Bulstrode, who also occupied the station of housekeeper, was to receive an annuity of £26 per annum, while 'Mrs Mary Perfect, spinster' was to receive £100 a year. The difference probably reflected both the different social backgrounds of the two women, and also their character: Elizabeth Bulstrode was, presumably, an upper servant before she became Conyngham's mistress, while Mrs Perfect was the daughter of a clergyman and had sufficient initiative and resources to take legal advice on the terms of the contract and to insist on changes to several clauses. Conyngham's lawyer was taken aback by this independence, but Conyngham replied that she had turned down several more valuable offers from other gentlemen for his sake and that he felt bound to compensate her. He was therefore prepared to leave her £2,000 on his death, subject to the conditions that she continued to live with him until then, not marry anyone without his consent and did not alienate or dispose of the bond. It was not unusual for men to seek to maintain control over their mistress with such provisions, but Mrs

Perfect soon threw off her shackles and married someone else while still trying (apparently unsuccessfully) to claim her income from Conyngham. The experience did not prevent Conyngham from coming to a similar arrangement, this time worth only £50 a year, with another clergyman's daughter, Miss Ann Barker, in 1771.[19]

Some men had scruples about seducing inexperienced young women, even from a much lower social class. James Boswell, who had frequently made use of prostitutes, was much taken by the beauty of the gardener's daughter at Auchinleck, his father's Ayrshire estate. However, he resisted the temptation of attempting to make her his mistress as he had always opposed ruining innocent virgins, in practice as well as in principle. He was so smitten that he even briefly fantasised about marrying the young woman, telling a friend, 'Only think of the proud Boswell, with all that you know of him, the fervent adorer of a country girl of three and twenty. I rave about her. I was never so much in love as I am now. My fancy is quite inflamed. It riots in extravagance.' Yet even at the height of his enchantment he knew that the dream would not survive ten days if put to the test. A few weeks later he found a more suitable outlet for his sexual energy: a young married woman of his own class who lived apart from her husband and who was as eager as he for an affair. Mrs Dodds had raven-black hair and was 'paradisial in bed'. She had no thought of divorce or marriage and was 'at full liberty' – in other words, the perfect mistress. Boswell set her up in lodgings in Edinburgh and was delightfully happy for a time, despite slight twinges of guilt about committing adultery, a little grumbling over the expense and a sense that the whole affair was a little too premediated and sensible, 'a settled plan of licentiousness', rather than a spontaneous fling. The affair did not last very long, and unfortunately we do not know what happened to Mrs Dodds afterwards, but such arrangements were probably not uncommon and may have been closer to the norm than Blandford's elaborate seduction of Susannah Law.[20]

The recent discovery by the historian Kate Gibson of twenty-seven letters from Lord Tyrconnel's mistress, known to us only as 'E.B.', written to him during their affair, which ended in 1790, gives some insight into how one woman at least perceived her position. Tyrconnel was in his late forties and was married, although he and his wife appear to have lived largely separate lives, and she had several affairs of her own, including with the Duke of York. The letters from E.B. portray a relationship marked more by domestic comfort and companionship than sexual passion, with her telling Tyrconnel at one point that 'it is my wish that I cou'd be your partner for life as well as for dancing' and that she frequently looked forward to an unspecified time when they could be constantly together. Yet her language was also emotionally intense, writing to 'My Dearest Love' and 'My Dearest Life', and repeatedly assuring him of her affection, probably in the hope of eliciting similar avowals in return. She clearly felt insecure in his absence, fearing that he would forget her, and made a point of her frugality and lack of interest in money – it was obviously very important to her to make clear that her motives were not mercenary. She wrote that it was natural for both men and women to pursue love and happiness, that 'you deserve to be happy if ever any one did' and that not to be happy was 'a sin'. 'I cannot bear your absence nor coud [*sic*] I exist long without seeing you . . . I can not live without you, and shall be miserable till I am to [find] my dearest love in my armes [*sic*] again.' She discounted his marriage, rejecting the idea of a reconciliation between Tyrconnel and his wife, in a way that helped justify her own position and was quick to note examples in literature and the world where such extra-marital love affairs were presented as not immoral. Nonetheless she went to some trouble to keep their relationship secret, or at least discreet, addressing her letters to his manservant and sending them to different post offices, while when one of her letters was lost she expressed alarm that it might fall into the hands of Lady Tyrconnel. In fact Lady Tyrconnel appears to have known of the affair, but turned a blind eye to it.[21]

E.B. lived with her mother and sister in a house paid for by Tyrconnel, and so long as she saw her lover frequently and had hopes of the future she felt able to defy convention, telling him boldly that 'I would give up the world for you alone', and that she did not mind the damage to her character 'as long as you continue to love me'. When she became pregnant she welcomed – or claimed to welcome – the prospect of having a child who would form another bond between them: 'I am sure it will be your little darling . . .' and 'a pledge of love'. However, Tyrconnel's visits became less frequent and her confidence waned as her pregnancy advanced and could not be concealed from strangers. She was daunted by the prospect of looking for new, cheaper, accommodation and was disconcerted and hurt when 'The people stare at my big belly and always ask where my husband is. I tell them he is forced to be in the country on business, I fear we shall find some difficulty in getting a lodging as they all seem very unwilling to take us in not knowing what to make of us.' By this point she was in real need for money to cover her medical and other expenses, and for emotional support and reassurance, and there is little evidence that she obtained either. The last letter, dated 14 December 1790, was written as E.B. went into labour, and we have no certain knowledge of her fate or that of her child. It is all too easy to imagine the story ending very badly, but Tyrconnel was apparently not completely heartless, for a few years later he commissioned the artist John Downman to paint portraits of his illegitimate children and their mothers. Among them is the painting *Mrs Beauville and her son* (1794), which strongly suggests that E.B. and her baby survived, and also that he made some provision for them.[22]

Nonetheless a woman in E.B.'s position was extremely vulnerable, dependent on her lover for money and for the recognition that would enable her to defy the condemnation of society. Without marriage even twenty years of happy domesticity could be extinguished in a moment as Mrs Jordan, the celebrated actress who had lived openly with the Duke of Clarence – the future King William IV – and borne him at least ten children, found when he abandoned her in 1811. She was, at least, promised a substantial pension, although a combination of folly and misplaced generosity to her daughter and dishonest son-in-law left her impoverished and living in exile in France.[23]

Most men could not afford to pension off an ex-mistress on a generous scale, even if they wished to do so. They would frequently get rid of an unwanted lover by passing her on to another man with more or less subtlety and tact. Sometimes, of course, the mistress would pre-empt them by transferring her affections of her own accord – Harriette Wilson's *Memoirs* are full of such shifts of allegiance, but she was a professional, and most mistresses were not. Lord Palmerston (the 2nd Viscount, not his more famous son) had several mistresses in the years between the death of his first wife and his second marriage. Among them was Madame

Gallina, the daughter of an Italian officer of dragoons and the wife of a surgeon in Milan. She met Palmerston in London in 1778 and soon became his mistress, but within two years the affair was over. He then found her a post as a governess with a family; however, she soon left after the husband made improper advances to her. She again turned to Palmerston for help, and he paid her expenses to travel back to Geneva, where she was 'fortuitously' met by her husband who wanted her back. The encounter was evidently set up by Palmerston and it appears to have been a successful resolution for all parties.[24]

Another of Palmerston's mistresses, Anna Crewe, later attempted to blackmail him, and a number of other gentlemen, by threatening to publish her memoirs. Her demands were remarkably modest: a pension of £50 a year paid for by the gentlemen together, but there was the obvious risk that once an initial demand was granted it might easily escalate. Palmerston's reply was a decorous and polite version of 'publish and be damned', with the addition of a small and uncertain carrot.

> In answer to this as far as regards myself I have only to say that anything that ever passed between us was of so trifling and unimportant a nature that I feel very little interested about the publication of it. I am sorry that the mode of application you have adopted makes it impossible for me with propriety to afford you any assistance at present. All I can say is that when your book appears, if I find you have omitted mentioning my name, I shall look upon it as a mark of delicacy and attention on your part which would give you a just claim to some pecuniary assistance from me, which in that case I should not refuse to afford you.

A second letter was marked 'not answered'.[25]

Quite a few men, including many from aristocratic families, were willing to acknowledge and take care of their illegitimate children. For example, the 4th Duke of Gordon had two sons and five daughters by his wife, the match-making duchess, and a further two sons and seven daughters by four different mistresses, whom he recognised, baptised with the name Gordon and provided with marriage portions for the girls and commissions in the army for the boys. His son, Lord Huntly, maintained the tradition in a more modest way, acknowledging a son and a daughter to one mistress and a daughter to another. The 3rd Earl of Aberdeen left most of his disposable (that is, not entailed) property to his illegitimate children as well as making some provisions for their mothers – an act of generosity and justice which rankled deeply with his grandson the 4th Earl, despite the fact that the 4th Earl inherited vast estates that made him, unlike his brothers and cousins, a very wealthy man. The 10th Earl of Pembroke had children by two mistresses whom he acknowledged, and one of his illegitimate sons not only had a successful naval career but was on excellent terms with the Earl's heir, his half-brother, and with the Countess. Similarly, the Marquess of Waterford's illegitimate sons John and William, born before his marriage, took the family name of Beresford and were always regarded as members of the family. John rose to be an admiral and William a general, marshal of Portugal and Wellington's right-hand man in the Peninsular War.[26]

However, there were also men who washed their hands of a discarded mistress and took no responsibility for their illegitimate children, while others lacked the means to give much useful assistance. Illegitimacy in itself was not a great bar in British society of the period, but it needed money and preferably the countenance of a family to wipe away the vestigial stigma, and those who had neither would only rise from obscurity through great good fortune or a touch of genius.

Men frequently did not marry until they were in their late twenties or even older, and while society did not explicitly approve of their having sex outside marriage, it did not expect that they would all remain celibate. Maria Edgeworth has one of her characters declare that 'the most moral ladies in the world do not expect men to be as moral as themselves', while in the same novel a lady's maid assures the heroine that 'no one, that has lived in the world, thinks anything of that', where 'that' is the fact that the hero has a mistress. The worldly Lady Delacour continues her protégé's education, 'do not look so shocked, my dear, I really cannot help laughing . . . it is all in rule and in course – when a man marries he sets up new equipages, and casts off old mistresses – or if you like to see the thing as a woman of sentiment, rather than as a woman of the world, here is the prettiest opportunity for your lover's making a sacrifice . . .'. Edgeworth does not endorse this outlook, but it is still presented as an accurate representation of the outlook of worldly society of the day, and while the less elastic morals of the middling orders in the provinces placed a higher emphasis on marital fidelity, they were less inclined to pronounce with confidence about the behaviour of unmarried men so long as they were discreet.[27]

Mistresses were a fact of life, a reality, but they were not respectable and would not normally be acknowledged by a woman who cared for her reputation. Jane Austen noted that her cousin Eliza had met Lord Craven and 'found his manners very pleasing indeed. – The little flaw of having a Mistress now living with him at Ashdown Park, seems to be the only unpleasing circumstance about him.' And her character Mary Crawford was forced to leave her uncle's house when he brought his mistress to live with him. A man might boast of his mistress to his male friends, and even introduce them to her, but he would not think of expecting his mother or sister to meet her. In late middle age the 5th Duke of Marlborough (Blandford's father) found comfort and domestic happiness in a relationship with a mistress, Matilda Glover, with whom he lived for the last twenty years of his life, moving her first into the Home Lodge, and ultimately into Blenheim (the Duchess, who had money of her own, already lived independently). The Duke and Matilda had at least six children, and as he grew old and his health deteriorated her position became accepted, with his doctor, for example, turning to her to influence the Duke's diet. Nonetheless Matilda's presence placed an additional strain on the already difficult relationship between the Duke and his legitimate children.[28]

Keeping a mistress was only one way, and almost certainly not the most common, in which an unmarried man, or a man who lived apart from his wife, could have sex. London and other towns and cities across Britain supported large numbers of prostitutes, and it is clear that they drew their clientele from right across the social spectrum. Equally, some married women took lovers without any intention of leaving their husband. But for many men an established mistress offered something more than sex: companionship and domestic comfort, even love, were just as important in some of these relationships. But a mistress was also in a much weaker position than a wife: she could be dismissed at any time and had nothing to claim by right from her lover. Some men probably found this ascendancy reassuring, especially if they were emotionally insecure or had been surprised to discover that their wife was less adoring than they had expected. But for the mistress, her lack of rights tilted the always unequal position of the sexes to an extreme. Even if their lover was generous, both materially and emotionally, the inequality of the relationship was marked, and they naturally worried about their own future and that of their children. Inevitably many hoped that the relationship would end in marriage, the only step that would give them some real security. Occasionally these hopes were realised, although as we shall see such *mésalliances* were not without problems of their own. But for most mistresses, the hope of marriage was an illusion which, while it may have sometimes saved them from despair, may also have induced them to sacrifice their own interests in favour of those of an often ungrateful lover. The fact that Lydia's family and friends were willing to go to great trouble and expense to pressure Wickham into marrying her, despite knowing that he was a rogue and that he would certainly be an indifferent husband, shows the weakness of the position in which she had placed herself.

Marriages where there was a great disparity in the social background between the couple – *mésalliances* – attracted far more attention than marriages where there was a great disparity of age, or where the couple belonged to different churches. The most common cases were gentlemen, or noblemen, marrying their humbly born mistresses: this in itself was enough to delight the gossips, but if she was already well known as one of the leading actresses of the day – as happened on a number of occasions – the public interest was all the greater. The potency of the mixture of sex, scandal, power and celebrity was already familiar by the beginning of the eighteenth century. The possibility that the son of an actress or a servant girl might inherit a title and become a peer of the realm stood social conventions on their head, although there was no shortage of precedents for those who looked for them. But what gave the idea of a *mésalliance* an even greater frisson was that the social superiority was not always on the side of the husband. There were cases of well-born women running off and marrying servants, tutors or grooms, which raised all kinds of disturbing but secretly exciting ideas of sex across class barriers, in a way that well-born men seducing or even marrying poor girls did not.

The literary potential of a *mésalliance* was obvious, and the story of a poor girl raised to riches and gentility through her good conduct and an advantageous marriage was a staple of novels since at least Samuel Richardson's *Pamela: or, Virtue Rewarded* appeared in 1740. Jane Austen played with the genre, and her heroines all married well, but no one, except Lady Catherine de Bourgh, would have claimed that these matches were *mésalliances*. Some of the marriages of subsidiary characters in Austen's novels make a greater leap across the social classes, but neither the marriage of Fanny Price's mother to a penniless lieutenant of marines nor that of Miss Taylor to Mr Weston can really be described as a *mésalliance*. We get a bit closer, although still not quite there, with the idea of a marriage between Harriet Smith and Mr Knightley, and between Mrs Clay and either Sir Walter Elliot or his nephew and namesake. Emma's reaction to the first possibility gives a sense of how such matches might be viewed, although her view is distorted by her own, unacknowledged feelings for Mr Knightley.

> Mr. Knightley and Harriet Smith! – It was an union to distance every wonder of the kind. . . . Such an elevation on her side! Such a debasement on his! – It was horrible to Emma to think how it must sink him in the general opinion, to foresee the smiles, the sneers, the merriment it would prompt at his expense; the mortification and disdain of his brother, the thousand inconveniences to himself. – Could it be? – No; it was impossible. And yet it was far, very far, from impossible. – Was it a new circumstance for a man of first-rate abilities to be captivated by very inferior powers?

It is obvious that this is how Emma views such a marriage, not the view of the author; but this distinction is less clear when, in *Persuasion*, Mrs Smith describes Mr Walter Elliot's marriage to 'a fine woman, [who] had had a decent education' but who was the daughter of a grazier and the granddaughter of a butcher. Mr Elliot married purely for money, and we condemn his mercenary motives, but are we also meant to condemn his disdain for the honour of his family, which he 'held as cheap as dirt', and that he felt 'not a difficulty or a scruple . . . on his side, with respect to her birth'?[29]

In real life Austen was sympathetic although characteristically playful when passing on the news of a *mésalliance* to Cassandra: 'Miss Sawbridge is married . . . Mr Maxwell *was* Tutor to the young Gregorys – consequently they must be one of the happiest Couple in the World, & either of them worthy of Envy – for *she* must be excessively in love, & *he* mounts from nothing to a comfortable Home. – Martha has heard him very highly spoken of.'[30]

Twelve years earlier, Lady Lucy Stanhope, youngest daughter of Charles, 3rd Earl Stanhope, caused consternation in her wider family when she ran off with Thomas Taylor, an apothecary-surgeon at Sevenoaks. The affair attracted a good deal of attention: Lady Lucy was the niece of the prime minister, Pitt the Younger, while her father was notorious for his radical, egalitarian views, so that it was widely felt that she was showing him the practical implications of his theories. Lord Stanhope appears not to have been very pleased with his daughter when the news first broke – although this may have been as much due to the fact that she was barely sixteen at the time of her marriage in April 1796 as with the social status of her husband – but he did not oppose the match, and went so far as to tell a friend that 'Her Mind is liberal, and she despises Rank and *Aristocracy*, as much as I do. I have seen much both here and abroad, of the middling classes; and I have observed, by far, more happiness there, as well as virtue, than amongst those Ranks of Men who insolently term themselves their *betters*.' Lady Lucy herself replied to a remonstrance from her aunt:

I have been well aware that with many of my station, Mr Taylor's situation would be an insuperable objection; but with me, that objection has no weight. And whatever respect I may feel for your opinion, and however I may regret acting contrary to your wishes . . . my first consideration ought certainly to be, for my own happiness; and since I have the sanction of a good father, I know no one whose disapprobation can influence me. I prefer happiness to Splendour and Riches, and had they any charms for me I would gladly sacrifice them all for Mr Taylor's sake. Affection for him, has been the guide, and the *sole* guide of my conduct.[31]

The striking thing about the affair, especially to modern eyes, is that Taylor's position as an apothecary-surgeon (the equivalent of a modern GP) was regarded as so far below hers. He had trained in London under Sir Henry Cline; and he was described by Sir Astley Cooper, one of the most famous surgeons of the day, as 'a clever fellow, but entirely a man of pleasure . . . much sought after by the ladies of the west-end of the town, who used to fetch him in their carriages'. Yet Gillray depicted the wedding in a satirical print entitled *Democratic Levelling — Alliance a la Françoise — or The Union of the Coronet & Clyster-pipe*, and a family friend wrote that 'Lady Chatham now has an account of her poor granddaughter, disposed of (with ten thousand pounds) to a dirty Apothecary in whose shop she is to reside in Sevenoaks.' Evidently her wider family felt the same way, for Taylor was persuaded to give up his medical practice and was appointed, presumably through the influence of her uncle, to the sinecure position of Comptroller General of the Customs, an office worth about £1,000 a year. A few years later her sister wrote that 'Mr Taylor is a most excellent good sort of man, and the whole of his conduct deserves much praise. Lucy is certainly very happy. What would have become of them without Mr Pitt, God only knows.' After Pitt's death in 1806 she was given an annuity of £600, so that her fall from the elevated heights of her upbringing was well cushioned: indeed she did considerably better than most of the daughters of less radical earls who married more conventionally.[32]

A generation earlier, two well-known *mésalliances* had shown the different ways in which a woman might handle her marriage to a man from a humble background. In 1764 Lady Harriet Wentworth, sister of Lord Rockingham, the Whig leader who would twice serve as prime minister, married William Sturgeon, her footman. He was a handsome young Irishman, totally without education, and the affair began when she started to teach him to read and write. She gave up her fine clothes and retired from society, eventually settling in Rouen, where Sturgeon set up a successful pottery business. But according to Horace Walpole's rather waspish account, she was careful to retain control of her money:

Lady Harriot . . . has mixed a wonderful degree of prudence with her potion, and considering how plain she is, has not, I think, sweetened the draught too much for her lover: she settles a single hundred pound a year upon him for his life, entails her whole fortune on their children, if they have any; and, if not, on her own family; – nay, in the height of the novel, provides for a separation, and ensures that same pin-money to Damon, in case they part. This deed she has vested out of her power, by sending it to Lord Mansfield, whom she makes her trustee; it is drawn up in her own hand, and Lord Mansfield says it is as binding as any lawyer could make it.[33]

She died in 1789 and the pottery business was ruined by the Revolution. Sturgeon returned to Ireland and took up farming, outliving his wife by more than forty years, and being described as 'a hale, venerable old man, of stately presence, and with the remains of much personal beauty'. They had five children, and for some time the eldest boy was the heir presumptive to the titles and estates of Earl Fitzwilliam (Rockingham's heir), until the late and rather unexpected birth of Lord Milton in 1786 saved the proud family from that embarrassing possibility. One of their sons was Lieutenant-Colonel Henry Sturgeon, who served with great distinction under Wellington in the Peninsula.[34]

Emily Fitzgerald, Duchess of Leinster, by contrast, saw no reason to accept the slightest lowering of her social standing following her marriage – soon after the Duke's death – to William Ogilvie, her children's tutor. They had been lovers for some time, and remained deeply in love for the rest of their lives, making this a supremely successful *mésalliance*. Naturally the news was greeted with considerable interest, with one observer commenting that 'People wonder at her marriage, as she is reckoned one of the proudest and most expensive women in the world. But perhaps she thought it incumbent (as Lady Brown says of her Grace) "to marry and make an honest man of him".' After their marriage they spent some years in France, but there, in England and in Ireland, they were received at court and in the highest flights of society, in which she was quite at home, her brother being the Duke of Richmond and her sister Lady Holland. Thanks to a generous marriage settlement, and the provisions of her first husband's will, her financial position was very comfortable – much more so, indeed, than that of her son, the 2nd Duke – and her considerable self-assurance enabled her to live down the sensation caused by her marriage. Ogilvie was elected to the Irish parliament, although he was more interested in family matters and making sound investments than in making a mark in public affairs. Their two surviving daughters both made good marriages despite their father's modest background.[35]

As these cases show, ladies who married beneath them might retain a privileged place in society, although they would have to defy some gossip and unkindness that they would have avoided if they had married a man of their own class. Much depended on their individual circumstances. Clearly a young woman whose inheritance depended on her marriage being approved by her parents was less secure than a widow who took the precaution of securing her position before making her second marriage. But even families who disapproved of a runaway match might still rally round to secure and protect a lady's future, either from genuine concern for her welfare or to protect themselves from the embarrassment of having a relative living above an apothecary's shop and relying on trade for her support. No general rule applied: neither that a woman automatically took her husband's station, nor that she raised him to her position in society; just as it is impossible to say these marriages were more or less happy than others, or that the women who made them either repented or did not repent their action.

Men suffered far less than women from an imprudent marriage. They would almost never be cut or disdained because they chose to marry their mistress or a servant girl. However, their wife was not so immune, and it took considerable courage, a thick skin and a good knowledge of upper-class manners and habits for a woman from a humble background to break into 'polite society'. Actresses seem the most likely to make the leap successfully. Presumably their professional experience gave them confidence and poise, and they were more likely to be familiar with the ways of the *bon ton* than a more respectable but bourgeois woman. Elizabeth Farren spent twenty years on the London stage and was one of the most successful actresses of the day before she married the Earl of Derby in 1797; and Lord Craven married Louisa Brunton in 1807, just days after her farewell performance. Neither man's career or position in society suffered from their marriages, and Miss Farren stormed society with a high hand, being presented to Queen Charlotte only ten days after her wedding, and soon afterwards taking part in the wedding procession of Princess Charlotte. Such royal patronage, from a queen famous for her concern with propriety, silenced most critics, while some years later Thomas Creevey commented that Lady Derby surpassed 'all your hereditary nobility I have ever seen, tho' she came from the stage to her title'.[36]

Even more striking was the example of Harriet Mellon, the actress who married the wealthy banker Thomas Coutts, inherited his fortune and then married the Duke of St Albans, a man twenty-three years her junior. In this second marriage she carefully retained control of her fortune and, after careful consideration and making a suitable settlement for her husband, she left it to her niece, Angela Burdett-Coutts. Soon after her second marriage she wrote to Walter Scott, an old and trusted friend, 'What a strange, eventful life has mine been, from a poor little player child, with just food and clothes to cover me, dependent on a very precarious profession, without talent or a friend in the world . . . first the wife of the best, the most perfect, being that ever breathed . . . and now the wife of a Duke!'[37]

Sometimes the leap appeared unbridgeable. When 'Poodle' Byng, son of Viscount Torrington and a member of Beau Brummell's set, married his mother's lady's maid, whom he had got pregnant, he made little attempt to introduce her into the fashionable world. Was he ashamed of his wife, or keen to protect her from insult? Or was it his wife who preferred to stay home? A sense of the difficulties she might face comes in a comment from Thomas Creevey – the same man who so admired the Countess of Derby – who responded to an invitation to dine with the Byngs and some male friends, men who might not scruple to dine with a comrade's mistress: that 'I have the greatest aversion to playing company with such kind of *tits*; but as Charles Greville, Cullen Smith and Luttrell, and two or three more of your men upon town took no objection, it was not for me to find fault.'[38]

When Edward Pedder, the son of a prominent banking family in Preston, married dairymaid maid, Mary Robinson, in 1809, he determined to educate her thoroughly before introducing her to his family. He was a widower with a ten-year-old daughter, and his new wife was only seventeen, exactly half his age. So he engaged a governess, Nelly Weeton, to attend to the different needs of wife and daughter. At first, all went well, and Miss Weeton thought that Mrs Pedder was in 'every way worthy [of] her present rank', and that 'her improvement is so rapid, her application so close, and her disposition and understanding so superior, that a little time will make her all he wishes'. Yet only a couple of months later Miss Weeton told a friend, 'if you knew the sorrow that [a] person must undergo who marries above herself, you would never be ambitious to marry out of your own rank; people call it doing well; they are most egregiously mistaken. Let the husband be ever so kind, it cannot compensate for the numberless mortifications a woman so raised must endure. Those married people have the greatest chance of being happy whose original rank was most nearly equal.' Matters went from bad to worse, especially after Miss Pedder died in an accident. Mr Pedder lost interest in playing Pygmalion and became drunken and abusive, while Mrs Pedder preferred playing cards to reading and gave up her lessons, so that Miss Weeton felt redundant, although neither of the Pedders wished her to leave them. It is not clear if Mrs Pedder was ever well received by her husband's family or by local society, although it does appear that she and her husband remained together and there is some reason to hope that their marriage improved with the birth of four children between 1826 and 1833.[39]

Miss Weeton's reflections on the disadvantages suffered by those — women or men — raised by marriage far above the class in which they had been born were not unjustified, but they were not a universal truth. Here as elsewhere individual circumstances differed so much as to make general conclusions almost impossible. Some *mésalliances* were painful and unhappy, but others, such as Harriet Mellon's, appear to have been very successful. But the essence of success lay less in the wealth and social position gained through the marriage, and more in the happiness, delight and pride which husband and wife felt in each other, whoever came from the more distinguished family.

CHAPTER EIGHT

SPINSTERS AND BACHELORS

The Alternative to Marriage

NOT EVERYONE GOT MARRIED. There are no definitive figures; however, it appears that something between one in four and one in eight (between 12 and 25 per cent) of upper-class men and women of this period, respectively, who lived to maturity died unmarried. Women were slightly more likely to remain unmarried than their brothers (a few more men than women married someone from a much lower social class), but the difference was not very great. And the numbers of those who remained unmarried had risen sharply over the long term: it had been rare (perhaps only one in twenty) in the late sixteenth century when Queen Elizabeth I was on the throne.[1]

Unmarried women as a group were not highly regarded by society once they had passed the age at which they were seen as likely to marry, perhaps when they were about thirty years old. They were commonly called 'old maids', and the term was loaded with negative connotations, some of which reflected the reality of their position and some of which were merely pejorative. Dr John Gregory, that eminent pontificator on morals, wrote of 'the forlorn and unprotected situation of an old maid, the chagrin and peevishness which are apt to infect their tempers'. And Nelly Weeton, unmarried and thirty-three, told her brother that 'An old maid is a stock for everyone to laugh at. Every article of dress, every word, every movement is satirized. Boys play tricks upon them, and are applauded. Girls sneer at them, and are unreproved.' Occasionally things might go even further: in one Cheshire town in the early nineteenth century the local hoodlums 'would stop ladies returning from the card-parties, which were the staple gaiety of the place . . . and whip them; literally whip them as you whip a little child' until the local magistrates intervened and suppressed the disorder, although instances of actual violence such as this were probably rare.[2]

Jane Austen acknowledged the difficulties facing spinsters, but identified the core of the problem as lack of money, not their marital status. One of her poorer characters, Elizabeth Watson in *The Watsons*, says, 'you know we must marry. I could do very well single for my own part; a little company, and a pleasant ball now and then, would be enough for me, if one could be young for ever; but my father cannot provide for us, and it is very bad to grow old and be poor and laughed at.' And Emma Woodhouse explained to Harriet Smith that not all 'old maids' were equal:

Never mind, Harriet, I shall not be a poor old maid; and it is poverty only which makes celibacy contemptible to a generous public! A single woman, with a very narrow income, must be a ridiculous, disagreeable, old maid! the proper sport of boys and girls; but a single woman, of good fortune, is always respectable, and may be as sensible and pleasant as anybody else. And the distinction is not quite so much against the candour and common sense of the world as appears at first; for a very narrow income has a tendency to contract the mind, and sour the temper. Those who can barely live, and who live perforce in a very small, and generally very inferior, society, may well be illiberal and cross.

And Austen told her niece Fanny Knight that 'Single Women have a dreadful propensity for being poor – which is one very strong argument in favour of Matrimony . . . .'[3]

Jane Austen was not alone in her insight: a generation earlier Jean Marishall had made the same point: 'What is the reason, it is alleged, there are so many fretful, ill-looking, discontented old maids? Is it because they have not got husbands? No. If they have money enough to ensure their consequence, entertain their friends, dress in the mode of the times; take my word for it, they will neither be particularly ill-looking, fretful, nor discontented.' Far from making things better, patronising comments like Dr Gregory's simply reinforced existing prejudices; nonetheless many women, even those with modest fortunes such as Austen herself, still chose not to marry when offered the chance by a man who they did not love or sufficiently esteem.[4]

Jane Austen's own experiences show that the life of a spinster was not so lonely, impoverished and miserable as some of the stereotypes suggest. She was fortunate in being part of a large and generally loving family. After the death of her father, she had a home with her mother, her sister and their friend Martha Lloyd, settling ultimately at Chawton in a comfortable cottage provided by her wealthy brother Edward Knight. The household's finances, which would have been straitened, were supported to a comfortable level (around £500 a year) by contributions from the more prosperous of Jane's brothers. This was not sufficient for Mrs Austen and her daughters to keep a carriage – something the family had only done for a few years in Mr Austen's life – and this restriction on their mobility was sometimes inconvenient; however, it was an inconvenience which a great many married women also had to endure. Living at Chawton, Jane had leisure to pursue her writing and her music: something that would have been much more difficult if she had been a married woman and mother, managing a household and attending to the education of her children. She had emotional support from her mother, her sister and their friend Martha, and their life was varied by visits to and from relatives, and to London. Intellectual stimulus came from her work, visits to the capital, conversations and correspondence with friends, and from the local circulating library which enabled her to read such topical works as Sir John Carr's *Descriptive Travels in the Southern and Eastern Parts of Spain* and Captain Pasley's *Essay on the Military Policy and Institutions of the British Empire* (which she found 'delightfully written & highly entertaining') as well as the latest novels and poetry. According to the second-hand testimony from one of her nieces, Jane Austen 'always said her books were her children, and supplied her [with] sufficient interest for happiness', while in one of her own letters she describes *Pride and Prejudice* as 'my own darling Child'.[5]

Jane Austen died in 1817 when she was only forty-one years old. Perhaps her sister Cassandra's later life might resemble the stereotype more closely? To some extent, it may have. For a decade after her sister's death, Cassandra Austen was kept largely at home at Chawton by the need to attend to her mother, who was then in her late seventies and eighties. And then, eighteen months after Mrs Austen's death at the age of eighty-seven in 1827, Martha Lloyd married Francis Austen, Jane's and Cassandra's brother, leaving Cassandra alone at Chawton. These successive losses must have caused grief and sadness, yet a few years later Cassandra gave an account of her life which does not suggest that she felt lonely or despondent.

> I continue to live in this cottage which I have now inhabited more than twenty years, and I can say with thankfulness that my health is tolerably good, better perhaps than I have any right to expect at my time of life, and considering that I have never been otherwise than a little ailing. I have no constant inmate, but am frequently visited by brothers and nephews and nieces and am likewise a visitor in my turn.
>
> I spent five months last year (from June till November) at Godmersham and have since passed a fortnight at Steventon, of which place one of my Knight nephews is Rector. . . .
>
> Henry resides on his little piece of preferment between six and seven miles from me and is a very good neighbour. He makes an excellent parish priest, and is indefatigable in his exertions . . .

At the time of writing the fifteen-year-old daughter of one of Cassandra's nieces (Julia Cassandra Lefroy, daughter of Anna Lefroy) was spending some time staying with her.[6]

In the following year Cassandra is even more explicit in stating her contentment with her life:

> I passed the greater part of the year *thirty-two* at home, but I have begun *thirty-three* in a different style, having set off to pay visits on the 7th of January. I have already passed three weeks with my brother Frank at his house in the neighbourhood of Portsmouth and am now finishing my excursion by a visit to Charles who is settled at this place . . .

I propose leaving them in the course of a few days and returning to my own cottage, which is about thirty miles distant. I shall of course, miss the cheerfulness of a large family, but home always ought to have its comforts, and it certainly has for me, and although I have no inmate in my house, my nephew Edward Knight lives so near, that I never need be more alone that I like. . . .

I am pleased to find that you still derive amusement from needle-work. I am likewise a great worker and have varieties of knitting and worsted work in hand. My garden is also a constant object of interest and at suitable seasons of the year of employ likewise.[7]

At around this time Cassandra Austen made a tour of the Wye Valley with her brother Charles, taking with them two of Charles's daughters and a niece (one of Francis's daughters). Finally we have the recollections of John White, a farmworker, who recalled that when he was a boy, 'Miss Cassandra Austen lived at the corner house by the Pond. She took a great interest in young girls, and taught them reading, the catechism and sewing. I remember a nice dog, his name was "Link", that she had. He always went with her manservant, William Littleworth, to Chawton House for milk, and carried it home in his mouth.'[8]

Nothing in this suggests that Cassandra's life was, in Dr Gregory's words, 'forlorn and unprotected' let alone filled with 'chagrin and peevishness' – on the contrary she appears self-confident and contented. Underpinning this contentment was a secure financial position, not dependent on the generosity of her brothers. Just how this was achieved is not entirely clear, for in 1816 Cassandra had only 1,100 Navy 5 per cent stocks yielding an income of £55 in her own name. She inherited more capital on her mother's death, and a further £5,000, which was given to her by Mrs Jane Leigh Perrot in 1833. When she died in 1845 Cassandra's estate was worth £14,700, which would have yielded a very comfortable income for a single woman of modest tastes. Nor were such investments unusual: one-third of all investors in Bank stocks in 1810 were women, rising to almost half by 1840, although their holdings were typically smaller than those of men – or of Cassandra Austen. Some advice books directed to women even began to include sections on managing money and property, and there is evidence that women were not as cautious investors as they are often represented. Cassandra Austen's portfolio included Brazilian bonds, while many women looked to mortgages and annuities when they gained control of their capital, rather than simply leaving it in the low-yielding but very safe stocks preferred by their trustees.[9]

Spinsters who were wealthier and better connected than Cassandra Austen might visit London for the season, either living in accommodation of their own or with family, and travel extensively both at home and abroad in the rest of the year, either by themselves, with relatives or with a paid companion. Many spinsters and widows chose to live in Bath or in other provincial watering and cathedral towns, where they were assured of plentiful society and had ready access to tradesmen and professional services such as doctors and lawyers. In itself, their marital status posed few limitations on their behaviour, but few unmarried women owned landed estates or country houses (which generally passed through the male line), or had enough money to keep a house in London for the season and cover all the other costs of cutting a figure in the *beau monde*. Some may also have been wearied of the forced gaieties by years of failing to find an appealing suitor in their youth, while even many married couples only returned to the capital when it was time to launch their daughters into society. However, spinsters did hold a number of positions at court.[10]

Mrs Gaskell gives an affectionate, if rather patronising, account of the lives of spinsters and widows in Knutsford in her youth, both in non-fiction ('The Last Generation in England') and lightly dressed as fiction in *Cranford*. Money in this circle was limited and many 'elegant econo-mies' had to be practised, especially by the more aristocratic and socially elevated members, who were also generally the least wealthy. Nonetheless blood counted more than brass, and those with connections to the aris-tocracy were treated with a deference bordering on obsequiousness by those who could boast only of professional relatives. The lives of these women were very sociable, with a constant round of visiting, tea, conver-sation and, above all, cards. Such society could be narrow and riven by petty quarrels and jealousies, but it could also be affectionate and caring, providing a network of support in times of illness and bereavement. Nor was there any significant distinction in the lives of spinsters and widows.[11]

Some spinsters remained with their family, running the house for their father when their mother died, or for a bachelor brother or uncle. Their position varied enormously according to individual circumstances: some were stifled, impoverished and treated as a dependant, little better than a servant; others were loved, valued and had as much authority and more independence than a wife. Their position in society might be destroyed when their father died or brother married, or they might be liberated to pursue their own preferences for the first time. Anne Lister's unmarried aunt and namesake kept house for her brother for many years, but still accompanied her niece to Paris and on a visit to Wales, and there is no reason to assume that her life was obviously better or worse than it would have been if she had married. Mary Lamb and Dorothy Wordsworth both lived with brothers who were the most important figure in their lives: Charles Lamb remained a bachelor and devoted himself to caring for his sister after she had, while mentally ill, murdered their mother; but William Wordsworth married when Dorothy was thirty years old, which at once devalued their close relationship and reduced her to a subordinate position in her own home. Most spinsters who continued to live with their family were less well off financially than their nearest male relative, and many – although not all – must have felt that they were to some extent subordinate to him. Their financial position and their social status was generally inferior to that of a wife, although in practice the difference was usually not great, and the disadvantage of marital status was much less than that arising from their gender.[12]

Other unmarried women were compelled to earn their living. The only careers open to them without entirely sacrificing their social status were to work as a governess, a school teacher or a companion to a lady. These were all very poorly paid and implied a great degree of subordination, and they normally required the woman to reside with their employer, so that her opportunity for a private life of her own was greatly circumscribed. Governesses notoriously inhabited an uneasy hinterland, below the family but above the servants. They might or might not dine with the parents of their charges, but did not usually spend the rest of the evening with them, and were the lowest of the low when there was company. Although the menial tasks of bathing and dressing the children, cleaning, making beds and the like were done by a nursery maid, the governess was expected to spend almost all her waking hours supervising the children. Nelly Weeton told a friend that:

> I often feel so jaded at night when the children are gone to bed, that I cannot exert resolution enough to take up a pen. When there is no company, I sit alone in an evening, in the school-room. This was part of my stipulation before I came, to have the evening to myself (imagining Mr. & Mrs. A. would not be sorry to be without a third person); and I wished to be at liberty to read, or write, and be at peace after the exercise of mind during the day. Yet really I should be very glad of some society in an evening, it would be such an enjoyment; but there is nobody in the house with whom I can be on equal terms, and I know nobody out of it, so I must make myself contented.[13]

School teachers were no better off. Most schools took as many boarders as day pupils and were generally crowded, while the teachers were expected to live on the premises and sleep in the same bedrooms as the girls. In many cases — even in good, successful girls' schools — the pupils slept two to a bed, and sometimes a school mistress did not even have a bed of her own but was expected to share it with one of the students. In an Edinburgh school in 1810, five girls and one mistress slept in three beds in one bedroom, and four girls and another mistress slept in the three beds in the other room. Schools were small: Mrs Goddard's school in *Emma* was successful, having forty students and three teachers besides Mrs Goddard and several servants; while Miss Pirie and Miss Woods' school was doing well, having as many as fourteen pupils the year after it opened. Like governesses, school teachers had little time free of their charges and almost no privacy. Not surprisingly, intense friendships and feuds blossomed among both the students and the teachers, and the atmosphere was often highly charged. Students boasted of the wealth or social standing of their parents, triumphing over each other, and looking down on their teachers, so that Miss Weeton commented wearily, 'I know very well from former experience what the insults of girls to a subordinate teacher can be.' And when Emma Watson tells her sister that 'I would rather be teacher at a school (and I can think of nothing worse), than marry a man I did not like', her sister replies, '*I* have been at school, Emma, and know what a life they lead; *you* never have.'[14]

Acting as a paid companion might be preferable, although much obviously depended on the characters involved and the element of subordination was inescapable. In 1805 Jane Austen commented on the position of Mrs Stent, the elderly companion to the equally elderly Mrs Lloyd, 'Poor Mrs Stent! it has been her lot to be always in the way; but we must be merciful, for perhaps in time we may come to be Mrs Stents ourselves, unequal to anything & unwelcome to everybody.' And Anne Platt, the daughter of a Rotherham stonemason, was even more emphatic: 'Of all the situations in life, that of being humble companion to any lady is the most slavish, the most mortifying, the most disagreeable, of any I ever knew or experienced', declaring that she would not accept it even 'if I was reduced to live upon water gruel' instead. Yet Agnes Porter spent nine months as companion to her friend Mrs Upcher and appears to have been happy there, only leaving after Mrs Upcher's unexpected death (before the age of fifty).[15]

Employment, whether as governess, school teacher or companion, greatly reduced a woman's chances of marriage, let alone marrying a gentleman. Agnes Porter's sister was thought to have been fortunate to marry a curate, the Rev. Thomas Richards, when she was working as a governess to the Hicks Beach family, but Richards remained a curate for the next twenty-eight years and took in pupils to supplement his stipend. And according to Harriet Smith, Miss Nash, one of the teachers at Mrs Goddard's school, 'thinks her own sister very well married, and it is only [to] a linen-draper'. To which Emma Woodhouse replies, 'One should be sorry to see greater pride or refinement in the teacher of a school, Harriet. I dare say Miss Nash would envy you such an opportunity as this of being married. Even this conquest [Robert Martin] would appear valuable in her eyes.' We note that Emma was being insufferably snobbish, but have little doubt that she was voicing a common prejudice. Miss Taylor marrying Mr Weston was the exception to rule, and Jane Austen's niece, Lady Knatchbull, instantly dismissed two governesses who appeared to be forming attachments to unmarried members of her family, and nothing more was heard of them.[16]

Some spinsters had no interest in marriage or, like Cassandra Austen, put the possibility completely to one side after they had lost (to death or through unrequited love) the chance of marrying the man they loved. But most probably shared the outlook of Miss Weeton, who answered a probing question from a friend by denying that she was hostile to the idea of marriage and that, 'could I meet with the man I could esteem as well as love, I would marry tomorrow if I could, and hope to be a mother too, in due time. But – lack a day! I may think, and talk, and wish to no purpose. I have no admirer that I know of – at least, he tells it not to me – so pray do not tantalise me by putting such thoughts into my head.' And, she added, 'Women *are* something better than rotten potatoes too, though they are often treated, and *suffer themselves* to be treated, as little better.' But when she was attracted to a gentleman while she was working as a governess/companion several years later, she avoided him: 'I cannot say I ever met with a man I thought so agreeable; the great difference between a governess and a clergyman of family and fortune, made me cautious of being in his company more than I could help, lest my heart should involuntarily form an attachment that might cause me years of unhappiness. I never did before feel such a sentiment, as I did whilst he was here; as I still yet do.' The probability of his reciprocating and proposing marriage seemed too low to run the risk of a broken heart, and so he disappears from her diary, leaving nothing more than the regret at what might have been.[17]

Spinsters sometimes feared for their future, and particularly the lack of children to look after them in their old age. Agnes Porter was much struck by accounts of the miserable end of Mrs Hayes, who had been housekeeper at Lord Ilchester's house and who retired to Bath where she was very badly treated by relatives in her final illness. Yet research by the historian Amy Froide shows that, in general, the position of single women improved as they grew older, gaining financial and social independence and often a home that was truly their own for the first time. They used their middle age to develop a network of support with wider family, friends and neighbours which might prove as resilient and reliable as adult children in easing the difficulties of old age. And this more positive interpretation is supported by the first-hand account of at least one spinster, Serena Holroyd, who wrote to her beloved niece Maria Stanley in 1817:

I am most thankful to God for such a happy close of life, surrounded by blessings and comforts of every kind, and though losing memory, yet my spirits, my state of mind, my sleep &c., all most comfortable, and, as my gaieties are innocent, I hope my friends will not be scandalized by hearing that poor Mrs. H. died one morn after having had a very agreeable party only a few days before. I seriously do think, please God, this may be the case, as I do not think the cheerful life I lead prevents my recollecting that I am to die, and that last Twelfth Day was my entrance into my 80th year. What I most regret is that I, who love writing and talking, suffer from both if I indulge any time. I really can only add blessings to you all.[18]

There was much less stigma attached to being a middle-aged or elderly bachelor than a spinster of similar age, although there was still some. It was commonly thought that older bachelors might become eccentric, careless of their dress and appearance, and pursue an intellectual or artistic interest with excessive, almost obsessive, enthusiasm, so that they were unfit for general society. The Rev. Josiah Cargill in Walter Scott's *St Ronan's Well* is just such a character. Early in life he had been disappointed in love and since then had not looked at another woman but buried himself in antiquarian research. For many years his mother had kept house for him and ensured his respectability, but after her death he became increasingly neglected, and as the servants took advantage of his inattention, the house, garden and everything else gradually became ruined about him. He forgot to eat or dress properly and it was hard to arouse his attention. He performed his clerical duties conscientiously, but was often forgetful, mistaking people and losing touch with the world around him.[19]

Scott's picture was exaggerated for comic effect, but it sometimes found an echo in the lives of actual bachelors. John Clerk was a highly successful Edinburgh advocate who was ultimately made a judge and created Lord Eldin (not to be confused with the Lord Chancellor, Lord Eldon). He was renowned for his rough sarcastic humour, often directing it at the judge presiding over a case in which he was appearing, apparently without damage to his cause or his career. He also had a taste for the fine arts and drew as well as forming a fine collection of pictures and prints. When the collection was sold after his death, in a sale that lasted fourteen days, the floor of his apartment gave way and a number of people were injured and one killed. He paid no attention to his dress and was not a good-looking man, with 'very bushy eyebrows, coarse grizzly hair, always in disorder, and firm and projecting features'. He also developed an 'old-maid like' fondness for cats, keeping half-a-dozen or more at any one time, while clients frequently found him 'seated in his study, with a favourite *Tom* elevated on his shoulder, and purring about his ears'.[20]

Examples such as this supported a common belief that marriage was necessary for a man's comfort and important to keep him respectable. Dr Johnson declared that 'Marriage, Sir, is more necessary to a man than to a woman; for he is much less able to supply himself with domestick comforts.' And Emily Cowper believed that 'marriage . . . at best . . . must always be a lottery'. 'I think', she went on, 'for a man's comfort it is almost better to have a bad wife than to have no wife – besides it is always a man's own fault if his wife is *very* bad.' While in the aftermath of Waterloo Georgiana Capel wrote to her grandmother from Brussels that 'Papa's illness makes me more than ever pity *Batchelors*; for after all, what is so kind, so useful as a woman, and what miserable helpless wretches men are without them, if they require any sort of comfort or attendance.'[21]

Some bachelors lived in institutions, such as the Inns of Court or Oxford or Cambridge colleges, where their domestic needs were supplied. Others established their own homes, either renting or buying properties in town or the country. In many cases a mother, sister or niece managed their household for them, but other men proved perfectly capable of supervising their own servants without falling into the neglect and disorder of the Rev. Cargill. A study by Dr Helen Metcalfe shows that bachelors were keenly aware both of practical considerations and social standing in choosing their accommodation: it should be clean and comfortable, providing the amenities they desired (ranging from plenty of sunlight to cooked meals if desired) and in a location which was both convenient and appropriate to their status and their ambitions. For example, in 1772, the thirty-five-year-old Edward Gibbon told his stepmother that 'I have at last pitched on Lady Rouse's house in Bentinck Street, which I have only taken till I find whether the place, situation &c will suit me.' Nonetheless he at once set about redecorating it and for some time his correspondence was full of bookcases and wallpaper. The result was pleasing and bolstered his self-confidence: 'I glory in thinking that although my house is small, it is just of a sufficient size to hold my real friends.' He remained at Bentinck Street for the next decade.[22]

Marriage was an important milestone in a man's life and it often marked the moment when he established an independent household and took control of his finances, which together identified him as a fully adult citizen. But it was not necessary for a man to marry to achieve this position. Men in the professions achieved independent status through their careers, and marriage was often a delayed result, not a catalyst, of their success. Nor is it really possible to argue that unmarried men were not full members of the community in an era when the dominant politician of the age was a bachelor, William Pitt the Younger, prime minister 1784–1801, 1804–6. Pitt was unusual, but not unique. Another bachelor, Thomas Grenville, was a close friend of Fox and an important member of the Buckingham–Grenville family connection. He served as President of the Board of Control and then First Lord of the Admiralty in the Ministry of All the Talents, and would have held other high offices if his political sympathies did not generally lie with the opposition. Indeed, more than one-third of all Members of Parliament serving in the Commons between 1790 and 1820 were unmarried when they were first elected, and 320 (out of 2,143) are not known to have married at all. Successful bachelors were also not unknown outside the world of politics, with examples including Lieutenant-General Sir John Moore, who was killed at the Battle of Coruña in 1809 at the age of forty-eight, and the 6th Duke of Devonshire (son of Georgiana, Duchess of Devonshire), who died unmarried at the age of sixty-seven in 1858.[23]

Bachelors lived very diverse lives: there was not much in common between James Boswell alternating between his mistress and prostitutes in Edinburgh and taking notes of Samuel Johnson's conversation in the coffeehouses of London, and James Lister, living a quiet domestic life at Shibden Hall in Yorkshire; or between either of them and Sir John Moore, studying the profession of arms and training his men at Shorncliffe, or getting on the wrong side of Britain's allies from Sicily to Sweden to Spain.

Their marital status affected their comfort and their happiness, their finances and possibly their sense of self-worth, but both married men and bachelors pursued the same careers or lived very similar lives. Marrying, or not marrying, played a much greater role in determining the life and position of women, although, even so, few women can be adequately defined simply by their husband or their marital status: whether they were a writer like Jane Austen, a leader of the *beau monde* like the Duchess of Devonshire or a quieter figure whom we know mostly through her connection with others, such as Cassandra Austen, their husband, or lack of one, was seldom the most interesting or important thing about them.[24]

It is reasonable to assume that some bachelors and spinsters remained unmarried because they were not sexually attracted to members of the opposite sex; however, the correlation between sexual orientation and marriage was probably not very high. In other words, many men and women who were primarily attracted to their own sex nonetheless married, for a variety of reasons, while many of those who remained unmarried were heterosexual. Some of those who married went on to have either casual sex or more lasting affairs with persons of their own gender, while others suppressed their desire. However, none of this is well documented, and there is no way of forming even a rough estimate of the numbers of people in this situation.

Men who wanted to have casual sex with other men had many opportunities to do so in London, either by picking up male prostitutes (who were reputedly often soldiers in the Guards, earning extra money) at recognised venues such as the city's parks, or at 'molly houses', which catered specifically to their tastes. Such molly houses had been a discreet feature of the capital throughout the eighteenth century, and their patrons ranged across the social classes, while their activities included organising mock weddings. There were fewer opportunities outside London, although we know of a group of men from across the north west of England who met regularly at the village of Great Sankey, near Warrington in Cheshire, and who copied many of the forms of the Freemasons in an endeavour to ensure their secrecy. Probably there were many other, similar groups, while the larger towns and cities probably had established places of rendezvous, although the surviving evidence is thin and patchy.[25]

It seems likely that it was much harder for a gay man to have a serious long-term relationship with another man than to have casual sex. Unrelated women could choose to live together without raising an eyebrow, but it was more difficult for two gentlemen to form a household together. It was a little easier if one was, or appeared to be, the domestic chaplain, secretary or servant of the other, but even in this case the household would usually have female servants to cook, clean and make the beds, and they would certainly notice what was going on and would probably disapprove.[26] This was also relevant to officers, let alone ordinary soldiers and sailors in the army and navy, who seldom had much privacy; and social historians of the navy in the eighteenth and early nineteenth century have found little evidence that sodomy was widespread or tolerated, let alone an established tradition.[27]

Male homosexuality of any kind, and particularly sodomy, was viewed with repugnance by society as a whole and was illegal. Prosecutions, which had been rare at the beginning of the eighteenth century, increased markedly from the 1780s, while between 1806 and 1861 no fewer than 404 men were sentenced to death for sodomy of whom 56 were executed (all before 1836). In 1810 a molly house in Clerkenwell, the White Swan, was raided and a group of men were arrested. Two were hanged and six sentenced to stand in the pillory, where a large crowd pelted them with rotten eggs and vegetables, stones, dead cats and buckets filled with blood, offal, dung and other filth, treatment which left them with significant injuries. A few years later Percy Jocelyn, the Anglican Bishop of Clogher, was arrested after being caught in a compromising position in the back room of a tavern in St James with a soldier named Moverley. The case attracted a great deal of publicity, including a number of satirical prints and pamphlets which sold in large numbers. Jocelyn was released on bail and disappeared, but was then stripped of his see, and is reported to have lived for the remainder of his life (another twenty years) under a false name in Scotland, working as a butler. He was buried in Edinburgh, but it appears that his body was re-interred in the family vault in Ireland, suggesting either that his family did not totally disown him or at least reclaimed him in death.[28]

Not everyone accepted the prevailing view without question. A Yorkshire farmer, Matthew Tomlinson, wondered in his diary in 1810 whether it was right to punish men for urges and desires that were innate, although he was uncertain of the answer; and the radical philosopher Jeremy Bentham believed that homosexuality should be decriminalised, although he never dared to publish these views in his lifetime. Some occupations, such as trades connected with women's hair and clothes, attracted effeminate men whose presence did nothing to harm the business, even if some writers felt obliged to deplore them as 'delicate, contemptible beings' unworthy of 'the masculine character'. And for everyone who went along to jeer and pelt the men in the pillory there were many more who stayed at home or went about their business, feeling either indifference or even pity for the 'criminals'.[29]

Nonetheless there was little if any open disagreement with the public condemnation and abhorrence of sodomy, which was buttressed by biblical prohibitions. This made it a powerful accusation in the hurly-burly of political debate on the hustings. For example, in 1801, Sir Thomas Turton, Member of Parliament for Southwark, was attacked in a squib with the claim that he did not love women. The charge resurfaced as late as 1820 when, *The Times* reported, he defended himself by entering into an account of his youthful adventures with the opposite sex 'a little more explicitly than we can decently report'. Given that Turton was not only married with seven children but had also gained notoriety by his affair with Mrs Dunnage, the wife of a City merchant, which is reported to have cost him £5,000 in 'criminal conversation' (*crim. con.*) damages, it is clear that such attacks were not restricted to bachelors or other obvious targets.[30]

These attitudes created a tempting opportunity for blackmail, whether or not the victim was actually homosexual. In one case, in the 1790s, a soldier alleged that Sir John Riddle had tried to pick him up, while Riddle countered by accusing the soldier of attempting to black-mail him. As the evidence was ambiguous the law sided with the man in the more powerful position, and the soldier was tried, convicted and sentenced to death as a warning to others. But cases where the blackmail succeeded leave fewer traces. The most famous, but also ambiguous, example is that of Castlereagh, by then Lord Londonderry, who, in 1822, told the King that he was being blackmailed for committing the same crime as the Bishop of Clogher, having been lured into a house of ill repute by a man dressed as a woman. However, Londonderry was suffering from mental illness at the time and committed suicide soon after, and we do not know whether this was precipitated by something that actually happened or if the whole story was a delusion.[31]

Some gay men felt obliged to live abroad in order to escape the expectations of British society. Lord Deskford, the son of Earl Findlater, was an early suitor of Lady Anne Lindsay. Tall, stiff, resembling 'a young Van Dyke lord with a Roman nose', he was considered a good match, but before the courtship progressed to a conclusion he left Scotland for the Continent, officially to recover from an illness in a warmer climate, but in fact to escape a scandal caused by his homosexual activities. Henry Grey Bennet, the fourth son of Lord Tankerville, resigned his seat in parliament and retired to the Continent, where he remained for the rest of his life, following accusations that he had 'mistaken a boy for a girl at Brussels'. For men from a humbler background it was often sufficient to move to London or another part of the country, just as a young woman who had 'lost her reputation' might do. On the other hand, Lord George Germain (previously Lord George Sackville) rose to high office in Lord North's Cabinet, despite the widespread belief that he was a sodomite *and* that he had behaved in a cowardly fashion at the Battle of Minden in 1759. However, it is possible that attitudes had hardened in the aftermath of the loss of America, and that he might not have been so successful a generation later.[32]

Our understanding of the position of lesbians in Regency England has been transformed by the decoding and publication of the diaries of Anne Lister. Where previously there was little beyond hints, innuendo and unprovable assumptions there is now a large body of detailed and explicit evidence which at many points can be verified from other sources, and whose authenticity cannot seriously be questioned. It is still dangerous to generalise too much from a single source, but Lister's diary shifts the starting point for any discussion by showing that quite a few women of her class were happy to have sex with her or other women, and that they did not need to practise much discretion to avoid an open scandal.

Anne Lister was born in 1791, the daughter of an army officer who was a younger son of a Yorkshire gentry family. She had several brothers who died prematurely (the last one when she was in her early twenties), and her uncle, the head of the family, was a bachelor, which meant that although she was not bound to inherit the family estate, there was no one who had an obviously better claim. She was highly intelligent and studied Latin, Greek, algebra, geometry and modern languages with coaching from a local clergyman. She began keeping a diary at the age of fifteen, although the unbroken run only began a decade later. The surviving diary is immense: twenty-seven volumes amounting to some 4 million words, about one-sixth of which are in code – passages relating to sex, money and clothes. Her handwriting is not easy, and the task of transcribing the full text is being undertaken by a team of volunteers, with the results steadily appearing online. A considerable collection of her letters has also survived, although only a selection has yet been published, so that her life is remarkably well documented.[33]

When Anne Lister was fourteen or fifteen she was a boarder at the Manor School in York, where she and another student slept in a little attic room by themselves. This other girl was Eliza Raine, who had been born in Madras, the daughter of an English surgeon and his Indian mistress. Anne soon fell in love with her, remarking many years later that she was 'the most beautiful girl I ever saw'. The two girls exchanged rings, swore to stay together forever and refused to be parted even in the holidays, when they continued to share a bed, as girls and women often did. Looking back Anne was clear that her attraction to Eliza and other women was innate: 'My conduct & feelings being surely natural to me inasmuch as they were not taught, not fictitious but instinctive. I had always the same turn from infancy . . . I had never varied & no effort on my part had been able to counteract it.' Anne did not return to the school after these holidays, although the reason is not clear and may simply have been lack of money for the fees, but she and Eliza continued to correspond, making plans to set up house together as soon as Eliza turned twenty-one and gained control of her fortune. Meanwhile Anne studied the classics and found much to interest and enlighten her in references to Sappho and lesbian love in works by Horace, Juvenal and Martial, which contained explicit if hostile accounts of women having sex with other women. In 1809, Anne stayed with Eliza and her guardian in York, and the two young women 'came out' together in December and enjoyed the whirl of local society, until the fatal illness of one of her brothers forced Anne to go home. Eliza's letters showed that there was no diminution of affection on her side, and she referred to Anne as her 'husband', but, in a pattern that would become familiar, Anne was growing tired of her and allowed the relationship to atrophy without having the courage to make an open break.[34]

Eliza Raine was just the first of Anne Lister's many lovers as she moved from relationship to relationship in a way that seems remarkably modern. Anne shows little or no guilt or qualms about her sexuality in her diary. 'I love & only love, the fairer sex & thus, beloved by them in turn, my heart revolts from any other love but theirs.' When one of her lovers, Nantz Belcombe, 'asked if I thought the thing was wrong – if it was forbidden in the bible', Anne responded that she thought it would be 'infamous to be connected with both sexes – but that there were beings who were so unfortunate as to be not quite so perfect &, supposing they kept to one side [of] the question, was there no excuse for them. It would be hard to deny them a gratification of this kind. I urged in my own defence the strength of natural feeling & instinct, for so I might call it.' But the disapproval of women who slept with both men and women was not consistent: one of Anne's longest lasting lovers was Nantz's sister Mariana, who married Charles Lawton (a wealthy landowner twenty years older than her) in order to gain financial security and a place in society, but who continued to sleep with Anne at every opportunity and to plan their life together as soon as Charles should have the good grace to die.[35]

Like some men, Anne enjoyed the pursuit, courting and flattering a woman until she agreed to have sex and then sometimes losing interest quite rapidly. One of her lovers, Isabella Norcliffe, remarked that 'It would be unnatural in you not to like sleeping with a pretty girl.' While Anne once criticised herself for some indiscreet flirtation, 'But somehow I seem as if I could never resist the opportunity. A woman tête-à-tête is a dangerous animal to me.' She also acknowledged that she was not really looking for an equal: 'I am not an admirer of learned ladies . . . I would rather have a pretty girl to flirt with.' And she was very taken aback when Maria Barlow took the initiative, and Anne firmly declined an offer that Maria penetrate *her* – that was not at all what she wanted or had experienced with any previous lover. But at the same time that Anne was promiscuous she always dreamt of establishing a permanent relationship akin to marriage: 'my heart longs after a companion & how I often wish for an establishment of my own . . . .' In the end she achieved this when she inherited Shibden Hall from her uncle and took as her partner a wealthy woman, Ann Walker, who was twelve years her junior.[36]

There was, however, much more to Anne Lister's life than her many love affairs, and at times they take second or even third place in her diary to her relations with her uncle and aunt (with whom she lived from 1815), her parents and her many other interests. Once she took over part of the daily management of the estate from her uncle in about 1822 business matters absorbed a great deal of her attention, and diary entries in later years dwell heavily on matters such as the drainage of agricultural land, the maintenance of farm buildings, the development of stone quarries and coal mines, renovations to the hall and landscaping of the park. She also took a keen interest in local and national politics, in which she was an old-fashioned Tory. It was unusual for a spinster to inherit and directly manage a landed estate in this way, and Anne's self-consciously masculine outlook probably assisted her in doing so, where a more conventional woman might have relied more heavily on a male agent. Anne also greatly enjoyed travelling, visiting France, Switzerland, the Netherlands, Germany, Italy and Spain, not only visiting famous places but also factories, prisons and mines, and climbing mountains in the Pyrenees. In 1839 she and Ann Walker set off on an expedition which took them through Germany and Sweden to Russia and thence down to the Caucasus and Persia. She fell ill and died in Georgia on 22 September 1840 at the age of forty-nine. Ann Walker brought her body home and she was interred in the Halifax parish church.[37]

Lister was a well-known figure in local society, first and foremost as the heir presumptive and then the owner of a landed estate. She was accepted in Halifax society, although her dress and manner were regarded as a little odd and sometimes embarrassed her more conventional companions. (She always dressed in black, an unusual colour for women not in mourning, and seldom wore a bonnet preferring a round hat, but her clothes were not overtly masculine.) Although she was generally treated with respect, there were instances where she was abused, and she was sometimes referred to as 'Gentleman Jack' and comments made that she looked like a man (which she quite liked). Occasional abusive letters arrived, which she did not read and tried not to be troubled by; yet she braced herself for the possibility of physical attack on some of her long unaccompanied walks. Her uncle and aunt were very supportive in the face of this, never suggesting that she adopt a more discreet appearance or manner. They were also sympathetic to her friendship with other women, while asking few questions and wanting no details, and her uncle was content for her to inherit the estate while knowing that she would never marry or have a child. She even confided in them when she caught a venereal disease and needed treatment, although her aunt either believed that this could be caught in other ways or pretended to believe this to avoid embarrassing disclosures.[38]

A similar preference for discretion can be seen in the response of British society to the 'Ladies of Llangollen', the two aristocratic Irish ladies who, in 1778, ran away together and set up house in north Wales. Lady Eleanor Butler and the Hon. Sarah Ponsonby made no demands on society and, after a time, society chose to treat them, not as outcasts or disreputable, but as admirable eccentrics. Their idyllic retreat was not far from the main route for British and Irish politicians heading to and from Dublin, and they received many well-connected visitors and gained greater fame than they would ever have achieved if they had lived conventional lives. Whatever they did in the privacy of their bedroom remained private, and society applauded their discretion and liked to think of them as embodying romantic friendship.[39]

Although there were occasional references to lesbianism in literature and satirical prints, and even Scottish judges knew that women were capable of giving each other sexual pleasure, society preferred to work on the assumption that relations between women were innocent unless there was very strong evidence to the contrary. Over the course of the eighteenth century ideas about women's sexuality had changed from depicting women as inherently lustful (possibly more so than men) to regarding them as largely passive and a-sexual, at least until they were aroused by a (male) husband or lover. The thought that any woman might actively prefer to have sex with another woman rather than with a man was altogether too threatening to male *amour propre* to be allowed to take root. Much better that the fantastical notion be pushed out of sight before it gave anyone dangerous ideas.[40]

Most people growing up in England in the late eighteenth and early nineteenth centuries took for granted that they would eventually marry, but many ended up remaining single, some because they fixed on a person who did not reciprocate their affections and they would have no other; some because money or other material circumstances made marriage imprudent; some because they never found anyone to whom they were willing to entrust their happiness; and others because of their sexual orientation. Some of these spinsters and bachelors went on to have lives that were impoverished, financially, emotionally and in other ways, just as some of those who married lived to regret it. But many spinsters and bachelors – it is probably safe to say 'most', although that cannot be proved – had lives with a pretty normal share of pleasures and pains, interests and tedium. There was almost always an alternative to marriage.

CHAPTER NINE

EARLY MARRIED LIFE

ADJUSTING TO MARRIED LIFE presented many challenges as couples learnt to live with each other and adapt to their new roles in an unfamiliar environment. But this was also a very happy time for most couples, filled with the love and passion of a relationship that was still fresh and exciting. Looking back, Frances Calvert wrote, 'I really think this was the happiest time of my life', and Lady Charlotte Bury, encountering Charles and Harriet Arbuthnot in the early days of their marriage, wrote that 'she is very pretty . . . He is all fire and flames and love . . . and so very proud of her. It is rather agreeable to see any person so completely happy.' Even James Boswell, not the most naturally uxorious of men, was so glutted with happiness in the first years of his marriage that the compulsion to write about himself evaporated. He disliked parting from Margaret even briefly, writing to her, 'the short absence which I have now suffered has convinced me still more feelingly than before how much I love you . . . how ill I can do without you.' His grievances and insecurities retreated into the furthest recesses of his consciousness, and for a time he did not hanker after the delights of London or the reflected glow of Dr Johnson's greatness.[1]

It was not only the young who might be enchanted with each other. Hester Mundy was almost forty when she married the fifty-seven-year-old Sir Roger Newdigate in 1776. A few months later he went up to London, possibly for the meeting of parliament, while she stayed with her friends

Lord and Lady Denbigh. She opened her first letter to him, 'My dear, dear Runaway', and admits that her spirits had been very low when she first arrived and so did not write at once, in case he perceived this, and 'your Vanity wd lead you to suspect that your absence was ye cause . . .'. At 'Supper everybody was jolly & happy excepting myself & I felt a weight at my Heart that would not let it rise . . .'. But she felt better now: 'I . . . think of you no more & have been trotting round my old Acquaintance in ye Shrubery [*sic*] with as much Glee as if I had not been transplanted into another Soil.' She even felt tempted to ride, but did not, out of deference to his often expressed anxiety for her safety. They drank his health at dinner, and when, at half-past nine, Lady Denbigh wondered what he was doing at that moment, 'I boldly answer'd "he is writing to me". I shall often have that absurd fancy if you do not cure me of it.'[2]

Her confidence was not misplaced and very late the next day she added, 'Tho' I am so sleepy I can hardly hold my eyes open I cannot go to bed till I have thanked my Dear Soul for a most sweet & kind Letter which I have just read over for ye third time & now I will pray for your preservation & happiness & then try if I can dream of you. Good night.' And the ending of her next letter suggests that he was equally affectionate in writing to her: 'You begin your Letter like a dear Goose, & end it in the same stile . . .'.[3]

This was a time when couples established patterns of behaviour and ways of dealing with each other that might go on to last a lifetime, or might subsequently fall by the wayside as old habits reasserted themselves, or the husband's career imposed its demands, or the arrival of children added new responsibilities. In the middle of July 1799, less than four months after her marriage, Lady Caroline Stuart Wortley described her daily routine to her mother, Lady Erne:

> I am sorry to say that from nine o'clock, which was the breakfast hour, we are now come to ten, for tho' we are called a little after eight, that villain Zac [her husband, James Stuart Wortley] frustrates all my efforts by it being impossible to wake him. However to proceed, having breakfasted we come into the Library & I begin by writing, because the morning is so short that if I put it off I never find another moment, as was the case yesterday. When the courier [a

newspaper] is finished, we all work [i.e. sew] & Zac reads to us, after which or sometimes before it, Louisa [her sister-in-law] & I sing together, & this with a little chatting brings us to dinner at 3 o'clock, by which hour we are all famished. At about 5 or a little after, we go out in the open carriages, & come in to tea & bread & butter between seven & eight. Between that hour and ten o'clock when we sup we talk & laugh not a little, sometimes sing, or take up a book & read to ourselves, and very often *nothing do*, but *talk*. By eleven we generally feel all enclined [*sic*] to go to our beds – in short it is a life that suits me in every respect, & seems to agree most perfectly with us all . . .

I don't know what you call summer like weather at Ickworth, but here we have not had any appearance of it, & indeed very little else than constant rain, & a continual demand for fire, which however we never obtain . . .[4]

Just a few months later, in October, their life was thrown in to turmoil by the prospect that James Stuart Wortley might be sent on active service in the Anglo-Russian expedition to the Low Countries.

We have been reading the Gazette together, I studying the map of Holland . . . one dreads I think seeing details & knowing the extent of our loss. Col. Wortley is just gone down to the orderly room to try & learn some particulars, especially concerning the officers who have fallen. How thankful I am that he should have escaped at least the dangers of these two severe actions – surely they can never have a third like them! . . . I am very well, all but a little nervousness occasioned by extreme anxiety & alarm.

Stuart Wortley set off for the Continent and Lady Caroline later admitted that she felt sure that he would be killed and she would never see him again. But even before he had embarked orders came for him and his men to return to London, and he obtained leave to go ahead and arrived home just as Lady Caroline was having supper. She was immensely relieved and delighted, but decided that if he was again sent abroad she would endeavour to follow him as far as she could: to Rome or to Naples if he was sent to Egypt, or to accompany him if he went to Ireland.[5]

In the meantime a new routine was established which evidently proved amusing:

> Louisa & I have begun di bel nuovo our education & Zac is schoolmaster – he is going thro' a regular course of history with me, & we are now reading Stangan's Grecian history – he reads it out to me & makes me make extracts as we go along – in the even[in]g he gives Louisa & me, a long lesson of Arithmetic – wch. occasions the greatest mirth, to the whole society, tho' sometimes it try's *his* exemplary patience; for à force d'etre *witty* & of laughing, Louisa & I get into the most complete and unconquerable giggles – you wd die, to see poor dear Mrs. W., trying to put on a grave manner, & scolding us, *forced* to laugh whether she will or no.[6]

Many couples enjoyed reading aloud to each other as a way of sharing a pleasure, and it was not uncommon for young women (who were often still in their teens or, like Lady Caroline, had just turned twenty), and who had married men with intellectual interests, to wish to continue their education, although it is reassuring to see that arithmetic was approached with an appropriate degree of levity.

John Stanley was only an officer in the Cheshire Militia, not the regular army, but even this was not without its duties, some of which his wife Maria Josepha (née Holroyd) rather resented. She grumbled to her sister Louisa, 'My rogue came home at eight. He gave the mess claret when he was there the first time upon his becoming major, and they drank him eight pounds' worth.' And, 'These nasty . . . dinners are shocking bores, for he cannot excuse himself if inclined, and I have very little of his company now with one vile duty or another. He is drilling with Major Atherton every morning, learning six ways of cutting down a man, and not having yet made himself an adept in one cut of three motions, I suppose many days will be required to make him perfect in all.'[7]

Nonetheless Maria Stanley was intensely happy, devoted to her husband and basking in his love of her, which was a characteristic of this early stage of marriage for many couples. She told Louisa, 'I wish you may find three months' marriage increase a husband's love and admiration as much as I have found they have.' And nine months later, a year after the wedding, she wrote to her Aunt Serena, reflecting on the chances of fate and the importance of finding the right partner:

> Were you an entirely indifferent person to me, and had you but an inch of heart, I think you would find it a gratifying spectacle to see me so loved by such a being as him, who does love me so. And as you are not at all indifferent and have a pretty large portion of heart, methinks would be in an ecstasy of pleasure. Do tell me how I can possibly have deserved to have such a lot, as to be united to the man in the world most calculated to make me happy and good for something; which might not have been the case, perhaps, had I less entirely loved, esteemed, and respected the partner of my life.[8]

She describes walking on a beach at Blyth (north of Newcastle) 'by the side of my lover, my husband', while she was equally happy the next day, when it rained, and 'he read to me; I went to our child, and wished for nothing more in the wide world'.[9]

While less open in expressing his feelings, John Stanley was equally happy, writing that 'My present enjoyments are great. I have found my child well. Maria is happy and placid, and pleased with everything about her. To live at Alderley with such a being to love, has ever been the wish of my heart.' And when he visited them at the end of the year, Maria's father, Lord Sheffield, commented on their contentment: 'There is nothing but what is highly pleasant to mention from this place. The good sense the dear Pol [i.e. Maria] thinks proper to display; the propriety; and attention to the Man is everything that could be desired. They seem eminently made for each other. She strokes and pats him, and does not seem particularly to prefer her own way.' Although Lord Sheffield particularly praised his daughter's efforts to please her husband, it seems clear that in this case and in many others, such efforts were made in both directions, with John Stanley as keen to please Maria as she was to please him. However, not all marriages worked in this way or were as happy.[10]

Lady Shelley (née Frances Winckley) had little reason to regret her determination to marry Sir John Shelley, against the advice of her family, in the first days of her marriage. She was presented at court and 'Every one seemed to rejoice with our happiness, and life then appeared to me to be a real Paradise.' But this contentment proved short-lived. A visit to Osterley was prolonged when Sir John twisted his ankle playing tennis at Hampton Court and was forced to use crutches. Lady Shelley disliked her hostess, Lady Jersey, who she found overbearing, but in 'deference to my husband's request I patiently swallowed every affront, and bore her impertinent curiosity with humility, which was more feigned than real. She inquired into the amount of my fortune, and of our expenditure, giving her opinion as to what we should, or should not, do.' This was bad enough, but Sir John's injury left him temporarily lame, which drew attention to the seventeen-year age difference between them and 'set all the gossips giggling'. Things did not improve during a stay at Holkham, where, 'I had an even more *triste* experience of the jealousy and spite of the worldly people of that period, who were prepared to hate me for having robbed them of their former flirt and gay *convive*. These ladies practiced the refined art of social torture, without attracting my husband's attention, and I had much to bear in silence.'[11]

Sir John made little effort to change his lifestyle to accommodate his wife, continuing to devote a great deal of time and money to horse racing – his horses would go on to win the Derby twice, in 1811 and 1825. Frances accepted this, but before they were married she had made him promise to give up gambling at cards, and he kept his word. Whist had been exempted from this promise as a sociable game that was widely played for low stakes; however, Lord Peterborough then introduced a new form of the game, 'short whist', which was much more dangerous. A more honourable, less self-indulgent man than Sir John might have abided by the spirit not the letter of his agreement, but that was not his way, and he 'contrived to lose thousands [of pounds] in a single night, sitting up until daylight chained to his chair by the fascination of the game!' Nor was this a solitary lapse, and his wife recalled, 'I passed many wretched nights, wasting the midnight oil, and waiting for my husband's return.' She followed some advice from Lady Sefton and 'never went to sleep until my husband came home', reading through the night, something which she felt 'affected my eyesight'. Looking back she commented, with more than a touch of melodrama, that 'Those eyes which, according to Saunders's miniature, were once so large and brilliant, began insensibly to grow dim.'[12]

Gossips and false friends preyed on the neglected nineteen-year-old bride, whispering tales in her ears of Sir John's unworthiness and arguing that if he was not faithful to her, why should she be faithful to him? Lady Boringdon (Lady Jersey's sister) was 'desperately in love with my husband. She tried, by every artifice, to induce him to go off with her. . . . I was not, at that time, aware of her motives in breathing poisonous insinuations into my unwilling ears. If only I had known I should not have been so unhappy!' However, Sir John was still in thrall to Lady Haggerston who had been his mistress before his marriage and who looked upon Frances 'as a mere "country girl" who could be managed under her skilful guidance'. 'One of the first struggles of my young married life was to break her chains.' None of this shook Lady Shelley's passionate love of her husband, and she resolved to win him at all costs, by making him 'so happy in his home that he would not crave for the love of other women. I exerted every power with which nature and study had endowed me, to fascinate him as a mistress, and to enchain his affections as a wife.' Moreover, 'I made it a point never to interfere in any way with my husband's mode of life; and I never kept him from the society even of persons whose conduct I could not admire. Often have I urged him to accept invitations, and go alone to dinner-parties where I knew that he was more than welcome. In this I feel sure that I acted wisely.' She also 'entreated him not to *tell me* if he were ever unfaithful to me', and she believed that once he had broken with Lady Haggerston, he remained loyal to her. It was a strange struggle between two apparently ill-matched adversaries, but Lady Shelley was not as naïve as she looked, and she was fiercely determined to make her husband love her as much as she loved him and – strange as it may seem to us – she succeeded, forging a happy marriage, in which she was the dominant partner, from such unpromising materials.[13]

Many couples, even from wealthy, aristocratic families, did not at once set up a home of their own when they were married. It was quite common for them to live for a time with the groom's family, despite the obvious danger of quarrels and discontent that this entailed. Lady Caroline Stuart-

Wortley evidently did not object to sharing her arithmetic lessons with her sister-in-law Louisa, or teasing her husband until even his mother broke down in laughter, but she may well have preferred to have this time with him alone. Lord and Lady Belgrave, the heirs to the Grosvenor estate and fortune, were expected to live for most of the year with his parents at Eaton Hall in Cheshire. Elizabeth, Lady Belgrave, took care to remain on excellent terms with her parents-in-law, but it is clear that she craved more independence, and delighted to have the house to herself when the Grosvenors were away. On one such occasion she told her mother, 'our life here is so very comfortable and pleasant – quite alone and doing what *we* like, with long rides and drives to dissipate us and puppies to educate in our more serious hours'. But it required all her patience to get through times when her husband was absent and she was left with Lady Grosvernor, listening to 'Mr. Aychbourn reading aloud "The Last of the Mohicans" or "Rokeby" in so lachrymose a manner that Dido [her terrier] cried'. She also greatly disliked some of Lady Grosvenor's friends, especially 'Those vile harpies the Miss Luxmoores – vulgar and detestable in every way', but as it was not her house, she had no choice but to be polite to her mother-in-law's guests, while avoiding them as much as civility permitted. Even so, 'The evenings are a mortal bore, but luckily they generally retire early after their daily fatigues and we see no more of them.'[14]

The Belgraves did not get a country house of their own for twelve years after their wedding. This was certainly unusual, but many wives had to wait a year or two before they could put down roots, especially if their husbands were officers in the army or navy. Betsey Fremantle spent the first year of her married life either on board ship (first the *Inconstant*, Captain Fremantle's ominously named frigate, and later the more promising *Seahorse*) or in a little rented cottage on Elba. Life at sea for a young bride had many inconveniences and rather less privacy than was desirable, although the captain's quarters were relatively spacious. Nonetheless they were both generally very happy. On Elba, Betsey declined going to the ball that marked the end of the carnival season: 'I spent the whole day and evening tête à tête with Fremantle, it was cold and we wrote letters till supper time. I never thought of the Ball, last year I should have been distressed and miserable to finish the carnaval in my room but now I am never so happy when alone with Fremantle and have not the least desire to enjoy any other pleasure.' And Fremantle told his brother, 'We go very little out and if I am to judge of the future by the present time I think I shall never have cause to repent of having married. *My Wife* is perfectly what I could have wished, joined to every personal accomplishment she is possessed of more good nature than any woman I know . . .'. When, at the end of April, Fremantle spent a night on board another ship after dining with Nelson, Betsey, 'slept alone in the cabin all night, the first night I have slept alone since I have been married, did not like it'.[15]

A few months later Betsey Fremantle was still on board when British gunboats attacked the Spanish defences at Cadiz. Captain Fremantle took part in the attack, and his wife wrote after the first operation, 'I was anxious for Fremantle and did not go to bed until he returned.' She was more relaxed at the subsequent attack on Tenerife: 'As the taking of this place seemed an easy and almost sure thing, I went to bed after they were gone apprehending no danger for Fremantle.' However, the attack was repulsed with considerable loss. 'Fremantle returned at 4 this morning wounded in the arm, he was shot in the right arm the moment he had landed, came off in the first boat, and stayed on board the Zealous till day light, where his wound was dressed. Thank God as the ball only went through the flesh he will not lose his arm he managed it so well that I was not frightened, but I was not a little distressed and miserable when I heard what it was, and indeed he was in great pain and suffered cruelly all day.' Nelson was also wounded and his arm had to be amputated. Although Fremantle's arm was saved, his wound proved worse than first thought, and Betsey spent long hours nursing him as the ship made its way to England, where they disembarked at the beginning of September, more than a month after the action. Even then his recovery was slow and painful, affecting his temper and spirits. Betsey required a great deal of patience, but also judgement, for much responsibility fell squarely on her, and she was a stranger in England, not having lived there for almost ten years, and her family were far beyond reach on the Continent. She was also coming to terms with the fact that she was pregnant. She was nineteen years old.[16]

Not all the wives of naval officers tolerated life on board ship as cheerfully as Betsey Fremantle. Although she was the daughter of an admiral and had crossed the Atlantic, Louisa, Lady Hardy, wife of Sir Thomas Hardy, never forgot the discomforts she had endured spending the winter of 1807–8 on board his ship in Chesapeake Bay. Because relations with the Americans were bad, none of the British crew were allowed to land and the ship was kept constantly ready for action, and Lady Hardy accumulated a considerable number of grievances against her husband to add to his lack of social distinction. But this was an unhappy marriage from the outset, in which neither side was willing to do much to please the other, and love of any kind was noticeable by its absence.[17]

Most brides, however, were able to take undisputed possession of their new home from the outset of their marriage. Very often their husband would have redecorated and modernised it before the wedding, ideally with input from the bride-to-be, although some couples preferred to wait until after the ceremony when they were in residence and could determine the most urgent priorities. When Jane Austen's eldest brother James married Anne Mathew the happy couple spent £200 (equal to half their annual income, but probably a gift from her father) over five months on new furniture and necessities for their home at Deane parsonage.[18]

It was not uncommon for the groom's mother and unmarried sisters to vacate the premises in order to make way for the eldest son and his new wife. In *Mansfield Park* we are told that Mrs Rushworth senior 'removed herself, her maid, her footman, and her chariot, with true dowager propriety, to Bath – there to parade over the wonders of Sotherton in her evening-parties – enjoying them as thoroughly perhaps in the animation of the card-table as she had ever done on the spot'. That was a cheerful interpretation of something that must often have been quite heart-wrenching, even when the marriage and the choice of bride met with warm approval. When Maria Stanley was about to move into Alderley House her sister-in-law Isa wrote to her from London telling her some of the practical details about the house that they had left for her: the two female servants, their roles and wages; the lack of good, modern furniture, especially a sofa; two good cows and a calf; a favourite spaniel called Bounce, and a nice but not especial favourite called Punch (also a spaniel); nothing was needed for a sick room (or for her confinement?); and finally a tolerable piano belonging jointly to Isa and Lou 'who leave it for your use till you suit yourself with one to your fancy'. She 'fear[ed] you would find many inconveniences, being accustomed to so elegant and complete a mansion as Sheffield Place. With all its imperfections, I could not leave it without a selfish regret, though I felt glad it was to belong to those who would take interest in it and improve it. If ever you are rich enough, it may be made very beautiful.'[19]

Fortunately Maria Stanley liked her new home, telling her sister that 'I was surprised to find the house as comfortable as it is from the account he had given of it, and everything of furniture &c. left in plenty and in nice order; a good stock of linen to begin with, stores of all kinds, and wine. The dear old Man is as busy as fifty bees all day long, and plenty of employment there is, for it would vex anybody to see some of the most beautiful ground possible in a state of wilderness beyond anything you can conceive.' A few months later she told her Aunt Serena that 'We are as busy here as possible. He is making me seats and walks and bosquets, intermixed with more necessary operations of planting, fencing and draining, &c. . . . much has been accomplished, and yet the very first moment it can be done, we must build a quite new mansion. The dear old rogue sends his love to you. He delights in his idle, busy, lounging, active life. He is never indoors except at meals, and does not come in to dinner till six o'clock.'[20]

The disadvantage for a new wife in having a home of her own was that she was usually expected to manage the household, and although she had often absorbed much knowledge from assisting her mother, and there were plenty of advice books to give guidance, this might still be a considerable challenge, especially if there were well-established servants who resented her interference. An example of the problems which might occur comes from the experiences of Louisa, Lady Hopetoun, who wrote to her father Godfrey, Lord Macdonald, in May 1827 asking for his advice. 'The fact is my husband depends entirely on my regulating the household business, and I being a new hand the more experienced [servants] are taking advantage, however with your assistance I think I shall improve.' She proceeds to give a detailed account of the existing arrangements which show the scale on which a large, almost feudal, estate in Scotland might operate:

The Steward has been to me this morning with the larder book and complaining of the consumption of meat which of course, as he says

167

he cannot control as the Cook mentions it to me when meat is wanted and I give her a note to be sent to the grieve mentioning either a bullock or a sheep to be killed which is done and when it comes into the larder he is present at the cutting up and notes the weight in the larder book. I then give all over to the Cook who comes up to me every Monday, so you see the fault cannot lie with him, but again if the Cook tells me that if meat is killed now it will only just be ready by the time it is wanted what can I say? I know my dear Papa you will forgive this little bit of household business but your own house books and calculations are so managed like clock-work, that I cannot helping thinking *you* are the person that can best assist me in my difficulties. Now for example, we were away from home nearly a fortnight in Decr. yet the larder book for that month from the 2nd to the 30th runs as follows, 3 bullocks (making 128 stone of beef) 8 sheep (making 37 stone 7 pounds of mutton) 24 chickens 4 geese besides which the keeper sent in 67 Hares 32 rabbits 38 Pheasants, 15 Partridges and two woodcocks and I forgot to mention two does which the servants had to make merry with as it was Christmas but which the Cook told me she gave away to the poor as the servants did not like venison! And I also forgot to mention 40 dozen of eggs! but I must give you the number of servants or you cannot judge, 4 in the Stewards room, 15 men and 11 women making altogether 30 – our own party for the first fortnight we will average at 4 never more, and for the rest of the month we will be at Keith, Pinkie and Luffness. . . . Easby has discovered that Mrs Anderson the Cook certainly disposes of the game and he fancys also meat as the Porter found some ready packed and next carrier day Ld. H. intends having the cart searched when it is fairly en route. I have ten thousand pardons to ask and fear I have sadly tired you but as we shall get another Cook I should like to gain a little experience against she comes – My very best love to Mamma and my Sisters. Ever believe me my dearest Papa . . .[21]

Few wives faced challenges on this scale, but even managing a much smaller household might prove difficult. Many women came to take great pride in their success and concealed the care and scrutiny which it required. Hester Chapone advised that 'The best sign of a home being well governed is, that nobody's attention is called to any of the little affairs of it', and both incompetence and boasting were judged harshly by other women. Not all servants were honest, and even those who were might quarrel among themselves or prove incompetent, and in most cases it was the lady who headed the household who was expected to sort out these problems. There were exceptions, however, with Charles Arbuthnot, suggesting that he employ a maître d'hôtel to manage the household rather than expect Harriet to do so. She approved the plan without hesitation: 'you have *kept house* so long, you *must* understand all about it, & if you really will make me quite happy you will indulge my lazy disposition & you & your maître d'hôtel manage everything without my knowing anything about the matter'. She was also anxious that her arrival should not disrupt the lives of the children of his first marriage more than was necessary. '[L]et everything go on as it is, only take me & my maid in. I must have the latter for she is a treasure I should be lost without. I *entreat* you to make no alteration with regard to your children, remember there *is* a common prejudice against a mother in law [i.e. stepmother]; it is natural, & every act which can be supposed to be mine will . . . be scrutinized with a prejudicial eye.' She also expressed clear preferences when it came to redecorating, asking that the bed be 'perfectly plain; I have a horror of a bed that has a great deal of *dressing* on it, such as I know is the fashion now, I always suspect it must be dirty. I don't mean that such would actually be the case in your house but I should fancy it. Anything in the world & it is but *clean* will do for me.' And she was equally forthright and self-confident on the essential matter of their own relationship: 'You know you are to *spoil me*, at least you may try how we should get on in that way & in return I will give you advice whenever you ask it, & *torment* you as much as you like.' The strength of their love shines through the banter, as does Harriet's remarkable self-confidence and deftness with which they both defused problems even before they arose.[22]

Another problem that often made its first appearance early in the marriage but which might then become entrenched was relations with in-laws. This manifested in many different ways. Brides often greatly missed their family in the early days of their marriage, and it is likely that some husbands, like Lord Teviot in Emily Eden's novel *The Semi-Attached Couple*, were jealous of this emotional bond. Sometimes it was the bride's family that created the difficulty. Lord William Russell's wife, Elizabeth (Bessy) Rawdon, was an only child, and her mother made little attempt to bear the loss of her daughter stoically. Less than a month after the wedding, Lord William wrote to Mrs Rawdon chiding her for her 'melancholy & violent' letters which constantly upset Bessy. 'Certainly you must feel most acutely the loss of your daughter, but . . . Endeavour to make your letters a comfort & pleasure to her, & not a cause for weeping & repentance which they have too often been.' Lord William may have been biased, but Lady Granville, the wife of the British ambassador in Paris, noted that the '*exigeante* mother-in-law . . . talks all the time as if Lady William was dead. "From the time I lost my poor Bessy." It is clear Lord William will not love Mrs Rawdon.' She was right, and Mrs Rawdon's frequent presence did not help a marriage that was soon to develop other problems. At least Lord William and his wife did not have to live with either of their parents, which was probably the most frequent source of tension with in-laws in the early days of a marriage.[23]

Most close relatives recognised the delicacy of the moment and did their best to avoid trouble and to establish harmonious relations with someone who, for good or ill, would be inseparably tied to someone they loved. The mother or sister of the groom often welcomed his fiancée or new wife into the family with a letter expressing her approval of the match. For example, Mrs Austen, Jane's mother, wrote to Mary Lloyd when James Austen asked her to become his second wife eighteen months after the death of his first wife Anne. 'Had the selection been mine, you, my dear Mary, are the person I should have chosen for James's wife, Anna's mother and my daughter, being as certain as I can be of anything in this uncertain world, that you will greatly increase and promote the happiness of each of the three.' But despite this, and the family's long friendship with the Lloyds, relations between Mary Austen and her mother- and sisters-in-law were never entirely comfortable.[24]

A generation earlier Mrs Graham wrote to Mary Cathcart after she had become engaged to her son Thomas:

A thousand thanks for your partiality to my son, my dearest Mary, for how can I give you any other name (tho' so little acquainted) when we are now to stand in so near a relation to one another – a relation which I hope will be the source of infinite happiness to the two persons most dear to me in the world . . .

Had my son studied only to please me (but by his rapturous expression it is pretty evident he pleased himself) he could not have made a choice so perfectly agreeable to me; for though I had not had opportunity enough to know you personally, yet your education was intimately known to me, and the general voice confirmed the Miss Cathcarts the most amiable and the most accomplished of our young women of fashion.

Anxiously solicitous for the happiness of an only son, how pleasing must be the prospect of a union which ensures to that son the enjoyment of the greatest worldly happiness and gives me a daughter after my heart's desire. I think I know my son: he has an honest and good heart, and will never forfeit the good opinion you have of him. May God Almighty bless you both; and be assured, my dear Mary shall always find in me a most affectionate parent and sincere friend.[25]

Despite these good intentions, relations with the spouse's relatives were a point of friction in many marriages. This could take many forms. Sir Arthur Wellesley's trust in his wife Kitty was greatly shaken when he discovered that she had diverted money from the household accounts to pay her brother's debts, leaving tradesmen's bills unpaid. Captain Fremantle was exasperated by the succession of scrapes his sister-in-law Eugenia Wynne got into, and then the melodrama associated with her courtship. Lord William Russell's marriage was blighted not only by the demands of Mrs Rawdon, but also by tension within Lord William's family, especially the hostility of Lord William and his brothers to their stepmother, the Duchess of Bedford. The arrival of Lady William (another strong and volatile personality) did not calm the atmosphere, and she was often at the centre of the quarrels which followed. This seems to have been quite common: where family relations were already difficult, the incomer frequently became the focus for existing irritation. But equally, there were cases where the new member of the family might ease resentments (partly just by making their partner happy), or at least would give them comfort and assurance in the face of family quarrels. John Stanley's parents lived apart and Maria believed that many of her husband's crippling headaches were caused by his difficult father, but this led her to be more sympathetic to him, rather than creating a problem in their marriage.[26]

There were also many cases in which the appearance of good relations with the in-laws was maintained, but considerable friction and irritation existed just below the surface, especially if there was a frequent contact between the two households. Jane Austen gives us a fine example of how this might happen in *Persuasion*, describing the simmering tension between Mary Musgrove (Anne Elliot's sister) and Mrs Musgrove (Mary's mother-in-law). The two women disagreed over how to treat Mary's children, with Mary remarking, 'I hate sending the children to the Great House, though their grandmamma is always wanting to see them, for she humours and indulges them to such a degree, and gives them so much trash and sweet things, that they are sure to come back sick and cross for the rest of the day.' And Mrs Musgrove expressing the view that the children were spoilt, and that when they visited her she constantly had to correct and admonish them. Servants were another battleground, with Mary claiming that the housemaid and the laundry-maid from the Great House were 'gadding about the village, all day long'. In response, Mrs Musgrove confided to Anne that 'I have no very good opinion of Mrs. Charles's nursery-maid: I hear strange stories of her; she is always upon the gad: and from my own knowledge, I can declare, she is such a fine-dressing lady, that she is enough to ruin any servants she comes near.' Then there was the issue of the precedence which was Mary's by right (as the daughter of a baronet), but which it would have been kinder and more tactful to forgo in deference to the older woman. None of this stopped the two families seeing a great deal of each other, meeting every morning and almost every evening, so that a casual observer might have thought them a particularly close and happy family.[27]

However, it is wrong to suggest that relations with in-laws were invariably a source of trouble. Some people got on very well with their in-laws, even finding more love and support than they had ever experienced in their own family. Many men found that their career benefited from their wife's connections, and many political alliances, particularly at a local level, were forged through a successful marriage. As we have seen, some men even married their wife's sister if their wife died, while other widowers received great help in bringing up their children from their wife's family; widows might equally be assisted in this and other ways, including financially. A husband's or wife's siblings might benefit by being introduced into a new social circle, and there were cases where a second matrimonial alliance might follow the first, when the husband's brother (or sister) married his wife's sister (or brother). Many men, especially officers in the army or navy, were grateful that their wife and children had the support of her family when they were forced to leave them to serve overseas, while sometimes wives in this position were comforted and assisted by their husband's relatives. Marrying into a happy welcoming family was emotionally rewarding, while providing a source of comfort and support in the face of any sort of trouble.

Inevitably relatives by marriage varied widely, and most people went into a marriage with some relatives of whom they were proud and who were likely to get on well with their spouse, and others whom they felt were less attractive. Mr Darcy had his sister Georgiana, but also Lady Catherine de Bourg; while Elizabeth Bennet had her sister Jane, her uncle and aunt Gardiner, and even her father, to set on the scales against her mother and her sister Lydia and her husband Wickham. For any couple, however much in love, relations with the in-laws needed to be handled with care and consideration for the other's feelings, for this was delicate territory with the potential to cause hurt or create a running sore that might do permanent damage to the marriage. In this and in many other ways the first year was important in setting a pattern for the marriage: couples might recover from getting off to a bad start, and a good beginning might not be sustained, but it was much easier to build on success than to recover from disappointment.

CHAPTER TEN

'MY LOVE...'

IN MARCH 1797, HALF-WAY through the first year of her marriage, Maria Stanley concluded an account of the details of her daily life that she had written to her Aunt Serena with the comment, 'You must forgive my saying so much on one subject, but trifles are the sum of human life, you know, and certainly they make up the sum of domestic happiness or misery . . .'. She was not alone in recognising the importance of the small business of everyday life in setting the tone of a marriage and in shaping relations between wives and husbands. Walter Scott made much the same point in *St Ronan's Well* when he wrote that 'it is in trifles that disrespect and unkindness are shown', and Emily Eden adapted some lines of Hannah More's to make them say:

> Since trifles make the sum of human things,
> And half our misery from trifles springs –
> Oh! let the ungentle spirit learn from thence
> A small unkindness is a great offence.

Eden went on to illustrate the point with the example of the fictional Lord Teviot, who thought that his wife should be satisfied: 'he had done all he could to please her; she ought to make allowance for his manner, for he owned that it was at times rather taunting; but she ought to be above such trifles'. He was yet to learn that the manner can be as important as substance, and that giving way without grace can cause almost as much alienation as not giving way at all.[1]

Small kindnesses frequently conveyed messages of love and affection, especially in the early days of a marriage, when the spouses were still feeling their way. In Susan Ferrier's novel *Marriage*, Lady Juliana is deserted by her maid and at a loss how to dress herself without assistance, until her husband, Henry Douglas, offers to assist her. '"Dear Harry, will you really dress me? Oh! that will be delightful! I shall die with laughing at your awkwardness;" and her beautiful eyes sparkled with childish delight at the idea.' It is a moment of genuine tenderness, even though the marriage, made impulsively, does not prosper. Elizabeth Bigg and William Harness were a much happier couple outside the realm of fiction, and during the long years of their engagement Elizabeth made William's shirts for him, consulting his preference on their style, and he praised highly their 'beautiful workmanship' and assured her that 'Nothing can fit better.' Making a man's shirts – either in person or by supervising and finishing the work of others – was accepted as an essential female task, with mothers and sisters employed in the task for unmarried men. It is easy to see this as nothing more than drudgery, and no doubt many women found it a tiresome chore, but equally many others enjoyed the work, which could be quite companionable, while others found satisfaction in imagining the man they loved wearing the garment and perhaps thinking of them, especially if he was far from home.[2]

Sometimes the kindness did not need to be directed at the spouse for it to reflect and even add to the atmosphere of matrimonial harmony. Lord Grenville's marriage proved very happy. Visiting them in 1802 Lord Minto commented, 'Nothing can be pleasanter than the Grenville family at home . . . Lady Grenville is beautiful, and nice and pleasant in all ways . . . and Lord Grenville is entirely different in his family from the notion which his general manners have perhaps naturally given of him to the world.' Three years later, on another visit, he commented that 'there never was a more gallant or attentive husband', but he was even more struck by Grenville's behaviour when they went for a walk after dinner, 'where he patted and *poored* an old horse, which they are keeping alive by mashes and care, a full quarter of an hour. This was an old horse he had been used to ride himself in his youth; but he went half the length of a field out of the way to do the same by an old cart horse.' Loving animals is no guarantee of a happy marriage, but it can be endearing, especially when the emotional atmosphere is already full of mutual affection.[3]

Grenville was prepared to express his affection for Anne in words as well as deeds, usually beginning his letters to her 'my dearest angel' and ending them 'God bless you my dearest wife', or, less attractively, 'my dear little woman'. He was not alone. In 1811, when they had been married for over a decade, James Stuart Wortley began a letter to his wife Caroline, 'Many, Many happy returns of the new year to you, My angel wife . . .'. And when William Harness was serving with his regiment in the Channel Islands in 1794, he wrote to 'my tenderly dear wife', imploring her not to deny herself 'any of the few amusements within your reach'. He acknowledged 'the delights you must experience in *our own Children*' but urged 'my adored and everbeloved wife' not to withdraw too much from society, which might provide her with amusement in case she lost her taste for it.[4]

In September 1809, on the evening before his duel with Castlereagh, George Canning sat down to write a letter of farewell to Joan in case he did not survive the encounter. In it he repeatedly calls her his 'dearest love', 'my own beloved Joan' and 'my own best & dearest love'. He discusses the character and future of their children, with comments like 'I leave his lot, as well as that of his brother and sister cheerfully & confidently in my own beloved's hands'. He left all his property to Joan, while asking her to provide for his mother, preferably with a pension of £300 a year. And he ended the letter, 'And now, my own best, & dearest, & most beloved love, I think I have said nearly all that it is necessary to say. There would be no end of taking leave & of saying how dearly I have loved you. I hope I have made you sensible of this, dearest, dearest, Joan. I hope I have been good & kind & affectionate towards you. I hope I have made you happy. If you have been a happy wife – & if I leave you a happy mother & a *proud* widow, I am content. Adieu. Adieu.'[5]

These examples all come from husbands writing to their wives, but women were equally willing to commit their feelings on paper. In 1785 Mary Dickenson told her husband John, 'I love you as much it is possible for one human creature to love another'; while Emily, Duchess of Leinster, wrote to her second husband, William Ogilvie, when they were apart, 'Let me tell you ten thousand million times that I love you to distraction', and called him the 'joy of my heart, charm of my life, comfort of my soul.' She added, 'Come to my heart my dear husband, love, friend, all that is dear', signing herself 'ever your tender and affectionate wife', adding, 'how pleasant to write those words!' When Lady Anne Barnard reluctantly parted from her husband Andrew in January 1802, returning to England from Cape Town ahead of him, she left him a farewell note as the ship was about to sail:

> My Dearest and Best Beloved,
>
> Oh My B, should I never see you more do I not leave you an inestimable legacy in the full assurance you have made me since I was in your life as Happy as it is possible to be in the world . . . To serve your future interests I leave you – the sole notice that could have persuaded me from your side . . .
>
> Your Own Anne
>
> All is ready. They ask for my letter. Oh, God Bless You.[6]

In return John Dickenson told his wife Mary that, after fourteen years of marriage, her presence was 'perfect Bliss to the Man who doats upon You, & who's [sic] greatest Pride is to have it in his power to subscribe himself, Your affectionate Husband'; and in another letter, 'I shall talk no more of *Love*! 'tis a *Cold* word and cannot express what *I* feel. Your aff[ectionat]e Husband *adores, respects & doats* upon you.' William Ogilvie was even more explicit: 'I am really dying with impatience to see your beautiful face again and to hug your lovely person in my fond loving arms – to meet your warm tender embraces and to hang on your sweet balmy lips. I am dying to call you mine again, to feel you such and to assure you of my unalterable love and affection.'[7]

On the relatively rare occasions when they were apart, Castlereagh missed Emily intensely and would sometimes write to her two or even three times in the course of a single day. Few of her letters survive, not because he did not value them, but because he received them when he was away from home and would not take the risk that they would be read by others. This concern for the privacy of their personal communications also emerges, in a light-hearted way, in a love letter he wrote to her in October 1800, when he had just resigned from a particularly demanding political position:

> I cannot go to bed without telling you, dearest Emily, that I am really emancipated, I do it in the full confidence that you will read it with a sensation not less animated and satisfactory than that with which it is written – I don't know what you feel, but I am quite determined, unless you differ, never to pass from one Country to another [i.e. Ireland to England], even for a day, without you. You know how little given I am to professions, but I have really of late felt the deprivation with an acuteness which is only known to those who are separated from what they most love. But I find I am in danger of committing the intolerable barbarism of writing a love letter to my wife. I shall therefore, for the sake of my character in the Post Office, trust all my experience at this moment in the consideration of my return to that imagination which is best acquainted with me.[8]

When Hester Newdigate was in London on her husband's birthday in 1789 she wrote to him that 'I am just come from Church my dear Love & at ye Altar have implored for Blessings on your head & for many returns of this day more & more happy and accompany'd with all that your heart can wish . . .'. And Lady Anne Barnard entrusted a special letter to Andrew's servant to be delivered on his birthday when he was at sea: 'Where will this find you, my Best Beloved? More than half way to the Cape I dare say . . . O! Barnard, if this matter were to be acted over again I should not consent to a separation.' She went on to urge him 'to feel as much happiness as your situation can afford you in a place where you are so much beloved, where you have so much the power of doing good, and such field sports to amuse you and keep you in health.' To assist him in this, she enclosed a note for £50 so that he could buy 'the best horse in the colony, which you may have wished for but thought above your pocket.' To which Andrew responded, 'How kind and good it was in you Dearest and Best of Creatures to think of preparing so great a treat for me long before the time arrived when I was able to enjoy it. You are always employed in devising means by which you can make those you love Happy.'[9]

Wedding anniversaries, as well as birthdays, were marked by some couples in letters when they were apart. Major-General William Pringle wrote home to his wife Harriet from Lisbon in May 1812:

> I cannot let this day pass without writing you a line to assure you of the sentiments I feel on the return of this day, believe me my darling love, this day is as dear to me now, as it was our first wedding day[.] I look on it as the day that has given me all the happiness of my life, & every succeeding year, proves still more to me how happy, truly happy you have made me, I wish I had an opportunity of sending you over some little present today, but I can with truth assure you, my adored Harriet, that you have every feeling of affection fondness my heart is capable of, this is the first anniversary of this day we have been separated . . .[10]

Inevitably the theme of separation and its pangs loomed large in the letters between loving couples, for when they were together they had no need to write. In 1786 Mary, Countess Palmerston, wrote from the country to her husband who was in London:

> I am quite unhappy about you, and shall not feel the least comfortable till I see you. If you are in any degree afraid of leaving London, and like it better that we should come to town we will set off directly, for place is of no consideration, when your society can be obtained. Let me know your wishes and in this, as in every other instance, I can know no pleasure equal gratifying them. I am much better, but rather low and comfortless, in short I want to be *dandled* a little.

And in 1806 Betsey Fremantle recorded in her journal: 'Few joys can equal what I experienced on reading a Letter from Fremantle which he wrote at Sea in his way to Portsmouth where he wishes me to meet him.' Five years later he told her, 'If ever man had real comfort and was made completely happy by marriage you have made me so.'[11]

Even the happiest couples might be affected differently by a separation, and not always in predictable ways. Charles Arbuthnot was forty-seven when he married Harriet, an experienced man of the world, a diplomat and politician who had held many onerous and responsible government positions, but after his marriage he became anxious whenever he and Harriet were apart and was in 'a fuss & turmoil' until her daily letter arrived. He told her, 'I am nervous about you lest you shd be unwell . . .', while their friend, the Duke of Wellington, remarked that Charles depended on Harriet 'for advice, for consolation, for everything'. Harriet, the inexperienced bride who married before she turned twenty-one, was much more independent and self-reliant, although no less loving. She was quite equal to entertaining a houseful of guests, including figures from the highest rank of London society, while Charles was away, but still made it clear that she missed him. '[T]he house is very dull without you coming in and out, and I do not like yr being away at all. . . . I have never been away from you for so long before . . . since I have been married and I feel quite lost.' 'You cannot think how much we all miss you or how very desolated I felt when that nasty hackchaise drove off the other night.'[12]

Sir William Hamilton's first wife, Catherine, wrote him a series of notes when she was dying, expressing her feelings: 'how shall I express my love & tenderness to you, dearest of earthly blessings! my only attachment to this world has been my love to you, & you are my only regret in leaving it – my heart has followed your footsteps whereever [sic] you went, & you have been the source of all my joys, I would have preferred beggary with you to Kingdoms without you.' 'Why am I so unwilling to quit this mortal clay? Alas how can I bear the idea of leaving him whom my soul loveth; Oh Hamilton no tongue can tell how I have loved, & do still love you – to quit you, to *me* is a task too terrible.' 'God grant . . . that we may meet in a better world than this – my lips, my heart, my soul blesses you & prays for you dearest of earthly beings.'[13]

Happily married couples sometimes expressed their appreciation of each other, not just in letters to their spouse, but in the privacy of their diary, in letters to friends or even in public. Mrs Calvert confided to her diary that 'Mr C. and I breakfasted at eight and he set off soon after in a chaise with Byrne for Portsmouth. God preserve him! He is the tenderest and kindest of husbands.' Ann Flinders, reunited with her husband after many years in which they were separated by war, told a friend, 'Day after day, month after month passes, and I neither experience an angry look nor a dissatisfied word. Our domestic life is an unvaried line of peace and comfort. And o, may heaven continue it such, so long as it shall permit us to dwell together on this earth.' While Maria Stanley could not conceal her embarrassed pleasure in recounting the:

> silly speech which the Man, in the delirium of his headache, made to the assembly in the barn when my health was drunk. It was not fair to take one by surprise, when I was standing most conspicuously at the top of a bench, luckily with my little Lou in my arms very conveniently to hide my blushes – and he had just before been giving a little twitch to one's feelings in a speech about the boys. Whatever he says of this kind one knows to be so to a tittle the real inspiration of his heart, and not the production of his head only, and it adds very much to the effect of such a scene. I should have liked seeing how others took it, if I could possibly have seen or thought of anything but myself and him.[14]

The *Gentleman's Magazine*, that arbiter of good manners, approved of open expressions of affection, at least from husbands to their wives, regarding them as displaying as polite, manly feeling and sensibility. It printed poems such as 'On the anniversary of my Marriage', by a reader from Leicestershire, who wrote that his Lucy was 'My Joy! my Transport! and my Pride'. The Reverend Samuel Bishop, headmaster of Merchant Taylors' School, wrote a number of such anniversary poems to his wife, which were published after his death in 1796, and in which he described his wife Molly as his best friend to whom he could reveal his innermost secrets. A gentleman should feel no shame in proclaiming his love for all the world to see.[15]

Josiah and Sarah Wedgwood were 'married lovers', with Josiah acknowledging that 'I should have made up a poor figure amongst my Potts; not one of which of any consequence is finished without the Approbation of my Sally.' And Caroline Stuart Wortley told her mother that 'I never hear of any marriage without comparing the woman's lot with my own. And I know of none which altogether I think equal to it. Most grateful do I feel for the happiness I enjoy.' Her husband James was very busy with public affairs, which meant that she saw less of him than she would have liked, but she generally reacted to this with sympathy rather than resentment.

> My poor *dog* is gone to Barnsley to day – indeed his business multi-plys so fast that he is never at home. To-morrow he goes to Leeds, Friday to a great dinner at Sheffield, (at which he is to be *President* & means to give many *Loyal* toasts) & saturday somewhere else. *Next* week also I believe he is engaged for every day – in short he is tossed about . . . like a *foot ball*. He is one of those people, who from a strong sense of duty, & extreme good nature is imposed upon, & made to do *every* thing that his neighbours *ought* to do, also, & *won't*. It quite provokes me; & I think it often worries & fatigues him.

Her feelings were helped by the fact that he obviously regretted it when he was away from home, writing to her that 'I want nothing but you and *sweet Babs* to make everything delightful to me. But I find it more and more uncomfortable to me every day to leave you all. . . . God bless you, Dearest dear Love, kiss the babes for me with all your might and strength, and give my kindest love to your mother . . .'. And again, 'Indeed my dearest Angel, though my body may be at Edinburgh my soul is always at Wortley where all my happiness and all my joys centre. . . . God bless you, My most beloved wife, give my darling children each a kiss from me, and a hearty one.'[16]

Couples were generally reluctant to display affection physically in front of others, although occasional exceptions crop up in the sources. When staying with her brother and his wife in 1808, Nelly Weeton noted that 'He is not content with kissing and cuddling by moonlight, but he must do it by sun-light too. Every day, after dinner and supper, instead of a desert [*sic*] on his table, came his wife upon his knee, and her lips to his mouth, sweeter I dare say in his opinion than the finest garden fruit, and more grateful to his heart.' He had been married for five years at this time, and had three children, so this was not an overflowing of passion in the first months of a marriage. But most couples preferred to keep kissing and cuddling to moments when they were alone, and also endeav-oured to keep particularly loving passages of their letters private, even when the rest of the letter was written with an eye to being shared.

William Wordsworth told his wife Mary that a 'fever of thought and longing and affection and desire is strengthening in me. . . . I tremble with sensations that almost overpower me.' But when, by an oversight, he wrote some love passages in part of the letter he intended Mary to show to his sister Dorothy, he felt compelled to ink them over so that she would not see them.[17]

Very little evidence survives about the sex lives of happily married couples, but we get the occasional glimpse, often by reading between the lines. In 1778 Mary Rebow told her absent husband Isaac that she had been unable to get to sleep until 3 or 4 in the morning 'intirely [sic] owing to ye want of *my usual Method of going to Sleep*', and the rest of their correspondence suggests that she wasn't talking about a cup of cocoa! It is equally obvious from their letters that the bond between Emily, Duchess of Leinster, and William Ogilvie included a very strong sexual element, while Andrew Barnard and his wife Lady Anne went out of their way to tell a prospective host that they wanted to sleep in the same bed and would come at another time if necessary to make this possible. In their correspondence with each other the Barnards talked of 'when the pot boils' as a metaphor for their passion, while Andrew also wrote of 'that beautiful and enchanting retreat called Cuddle Hall'. They were delighted with each other, in love and full of surprise. She wrote, 'How easy it was to render such a man happy, and how sweet was the task of doing so.' When he was away on a hunting trip he wrote to Anne, 'How do you sleep? I wanted a Certain Something which I cannot now do without. My case here is desperate. Poor Bonny [a dog] is my only bedfellow and she is a bad substitute.' All of which suggests both sex and a pleasure in other physical contact as well, such as cuddling, holding and kissing, that constantly reinforced the bond between them, while making separation even harder to endure.[18]

Some of these happy couples remained intensely devoted to each other throughout their married lives; for others, the ardour eventually began to cool, leaving a bond of affection and shared experience, fondness without passion. But none of these couples treated their love as a static thing, kindled in courtship and put away in mothballs along with the wedding dress. By constantly expressing affection, in words and gestures, directly and indirectly, they reassured their beloved and helped keep their feelings alive.

CHAPTER ELEVEN

GETTING ALONG

ALL COUPLES, WHETHER HAPPY or not, took some time to work out the role each of them would play in the marriage, whose wishes would carry the greater weight, who would make the greater effort to please the other and who would have the final say when their views differed. Not that it was generally as simple as this: except in the most one-sided of relationships, the balance between husband and wife varied from one aspect of their marriage to another, partly depending on what mattered most to each of them, and partly according to social conventions: for example, the wife's views would normally be more influential on matters of interior decoration than on purchases for the cellar or the stable. Nor was this relationship static: it would continue to evolve throughout the marriage in multiple ways, and it was frequently understood in different ways by wife and husband.

The starting point for how the relationship would function was generally determined either during courtship or soon after the wedding when both spouses were likely to be trying hard to please each other, but even then there was ample scope for self-deception and misunderstanding. Before her marriage Eugenia Wynne wrote in her diary after one of her quarrels with Robert Campbell, 'I am well determined he never shall have reason to complain of me again . . . I shall not be surprised, if he takes it into his head to be *the Master* when we marry – but I shall willingly yield to him, and shall not quarrel for that.' But one does not need to know her very well to feel a certain scepticism about this resolution; nor is it a struggle to imagine how cynically her brother-in-law, Captain Fremantle, would have laughed if he had read it. Eliza de Feuillide probably erred almost as much in the other direction when, six weeks after her marriage to Henry Austen, she told her cousin that she expected 'the pleasure of having my own way in every thing, for Henry well knows that I have not been much accustomed to controul and should probably behave rather awkwardly under it, and therefore like a wise Man he has no will but mine, which to be sure some people would call spoiling me, but [I] know it is the best way of managing me.'[1]

Fanny Knight expected Sir Edward Knatchbull to take the lead in their marriage: 'You will, under Heaven, be the means of leading me to everything that is good in this world.' And, 'It will be my pride and pleasure to conform to your wishes in every respect.' But when a friend told her that Sir Edward always liked to get his own way, she admitted to being frightened 'out of her wits', even though she felt that it would suit her 'to be directed'. Jane Austen tells us that Sir Thomas Bertram was 'master at Mansfield Park', and that when 'he had really resolved on any measure, he could always carry it through', but in persuading his wife to allow Fanny Price to spend some time with her family at Portsmouth, he obtained her consent 'rather from submission, however, than conviction, for Lady Bertram was convinced of very little more than that Sir Thomas thought Fanny ought to go, and therefore that she must'. And in Emily Eden's *The Semi-Attached Couple*, Mr Douglas is 'what is called a good husband'. He let his wife 'have a reasonable share of her own way, and spend a reasonable portion of her own money; he abstained from all vivid admiration of beauty within her hearing; he had a great reliance on her judgment, and a high opinion of her talents; and . . . he seldom irritated her by contradiction, but kept his own opinion with a quiet regret that his wife was so hard to please'.[2]

In the seventeenth and early eighteenth centuries, wives had often referred to the vow of obedience they had taken in the wedding ceremony and to their duty of submission, even if their actions did not always match their words. This had become rare in the second half of the eighteenth century, except when used in jest, although it probably still had a residual influence in shaping expectations and attitudes of both husbands and wives: the wedding service did not suggest that the relationship they both entered into was founded on a recognition of their equality, but rather one of subordination. Most men probably still began their marriage with a presumption that in the end they would have the final say on major decisions; and most women might not have denied this, while expecting that their husband (unlike some husbands) would give full weight to their interests and wishes. But the messy reality of individual personalities and circumstances meant that these preconceptions soon had to be adjusted, often with some discomfort, until the couple came to an arrangement which worked for them.[3]

An extreme example of the manipulation of the principle of wifely submission is provided by the formidable Lady Spencer, who was unwilling to attend church on the occasion of the King's jubilee in 1809, 'for pray for King George she cannot and will not'. However, faced with the argument that she should go in order to set an example, she demanded that her husband command her to go with all the weight of his conjugal authority, so that her attendance 'will not be what she calls so hypocritical'! More common was the device of wives paying lip-service to their husband's authority, even while clearly being the dominant partner. Thus General Conway reported a visit to the Duke and Duchess of Norfolk in 1758, during which plans for building a large ornamental lake were discussed: 'The Duke does not positively know whether he shall do it or not, but the Duchess does and says, "My Lord Duke intends to do it very soon." I fancy she is in the right.' During the early nineteenth century the image of an easy-going husband overshadowed by a domineering wife was embodied by the example of Lord and Lady Holland, at the centre of Whig society: he was famously amiable, while she was renowned for her sharp tongue and imperious manner.[4]

Submissive husbands were viewed with a mixture of sympathy and contempt, and men sometimes refused to listen to their wives from a fear that they would be regarded as subordinate. In Maria Edgeworth's novel *Belinda*, the weak and foolish Lord Delacour took to contradicting his much more intelligent wife and disagreeing with whatever she proposed, simply because he feared being regarded as under her thumb. While this was fiction and simplistic, if not necessarily exaggerated, we find Lady William Russell telling an old friend of her husband's that 'Ld Wm is

sore as he dreads henpecking amazingly from its being in the family . . .
we have all our weaknesses, & I should say Ld William's peculiar one was
that of such a dread of being led that he will not be advized, & any
insinuation of the kind annoys him to death . . .'. Yet the reality was
more complicated than Lady William made it appear, and far from being
perpetually obdurate, there were times when Lord William appeared
painfully anxious for his wife's approval, for example, when he was
packing up his quarters in 1828, he wrote to her: 'Pray tell me what I
shall do with all the things, plate, linen, platters, wine, furniture – shall
I sell them, shall I give them away. Pray write & say for I tremble at the
thought of doing wrong. If I sell them I shall be mean, if I give them
away I shall be foolish & heedless, if I keep them I shall be stupid, this is
always my poor fate, so send me peremptory orders in writing & they
shall be obeyed.' Their relationship was not simple, but it is clear that
Lady William was the stronger personality, and that Lord William was
somewhat overawed by her.[5]

Most wives had no wish to appear to dominate their husbands like
this, but nor would they surrender their own judgement or opinion
without persuasion. This middle-of-the-road approach was well expressed
by Louisa Clinton, Maria Stanley's sister, who wrote in 1801 four years
after her marriage, 'For though I hope I am a *good* wife, I never can bring
myself to that necessary perfection of an excellent one, thinking it impossible for my husband to be mistaken like any other frail human creature,
and consequently defending to the death every opinion he chances to
hold, were it to change every fortnight . . .'. Equally, few husbands
expected unthinking obedience or brainless adoration from their wives.
Captain Fremantle was even at pains to explain and justify his right to
advise Betsey in his absence: 'As I have not lately dealt much in the
Sermonizing line, and I know no man in Europe who has less occasion to do
so to his wife than myself, still I am convinced you will feel better satisfied at hearing my opinions on many subjects, which will perhaps enable
you to form further conclusions, and this I do not do from Vanity or any
superior understanding, but from the experience of years, and of course,
longer intercourse with the world.' A significant age difference –
Fremantle was more than twelve years older than his wife, and as we have
seen such differences were not uncommon – certainly encouraged many

husbands to feel that their judgement was likely to be based on a greater knowledge of the world than that of their wives, especially early in a marriage when patterns of behaviour were being established. However, it is worth adding that Fremantle repeatedly went out of his way to acknowledge and praise his wife's ability and increasingly relied on her judgement.[6]

Husbands had many latent rights that it was seldom sensible for them to invoke. For example, a husband had the right to read his wife's letters, and in Emily Eden's *The Semi-Attached Couple* Lord Teviot disgusts his wife by implicitly asking to read a letter she is writing to her family. Far wiser, and surely far more common, was John Stanley's approach as described by his wife Maria:

> I believe I should infinitely prefer his insisting on seeing every letter I wrote or received, rather than that he should be indifferent and uninterested in them; but he takes great pleasure in reading all I show him. Those I do not show, he never expresses or implies the smallest curiosity to see, and I believe nothing would make him open or read a letter of mine first, though it were from his own sister. . . . In this way he preserves the medium, for with regard to his own letters he goes far beyond it on the indulgent side. Since we have been married he has never received one and scarcely written one which he has not shown me. Those few which he has not given me were those in which I was convinced he had spoken the most affectionately of me. The ease of my style would be lost were I to write with the idea of showing it to any person with whom I lived. I could never mention him in the manner I wished, least [*sic*] it should seem written for his eye.[7]

It was generally recognised that both husbands and wives were entitled to some privacy and some space within the marriage to pursue their own interests. As early as 1700, in Congreve's *The Way of the World* the heroine insists on the right to 'dine in my Dressing room when I'm out of Humour, without giving a reason' and adds that 'wherever I am, you shall always knock at the door before you come in'. And yet difficulties could still arise. Lady Delacour refuses to submit to a life-saving operation from the fear that no surgeon would be willing to perform it without first informing her husband, whose pity she dreads. And Mrs Calvert, that bastion of propriety, got herself into a scrape in 1809 by setting off for Ireland with her sister without first consulting her husband or even taking her maid with her. She had second thoughts and abandoned the journey before reaching Liverpool, but then had to wait several days to be rescued by her nephew. 'I trust Mr. C. will not be angry, but I do dread seeing him. If he is not angry, I shall not tell him I was afraid he would be, lest I should put it into his head.' When her nephew arrived he brought a kind note from Mr Calvert, but it was nonetheless clear when she returned to London that he was unhappy about the whole expedition, although this may have simply been because it had caused inconvenience to others and distress to herself without achieving anything, rather than from a feeling that she had acted improperly. Certainly there was no obstacle to married women travelling independently of their husbands, although they would usually be accompanied by at least a servant to maintain her dignity and protect her from insult and inconvenience.[8]

The state of a marriage coloured all the business of daily life, and in turn the joys and trials that the couple encountered in living their lives would influence their relations with each other. How they managed money, their views on politics and religion, where they lived and how they spent their time, whether together or apart, were all part of the fabric of a marriage. The rest of this chapter will look at how these potentially difficult subjects were managed, leaving the issues raised by careers and children to follow in subsequent chapters. The focus will generally be on couples who got along reasonably or very well: unhappy, dysfunctional marriages will be examined in chapters 14 and 15.

Every couple had to work out for themselves how they would handle their money. Legally the power and responsibility rested with the husband and the extent to which he shared information and decision-making with his wife was, at least in theory, his decision. However, Hester Chapone, the influential writer of conduct books for women, was clear on the importance of husbands confiding in their wives and the couple making joint decisions on their expenditure.

The first and greatest point is to lay out your general plan of living in a just proportion to your fortune and rank: if these two will not coincide, the last must certainly give way. . . . Perhaps it may be said, that the settling [of] the general scheme of expences is seldom the wife's province, and that many men do not choose even to acquaint her with the real state of their affairs. Where this is the case, a woman can be answerable for no more than is entrusted to her. But I think it a very ill sign, for one or both of the parties, where there is such a want of openness, in what equally concerns them. As I trust you will deserve the confidence of your husband; so I hope you will be allowed free consultation with him on your mutual interest: and, I believe, there are few men, who would not hearken to reason on their own affairs, when they saw a wife ready and desirous to give up her share of vanities and indulgences, and only earnest to promote the common good of the family.[9]

It is uncertain just how many husbands involved their wives fully in financial decisions: it is difficult to imagine Mr Bennet or Sir Thomas Bertram doing so, but easy to suppose that Mr Darcy, Captain Wentworth and Admiral Croft would regard marriage as a joint enterprise.

In practice, many men had no choice but to trust their wives to manage their finances, particularly officers on active service or others who were forced to spend long periods out of Britain. Captain Fremantle relied on Betsey not just to manage the family's day-to-day expenses, but also to undertake major purchases and readily acknowledged her ability on money matters great and small. 'I give you great credit for being so good a manager about coals, you surpass all my endeavours.' 'I think you sold King George [a carriage horse] very well, and I beg you will [do] whatever you find necessary about getting another.' 'I tell you in a few words that the Bankers receive annually from me £1,125 – all of which is perfectly at your disposal and command, and if you want more money they have my direction to answer your bills to any amount.' 'All my other bills except a small one at Morny's the Taylors [sic: tailor's] I have already paid so that you will perceive I have not been very extravagant . . .' And, 'I hope you have ere this purchased Orchards, Cottage and Garden, do pray do it before I come home, for you do everything with so much temper and steadiness that I should rather depend upon you for the accomplishment of the purchase than myself . . .'[10]

Another naval officer, Charles Paget, was so impressed with how his wife managed their finances in his absence that when he came ashore at the end of the war in 1814 he resolved to leave them entirely in her hands: 'I find Elizabeth, God bless her, so punctual, so exact, and so provident in the management of my resources, so infinitely more so than I ever could attain to, that I am persuaded it will be to the advantage of myself, and my family, to confide the management of every thing to her, and I hope to confine what I shall consider *my own personal* expenses to within the limits of my half-pay.' (Although it is interesting that even here he writes of 'my resources' not 'our resources'; but then, he was a Paget.) The Duke of Bedford would have approved of this resolution, writing to his daughter-in-law, Bessy, 'The sooner you can persuade him [Lord William Russell] to give up the arrangement of his affairs to you the better. I am sure you have a much better head than he has, but this perhaps is paying you no extravagant compliment.' And Mary Dickenson explained to her father-in-law that 'my Husband has done me the honor to make me his Banker', and that she managed their finances, insisting that they pay ready money for everything they purchased and accumulate no debts, while having a surplus at the end of every year. One wonders in how many upper-class families the finances were actually managed predominantly if not entirely by the wife, even if the orders she gave were given in the name of her husband?[11]

Of course, there were also men who did not confide in their wives. When John Harwood, the local squire at Steventon, died in 1813 it was discovered that he had contracted large debts, completely unsuspected by the family. For a time it seemed as if the estate would have to be sold, and his widow and sister both lost their capital, which had evidently not been placed in trust. Even more surprisingly, Eliza Jervoise of Herriard House, Hampshire, managed the extensive renovations to the property while her husband, an officer in the army, was away, without any inkling that he had accumulated such debts that, if his father did not bail him out, they would be forced to sell the house and take refuge from his creditors abroad. Evidently his father paid, or the debts were less pressing than Jervoise claimed, for the renovations continued and the Colonel was never forced to confess his extravagance to his wife.[12]

The economic turmoil of the long war with France and expensive tastes, especially for building work, gambling or cutting a figure in society, meant that many upper-class families were forced to economise at one time or another. In 1796, Lord Palmerston confided to his wife Mary that he was under considerable financial pressure. Her reaction was immediate and whole-hearted:

> All I can say is that if you think we should spend less money this year by the family staying in the country and your living in a bachelor style in London, I have no kind of objection, for I have no wish to see London, and here I have no desire to see company. And I should want no horses in the country, never liking to go out in the carriage and always preferring walking. In short I beg you will adopt any plan you think most advisable and be assured there is none (even to the parting with Broadlands if you thought it right) to which I should even in *thought* have the least objection. As long as you and my children are well and happy, places are perfectly indifferent to me.[13]

Some months later, when he was under pressure to repay a loan to Drummonds Bank, which he had believed they were happy to renew, she went further urging him to draw on the capital tied up in her settlement, while professing to be ignorant of the details involved. Her overriding message throughout was clear: she hated seeing him distressed by financial worries and would do anything she could to assist in resolving them, and was already making plans for stringent economies in the way their establishment was managed.

Palmerston replied with some good news: he had obtained a loan for £6,000 from a private gentleman (at 5 per cent interest, not a particularly high rate at the time) and had sold one of his farms in Yorkshire for £1,975. With this, and a mortgage on Broadlands, he had settled the most pressing demands of his bankers. He told Mary, 'You are very kind and considerate in what you say about reductions. I hope very few if any of those you are so ready to submit to are at all necessary. I think a good deal may done, for a time at least, by care to avoid extra expenses without trenching into real and substantial articles of comfort; and least of all in the manner and degree you mention in what relates to yourself.' With considerable anxiety and some inconvenience they rode out the storm, their marriage not only intact, but if anything strengthened.[14]

Mrs Calvert faced a similar test of her fortitude in 1810 when she and her husband decided that they needed to give up their nice house in Albemarle Street. 'Our object in doing so is to get our London establishment into a smaller scale, as in these hard times, we should find a large house in Town and a large one in the Country more than we could well afford. It is a bitter pill after being accustomed to this large mansion, but I take my physic well, and indeed it was my own proposal, for Mr. C. is so kind to me, that though he wished it, the suggestion never would have come from him.' As they moved to No. 5 Hanover Square we can, perhaps, afford to be moderate in our sympathy for her distress.[15]

However, many women faced much greater sacrifices. Lady Caroline Capel was forced to move, with her husband and large family, to Brussels in 1814 to avoid debts which were largely due to her husband's gambling. No whisper of reproach towards her husband survives in her letters, even though he had not stopped gambling and soon took a mistress in Brussels. But she does admit to her mother the strain of constantly seeking to control the household's expenses in order to keep them within their income. A single lady's maid attended to herself and her three eldest daughters; the cook had no assistant; and there was only a single housemaid. After two years of exile she told her mother, 'I pay every bill, & scold every Saturday but in spite of all, I am sometimes in a state of discouragement that requires my good spirits to shake off; I have really made myself a Slave to every Minutiae of Economy – I think I shall become, at last, narrow minded & stingy.' Success was far from certain, and – although she does not say so – any ground gained might be squandered by her husband in a single evening's play. It was not easy for a woman, brought up in an aristocratic family that expected the best of everything as a matter of course, to remain cheerful in these circumstances, especially as she soon discovered that she was pregnant with her thirteenth child.[16]

Men could also feel the pinch of economy. Lieutenant-General Sir George Murray had held high office under Wellington both in the

Peninsula and in cabinet, but he was not a rich man, and a few years after his late marriage (he was fifty-two when he married), he found it necessary to curtail his expenses, explaining to a friend:

> I find myself obliged to look much more narrowly into my pecuniary affairs more than I have ever been accustomed to do. In a great part of my life I had, as a single man, no cause for anxiety on that head, because I could shape my expenses to my income without any difficulty, or any inclination to consult but my own – and I always made my way, by good luck, to some Professional Appointment of emolument. Now, however I cannot so easily curtail my expenses at pleasure on a moment's notice, and the sphere of employment is much more narrowed than it used to be. A most heavy and unavoidable expense for many months past has been doctors fees, and apothecaries bills. However by parting with servants, and by giving up Carriage Horses, I hope to bring matters into such a shape as to keep clear of incurring debt.[17]

Even the Arbuthnots faced severe financial pressures in the early 1820s and were forced at one point to consider selling their beloved country home at Woodford. Harriet successfully opposed this desperate measure, telling Charles, 'Tho' I do not think this place so indispensable to my comfort as it is to yours, still even for myself I shd be very sorry indeed, & I know it wd be so horrible to you that I shd. be really in despair.' Instead she encouraged him: 'Pray keep up yr spirits, & do not talk of being broken down, my dearest. I look forward to our passing many happy years together, & if we can but get rid of these money concerns & make the farm pay *tolerably*, our next ten years will be happier than the last.' In the end an unlikely solution was found through the unexpected generosity of the King. Charles told Sir William Knighton, the King's private secretary, that he had transformed their position: 'With everything at home to make me happy I still was a wretched being; and you have turned me into a most happy one. But you have done more than this – you have made happy one of the best of women – one whose strength of mind has supported me under the severest trials, and one who will ever join with me in thanks and gratitude to you. May God bless you.' And Harriet wrote to Charles, 'Believe me I rejoice ten times more in the ease & comfort all this will procure to you, than for any advantages to myself. You were always so kind to me & took such care that *I* at least shd. feel no want of money that I have never wished for a comfort more than I have always had. . . . Dearest love, we shall indeed be rich & happy, but let us be *stingy* in future & take care that such distress shall never come upon us again.' Throughout the difficulty their first thought was always how any financial sacrifice would affect each other, which was typical of their whole marriage.[18]

In *Belinda*, Maria Edgeworth has one of her characters remark that 'love quarrels are easily made up – but of money quarrels there is no end . . .', and it is true that troubles over money marred and soured many marriages. It was all too easy for a husband or a wife to notice and resent the amount of money the other spent on personal pleasures, whether it was the husband's gambling, sport or politics, or the wife's clothes and social life (or, for that matter, the wife's gambling and the husband's social life and mistresses). And even if there was no obvious extravagance, families might face financial problems caused by the failure of a local bank, ill-judged investments or simply the volatile state of the economy, and it was hard for a wife not to blame her husband for incompetence if he had retained sole management of their finances and then incurred problems which necessitated sacrifices on her part. However, evidence for such recriminations is relatively scarce: possibly they were less likely to be written than spoken, and less likely to survive than more creditable letters; but perhaps also couples were inclined to come together in the face of financial problems.[19]

⋙━◆━⋘

In happy marriages women generally felt free to make their own purchases without first seeking the approval of their husbands, just as husbands felt able to spend a certain amount of money on themselves without consultation or being made to feel overly self-indulgent. In many cases, a woman had her own guaranteed income for her private expenses – her 'pin money' as set out in her marriage settlement. This was commonly used for clothes, decorations, presents and charity, but the essential point was that how she spent it was her own concern. In 1781 Lady Newdigate stayed at Buxton to take the waters while her husband, Sir Roger, having escorted her there, returned home. She proposed visiting Sheffield nearby to purchase some silver-plated cutlery; he disliked the idea, calling them 'shams'; but she persisted, arguing that 'ye Money you gave me is for no other purpose than to fool away as I like, and in ye second it is fit that every one sh'd pay for their own Whims. You must . . . [pay] still more dearly for yours whenever your *Magnificence* chuses to replace them with really Silver.' Rather abashed, he responded by sending her an additional 50 guineas – far more than she needed – joking that he didn't want her to be imprisoned for debt and so unable to come home. He also evidently apologised for seeming to question her right to spend the money as she chose, for she replied, 'I never cd have ye most distant thought of your wishing to interfere in or even to know anything of my Private expences; no one word or Action of your Life cd give birth to such an Idea.' Was she teasing or did she mean it literally? Either way she had asserted her financial independence and he had accepted it both in practice and principle.[20]

Some women went further than this, continuing to regard the fortune they brought to the marriage as their own. For example, Lady Shelley tells us that, 'In 1814, Sir John inherited Maresfield, a beautiful place near Uckfield, from his uncle Mr. Newnham. We laid out £70,000 in improving the place, which henceforth became our home. It was with real pleasure that I spent this enormous sum on Sir John's new property, for it gave him a good position in the county, and consoled him for his early errors which he never ceased to deplore.' Without knowing the details of her marriage settlement we cannot know whether in law this expenditure depended on her decision, that of her trustees or that of her husband, but it is clear that in her mind she took the initiative and had the power to grant or withhold the funds, and it may be that this sense of power was an important element in the unlikely success of their marriage.[21]

But most couples felt that they had united their fortunes, even if some husbands sought to monopolise the power of making major financial decisions. There were also numerous aristocratic and gentry families who ignored Hester Chapone's other main piece of advice and made no attempt to balance their expenditure with their income, with both husband and wife spending freely and accumulating debts in order to live in the style which they believed was required by their station in society. It was not a culture that encouraged prudent financial management and the accumulation of savings – those quintessentially bourgeois virtues – although many families, especially those without vast landed estates, were probably rather more careful than they liked to appear. Tensions might arise within the marriage where either the husband or the wife was more inclined to prudence and the other to extravagance, whoever filled which role, especially if the husband did not confide their true financial position to his wife. But the ideal marriage was based on mutual confidence and the sharing of both information and the responsibility for making decisions. Many couples, including some happy ones, fell short of this, and the ideal did not suit all personalities or circumstances, but the way couples managed money was often a good indication of how their marriage functioned more generally.

⟫⬦⟪

Religion and politics played an important part in the lives of many couples, and any differences in approach or belief needed to be handled with care if they were not to be a source of unease and tension. The writer Mrs Sherwood recalled in her memoirs that she was very assiduous in her religious observances early in her marriage, imposing twenty-one daily tasks on herself, including six forms of prayer and reading the Bible three times a day. 'I was not content with reading [the Bible] to myself, I must force Mr Sherwood to do the same. He must read also, and he was by no means disposed to do so. It was then, for the first time, whilst still at Sunderland, he very quietly and calmly let me know that he was not quite convinced that the whole of the Bible was true, although he thought parts of it might be so.' She was furious, demanding to know why he had not admitted this before they were married, but had 'made no objections whatever to hearing the Bible read, or to any religious observances whatever'. He replied that he would never interfere with her prayers and reading, but expected equal tolerance from her. 'I cried most bitterly at this, and probably made my religion anything but inviting by so doing . . . .' The rift that this created between them was only healed by the birth of their first child, when Mr Sherwood was so moved that he agreed to read the Bible every day, and they soon fell into a pattern of studying it together that became an important element in strengthening their marriage.[22]

Accounts such as this are less common than we might expect, and it seems that most couples understood each other well enough on the subject before they were married, or else trod carefully enough to avoid it becoming a significant problem in their marriage. This was true even in mixed marriages (between a Catholic and a Protestant), such as that of Betsey and Thomas Fremantle, where there is little or no evidence of their religious difference causing tension. In other cases, different levels of enthusiasm for religion, and perhaps a different view of the local clergyman, might have caused some concern or ill-feeling, but there is nothing to suggest that this was a common source of tension. Equally, an interest in religion might bring a couple together. Lady Caroline Stuart Wortley and her husband took great pleasure in reading Paley's defence of Christianity together, as well as '4 chapters of the Bible every Sunday evening'. But even references like this are not frequent: as the historian Katie Barclay notes about her sample of upper-class Scottish couples, 'overt discussions on religious matters were curiously rare in their correspondence with their spouses'.[23]

Politics figures more prominently than religion in the lives and correspondence of these couples, although that may be due to a distortion in the surviving evidence. Many young women had little or no interest in the subject before they were married: Emily Eden illustrates this in *The Semi-Attached Couple* when she has Eliza Douglas, on a visit to Lord and Lady Eskdale, write home to her mother, 'Please mention what papa's politics are. They talk a great deal about government and opposition, and I do not know which I am for.' And even after her marriage Eliza's sister, Lady Teviot, remarks, 'I should be puzzled to say what my party is, for at this moment I am very ignorant of all political matters; but if Lord Teviot comes into office, I suppose I shall grow as eager as most people are.' This was all very well in theory, enabling wives to adopt their husband's political views without thought or effort, but the reality was often less simple; after all, Emily Eden herself was from a highly political family, and her correspondence is full of politics on which she held firm views of her own.[24]

Harriet Arbuthnot became deeply absorbed by politics after her marriage, and while her political allegiances were aligned to those of her husband she was decidedly a figure in her own right, and was in the confidence first of Castlereagh and then of Wellington, not hesitating to give the latter forthright advice which he took seriously, for he valued her judgement and opinions. Many other women were equally important and influential in the political world throughout this period: sometimes their husbands were important politicians, sometimes complete nonentities and sometimes part way between these extremes, but the lack of a formal role in politics did not prevent women from wielding significant power and influence. Even women who were not particularly political, such as Mrs Calvert, felt empowered to take an independent line on occasion. She greatly disliked her husband's friend Sir John Sebright and, after one 'extremely disagreeable' conversation with him, she resolved that 'If I can possibly prevent it Sir John shall never represent our country again. A woman's talk can have great effect in a County Election, and I won't be sparing of mine!' The threat proved empty – Sebright remained the Member of Parliament for Hertfordshire for another quarter of a century – but it shows that she did not feel tied to following her husband's lead regardless of her private opinion.[25]

Nonetheless the most common way in which politics played a part in the lives of married couples was as a subject for discussion and a reason for travel: Members of Parliament attending its sessions in London with or without their wives, and visiting their electorate, which might be in a distant part of the country. Caroline Stuart Wortley accompanied her husband James to Cornwall in November 1806, when he visited Bossiney for the formality of his election. Caroline did not stay in the borough itself as there was no inn, but spent the night at Camelford, while her husband and the electoral agent, Mr Elford, attended the electors. 'He & the Doge [her nickname for her husband] are gone on horseback to Bossiney, but as there is a contested Election at Plymouth, Mr. Elford is impatient to get back, & will therefore be obliged to set off from Bossiney the *instant* the *Member* is *Elected*, leaving the poor Doge to dine by himself with the Electors!' There were nine electors for Bossiney at the time, and the election (for two Members of Parliament) was not contested, but some courtesies still had to be performed. 'Imagine what it must be! For it is a *very* small dirty Village & inhabited only by the lowest Class of people. He will have the happiness too of going round to all the Cottages & *kissing* the wives and daughters of the Worthy Electors. As the Election takes place to day, we shall be able to get away again to-morrow morning early . . . .' In this case Caroline's presence was not for any purpose of electioneering, but simply so that she and her husband could enjoy each other's company and not be apart during the journey. Women sometimes took a more active role on the hustings, especially when their husbands took part in contested elections, although the lack of decorum in a Georgian election meant that most preferred to observe from a distance or use their influence in advance of the actual poll.[26]

The wives of many politicians took a keen interest in political developments, and their husbands wrote at length to keep them informed and to consult their opinion. George Canning sent long confidential letters to Joan, discussing which office he might take when a government was being formed, or how he should respond to overtures from the opposition or government, as well as reporting on the success of his speeches and the mood of the house, and it is clear that he valued her opinions in making his decisions. Similarly, Lord Palmerston involved his wife Mary in his political life, sending her very detailed letters, especially at moments of high drama such as the Regency Crisis of 1788–89. Several years later she told him that 'The reading the debates in the Star takes up all my morning' and went on to comment on the impeachment of Warren Hastings. In November 1801 Palmerston was lobbying to be given an English peerage, mostly to save himself the trouble and bother of getting elected to the Commons. In a letter dated 3 November 1801 he discussed the tactics he should use, whether to make an approach to Addington and Pelham directly, or through Malmesbury. Having outlined the alternatives he went on, 'You will let me know your thoughts on the subject . . . .' She did so, writing that she was glad that he had approached Pelham (who was under an obligation to him) – 'However, if I was you I would follow it up now and if you do not succeed I shall say more shame for those who prevent it . . . .' Wives were often – although certainly not always – a politician's best ally, friend and adviser.[27]

Deciding where to live and purchasing a house were major decisions that usually involved consultation and agreement between a couple. When Captain Fremantle found a house he liked in August 1798, Betsey approved the idea of moving in principle and went to see the house the next day, declaring that 'it is a very nice place which should suit us on all accounts'. They soon completed the purchase for 900 guineas, which Betsey thought a bargain, as she felt it was worth fully £1,200. Early in their marriage James and Caroline Stuart Wortley were undecided where to live, with James explaining to his mother-in-law that 'Yorkshire is my first and favourite plan and till I have been there and found out whether I can make myself comfortable there I shall do nothing about it.' But he added that if Caroline preferred to take a little place they had seen in Surrey, 'and that it will add much to her comfort the thing will be very soon decided with me'. Many years later they bought a house in London, 15 Curzon Street, on a 900-year lease for £12,000. Caroline admitted to her mother that she had mixed feelings about the purchase, 'I am hurried and nervous with the suddenness of the decision, the more so as I hate the situation, tho' I like the House very much; and that there is an end for *ever* of all my dreams of a house in a Square or [close] to the Park! But this I must try to forget, and hope I shall *grow* to like my new house, especially as the Doge is enamour'd of it. . . . Don't take any notice in your answer of my dislike of Curzon Street . . . .' It is evident here, and perhaps also in the decision to live in Yorkshire, that Caroline had yielded to her husband's enthusiasm, although it is also clear that she chose not to object rather than her wishes being over-ruled. It is a subject on which some compromise is often necessary, and on which even an individual will often have mixed and uncertain feelings, liking one aspect of a property and disliking another.[28]

Sometimes the decision where to live, especially in the country, was already made and could not be altered: an eldest son inheriting the family estate or a clergyman living in the parsonage in his parish could not easily decide to move, and both he and his wife had to make the best of their situation even if they privately disliked it. Charles Arbuthnot had purchased a 600 acre estate at Woodford in Northamptonshire some years before his marriage to Harriet, and although it was not very profitable, there was little question of their selling and moving elsewhere, despite the fact that Harriet's first impression of the house was that it was 'perfectly hideous'. Rather than move she set to work to improve both the house and its setting, beginning with the gardens and grounds, planting trees and shrubs, including 1,000 laurel bushes and 1,000 acacias around her walks. A few years later she moved the farmyard and out-buildings away from the house, replacing them with a 'French parterre' and a flower garden in front of the house. She also added new stables and a dining room, and was satisfied that the result made 'a comfortable, very small dwelling' where she could have distinguished friends, such as Wellington, to stay. She took great pleasure in the results of her planning, being delighted when the garden was 'full of flowers & very pretty', and in hanging her own portrait by Sir Thomas Lawrence over the fireplace in the dining room, while Lawrence's portrait of Wellington (a present from the Duke) was hung in the drawing room. When she won £80 on the Derby in 1828 she spent the money on a japan[ned] cabinet which she painted herself, and on new curtains in the drawing room, which 'made my house here nearly complete'. It was 'a place, which, from having made myself, I am much attached to . . . Mr Arbuthnot left all the ornamental part for me to manage'.[29]

We do not know whether Mrs Arbuthnot took an active part in making any of the alterations to the house and garden at Woodford, or whether she limited herself to planning and directing others, but on at least one occasion Caroline Stuart Wortley 'took the hatchet into my own hands, and tired myself so completely with cutting down branches that I could hardly get home, and was obliged to strip entirely before dinner I was so hot'. This was certainly uncommon, although it was not so unusual for enthusiastic gentlemen to take a physical role in some new project that caught their fancy. While Harriet Arbuthnot improved the house and garden, her husband became an enthusiastic gentleman farmer. In 1824 he went on tour of farms and markets that took him as far afield as Yorkshire and Northumberland, with Harriet responding to his account of his progress, 'Going to Market! . . . I dare say you will smell of sheep for a week after yr return. I am delighted however you seem to enjoy yourself so much.' She urged him 'not to stand about in the wet, and catch cold. Remember how liable to cold you are and how angry I shall be if you come back less well than you went.' And when he seemed anxious that she would disapprove of the cost of a bull he had purchased, she responded by insisting on paying for it herself.[30]

Many women found long periods of life in the country, especially in winter, tedious, particularly if they stayed home and had few or no guests. Mrs Calvert lamented, 'I don't know what I should do if the Stronges [her daughter and son-in-law] were not here, it would be so dull! I miss a house in town very much. Living all the winter in the country is not to my taste, and when Mr. C. built this house my pleasure and comfort were considerably diminished. However, it will be all the same a hundred years hence!' This was in 1815, at the beginning of the post-war economic slump, and on the first day of the following year she added, 'The times make me often low. The tenants can't pay, and we are very poor. I fear we shall never be able to have a house in town, though I felt so sure of one this year.' Fifteen years earlier Maria Stanley had written to her Aunt Serena: 'we are all alive and well, which is about the sum total of events that I have to relate. What a fool of a thing human nature is! I did not like to be always going out, and in a bustle, and thought I should be mighty glad when we were quite quiet again; and now we are so, I think it is rather dull, and am considering what a long dreary winter there is between the present time and the chance of seeing any beings but our neighbours. . . . I depend, however, on seeing you here, I hope, in the spring . . .' And a few weeks later she added, 'It is terrible gloomy weather, for it has been raining and snowing without ceasing; and if there were ropes enough in the kingdom, all placed in tempting situations with convenient nooses, up and down the country, I should be surprised any English man or woman in the Campagne abstained from hanging themselves. Long evenings are not pleasant.'[31]

Hester Chapone recognised the dangers of boredom posed by months in the country, but could only recommend the pursuit of accomplishments – music, drawing, needlework and the like – to fill the gap. This suited some better than others, and Caroline Stuart Wortley used her leisure to become a capable artist, some of whose works are now held by the Tate Gallery.[32] But most women lacked the talent or the passion for such pursuits to give satisfaction day after day over a long winter. Company might help, but could bring its own tedium, especially when the quirks and foibles of neighbouring families had become all too familiar. Reading, especially if it could be shared with a spouse, was a more reliable resource. A similar taste in literature played a part in many courtships, and although it often faded away when couples were married and able to communicate their feelings more directly, it remained important for some. Even differences of taste could be stimulating and interesting if they led to discussion. For example, Caroline Stuart Wortley was unable to share her husband's enthusiasm for the works of Ossian – the enormously popular concoction of fake ancient Gaelic poetry which James Macpherson had supposedly discovered, but in fact largely written himself. She told her mother that her husband 'is trying to make me like Ossian, but I am still a goth upon that subject – tho' I like it rather better than I did, & shall go thro' it for the sake of good subjects for drawing'. And Maria Stanley was disappointed that her husband John would not finish Lady Morgan's novel *St Clair: or the Heiress of Desmond*, lamenting that 'my sober old fellow has so lost his taste for these kind of things. . . . He is a very different kind of animal to that which used to read poetry, pick off thorns from sweetbrier, and sing French songs. . . .' However, a few years later we find them enjoying Byron's *Childe Harold* together, Maria telling her daughter, 'your papa and I sat over the fire in the dining-room and fancied ourselves young people, with a baby, or two perhaps, in the cradle upstairs, and read together more beautiful poetry than any other pen I am acquainted with has yet produced; and he was not cross when I interrupted him in reading his newspaper with cries of "Never was anything so fine!" and very soon he laid down his newspaper and said, "Read more." '[33]

For many men life in the country was closely associated with field sports, especially hunting and shooting. Some women joined them. In November 1811 Caroline Stuart Wortley told her mother 'The Doge [her husband James] has had two good days hunting, & I was out to day with the foxhounds from Clumber, when we all assembled this morning just after breakfast. It was a very pretty sight, there were such a number of people & four carriages out. After hunting I return'd here to ride with Lady Newark who never rides *alone*, so that in all I was on my horse for above five hours – *"pretty well my dear"* – & I own I am rather tired.' Mrs Arbuthnot also rode to hounds on occasion, remarking when staying at Apethorpe for New Year in 1822 that 'we had a very good run for ladies & rode very hard'. Many years later Lady Hardy recalled that in 1818 'I rode thirty Miles and over such ridges and narrow Causeways as I should not have hardly liked to walk in cold blood. Lady Elizabeth Forbes rode very boldly and took all the leaps that the Gentlemen did.' But she added, 'I certainly enjoyed hunting thoroughly but I do not think it a desirable amusement for Women and after these few days I never did so since.' This ambivalence was quite common, with Tysoe Saul Hancock telling his wife in 1773, 'I am convinced that Riding is the most wholesome Exercise in the World, and tho' I think Fox hunting is not only dangerous but in some degree an indecent Amusement for a Lady, yet I wish my Daughter to sit gracefully on a Horse and to Ride without fear; both of which are Necessary to make Her sufficiently fond of the Exercise to promote her Health by Constantly using it.'[34]

But for most women, most of the time, sport was something that separated them from their husbands and other menfolk. At the beginning of September 1803, Caroline Stuart Wortley complained about 'the Dog whom I literally hardly ever see', as he only returned from shooting in time to eat dinner-supper with her at 8 o'clock; and that 'I think at last I am pretty well broke into being alone & really am grown not to mind it, except that I see so little of the *vile Dog*.' Lady Shelley recalled with gratitude that in her youth 'Lord Derby never allowed more than five brace of partridges to be killed by any one of his guests. He did this in order to ensure their returning to ride or drive with the ladies. Dear old man! his joyous temperament, and his love of society and good cheer, made his guests as happy and merry as himself.' And Jane Austen gives us a taste of what sport meant to all too many women when she describes how, in the absence of Henry Crawford, Maria Bertram was left to enjoy the undiluted company of her fiancé Mr Rushworth and was 'doomed' to hear 'the repeated details of his day's sport, good or bad, his boast of his dogs, his jealousy of his neighbours, his doubts of their qualification, and his zeal after poachers, – subjects which will not find their way to female feelings without some talent on one side, or some attachment on the other . . .'.[35]

Not surprisingly this meant that women were often more keen to travel, and especially to visit London for the season, than their husbands. At the beginning of June 1799, Maria Stanley wrote to her aunt from London. 'You know I have had all the winter a wish to migrate, and had only been quiescent in the country because I found it would have been unpleasant to the Man had I persevered in expressing that wish, since it would have given me no gratification to prevail with him *à contre-coeur*.' An opportunity arose when all the local business which had preoccupied John Stanley was concluded. 'I made the little observation how easy it would be to go to London, as things stood with us, for a very short time, before the Sheff[ield]s [her father and her stepmother] went into the country, and pass what time we could then spare at S[heffield]. P[lace – her father's house in Sussex].' The remark appeared to make little impression on her husband 'so there I left it to pursue its progress in his mind till the next day and tried again how it had acted. To my great surprise (if I can be surprised at kindness from him, when he knows how to oblige me) and pleasure, he said: "Well, we will go to London," but bid me take all the arrangements on myself.' These were quickly made and they soon set off, leaving the children behind them in care of the servants. The visit was a success, but after six weeks away from home Maria was satisfied, 'I do long to be at home again, and am almost sorry that I have promised to stay so much longer here than we intended, though indeed I am very happy and comfortable; but it is odd how I want to see all the things at Alderley.'[36]

The visit was not repeated for nearly a decade, but then the Stanleys began to visit London much more regularly, having purchased her father's house in Privy Gardens and redecorated it. Maria told her sister that she was eager for some intellectual stimulus after years of rustication.

It is what I look forward to with the most pleasure, that Sir John will pick up some old acquaintance and some new, and without form or ceremony bring them in to dinner that I may again hear conversation. For many years I have only heard discourses. As far as one man's mind may go, I have had within my hearing, knowledge, the fruit of reflection, and a very rare turn of thought, enough to satisfy any one; but I long to hear him converse with others who may in some degree be able to meet him in conversation.

Her wish was fulfilled and over the next few months her letters mention dinner guests, including Humphry Davy, Sir James Hall and Professor Playfair, with much scientific discussion over the dinner table. But they also mixed in London Society, and Maria recorded that 'London is very agreeable in this month of May, and we have been very gay. Sir John bears it better than I expected. He went with us to Lady Stafford on Friday, and was so much amused that at two o'clock he was not at all impatient to be gone. . . . Tonight we have two assemblies and a concert . . . .' Several years later Maria noted that time passed much more quickly and pleasantly in London than the country: 'an hour in London certainly consists of no more than thirty minutes according to country reckoning . . . .' It was a sentiment that many women, even those who were happily married and who loved their homes in the country, would have endorsed.[37]

No one pattern fits all these relatively happy marriages: in some one partner was clearly more dominant or more full of vitality than their spouse, in others there was a much more even balance; what is most apparent is a mutual concern for the other's happiness and a willingness to give way and compromise without playing the martyr. None of these marriages would have been perfectly smooth and contented: there would have been quarrels and arguments, sometimes based on significant differences of opinion or wishes, and sometimes arising simply from tiredness, ill-humour or genuine misunderstanding. But these disagreements were resolved without doing lasting harm; indeed they were sometimes necessary for each party to realise what mattered to the other and to find a mutually acceptable accommodation. The ability to express affection and to apologise when the other was hurt were great assets to any couple. Almost as important was working out a pattern of life that was reasonably satisfactory for them both: where they lived, how much they entertained or visited others, how much they spent and on what, and how much time they spent alone together. This would inevitably require some compromise, but they were much more likely to be happy if their inclinations on these points were similar, and if neither had to sacrifice too much to satisfy the other. Enjoying living with each other was just as important, in the long run, as loving each other.[38]

CHAPTER TWELVE

⟵◆⟶

CAREERS

MANY GENTLEMEN IN THE early nineteenth century had a career in one of the socially acceptable professions, such as the church, the army or the navy. The demands of these professions varied widely and were often rather different from the pattern of work we take for granted today, but they still had considerable implications for the man and for his wife and family. Clergymen might, if they wished, live fairly idle lives if they had a good living, but there was increasing social and official pressure for them to live in or near their parish. They could not, generally, go up to London for the season or visit Bath, coastal resorts or distant family, unless they employed a curate to take their place or made an arrangement with a neighbouring clergyman to fill in for them in their absence. Even then they had to explain their absence to their bishop, who might not be pleased if his indulgence was abused by frequent demands. So the wife of a clergyman was likely to spend most of her life living in the country, with the limited society of the neighbourhood. This suited some women, such as Fanny Price or even Catherine Tilney, better than others, and most readers can feel some sympathy for Mary Crawford's doubts that it was a life that would make her happy. The wife of a clergyman was expected to take an interest in his parishioners, to dole out comforts to the poor and the ill, and to set an example of respectability and good behaviour, if not piety, and again this suited some women better than others. She might have to accept a great deal of impertinent interference from an odious patron, such as Lady Catherine de Bourg, or tolerate long periods of isolation if there were no families of her own social standing who were close enough for her to visit, and there was little prospect that her social status would ever change, at least for the better.[1]

The wife of a barrister, such as Emma's sister Isabella Knightley, would generally live in or close to London, but had to accept that her husband would be away on circuit for six or seven weeks twice each year, whether or not this was convenient. This was also a most uncertain profession, with great rewards for the most successful barristers but failure for many; and failure often meant poverty for his wife and children. Much the same can be said of merchants and bankers, whether based in London or the provinces, except that even the most successful merchant or banker might be ruined almost overnight by a combination of adverse circumstances. The perils facing an officer in the army or the navy — and consequently the anxiety suffered by his wife — are more obvious, but they were very unevenly distributed. Even at the height of the war there were a great many naval officers living at home on half-pay, for the navy had more officers than it could use, and only those with recognised ability or good connections could be sure to be actively employed once they had reached the rank of commander or captain. Unemployed officers were often frustrated at their inability to pursue their career, and, unless they had significant private wealth, they were also financially constrained: the half-pay of even a senior officer was not generous. On the other hand, the wives of officers who were actively employed faced prolonged periods of separation, worrying about their husband's safety, not just in action but from the even greater risks posed by shipwreck and disease. Some officers in the army were also on half-pay, but the great majority held active commissions and were expected to serve with their regiment. This service varied widely: some regiments spent most of the war at home or in Ireland; others might be used to garrison distant colonies and could remain there for many years; while the brunt of active operations fell on a minority of regiments in the army. Wives and families of army officers sometimes accompanied them in Britain, and even followed them abroad, although most stayed home and endured prolonged or repeated separations. Even the wives of officers in the militia (a full-time home defence force not normally employed outside the British Isles) had to choose between long periods in which their husband would be absent on duty, or following him from temporary quarter to temporary quarter as his regiment was moved about the country.[2]

Not all men belonged to one of the professions, and some, like Mr Woodhouse, led idle lives, but most country gentlemen played an important role in their local community, and this entailed some obligations which affected their wives. Mr Knightley took a keen interest in farming and was a magistrate, which would have made it difficult for him to leave Highbury at certain times of the year. Sir Thomas Bertram was obliged to part from his wife and family to visit his estates in the West Indies, and was gone for about two years. He was also a Member of Parliament, and as such would have been obliged to spend some months in London each year. Early in his marriage his wife had accompanied him and they had spent the season together in London, but by the time Fanny Price arrived at Mansfield Park, Lady Bertram had given up her house in town and 'remained wholly in the country, leaving Sir Thomas to attend his duty in Parliament, with whatever increase or diminution of comfort might arise from her absence'. This was a choice which all Members of Parliament and their wives had to make, in which personal preference might be at odds with the need for economy, or with concerns for health, although that could cut both ways: London was regarded as unhealthy compared to the country, but the best doctors were readily to hand.[3]

Some women became closely involved in their husband's careers. We have already seen how women might become active in politics and this was frequently, although not always, in conjunction with their husband. Lady Torrington, the wife of the British minister at Brussels in 1789, took a close interest in her husband's work, superintended the activities of the *chargé d'affaires* when he was away and generally acted, in her husband's words, as 'the soul of my office'. Women might also seek patronage and appointments for their husbands, especially if they had family or other connections to those in power. Lady Anne Barnard spent two years lobbying her old friend Henry Dundas for a position for her husband Andrew, before Dundas finally obliged with a position in the newly conquered Dutch colony at the Cape of Good Hope. And when husbands were away on active service, wives such as Betsey Fremantle and Fanny Nelson circulated their letters home to remind patrons and other influential figures of the work they were doing and to ensure that their perspective on events was taken into account. Mary Buckland collaborated with her husband in his geological research, curating his collection of fossils and illustrating his books. At a much simpler level, women were often employed as unofficial secretaries, as when Joan Canning spent a 'bloody hot day' in August, copying a speech which her husband had given and then revised for publication in the *Parliamentary Register*. Even a gentleman without a formal career, such as Lord Sheffield, might ask his wife to help him in his correspondence. Indeed, Lord Sheffield's daughter, Maria Stanley, thought that he asked rather more than he should of her stepmother and hoped that he would soon get a paid secretary, 'for he does employ all the poor lady's time terribly, and has gained so many new correspondents at Liverpool, and so much infor-mation to disperse, that there is no end of his epistles'.[4]

Some other wives were much less committed to the success of their husband's career. Lavinia, Lady Spencer, disliked having to extend hospi-tality to the large number of naval captains who her husband, as First Lord of the Admiralty during the French Revolutionary Wars, invited to dinner and drew the line at receiving their wives, so as not to establish an acquaintance which might subsequently prove tiresome or embar-rassing. Lady Hawkesbury was distinctly unexcited when her husband was appointed Home Secretary in the Duke of Portland's government in 1807 after a year out of office. 'I find our year of Holyday has spoilt *me*. . . . I never can tell you how I shrink from ye renewal of hurry, bustle, anxiety and worry. . . .' And, 'Walmer Castle at *Easter* is of course, out of the question now. Alas I fear even in autumn it will be very different from ye tranquil séjour of last year. But I must not complain, tho' I cannot rejoice. If Lord Hawkesbury's health & Peace of mind do not suffer by this unexpected & unwish'd for return to Power I am content, & must again try to make the best of its advantages, & ye least of its worries.' And when, in 1829, Lord William Russell took up command of his regiment in Corfu and was then offered the position of Resident in Cephalonia he soon came to realise that his wife would never join him in these remote outposts, preferring life in the heart of Europe. He therefore declined the Cephalonia appointment, and after two years, most of it spent on leave, resigned his commission in the army in order to be free to live with her and their children.[5]

As this suggests there could be considerable tension between the demands of a career, the needs of a wife and family, and the private wishes of the husband. It was all very well for Nelson to proclaim grandly that 'Duty is the great business of a sea officer. All private considerations must give way to it however painful it is.' But later events showed that even Nelson did not always find it easy to subordinate his private feelings to his official duties, and most people – husbands and wives – recognised that a difficult balance had to be struck, and not just struck once, but repeatedly reconsidered as circumstances changed. Another naval officer, Philip Broke, promised his wife in 1812 that:

> I will come my Loo, as soon as duty will let me; for not all the fame of Nelson, or Lord Wellington would reconcile me to destroying the happiness of an affectionate wife, and whom duty has already compelled me to desert so long and so cruelly. Whenever I can retire without reproach conscious of having done my duty to my country, no view of honors however splendid shall tempt me to surrender my own happiness, and to sacrifice that of my beloved Loo to my ambition.

And Richard Bourke, a staff officer high in Wellington's favour, abandoned his chance of advancement and returned home in 1809 because his wife was ill, and only returned to the Peninsula three years later when she was somewhat better and could accompany him to a position far from the frontline.[6]

A few wives urged their husband to give up a career that led to separation and misery. In 1755, two years after her marriage, Jenny Rodney told her husband that 'without you life is not worth my care, nor would millions make me happy', and begged him to quit the navy, 'I hope you will then, as soon as you possibly can, give up that vile ship that causes us so much pain.' Louisa Broke also made her wishes obvious: 'My husband cannot stand higher in my opinion than he does, therefore nothing in this world can compensate me for the loss of his dear and valuable society, time never to be recalled, which now passes in constant anxiety, excluding the possibility of our happiness when separated.' But Elizabeth Paget had seen how unhappy her husband Charles – another naval officer – was onshore and urged him (in his words) 'in the strongest manner *never* to take into account *for her sake* the domestic sacrifices I am making, for *she never should* cease to be miserable if, by my seceding from Service, anything should occur in the interval which might make me condemn myself for having so withdrawn from it. The fact is the poor soul experienced, in a degree she probably never will forget, the misery I endured on a late occasion, which you also observed.'[7]

Women were conditioned to subordinate their needs to those of their husband, and in many cases financial necessity meant that there was no real alternative to his continuing his career. Matthew Flinders justified the prospect of a long separation from his newly married wife Ann with the simple argument that otherwise 'we could have barely existed in England'. They could only have obtained even the necessities of life through the charity of others, whereas his voyage of exploration to Australia would give them financial independence and prevent the necessity of a future separation. Two years later he wrote to her from the other side of the world, admitting that he was very ambitious, but assuring her that 'so soon as I can insure for us a moderate portion of the comforts of life, thou wilt see whether love or ambition have the greatest power over me. Before thou wast mine, I had engaged in this voyage; – without it we could not live. Thou knowest not the struggle in my bosom, before I consented to the necessity. There was no prospect of a permanent subsistence but in pursuing what I had undertaken, and I doubt not but that will it answer the end.'[8]

Many women refused to be separated from their husbands, especially early in their marriages. John Stanley was an officer in the Cheshire Militia at the time of his marriage, and in September 1797, eleven months after the wedding, Maria prepared to follow the regiment to Scotland while sending her month-old baby to Alderley with a nurse. 'I could not be tolerably easy if I did not follow the regiment, not knowing exactly what they would have to encounter, or where they may go, and fortunately my beloved, though he made a few prudent objections, is as desirous I should go with him as I am myself.' Nonetheless Maria soon concluded that 'I do not think lieutenant-colonels or majors of militia should be married men with families'. They had not been in Scotland for a month before they obtained leave for the winter and set off for Alderley, and John resigned his commission the following year. He was not alone: it was common for gentlemen with independent fortunes to serve in the army or militia for a few years, but to resign when they got married or soon afterwards.[9]

Life for a well-born army wife, even in a peaceful garrison, was some-times uncomfortable. In 1804 Lady Louisa Erskine wrote home to her mother, the Countess of Uxbridge, from Mallow in Ireland, complaining of her perpetual ill health, which she blamed on the climate and on the mice which infested their quarters: 'they run over our Bed every night, the House tho' quite new swarms with them. Everything we eat smells of them. They not only eat our food but devour my Gowns &c.' And even if the conditions in the lodgings were more salubrious, local society was generally very limited and provincial, and the other officers would either be unmarried or their wives would have stayed home. This meant long periods alone while their husbands were on duty and it took consid-erable character and mental resources for a wife in this position not to become bored and discontented.[10]

However, the greatest concern of most wives was the possibility that their husband's regiment might be sent overseas. Mrs Sherwood recalled that 'There was a constant dread at that time hanging over my mind that we should soon be ordered abroad, and that I must then part with my baby. I remember that I used often to watch her as she lay in her cradle, and weep most bitterly at the thought. Still, however, I had resolved, should such an event occur as our being sent from England, that I would leave this little one with my mother and sister, and so save her health from the effects of other climes.'[11]

Mrs Sherwood's fears were realised when orders arrived that the 53rd Foot were being sent to India. She spent a few days in London making preparations for the voyage and staying with her sister – a time which she remembered as 'a dream full of pain'. She wrote in her journal, 'The last time I saw my Mary she was sitting on her nurse's lap. She was eleven months and eighteen days old. Oh, my baby! my little baby! She could then walk a few paces alone. She could call mamma, and tell me what the lambs said. Oh, this state of bereavement – this parting – this life in which we are as dead to each other! My mother, my sister, you who have taken my infant under your care, you will feel for her and be tender with her. . . .' In all probability it would be years before Mrs Sherwood would see her daughter again, and it is hardly surprising that the 'parting from my mother, my brother, and my sister, and baby, filled up my whole thoughts. My mind had not any room for fears of the dangers of the deep . . . .'[12]

Voyages were not always pleasant. Susannah Middleton, the wife of a well-connected officer, who was going out to Gibraltar to take up a position as Commissioner of the Dockyard in 1805, wrote that after twelve days at sea, 'I think if we are a fortnight longer we shall not only be made distress'd for clean linen, but for provision, the water is getting now almost black, which makes the tea & coffee so bad at breakfast, that it is really difficult to get it down.' The cook was 'one of the nastiest creatures you ever saw', and the food he served was unappetising, the meat often rank. 'At supper I generally eat some biscuit and drink some wine & water soon after eight and go to bed at nine, for if I sit in any of the cabins below it makes me half sick, there are such a collection of dreadful nasty smells, in short we are all completely sick of living on board a ship.' Yet her position was better than Mrs Sherwood's whose husband had only managed to secure the carpenter's cabin for her on the long voyage to India. 'When the pumps were at work, the bilge water ran through this miserable place, this worse than a dog-kennel; and to finish the horrors of it, it was only separated by a canvas partition from the place where the soldiers sat, and, I believe, slept and dressed; so that it was absolutely necessary for me in all weathers to go down to this shocking place before any of the men were turned down for the night.' Being on the starboard side of the ship, the cabin was in almost constant darkness, so she spent as much time as she could on deck 'sit[ting] under the awning by the wheel, at the door of the dining-room'.[13]

It was not only the wives of officers in the army and navy who sometimes went with their husbands abroad. Charles Arbuthnot's first wife Marcia accompanied him on three successive diplomatic appointments: first to Lisbon in 1799, then to Stockholm in 1802 and finally to Constantinople in 1804. Their first child, Charles, was born on a navy frigate sailing home from Lisbon, and three further children followed who travelled with them. The journey to Constantinople was complicated and protracted by the decision to send them via Vienna, where Charles was to stand in for Arthur Paget who had sought leave to go home and a delay in securing a passage from Trieste to Constantinople on a navy ship. Having arrived at Constantinople they found that there was no suitable residence for the British ambassador, and Marcia's health deteriorated, although whether her illness was caused or made worse by the exertions of travelling, or by another pregnancy, is not clear. Their fifth child in seven years was born on 24 May 1806, but Marcia died in childbirth. Charles was devastated, and many years later told his children that 'time has not had the effect of reconciling me to her loss. To me it was dreadful. To you all it has been a misfortune beyond what I could make known to you. A more perfect creature never breathed . . . .' Marcia's mother, Mrs Lisle, offered to go to Constantinople to bring the children home if Charles wished, but it appears that he declined, and that the children remained with him until he gave up his diplomatic career and returned to England the following year.[14]

When Lord Burghersh was appointed British representative to the Austrian army in 1813, during the final climactic campaigns against Napoleon, his twenty-year-old wife Priscilla insisted on accompanying him, despite the more prudent advice of her father. The young couple travelled across Sweden, Germany and France through the autumn, winter and spring of 1813–14, enduring considerable hardships and some danger. More prosaically, the normally nervous Duchess of Wellington had no hesitation in deciding to accompany the Duke when he was appointed ambassador to France after Napoleon's fall in 1814: 'my wish would have been the same had your appointment been in any other part of the world to which you could, with safety, have permitted me to accompany you'. Ambassador's wives had an important role in the social side of diplomacy, and although the Duchess was not well suited to perform this with distinction, she clearly felt that it was better for her to make the attempt than to stay home.[15]

When the wives of military and naval officers accompanied their husbands abroad they did not normally follow them into the field of action, but remained in relative security at the port or city that formed the base of operations. For example, in North America most naval wives would divide their year between Halifax and Bermuda: Sir Thomas Hardy was unusual in expecting his wife to live with him on board his ship, which may help to explain her sense of grievance. Similarly, most of the wives of officers who went out to the Peninsula stayed in Lisbon, where there was a considerable expatriate community which one observer sourly described as 'corrupt and immoral'. A rare exception was Susanna Dalbiac, the wife of Lieutenant-Colonel Charles Dalbiac, the commander of the 4th Dragoons. Although her health had always been regarded as delicate, she flourished on campaign, sleeping beside her husband in a tent, in requisitioned quarters, or sometimes under the stars, and riding at the head of the regiment with a little haversack and bottle on the pommel of her saddle. In July 1812 the 4th Dragoons took a leading part in the Battle of Salamanca, and when the fighting was almost over she scoured the battlefield, escorted by a single dragoon, looking among the dead and wounded for her husband. He had survived unharmed and she set about nursing other wounded officers before rejoining the regiment for the advance on Madrid. She survived the war, but died in 1829 at the age of 45, and her husband erected a memorial tablet which declared that she had 'fulfilled in a pre-eminent degree all the duties which belong to the wife, the mother, the daughter, and the friend . . . to perpetuate the memory of so beloved an object, a mourning husband erects this monument, a faint memorial of his veneration for her virtues, a feeble testimony of his grief for her irreparable loss'.[16]

Susanna Dalbiac was unusual: most officers' wives stayed home and endured months, often years of separation and anxiety, while the men themselves often felt lonely and homesick. In March 1800, two-and-a-half years after being wounded at Tenerife, Thomas Fremantle felt sufficiently recovered to apply to the Admiralty for a new command. Almost six months passed before a letter arrived announcing that he had been given the command of the *Ganges*, a ship-of-the-line. Betsey wrote in her diary, 'I feel quite miserable at his going from me but still cannot help being flattered that he has so good a ship. It threw us in great confusion & misery.' A few years later, when the breakdown of the Peace of Amiens led to another parting, Betsey's sister was staying with them and noted that 'Capt. Fremantle was much affected during dinner and cried so that he was obliged to leave the room. We were all very dull at the thought of his going away.' After farewelling her husband at Spithead, Elizabeth Bass wrote to him that she felt as if 'I had lost every friend I had in the World', while Matthew Flinders told his wife Ann that without her he felt like 'one half of a pair of scissors without its fellow'. Anna Walker, the wife of an army officer, wrote in her diary after he had sailed on the Copenhagen Expedition in 1807 that 'in parting with him, I endured perhaps the most painful Moment of My Life. He was much affected, but endeavoured to keep up, & to persuade me his Absence would not be long – & that he saw Nothing to be done – but alas! Danger on every Side glared in My Face – I felt too strongly that all of my Happiness was at Stake – and the risque I run of losing all!'[17]

Captain Fremantle was an able, ambitious and responsible officer, but his letters home are often filled with his longing to be with his wife and children again: 'my mind hangs constantly towards you and your children, and I am at times so low I cannot hold up my head . . .'; 'my low spirits are excessive and I do nothing but take snuff and read Shakespeare, when I am off the deck, – thank you my dearest woman for your attention in sending me newspapers . . . you can't think how much I enjoy these periodical papers, and daily ones . . .' and:

> I just receive[d] your letter of the 4th, which you have the modesty to say contains nothing, I on the contrary think it contains everything as I am assured of the health and happiness of all I hold dear in the world, indeed I think it most interesting, and you can have no idea how an arrival revives and comforts my spirits which are not so good as they used to be . . . my only consolation is in the recollection that au dernier resort, I shall have the happiness of returning to the arms of the most affectionate wife, and children any man can be blessed with, I am horribly worried at times with ennui and bile, and still I flatter myself I am getting more reconciled to this dog's life . . .[18]

These letters were all written over the space of a few weeks when Fremantle was engaged in the dull work of blockading the French ports: there were other times when he was much more enthusiastic about his duty, but even then it is clear that part of him hankered to be at home.

Equally, Philip Broke thought of his family and dreamt of home even while he took pride in pursuing his career. He kept a rose bush in his cabin which acted both as a symbol and a reminder of home and told his wife Louisa (Loo) in July 1810 that 'I have just got my dear Loo's letters, of 23rd and 29th, and am charmed to hear so favourable account of the dear children, and so I put my rose by my side, and sat down and kissed the letters, and the rose, and the Loo, in imagination, and felt very happy for a few minutes, till I began to reflect that the real real [sic], true Loo was not there!' Sometimes the rose was too poignant, 'No! These roses must not stay! They haunt my imagination with wifish ideas, and won't leave me a moment for myself, or King George; if it was even a picture of Loo's soft countenance, I could shut it up; but these things flaunt their beauties in my face, and yet look so mild, and so innocent in their bloom, that I can't help thinking of her.' But the rose remained, and Broke never attempted to hide his love and longing for his wife in his letters home.[19]

Matthew Flinders was delighted with the parcel of letters from Ann that he found waiting for him when he returned to Port Jackson in 1803, and especially with 'the effusions of thy tenderness', admitting that she had outdone him in 'expressing affection'. He added, 'that very, very often my thoughts which are never expressed, are devoted to thee. In torture at thy great distance from me, I lay musing upon thee and whilst sighs of fervent love, compassion for thy suffering health, and admiration of thy excellencies in turn get utterance . . . my heart is with thee. . . .' Other officers were sometimes inhibited by the fear that their letters might be captured by the enemy and published in French newspapers (something which had happened), although Captain Fremantle acknowledged that he might not be able to restrain himself: 'I shall confine myself in future as *much as I can* to general subjects', and naval officers in particular seem to have been ready to acknowledge their feelings, possibly recognising that their wives needed some assurance that a long separation had not lessened their love.[20]

Letters were vital for both parties: Thomas Fremantle asked Betsey to write to him at least twice a week, while Philip Broke began a new letter each Sunday and added to it throughout the week. Both husbands and wives would frequently number their letters so that the recipient could read them in sequence and know if any had been lost, and some couples devised simple codes (usually involving a straightforward substitution of letters) for more intimate or delicate passages. The letters would commonly be read and re-read, with Thomas Fremantle assuring his wife that 'your letters are not thrown away, I read them over and over with pleasure, and would you believe that I was as great a fool as yourself when I read about poor Doddy's heart being so full the first night he was at school. What is there in Children that gets such entire possession of our hearts?' When, in the 1760s, one wife asked her husband to burn her letters, his reply shows how much they meant to him, 'How can you my dear, lay so hard an injunction on me as to burn your letters? I preserve them for my real friends sake; without regarding the hand writing; they contain sentiments truly noble, full of affection, and are highly worthy to be preserved. I value them much more than all the manuscript in the whole world and will keep them as I choose.' George Bass, who had set off on a long voyage a few weeks after his marriage, told Elizabeth, 'Since we could not add to the cement [of our love] by living together let us at least do it by frequent correspondence.' And Matthew Flinders asked Ann, 'Write to me constantly; write me pages and volumes. Tell me the dress thou wearest, tell me thy dreams, anything, so do but talk to me and of thyself.' For couples who were separated for months or years at a time, letters conveyed a sense of intimacy and allowed them to share at least part of their life and thoughts with the other. Not all couples wrote as much or as openly to each other – not all felt as close or were on good terms when together – while many marriages suffered from long separations, but the lifeline provided by correspondence seems to have been very effective in keeping some marriages in good repair in adverse circumstances.[21]

Opportunities for reunions, however brief, were eagerly anticipated and seized despite the risk of disappointment. In 1801 Sarah Collingwood travelled 500 miles from Morpeth to Plymouth in mid-winter with her eight-year-old daughter (and leaving a younger child at home) in order to see her husband. The day she arrived Admiral Collingwood had to sail, but she took lodgings in the town and he was able to join her a few weeks later. This was only the most extreme of many examples, although Betsey Fremantle's diary shows that she often felt so 'tired and stupified' by the hurried journey that she could not fully enjoy the occasion. Sometimes a wife might also have an underlying fear that a brief reunion might result in a pregnancy and childbirth, which she would have to get through without the support that the presence of a husband might provide.[22]

Disease and shipwreck both caused more deaths of naval officers and men than battle during this period, but fighting was what men trained for, the culmination of all their efforts, and the route to fame, glory and – sometimes – fortune, and it naturally figured large in their thoughts and hopes. Francis Austen, Jane's brother, wrote at length to his fiancée, Mary Gibson, explaining his disappointment at having missed Trafalgar, although he did not expect her to share this feeling. Three years later Admiral Collingwood, by then a veteran of many actions, told his wife that he wanted one last battle against the French before he was ready to come home and retire: a final victory to crown his career. (His hope was in vain and he died at sea in 1810, not having seen his wife and family for six years.) Yet there was a tension between the pursuit of glory and the love of family. Captain Fremantle, that devoted husband but ambitious officer, told Betsey after the Battle of Copenhagen in 1801 that 'I went through the action without reflecting *much* on those who were so much interested in my welfare but when everything was over I could not suppress tears which at this time again flow from my eyes.'[23]

Wives left at home, or on a foreign station, often knew that a battle was imminent beforehand and had much anxiety to endure before the result, and – crucially – the details of who was killed or wounded, reached them. Betsey Fremantle was relatively fortunate when the news of Trafalgar arrived, but her account still suggests the painful uncertainty that women suffered.

I was much alarmed by *Nelly's ghastly* appearance immediately after breakfast, who came in to say Dudley had brought from Winslow the account that a most dreadful action had been fought off Cadiz, Nelson & several Captains killed, & twenty ships were taken. I really felt undescribable misery until the arrival of the Post, but was relieved from such a wretched state of anxious suspence [*sic*] by a Letter from Lord Garlies, who congratulated me on Fremantle's safety & the conspicuous share he had in the Victory gained the 21st off Cadiz. He adds poor Nelson was no more, he lived to take the

Spanish Admiral his opponent & to know he was victorious. In the midst of my delight to hear Fremantle had been preserved in this severe action, I could not help feeling greatly distressed for the Fate of poor *Nelson* whose loss is irreparable. . . . How thankful I am Fremantle has once more escaped unhurt. The accounts greatly shook my nerves. . . . I long for a Letter from Fremantle, I am perfectly bewildered & can think & dream of nothing but the late Victory. Poor Nelson! had he survived, it would have been glorious indeed. Regret at his death is more severely felt than joy at the destruction of the Combined Fleets – ten ships only returned into Cadiz under the Command of Gravina.[24]

Betsey Fremantle's experience was relatively unusual, even among the wives of naval officers, while most other professions occasioned less anxiety and stress. Nonetheless, a husband's profession, or even his unpaid pastimes, played a very important role in shaping the terms of most marriages. The demands of a career often trumped the preferences of the wife, and while this was sometimes a matter of choice, on other occasions the arguments of financial necessity were overwhelming. Most men were already committed to a career before they met their wife, and in many cases could only change direction if they had an independent source of income. A woman would at least know that she was marrying a clergyman, a barrister or a naval officer and would have some general idea of what this implied. Subsequent decisions about his career would generally be the subject of discussion, and perhaps negotiation, although the final decision generally remained with the husband. Most women accepted this as inevitable, although some were undoubtedly frustrated or regretted the demands that their husband's career made on them and their family, especially if the marriage was not close or their husband did not consult them. But if women suffered on account of their husband's careers, so too did men. Most careers open to gentlemen in the early nineteenth century rewarded a few men extremely well, while the rest struggled to make a sufficient income to maintain their place in society. Professions might be dull or dangerous – some were both – but no career offered a certain path to even modest affluence, and success depended less on ability and hard work than on luck and connections. If some wives found life in a country vicarage dull, so did some of their husbands; and the miseries of separation and anxiety suffered by army and navy wives were mirrored by their homesick husbands; even the threat of danger was similar, for a husband would fret about his wife's giving birth as much as she would worry about the dangers of storm and battle. But the picture was not wholly negative: some men were well suited to their profession and took great delight in it, and sometimes their wives were proud of their achievements and identified strongly with it, finding that it provided them with a community, a sense of purpose or even a vocation, whether as the wife of a naval officer or a clergyman. At the end of *Persuasion* Anne Wentworth, as she had become, 'gloried in being a sailor's wife', and she was not alone.[25]

CHAPTER THIRTEEN

CHILDREN

CHILDREN PLAYED AN IMPORTANT part in the lives of most couples in the late eighteenth and early nineteenth centuries, although a significant minority of marriages – probably more than one in five – remained childless. The common assumption of couples getting married was that they would have children, and that this would be a good thing, although it is safe to assume that some people viewed the prospect with more enthusiasm than others. However, the lack of children did not necessarily undermine a marriage. Indeed, many childless couples had extremely happy marriages: examples include Harriet and Charles Arbuthnot, Lord and Lady Castlereagh, the Liverpools, Lord and Lady Grenville, Lady Anne and Andrew Barnard and Jane Austen's uncle James Leigh-Perrot and his wife Jane. To this list we might also add Admiral and Mrs Croft, the happiest married couple in any of Jane Austen's novels. In at least some of these cases it seems likely that the lack of children made the couple focus their affections more intensely on the other. Not that all childless marriages were happy: Sir James and Lady Louisa Erskine's marriage was not, and it does not seem that the union of Henry Austen and Eliza de Feuillide was especially successful, although the evidence here is not conclusive.[1]

A childless marriage could mean very different things, ranging from a surprising but not unwelcome outcome, to a heartbreaking succession of miscarriages or stillbirths. In the case of second marriages, where there was already a family from the first, the absence of a second batch of children might be a relief; but in other cases the pressure to produce a son and heir to inherit a title and an estate might be considerable. Lady Anne Lindsay was forty-three when she married Andrew Barnard, and so was not surprised when they did not have children, although she acknowledged some regret, commenting a few years later on seeing a baby, 'I wishd it had been my own, but one must not wish for anything now so improbable. Fortunately for my happiness, tho my B would have much rejoyced in having two or three, he is too reasonable to permit himself to be unhappy about what can't be helpd – it is no fault of his, poor fellow!' A few years later, when his career had stalled, Andrew reflected on the advantages of not having children: 'I have great comfort My Love in what at a former time I rather wished otherwise – that we have no children. You and I can make ourselves happy anywhere – in Africa, Wales, Russia. Had we children in the present position of the times our hearts would bleed for them. I feel now for you only. I can face any ill with you.'[2]

Couples were sometimes anxious or embarrassed when pregnancy did not follow in the year or so after the wedding, especially as family and friends were likely to be on the watch for the first hint and to make frequent leading enquiries and even make 'helpful' suggestions. Yet couples were also warned of the risks of pregnancy and childbirth, and attitudes were often complicated. Eliza Whitaker noted the comfort offered by a family friend: 'She gives many reasons why we should not be anxious to possess a family, She says she was 3 or 4 yrs before the birth of her daughter, which was an ecstasy of delight to herself and her husband. The little creature sickened and a month after its birth died, and for many months they were miserable and wished they had no family. How little we know whether the attainment of our wishes will bring us happiness.' And another friend confessed, 'I should be one of those to rejoice with you, if your illness proceeded from the *common cause* for once they come they are such a comfort, though I cannot help feeling thankful to have escaped so long. I should like to have several more yet if I had my choice. I do not know if I dare to choose to have them, but I am a terrible coward even in trifles.'[3]

Still most people, perhaps especially most women, were in favour of having children. Lady Sheffield, Maria Stanley's stepmother, wrote that

'It is certain no woman can be a wife without wishing to be a mother, at least according to my way of thinking.' And Maria herself, in writing to her sister about the book *Letters from the Mountains* by Mrs Grant of Laggan, said:

> I think I can discover that though she submitted to rear children, and even thought she took pleasure in them, that she looked upon it as a subordinate employment, and almost envied her childless friend in America. Well! *Dieu merci*! I do not make a virtue of necessity; but feel thoroughly convinced that no possible torment the eight I have can give me could be so irksome to me as having led a childless married life. Nothing could have carried me through my long exile but a family of children. I know, in the bottom of your heart you think this is a mark of want of high sentiment and of a strong philosophic turn of mind. Maybe so; but I do not wish to be otherwise, any more than I do to be a man, another proof of my grovelling disposition.

Yet even here there is an acknowledgement that not everyone would share this view and an understandable hint of ambivalence: having children or not having children is never an entirely unmixed blessing, although few parents will break the taboo and admit any regrets.[4]

Lady Caroline Lamb became pregnant soon after her marriage. The news delighted her husband William, the future Lord Melbourne, who 'loves her *much* better than ever, and they are if possible more like lovers even than before their marriage'. She asked her cousin Georgiana Morpeth whether 'it is bad for you to *sleep* with your husband at the time in the most significant sense of the word', adding that she still found William 'very beautiful'. Unfortunately the child was born prematurely and died on 30 January 1806, and a further miscarriage followed in 1809. Disappointments such as this were relatively common and caused much heartache. Anna Walker wrote in her diary for 4 September 1803: 'I was extremely ill all Night, but unwilling to disturb any One. In the Morning I got up, but was Soon obliged to go to Bed, & Send for Dr. McDonald, & in about the middle of the Day My poor little infant was born – but as I feared, had been dead Some time. My disappointment was great, notwithstanding I was So Much prepared for it. Walker was also Much hurt . . .' And twenty years later Bessy Russell confided to Lady Holland, 'I am I confess disappointed at my little mishap. . . . I wished for a daughter, & I cried bitterly when I saw my little foetus that would have been a rational & loveable little being. In short I am no heroine & have too thin spun nerves to attempt the character.' She was ill for some time after the miscarriage and did not recover her health or her spirits for more than six months.[5]

Even where the pregnancy went smoothly, many women understandably feared the ordeal and risk of childbirth. Lord William Russell wrote to his mother-in-law in 1819, when Bessy was pregnant for the second time, 'Pray give her all the encouragement you can about lying in, as she has all sorts of absurd fancies, & sits sometimes thinking & picking her lips, till her mind is bewildered & her lips scarified.' And Mrs Calvert, who had already had eight children and was again pregnant, was greatly upset by the death of Lady Sydney in childbirth, a young woman whom she had known since she was a girl. 'I am very low-spirited. Lady Sydney's death preys upon my mind. I try not to think of it, for it is no rule because she has died in her lying-in, that the same thing is to happen to me, but I can't banish the idea, and I feel most terribly frightened this time – however, God's will be done.' That was in August, and she had not recovered her spirits in January when the birth was imminent, writing, 'I suppose I shall not be able to write again for some time – if ever. If I die, my last prayer will be for my beloved husband and children. God grant me strength of mind and body to bear the pain I must necessarily endure!' Her son Richard was born later that day and she made a good and rapid recovery, but the baby died before it was a month old.[6]

Betsey Fremantle was characteristically stoical in her description of giving birth to her first child: 'I woke in great pain this morning, continued poorly all day, but minded it as little as possible. To my no small happiness and everybody's surprise I was brought to bed by seven o'clock in the evening of a boy, before Dr. Savage had time to come, the nurse delivered me. A small child but a sweet boy.' Bystanders might be less restrained. One woman wrote of her daughter's experience:

She is as well as we ought to expect, considering the sufferings she went thro' for two days & a half, she was wonderfully supported, her spirits & good humour never failed, except when nature was quite exhausted. The anxiety has been almost too much for her husband & Myself . . . Altho' I have not named it, yet I am a very proud Grandmother, the sweet Girl is already my darling, tho' till her Mother was safe, I did not care at all whether the baby was dead or alive . . .

And Fanny Knight reacted strongly to her sister's suffering, telling her trusted cousin Fanny Cage that:

I was in the next room during the worst and heard everything and the impression it made upon me will never be effaced . . . I who always doted upon everything belonging to babies, must acknowledge that I would rather forgo the happiness of becoming a Mother than have to endure what must be endured to accomplish it. I could not for the world have anybody know but yourself how miserable it made me, because it is a sort of thing people always think it witty to laugh at or treat lightly – but I literally have not been myself in body or mind ever since, and instead of the joy one is supposed to feel on such occasions, the irritability of my mind has been such that I have almost hated all the congratulatory letters which have arrived and have been more disposed to cry than to rejoice . . .[7]

Nonetheless she married Sir Edward Knatchbull the following year and went on to have nine children of her own.

The risk of the mother dying in childbirth or as a result of complications afterwards was not as high as might be expected: something in the order of 1 in 100 per childbirth, which, as married women averaged about six children, meant that 6 or 7 per cent of married women died from this cause. Three of Jane Austen's sisters-in-law – Edward's wife Elizabeth, Francis's wife Mary and Charles's wife Fanny – died either in childbirth or soon afterwards; and so did Frances Poole, the first wife of Lord Palmerston, and Esther Acklom, the confident flirt who had found great happiness in her marriage to Lord Althorp.[8]

Husbands were not normally present at the birth, but would generally be in the house waiting anxiously for news.[9] Maria Stanley's Aunt

Serena commented sharply that 'It must be a great affront to produce a child and not have a husband to say "Thank ye, my love,"' although, of course, this often happened when a husband was away on active service. At Christmas 1788 Lord Palmerston was attending parliament in London while Mary, his second wife, was at Broadlands and expecting soon to give birth, and she made it clear that she wanted him present, even if she had to travel up to London and join him. 'If you have any idea that it will not be in your power to give your daughter Mary the meeting on her first arrival I must come up, as I shall be miserable to go through that trial without your being in the same house. I am perhaps absurd, but I only can answer for my feelings and not for the propriety of them . . . .' Palmerston assured her that he would come home in time, but delayed his departure for another fortnight as he waited to recover from a cold. Fortunately he did get home before Mary gave birth – to their fourth child, a daughter, on 15 January 1789. Fourteen months later Mary gave birth safely again, and his diary for the day reads: 'Lady Palmerston delivered of daughter (Elizabeth) at three this morning; dined at Lord Malmesbury's' – so it is clear that he did not allow the events of the day to disrupt his plans or social life too much.[10]

Women were expected to take some time to recover from the ordeal of giving birth. After giving birth on 11 March 1798, Betsey Fremantle noted two days later that she was 'doing extremely well, so is the child . . . I got up to have my bed made this afternoon.' On the following day (the 14th), 'My little boy begins to suck very nicely and I am not at all troubled with my milk, he is a charming child and never cries. Got up for half an hour in the afternoon.' By the 18th she was up all day, although still in keeping to her room, and found it 'very tiresome to be so much alone, and the nurse's gossip a great bore'. On the 24th, 'I dined with F, in his little parlour. I am getting stout quite fast and my little boy improving every day.' While on the 31st she went out for the first time and was Churched, and then slowly picked up the threads of her life, although she found that the baby left her little time for her music and other pursuits.[11]

Maria Stanley had a relatively easy time with the birth of her first child ('a dream of about an hour and a half, somewhat unpleasant') and was impatient to go out before the end of the customary month's recuperation, but found it best not to flout local opinion:

I sacrifice my inclinations to a sense of propriety and fear of old grimalkins, inasmuch as it is within two days before the expiration of the month. All the gossiping old women in Christendom shall not prevent my doing like other folks after Thursday; but I found that unless I would be wondered at by all the town (and perhaps it might have reached the judges and gone the circuit with the lawyers) I must not stir out into the haunts of men before that time.[12]

On the other hand, Emily Eden's friend Pamela, Lady Campbell, regretted that her period of enforced leisure was not longer:

Here, alas, my reign is over, my role of lying-in. . . . One month, one little month, was scarce allowed me; and I was again dragged into the vulgar tumult of common barren life. Provoking and vexatious events are no longer kept from my knowledge, the hush and tiptoe are forgotten, the terror of my agitation has ceased, the glory of Israel is departed! The truth is I am too well; there is no pathos, no dignity, no interest, in rude health, and consequently I meet with no respect. I have not even been allowed to read *Redgauntlet* in seclusion, and chickens and tit-bits have given way to mutton chops and the coarse nutrition adapted to an unimpaired constitution.[13]

However, it is likely that many women who had experienced a more difficult labour needed the full month to recover and could probably have done with longer and more attention.

——>◆<——

Large families were quite common. George and Cassandra Austen had eight children of whom three (Jane, Cassandra and their brother George) never married. Of the five boys who married, Henry had no children, James had three (one from his first marriage and two from his second), Edward had eleven, Francis also had eleven and Charles had eight (four with each of his wives), a total of thirty-three children. As Jane Austen light-heartedly remarked on the opening page of *Northanger Abbey*, 'A family of ten children will always be called a fine family, where there are

heads and arms and legs enough for the number . . . .' Lady Uxbridge
and her progeny far exceeded the Austen's fertility: she had ten surviving
children, all but one of whom went on to have large families of their
own, giving her seventy-five grandchildren – no wonder that Thomas
Malthus thought that the world could never sustain such population
increases.[14]

Contemporaries were not unaware of the financial cost of having so
many children. Jane Austen's uncle, Tysoe Saul Hancock, commented
that George Austen (Jane's father) 'will find it easier to get a family than
to provide for them . . .'. Jane Austen herself made the same point in
Sanditon when she observed that 'The Heywoods were a thoroughly
respectable family . . .', but:

Mr & Mrs H. never left home. Marrying early & having a very
numerous Family, their movements had been long limited to one
small circle; & they were older in Habits than in Age. Excepting two
Journeys to London in the year, to receive his Dividends, Mr H. went
no farther than his feet or his well-tried old Horse could carry him,
and Mrs Heywood's Adventurings were only now & then to visit her
Neighbours, in the old Coach which had been new when they married
& fresh lined on their eldest son's coming of age 10 years ago. – They
had very pretty Property – enough, had their family been of reasonable Limits to have allowed them a very gentlemanlike share of
Luxuries & Change – enough for them to have indulged in a new
Carriage & better roads, an occasional month at Tunbridge Wells, &
symptoms of the Gout and a Winter at Bath; – but the maintenance,
Education & fitting out of 14 Children demanded a very quiet,
settled, careful course of Life – & obliged them to be stationary and
healthy at Willingden.[15]

Some couples endeavoured to limit the size of their families, although
we know frustratingly little about how common this was or the popularity of the various methods they employed. Breast feeding was known
to reduce the likelihood of falling pregnant, and was approved by
doctors, but not all women were willing to continue breast feeding for a
year or more when this would tie them close to their baby; while husbands

were also likely to be unenthusiastic, as doctors argued against sexual relations while the mother was suckling, claiming that this would spoil the milk and endanger the child. Condoms were fairly readily available, at least in London, but were expensive and unreliable, and it seems that they were mainly used as a protection against sexually transmitted diseases, generally when a man was having sex with a prostitute. Coitus interruptus was also known and was practised by at least some couples. Other options, such as oral, anal or digital sex, are seldom if ever mentioned in the context of married couples and carried more than a hint of the irresponsible sex which a man had with a mistress or prostitute. In the event of an unwanted pregnancy a woman might seek to induce a miscarriage. The eighteenth-century press contained many advertisements for concoctions of drugs to treat female problems with prominent warnings that they should not be taken if pregnant as it would lead to a miscarriage. Abortions were only made illegal in 1803, and even then the advertisements continued, and it appears that women generally did not regard a foetus as alive until they could detect movement, although doctors disagreed. These drugs were not entirely safe, nor entirely effective. Lady Strathmore successfully dealt with an unwanted pregnancy in 1776, only to again find herself pregnant a few months later, and this time all the measures she adopted failed to produce a miscarriage. Nor is it clear how easy it was to procure such drugs outside London and other large centres.[16]

Sometimes it was pressure from the husband that induced a woman to attempt to end her pregnancy. Eugenia Wynne recorded the example of Mrs Manners who 'talks cooly [sic] of riding hard to procure a miscarriage, and this because [her husband] hates children and beats her for having some'. Other cases are more ambiguous. When the pregnant Emily Somerset was dancing vigorously in Brussels in November 1814 was she simply acting with the high spirits of youth (she was only twenty-one) or trying to get rid of a child who – if later gossip was well founded – may not have been fathered by her adoring husband?[17]

However, the most common, respectable and effective form of contraception was, in Jane Austen's phrase, 'the simple regimen of separate rooms'. This does seem to have been a widespread expedient, with many references to couples sleeping separately, although, of course, this does not necessarily mean that they did not sometimes have sex and even spend the occasional night together. Nor was abstention always easy for either party. In 1777, after Emily, Duchess of Leinster, who was then in her mid-forties, suffered three miscarriages in rapid succession and a child who died young, William Ogilvie insisted that they part for a few months to allow her to recover. He felt they could not risk another pregnancy, but that he could only resist passion's call if they put at least one sea between them. However, the temporary separation made her intensely miserable – so much so that it made her ill – and produced an outpouring of abject appeals for him to return. And yet she was pregnant again only a few weeks after his return and in May 1778 gave birth to her twenty-second child.[18]

Babies and children often gave their parents intense pleasure. Mrs Calvert looked back on the birth of her first child as 'Oh joyful moment! never, never to be forgotten'. Lady William Russell wrote of her almost two-year-old son, 'My boy grows charming, I adore him, we do nothing but play with him all day long . . . .' A month later her husband added, 'Bessy is so fond of him, she would die if we were to lose him. But he is healthy, strong, full of spirits, & every thing I could wish . . . he is handsome & jabbers like a magpie – he has all the quickness & *esprit* of his mother, & is quite a little prodigy.' And in the following year Lord William boasted, 'My little boy is a dear little fellow, at least we think it, so much so that he breakfasts dines & lives with us as if he were 20 years old, to the horror & amazement of English mothers . . . .' Similarly, Caroline Stuart Wortley wrote four months after the birth of her first child, 'Every time I leave that child I feel more lost without him, he really grows too amiable & agreeable to be parted from him at all.' Her husband James was equally smitten and a few years later told her, 'I must not forget to tell you *but quite between ourselves* that I now never see a child in arms without being tempted to go and kiss it as a sort of type of pretty dear *Miss Wortley* . . . .' Yet this very devotion to her children made Caroline fear for the state of the world and worry for the future.[19]

Children were loved whether they were boys or girls, although parents were most likely to go into raptures about their eldest child, before the novelty had worn off. However, there were cases in which parents passionately desired a son and heir and regarded the appearance of a daughter as a disappointment. Lord and Lady Belgrave had two girls, then a miscarriage, then a son who died at nine months and then a third girl. When the next baby proved to be a boy, Lord Belgrave wrote to his mother-in-law with obvious delight and excitement, 'A son! A son! Born at 4 o clock this morning after three hours' labour, both mother and child doing as well as possible – a fine healthy boy.' Lady Elizabeth had resigned herself to another girl and apologised to her mother, 'for telling you it would be a girl, and I am so glad to have been mistaken. It is a terrible uncertainty to be under when the time gets near as I can witness.' Four further children followed over the next six years, but they were all girls, and in the privacy of her diary Lady Elizabeth did not attempt to conceal her reaction: 'Alas, 100 times'; 'a provoking catastrophe'; and finally 'horror!' A son then provided some consolation (and insurance in case any misfortune happened to the heir), but was soon followed by an eighth daughter: 'The catastrophe of a daughter was a bore,' Lady Elizabeth wrote, 'but what can't be cured must be endured, for ever abjured and never mentioned.' Another son and daughter rounded off the family.[20]

Other instances of a marked preference for boys tend to be in families where – like the Belgraves – there was already a predominance of girls. When Lady Caroline Capel had her sixth daughter, without having a single son, one of her uncles wrote, 'Caroline has just produc'd *another girl* . . . much to the mortification of Capel and herself.' And when she completed her family with her thirteenth child (of whom three were boys), she herself kissed it and said 'Poor little thing I forgive you for being a Girl.' The following day she wrote to her mother, 'As well as the little *Girl*, who I am rather provoked is not a young *Hero* as you had predicted. However I suppose it is right as it is; and I am too happy to have it over.' On the other hand, there are cases of a preference for girls, especially where there were already sons. The Duke of Bedford finished a letter to Bessy Russell, when she was pregnant with her third child, having had two boys, 'With best wishes for a *petite fille* rather than another *gros garcon.*' Betsey Fremantle was delighted that her sister Eugenia had 'a Girl this time, after three Boys; it proves quite a treasure and she is as happy as possible.' And Captain Fremantle, having three sons and two daughters, still wrote home when the news of the birth of his third daughter, 'what is it that makes me think so much more of my Girls than my boys? Lord Nelson on presenting me with Harriet's letter asked me if I would have a Girl or a boy, I answd, the former, when he put letter into my hand and told me to be satisfied . . . .'[21]

Most children were given fairly traditional names, quite often those of their parents or grandparents. Sometimes a wealthy, childless relative might express a wish that a child might be named after them, with the implication that they would be more inclined to remember their name-sake in their will than a child bearing a different name. Mrs Calvert greatly disliked her husband's relatives Mr and Mrs Tash, but tolerated them as guests as they were rich, able to dispose of their fortune as they wished and had no other relatives with a better claim on it. However, when Mr Calvert passed on a suggestion that their next baby be named Honor (Mrs Tash's name), 'I actually screamed . . . and he has promised to tell Mr. Tash I cannot bear the name, especially as I have set my heart on calling her after my angel Mary. But if it gives him any pleasure, she shall be called Mary Honor.' Mr Tash took the blow well and suggested reserving the name for a later occasion, and despite the snub went on to leave the Calverts £20,000 together with a very comfortable house in town.[22]

The responsibility for caring for children normally fell on the mother, who would be assisted to a greater or lesser extent by a nursery maid and other servants. The health of the mother, the number of children, personal preference and financial circumstances all influenced the way this worked in practice, but it is clear that in most cases mothers spent a great deal of time actively engaged in tending to their babies, toddlers and older children, although in a large family, where the mother was frequently pregnant, the amount of maternal attention any individual child received was necessarily limited. The cliché of the upper-class mother who only saw her children for an hour or so each day when they were brought down from the nursery, scrubbed and on their best behaviour may have been true in some families in this period, but it was not the norm. Most mothers appear to have been fully engaged, physically, emotionally and intellectually, with their children. Fathers varied more in the way they related to their offspring: some took little interest, but others were heavily involved, although the paternal role always ran more to romping and strictures than the daily chores of washing, dressing and feeding.[23]

There is an undeniable warmth in the way many parents write of their children. In 1807 James and Caroline Stuart Wortley took their two eldest children with them on a visit to the Duke and Duchess of Leeds at Hornby Castle. When James left, Caroline told her mother that she had John, the older child, sleep in her bed 'which is a great treat. Ta [Charles, her second child, who was five] was to have taken his turn last night, but he did not choose to be in the room alone till I came to bed, so John slept with me again, & I was not sorry for the change, as Ta is a most riotous creature in bed. They are very happy here, & I go on with their reading & writing in my own room every morning . . . .' In November 1812 Wellington's wife Kitty described the benefit for her young sons (aged four and five) in staying in the country:

> I wish you could see the delight, hear the shout of joy, with which they fly out of the house after the confinement of a day of rain. They are absolutely wild. Woe to the old lady who happens to be turning the corner as Charley dashes round it! After running about the Common as long as they like, they return to me glowing with exercise and health. They are beautiful and good and a thousand times happier than they would be confined to town.

Captain Fremantle would have approved, telling his wife that 'nothing tends more to health than exercise and Air, and that the more they are out of the house the better.' Maria Stanley told her sister that 'I should be very glad if my breed had not so much game in it! But the chicks fight, kick and cuff as soon as they can move, as naturally as the fighting-cock race peck each other before they are full-fledged. The future hero, Edward, is a troublesome boy as needs be. Maud is a great favourite and prime scholar of his. For sure there never centred in so many little human beings so much quicksilver.' And Betsey Fremantle was determined that her eldest daughter should not be forced into ladylike ways too early, writing in 1812, when Emma was twelve, '[I am] so delighted to see her amuse herself like a perfect child that I let her fly her kite, & brush down her poney, provided she holds herself up like a *Gentlewoman* in the drawing room, & plays upon the Piano Forte, *à ma façon*, if you were here, you would do the same.'[24]

Good parents treated each child as an individual, recognising their strengths and weaknesses and, in the case of the boys, seeking to find a career that would suit them, rather than forcing them into a predeter-mined path. When George Canning wrote to his wife Joan on the eve of his duel with Castlereagh in 1809, he was clear in recognising that his invalid eldest son was completely unsuited to follow in his footsteps: 'His feelings are too sensitive for publick life even if (which God grant!) his health should admit of his being anything else than a sedentary scholar. . . . I could almost wish him to be a clergyman: but not unless he wished it too.' And Betsey Fremantle's letters contained many vivid glimpses of one child or another, that not only showed their character but included her husband in the family circle even when he had been at sea for months or even years. 'I wish you could see Your Daughter [Emma] at this moment, pasting some papers in the inside of her writing desk, where she unfortunately spilt some ink this morng[?]. She is *vrai fille de son père* & is working & slaving as you would yourself.' Emma's younger brother Billy was obstreperous, 'always out & runs away from us all; he wants you much to keep him in order'. But Tom, the oldest boy, was 'perfection if you could see how very attentive he is, to me, full of spirits & fun & still always tractable & obedient, you would be delighted with him, & he grows remarkably handsome'.[25]

Betsey Fremantle's letters give us a rich and engaging picture of family life in the period, in which exuberance and high spirits are more evident than formality and decorum. In February 1812 she told her husband that Emma and Charles 'are making so intolerable a noise in *conversation* with their Cousin Fanny that I scarcely know what I am writing at this moment, luckily it has struck ten & I shall send them to Bed, when I hope to have a moment's peace'. Emma then added a message of her own: 'Dear Papa, Indeed we are very agreeable company and I only wish you were here to make more noise but I must go to bed or else

Mama will be in a pet.' Betsey continued the letter, presumably after packing the children off to bed, recounting an incident from the previous day: 'yesterday when Charles led in the Shetland Poney into the library I would not allow him to go through, for fear of *my carpet*, & insisted on the poor beast going out the way it came in through your dressing room, Emma almost in tears as she was certain the poney would break his legs, going down the steps, it certainly was *a dangerous leap*, but he went safe out of the House.' And she ended the letter with the assurance that 'our children improve daily in appearance & looking at them I quite forget that I myself am growing an old woman [she was thirty-three], I dance & play with them & you would be amused to see me become so active'.[26]

Not all parents were as loving or conscientious as the Fremantles. Lady Shelley's father was often absent, and when present, often drunk, and encouraged his daughter (then little more than a toddler) to 'toss off a bumper of port, and throw the glass over her shoulder to the toast of "Church and King, and down with the Rump"'! Her mother was less irresponsible, but spoiled her daughter who disliked 'her impetuous caressing, and [I] early learnt to allow myself, as a favour to *her*, to be kissed; and not, as is usual with most children, to receive a caress as the reward of good conduct and maternal affection'. The Duchess of Wellington also indulged her sons to a degree that was unhealthy, 'carrying their fishing-nets, their bats, balls, and stumps, apparently not perceiving how bad it was for them to regard a woman, far less their mother, as a simple drudge, fit only to minister to their pleasures. In consequence her sons pitied, without respecting her'. When her younger son Charles was nine he wrote to her from school, 'My dear Mama, You must have everything ready as ready as possible or dread the most severe punishment from me.' And two years later the older boy felt that it was acceptable for him to address his mother as follows: 'You shall get up every morning at eight o'clock precisely if you are good and obey my orders, but if you are bad . . . you shall get up at 6 o'clock without any fire or warm water and then stand in the corner with a fool's cap upon your head till breakfast time.'[27]

Parents were often closely involved in the education of their children: many boys and even more girls were taught at home, while even those who were sent to school might, like Jane Austen, stay there only for a

Drawn by Huet Villiers.   Engraved by W. Blake.

1. Portrait of Mrs Harriet Quentin, after François Hüet Villiers, print by William Blake (1820). This is believed to be the painting Jane Austen saw in London in spring 1813 and described as 'excessively like' Jane Bennet, the character she had created in *Pride and Prejudice*. (Jane Austen to her sister Cassandra, Sloane St, 24 May 1813, *Jane Austen's Letters*, p. 220.)

A RECEIPT for COURTSHIP

Two or three dears, and two or three sweets;
Two or three balls, and two or three treats;
Two or three serenades, given as a lure;
Two or three oaths how much they endure;
Two or three messages sent in a day;
Two or three times led out from the play;
Two or three soft speeches made by the way;

Two or three tickets for two or three times;
Two or three love letters writ all in rhymes;
Two or three months keeping strict to these rules,
Can never fail making a couple of fools.

Published Dec'r 1805,
by LAURIE & WHITTLE, 53,
Fleet Street, London.

2. *A Receipt for Courtship*, by Thomas Rowlandson (1805), describes the ingredients in courtship with, inevitably, a satirical sting in its tail.

3. *The Comforts of Matrimony: A Good Toast*, by Rowlandson (1809). An idealised picture of a happy marriage in modest circumstances, but 'love in a cottage' could be perilous.

4. *Fillial* [*sic*] *Affection, or a Trip to Gretna Green*, by Rowlandson (1785). Elopements were surprisingly common, although seldom as dramatic as the one depicted here.

5. *Reconciliation or the Return from Scotland*, by Rowlandson (1793). Most families were soon reconciled to their children after an elopement and made the best of the situation.

6. A joint wedding in Oliver Goldsmith's *The Vicar of Wakefield* (1766), illustrated by Rowlandson (1817). By the late eighteenth century, the fashion was to keep weddings small and quiet.

7. *The Four Seasons of Love*, by Rowlandson (1814). This is a typically satirical view of how romance could end in acrimony and separation.

8. *The Arrival of Country Relations*, by Alexander Carse (*c*. 1812),
illustrates the contrast between a fashionable urban family and
their rural cousins. Among other attractions, coming to town
offered the chance to make new friends and acquaintances
which might blossom into courtship and marriage.

9. John Thomas Stanley
(1766–1850), Lord Stanley
of Alderley, in later life.

10. Maria Josepha Stanley
(1771–1863), née
Holroyd, in later life.

11. William Henry Lyttelton,
Lord Lyttelton (1782–1837).

12. Sarah, Lady Lyttelton (1787–
1870), née Lady Sarah Spencer.

13. Harriet Arbuthnot
(1793–1834), née Fane.

14. Charles Arbuthnot
(1767–1850).

15. Henry William Paget,
Lord Paget (1768–1854),
later Earl of Uxbridge and
Marquess of Anglesey.

16. Caroline, Lady Paget
(1774–1835), née Lady Caroline
Villiers, later Duchess of Argyll.

17. Thomas Clover and his bride, Maria Cook, painted on their wedding day in 1804 by the groom's brother, Joseph Clover, in the porch of Thwaite Church – an unusual precursor of the modern wedding photograph. Joseph Clover was a successful artist who never married after his fiancée died.

year or two. In *Northanger Abbey* we are told that Catherine Morland was educated at home: 'Writing and accounts she was taught by her father; French by her mother: her proficiency in either was not remarkable, and she shirked her lessons in both whenever she could . . . .' Later in the novel she recognises that the task of teaching the children was no sine-cure, telling a sceptical Henry Tilney, 'You think me foolish to call instruction a torment, but if you had been as much used as myself to hear poor little children first learning their letters and then learning to spell, if you had ever seen how stupid they can be a whole morning together, and how tired my poor mother is at the end of it, as I am in the habit of seeing almost every day of my life at home, you would allow that to *torment* and to *instruct* might sometimes be used as synonimous [*sic*] words.' Maria Stanley might have agreed, telling her aunt that 'Rianette [her eldest child] and I get on tolerably well, considering my want of patience and her want of application in b-a ba, and a-b ab. I have got a delightful new-invented spelling book, and expect a new-invented spelling box, which makes these studies much easier than before.' Nonetheless, 'I am not equal to having them all day with me, nor have I patience to teach. I speak very feelingly just now, for Lucy has been plaguing me with questions without end, and now I have exchanged her for Rianette, and have not mended myself one bit.' And, a few years later, 'Upon my word, six children under six years would have tired Job's patience sufficiently, without Devil or wife to help . . . .'[28]

Like most parents who could afford it, the Stanleys eased the burden of teaching by employing a governess, and Maria acknowledged the difference this made in a later letter to her aunt: 'till my governess came, my days were quite employed, and I was not disposed to write in the short happy period after the children retired to rest. Since she came I have given a good deal of attention to my dear little Lou-Dolly, who is really the cleverest, most engaging child I ever saw, and of whose company I had less than I wished, because her sisters required attention still more.' The decision whether or not to send children to school was often complicated by the costs involved. While some schools, especially for girls and younger boys, charged relatively low fees, the traditional public schools for boys were expensive, charging something in the order of £200 per pupil a year, at a time when £500 was a perfectly respectable income for a man in one of the gentlemanly professions. Governesses, of course, were very much cheaper, and even a good private tutor might be engaged for a similar sum, although there was the additional cost and inconvenience of having him in residence. Education was a serious expense for a large family, especially one with many boys.[29]

Many parents became less loving towards their children as they grew up, but others remained closely bonded. When the Palmerstons left their sixteen-year-old son in Edinburgh for a year's study with Dugald Stewart, Lady Palmerston wrote that 'The pain I felt at bidding him adieu made me so wretched that I had no spirits to enjoy a very fine drive, for I wept the whole way. It is impossible to leave so amiable a being without regret, and when that being is one of the most affectionate sons, the pain must be acute . . . .' And when Spencer Madan, then a man in his early twenties, left to take up a position as tutor to the family of the Duke of Richmond, his father wrote to him, 'My *own* loss of you is irreparable when I think of you in the light of a *Son so uniformly affectionate & dutiful*; but this is a subject which I _cannot attempt_, so I will only beg you to believe that I love & esteem you beyond all expression!' Three months later Dr Madan was even more explicit: 'I am deeply sensible of my *rare* degree of happiness in having two such Sons. In the letters which I receive from various correspondents this is the constant theme of congratulation & of envy; & it is indeed _no common case_! Your old Daddy, with inexpressible pride, thanks you Both most cordially with overflowing eyes, & will bless you with his latest breath! But my very pen falters (as my voice would do) in touching these sources of parental tenderness.'[30]

As this suggests, children could give their parents a great deal of continuing pleasure, and while Dr Madan's delight in his adult children was expressed with unusual force, a happy relationship with adult children was not uncommon. The effect of children on their parents' marriage was more uncertain. As we have seen, many childless couples seem to have been unusually happy; but equally children acted as a bond uniting some couples: Betsey Fremantle wrote to her husband: 'I must say something of my brats, the inexhaustible Subject & certainly the pleasantest to us.' Nonetheless there were other marriages in which the husband, or, more rarely the wife, felt usurped by the children in the affection of their spouse. Lord William Russell was devoted to his wife and children, and praised his wife's care of their children lavishly, but it is clear that he felt neglected by comparison, and with some reason. There was no universal agreement whether the role of wife or mother was more important: some women struggled to balance their obligations to husbands and children, while others played one competing demand off against the other in order to gain some freedom of manoeuvre. In theory the same was true of men – was the role of father or husband more important? – but conflict between the two roles was much less likely to arise, and in any case men were less constrained in their choices. Even so, the overriding impression is of parents who loved their children and conscientiously endeavoured to look after them as well as they could, while balancing the children's needs against other demands, including the husband's career, financial necessity, obligations to wider family and local society, their own personal wishes and the claims of their spouse. It was not always possible, let alone easy, to strike a happy balance.[31]

CHAPTER FOURTEEN

UNHAPPY MARRIAGES

THE GREAT MAJORITY OF people got married with high hopes of happiness. Even those like Charlotte Lucas or Maria Bertram who married for position or other worldly motives without any great love for their spouse, felt that they were making a good bargain and anticipated that its pleasures would outweigh the less attractive aspects of married life. But most people seem to have been genuinely enthusiastic about their partner, believing that they had found someone who would make them happy, and with whom they would have a good life at the centre of a new family. And yet they were often mistaken, and many marriages – it is impossible to say how many – ultimately proved disappointing and unhappy. This unhappiness might begin almost at once or come on slowly as delight subsided into contentment and then apathy and finally weariness. It might be relatively mild: impatience with the spouse's foibles and pervasive discontent; or it might escalate into violence, infidelity, separation and even divorce (subjects which will be explored in the next chapter). Couples might quarrel vehemently, treat each other with studied coldness or rub along with steady level of friction which both were able to take in their stride. Occasionally one spouse might be completely unaware of the unhappiness of the other, but this was unusual, for discontent was as infectious as love in making or marring a marriage. More often, feelings were far from simple, with affection and irritation mixed confusingly together, while a backlog of accumulated grievances battled with a sense of duty, the memory of better times and a commitment to making the marriage work even at the sacrifice of many personal preferences.

Emily Eden describes how a marriage could descend into unhappiness almost from the outset in her novel *The Semi-Attached Couple*, which, although it was not published until 1860, was written in 1829, and if anything reflected the outlook of a slightly earlier period. Lord Teviot is rich, fashionable and rather spoilt. He falls in love with the young and inexperienced Helen Beaufort, who accepts his proposal to the universal satisfaction of her family and friends. However, as the wedding approaches she has doubts, disliking his temper and feeling that she does not love him as much as her sisters love their husbands. His ardour frightens her, and her comparative coolness offends him: he reproaches her, and she is intimidated and further alienated. She attempts to confide in one of her sisters, but the sister dismisses her fears as natural nerves and does not take them seriously. Helen even considers breaking off the engagement, but cannot summon the resolution to do so when the wedding is so close and everyone she trusts is enthusiastic about the marriage. And so she marries Lord Teviot and they spend the honeymoon at the grandest of his houses, but they are ill at ease with each other. He craves more signs of affection, but his demands make her more uncomfortable, and they begin to behave badly to each other. As he grows irritable, she withdraws from him, refusing to contradict him on anything, and he is intelligent enough to notice this and to be further offended by it: that his wife should be so absurd as to be afraid of him! The arrival of guests – fashionable friends of his, some of whom are bent on mischief – increases their growing alienation, as does Helen's all too obvious wish to spend time with her family rather than with her husband. Of course, in the end – for it is a novel – everything is happily resolved and they learn to understand and love one another as equals, but it is the depiction of the speed with which disillusionment might set in that stays with the reader.[1]

A similar sequence of events, without the happy ending, marked the marriage of the heiress Mary Bowes to John Lyon, 9th Earl of Strathmore, in 1767. Mary had accepted his proposal against her mother's advice, but before the prolonged negotiations over their marriage settlement had been completed she regretted her decision. 'I found', she later wrote, 'our tempers, dispositions and turns differed. I wished to retract (and would [have] if I durst have consulted with my mother), but my pride, and sometimes my weakness, would not let me.' She was married at St George's, Hanover Square, on 27 February, her eighteenth birthday, and over the next nine years the Strathmores had five children, two boys and three girls. They were both extravagant and ran up considerable debts, while his family took a marked and persistent dislike to her. He was out of sympathy with her intellectual interests, making her give up her friendship with her blue-stocking friends, whom he thought ridiculous, although she continued to pursue her botanical studies. For her part, she engaged in a number of flirtations which probably did not extend to infidelity, at least until the last months of their marriage. They lived apart for much of the time, and she did not accompany him when he went to Bath and Bristol seeking medical treatment, for he was ill with consumption. Finally he sailed for Lisbon without her, in a forlorn hope of a cure in late February 1776, but died at sea. Before he died he wrote a letter of farewell in which, as well as pointing out some of her faults (an unreasonable partiality for her daughters and dislike of her sons; an unrestrained weakness for making cruel but funny remarks, regardless of the pain they inflicted), he very sensibly advised her to put her estates into trust in order to protect herself from fortune hunters and to lessen the attention she needed to devote to their management. All of which suggests rather more sense and goodwill than might have been expected, although Lady Strathmore's doubts before the wedding were clearly well founded: whatever their virtues and vices the Strathmores were unsuited and their marriage was destined to be unhappy.[2]

But if an unhappy outcome sometimes appeared inevitable, other marriages, that began in a great glow of romantic excitement and passion, might also end in tears. Consider the case of Lady Louisa Paget who, at the age of twenty-one fell head over heels in love with James Erskine, a good-looking soldier, five years her senior. Unfortunately he was a younger son, with little fortune and living mainly on his pay. Lady Louisa's parents disapproved of the match and kept her in close confinement, but the young couple found ways to communicate – messages smuggled to and fro by sympathetic servants, and the occasional, brief meeting as if by chance. Finally, after three years of persistence, the

Pagets were persuaded to relent, with pressure coming among others from the Royal Family (Lady Louisa had been a lady-in-waiting to Queen Charlotte), who obtained a pension of £509 for Lady Louisa, and appointed James as aide-de-camp to the King. Lady Louisa's father, Lord Uxbridge, settled a handsome sum on his daughter and the couple were married on 5 March 1801. After this excitement, married life may have proved an anti-climax, but for a few years they appear to have been a fairly happy couple, although the absence of children and growing debts may have contributed to creeping disillusionment. Few of the Pagets found marriage easy, and rumours eventually reached even the Royal Family that Lady Louisa was having an affair with her brother-in-law General Wemyss. Erskine later wrote, 'I knew not how to act. I had seen the thing long myself . . . and knowing how delicate the knot is which really binds the married state, I delayed speaking perhaps too long, unwilling to show any want of confidence . . . I saw with undescribable pain that she did not feel it as I did, but her natural irritation of disposition was augmented to a degree that, day after day, I left the house to seek quiet out of doors . . . .' Intimidated by his wife, unwilling to force a confrontation that could only make matters worse, Erskine chose to turn a blind eye, and the marriage limped on unhappily.[3]

Unhappiness did not always, or even usually, take such extreme forms: it was often a matter of couples irritating each other, unconsciously flicking at their spouse's sore spots without any sense of behaving badly. Eugenia Wynne preserved a trivial incident that shed light on the state of her parents' marriage:

In the evening Mamma had a little argument with Jaegle [the tutor and family companion] on account of the Religion. Papa interfered and turned it in a manner which Mamma took as serious and offending and it finished by tears and distress on her side, a thing which made me reflect with sorrow on the natural consequences of a great sensibility when it is too much indulged. Mamma is of a temper to take everything of the bad side, therefore what to others would be a jest to which a smile alone would answer, is for her an offence which grieves her excessively and prompts her to weep. Papa is of a disposition quite contrary to hers and never scruples to jest in a manner which he knows must offend her. Thus two opposite characters have been matched together in a manner to make one another perpetually unhappy. Papa has too much egotism and carelessness to suffer himself to be made so, but neither is he happy, and Mamma is the sufferer for both.

However, on the following day, Eugenia was less perceptive and more inclined to blame her mother than her father for their unhappiness: 'Mamma pouts, Papa tries to make it up. I think it really wrong of her to attach so much consequence to a trifle.'[4]

Many of the marriages depicted in Jane Austen's novels are marked by similar tensions, leading to an undercurrent of unhappiness: Dr Grant in *Mansfield Park* was a self-indulgent bon vivant who 'will not stir a finger for the convenience of any one, and who, moreover, if the cook makes a blunder, is out of humour with his excellent wife'. John Knightley in *Emma* was 'not an ill-tempered man, not so often unreasonably cross as to deserve such a reproach; but his temper was not his great perfection; and, indeed, with such a worshipping wife, it was hardly possible that any natural defects in it should not be increased'. And Thomas Palmer in *Sense and Sensibility* affected even more ill-nature than he really possessed in the hope of gaining distinction, although his 'very silly' wife simply laughed at his remarks, dismissing them as 'droll' and, by refusing to be disconcerted, possibly kept the reality as well as the appearance of contentment in her marriage. Of course, it was not only husbands who were at fault, and the unhappiness of the Bennet's marriage is one of the shadows that adds depth to *Pride and Prejudice*.[5]

It was widely accepted at the time that upper-class men were, in general, rather less civilised and well behaved than comparable women, and that a feminine touch was needed to add elegance and decorum to a gathering. When men congregated by themselves, the result might be expected to be rowdy and often drunken, with coarse jokes and a level of behaviour that would not be acceptable in mixed society. This (often well-founded) prejudice gave women a valuable weapon in domestic disputes, and many a husband was rebuked for his boorish and even vulgar manners. However, it was a double-edged sword, for this expectation also permitted men – even men like John Knightley and Dr Grant

– to behave badly to their wives without transgressing the code of acceptable behaviour or damaging their self-respect. The range of misbehaviour that wives were expected to tolerate was much broader than that which husbands should endure, and society encouraged women to be long-suffering, while it was quick to deride a 'hen-pecked' husband who failed to exert his 'proper' authority.[6]

Some men alienated their wives simply through neglect. Eliza Chute complained that her husband expected her to dance attendance on him whenever he was present, but had no hesitation in absenting himself whenever he wished. '[H]e seems to think it strange that I should absent myself from him for four & twenty hours when he is at home, tho' it appears in the natural order of things that he should quit me for business or pleasure; such is the difference between husbands & wives. The latter are sort of tame animals, whom the men always expect to find at home ready to receive them: the former are lords of the creation free to go where they please.' So the double standard did not pass unnoticed, nor without arousing resentment, although many women probably felt that it was utopian folly to imagine that it might be generally abolished, however much they hoped for a more equal relationship within their own marriage. And some men were well aware of the danger of pushing their luck: as Admiral Sir William Young remarked to a fellow admiral, 'Never forget that an inattentive husband has no case of complaint against a negligent wife.'[7]

Other husbands offended their wives by rudeness and presumption. Alexander Fordyce was a successful banker who, at the age of forty, married Lady Margaret Lindsay, when she was barely seventeen. When Margaret's sister Anne visited them in London the following year she found that the young bride was far from happy, and that Fordyce was 'bizarre when in good humour, indelicate when in spirits, and brutal when out of sorts'. He treated Margaret with a mixture of petty unkindness, ill-judged generosity and disdain that could not help but make her miserable, although she was resolved to endure it quietly. Margaret's mother, Lady Balcarres, disliked her son-in-law's behaviour, but did not object as he was giving her considerable assistance in starting her sons in their careers. Curiously, Alexander's brother, James Fordyce, thought himself qualified to advise young women on their conduct in a series of published, and surprisingly popular, sermons, rather than noticing and reforming his brother's conduct.[8]

Other husbands, such as Lord Boringdon, were controlling. Lady Bessborough commented, 'he directs not only her visits, but the hours she is to pay them. I imagine that he gives out his orders like a General, and that he points out her *route* and where her stations are to be. Attention! – turn to the Right; Halt at Ly. Bessboro's at 3, D. House at 4, &c'. This may be no more than a *jeu d'esprit* – Lady Bessborough's letters are playful and entertaining but not always intended to be read literally – but the Boringdon marriage was unhappy from very early on, and only a few months after the wedding Mrs Calvert reported that 'Lord and Lady Boringdon are going to part – that she says he is so cross she can't live with him. They are only married a few months; what a pity it is that people don't consider more than they do their tempers before they marry!' In fact the marriage lasted a few more years until Lady Boringdon ran away with Arthur Paget and, remarkably (for he was a confirmed womaniser as well as being a Paget), had a much happier second marriage.[9]

Margaret, Lady Stanley – Maria Stanley's mother-in-law – spent twenty years in an unhappy marriage to an inconsiderate husband whose tastes were very different to her own, before she finally parted from him. Explaining her decision to her mother she wrote that she had done everything she could to please him: 'My every Taste and Inclination I sacrificed to his, contending no point however desirable to me and conforming as well as I could in all things (& with chearfulness too) to his humour, different as it was to my own,' but he was never satisfied. He 'never consulted me on any concern respecting either my family, my children or my satisfaction' and 'always appear[ed] gloomy reserved dissatisfied & full of Duplicity'. She craved more company and social life, but he would not hear of it: 'you well know the very inhospitable manner of our house, no friend, no social Guest frequented it, we lived for ourselves and for ourselves alone, and though our Fortune was considerable, we live obscurely, cheerlessly, unbefriended and unbefriending'. Recently he had been a little more conciliatory, but it was far too little and too late: 'with Health declined, my spirits broken & my mind disgusted by continual disregards it matter'd to me not', and she resolved to make a break, leaving Sir John and retreating to Lisbon for a time, before ultimately settling in north Wales.[10]

The expectation that wives would tolerate bad behaviour was taught by example as well as by precept. The young Frances Winckley observed that her half-brother, Sir Thomas Hesketh, with whom she lived for a time, behaved very badly to his 'sweet, unselfish' wife, flirting terribly with other women in front of her. Lady Hesketh forgave him everything and kept on loving him, in the hope of 'bringing her husband round to a proper sense of his duties, and obligations towards her'. Frances was deeply impressed by her conduct and drew upon it in the difficult early years of her marriage to Sir John Shelley. And women should not only endure their husband's misconduct, they should, ideally at least, do so without complaint, although this injunction applied to husbands as well. It was regarded as both bad form and unwise to discuss, or criticise, your spouse with anyone else: in *The Semi-Attached Couple*, Helen prudently rebuffs the false overtures of Lady Portmore, citing advice to this effect from her mother, but Lord Teviot is less restrained and suffers from it, as Lady Portmore's 'sympathy' helps poison his mind against Helen; he is repelled and humiliated at the same time, which only adds to his discontent. Of course, it was unrealistic to expect that aggrieved spouses would never complain or confide in anyone, and it is likely that many wives told their lady's maid rather more than was discreet, and that the maids often benefited indirectly from their mistress's confidence.[11]

Some men appear to have enjoyed taunting and humiliating their wives in front of company. Andrew Robinson Stoney married an heiress, Hannah Newton, and soon broke her heart. 'He knew secret ways of provoking her before company and then, if she looked displeased, or said anything tart, he appealed to the company.' Similarly, Sir John Sebright's behaviour to his wife made Frances Calvert furious, 'Oh, how I should hate to be married to Sir John!! He is, I think, the most disagreeable husband I ever saw. He was very cross to her [Lady Sebright] this morning when she cried.' In both these cases, this behaviour was surpassed by the husband's misconduct in private: Stoney appears to have been violent, while Sir John seduced (or possibly raped) the maids and governesses employed in the house.[12]

The behaviour for which wives were customarily blamed seldom reached comparable levels. Nagging, extravagance, ill-humour and coldness were faults most commonly attributed to wives, not least by husbands who were not themselves blameless. But there is no doubt that some wives did make their husband's lives miserable. A simple example is provided by Mr Bannister, a clergyman who married a woman who was both older and richer than himself. Unfortunately Mrs Bannister 'was of an unsocial disposition', disliked his old friends and acquaintance and was 'such a devotee of cleanliness that Mr. B. could scarcely bring an individual into the house, lest footmarks should be made'. One day he returned home to find his wife out and took advantage of the occasion to invite in some of his church singers and musicians and an impromptu concert was under way when Mrs Bannister returned and promptly expelled the guests from the house: the experiment was not repeated.[13]

Even when a marriage appeared to be settled into a state of mutual contentment, there was no guarantee that this would last. William and Clara Middleton of Stockeld Park, Yorkshire, appeared well suited and prosperous. Accounts agree that Clara was an affectionate, considerate and faithful wife and a devoted mother, who also played a beneficent role in the local community. William was a loving and indulgent husband – rather too much so in the view of their butler, who told his fellow servants that William gave in to his wife all the time and 'No man on earth would give their wife so much their own way as he did.' The Middletons did not often leave home and had few close friends, but saw plenty of company – their estate was on the Great North Road and many acquaintances stayed with them when travelling. Clara in particular was bright and sociable, and the house had a reputation for warm hospitality. They had eight children in twelve years, although three of them died young. And then, after ten years of apparent happiness, Clara fell passionately in love with a handsome young groom who had recently joined the staff, and the marriage dissolved amidst scandal and acrimony. Was their marriage actually much less happy than it appeared, or was Clara's infatuation a random stroke of malevolent fortune, built on little more than *ennui* at the even pace of married life? We simply don't know, although if it was the husband who had taken a mistress after ten years of marriage, society would have been much less surprised or outraged and the marriage would probably have survived, even if not happily.[14]

In many unhappy marriages bad behaviour on one side led to bad behaviour on the other, until it was profitless to enquire who was more to blame. The Duchess of Richmond is famous for the ball she gave on the eve of the Waterloo campaign, but at the time she was well known for being extremely proud, touchy, with a formidable temper and some inclination for mischievous gossip: altogether a thoroughly uncomfortable woman. The Duke, on the other hand, had been a dashing sportsman in his youth, amusing and good company. However, as the years passed he also became notorious for drinking far too heavily (which given the standards of the time was no mean feat) and for uninhibited flirting – even inviting pretty shop girls to vice-regal balls when he was Lord Lieutenant of Ireland, outraging local society: altogether a thoroughly uncomfortable husband. Together their extravagance and gambling reduced them to such financial straits that they could not afford to live in England or to properly provide for their children, which cannot have made their marriage any happier, although no open breach occurred, and possibly neither ever contemplated the possibility of leaving the other.[15]

Lord Malmesbury was Britain's leading diplomat in the 1790s, charged with several abortive rounds of peace negotiations with revolutionary France; however, his skills were not sufficient to bring peace to his own marriage. Long absences from home when serving abroad cannot have helped, but neither of the Malmesburys behaved well, and their personalities were not compatible. Harriet Malmesbury was, apparently, known as the 'kettle-drum' due to her loud voice and 'unceasing *clack*'. According to an unfriendly observer, 'She is . . . used to domineer through life [and] delivers opinions without appeal, in the voice of a pea-hen.' Her husband was deaf (an unfortunate failing in a diplomat) and evidently unfaithful to her, and she responded with infidelities of her own. It seems that he had also struck her on more than one occasion, and for a time relations between them had bordered on hatred, although eventually they had cooled to a 'rooted, incurable alienation'; but they did not separate, probably in order to protect their daughters from scandal, although they may also have calculated that they could live largely separate lives together more economically under the same roof than if they had to maintain two different establishments.[16]

A sense of the day-to-day realities of living in such an unhappy marriage comes from a succession of entries in Lord William Russell's diary for July and August 1830, when he and his family were in Genoa and then Geneva:

26 July 1830 'I shall fail. Have not animal spirits.'
27 July 1830 'Worse & worse. sad scene A [Bessy, his wife] says I have a bad heart, no principles, selfish, malignant, torpid & hates me. It's impossible, I give up, must flee. Spirits not equal to her dreadful temper. All resolutions useless. Hopes I may be absent with my regiment often & long. Sad, sad, sad. God help me, God help me.'
29 July 1830 'Repetition of yesterday very sad. Try taming shrew.'
30 July 1830 'Old scene. mutual reproaches.'
1 August 1830 'Reconciliation'.
2 August 1830 'Terrible scene about 5 – sad, sad, sad, I have not spirits for it.'
4 August 1830 [family sets off for Geneva]
8 August 1830 'Travelled thro' the beautiful valley of Morienne on the banks of the rushing roaring Isère – discoursing agreably [sic] with my dear wife, & playing with my dear boys. This is a state of existence that makes one's heart overflow with gratitude to God, it is the ne plus ultra of moral & physical happiness. Arrived at Geneva at the Campagne Baumgarten at St Jean at 8 p.m.'[17]

As this suggests, the accumulation of unhappiness in a marriage often progressed in an irregular fashion, now advancing, now retreating as conflicting emotions and interests battled inside both the husband and wife. In this case Lord William appears to have always been much more in love with his wife than she was with him, to have admired her greatly and to have regarded her as an exemplary mother of their children. However, he also felt slighted and neglected (with reason) and at times behaved badly; on one occasion admitting to 'brutality' in a context which suggests that he enforced his conjugal rights, or, in plain language, that he raped her. They spent considerable periods living apart, but never completely separated, although the bond between them was greatly loosened when he began a very public, and lasting, affair in 1835.[18]

James Boswell was intensely happy in the first couple of years of his marriage, abandoning many of the habits of his bachelor life, such as whoring, drinking to excess and even writing his journal, as he found an inner peace that he had seldom known. Old grievances about his father's second marriage, about living in Scotland and about his life as an advocate faded into insignificance, although they did not totally disappear. The death of their first child soon after its birth affected both James and Margaret greatly, and Margaret's recovery from her confinement was slow, but the glow of contentment remained in the background. In August 1771, an expedition into the border country and northern England delighted Margaret and strengthened their sense of companionship. A miscarriage darkened the mood for a time, and Boswell began to hanker for his literary and artistic friends in London. Margaret did not fully recover from the miscarriage – her health in the winter of 1771–2 was not good – but Boswell nonetheless planned a solo expedition to London for the beginning of spring. He felt guilty at leaving her, but went anyway, excited at the thought of returning to the sophisticated society he knew in London. In his journal he acknowledged that the sexual temptations of the metropolis would pose a challenge, but felt that the 'present firmness and cheerfulness of [his] mind' would enable him to resist them. Nonetheless marriage to a woman he truly loved had not made him impervious to the sight of a pretty young woman. When he encountered the attractive daughter of a clergyman on the journey south he noted that 'I cannot help being instantaneously affected by the sight of beauty . . . a glance from a fine eye can yet affect my assurance'; and in London he watched the prostitutes with avidity and even conversed with them, although he managed to restrain himself from acting on his desires. At the same time he wrote constantly to Margaret – dozens of letters over seven weeks – which he declared was 'a great happiness to me', although the news he received from home should have given him concern: Margaret was lonely and unhappy without him. He greatly enjoyed himself in London, more even than on his previous visits, and felt that he had the best of both worlds.[19]

That perhaps was the problem, for after he returned to Edinburgh – to a loving welcome from Margaret – Boswell increasingly sought to have his cake and eat it: to rely utterly on Margaret's love, but at the same time indulge himself, first with card playing, even though he knew she disliked it; then with drinking too much; and finally by having sex with prostitutes in Edinburgh. He confessed it all to Margaret who reacted with a mixture of love, practicality and forgiveness, insisting that his surgeon give him a clear bill of health before she would sleep with him, but refusing to berate him. Boswell fully appreciated her goodness, but his resolutions to do better in the future did not last long. Meanwhile Margaret was again pregnant and Boswell hankering for another trip to London. On 15 March 1773, Margaret gave birth to a healthy daughter and two weeks later, before she had properly recovered, he set out for London.

> I had still the awful thought that I might never return to Scotland and meet my dearest wife. Either of us might die during our separation. This thought, when it presses strongly upon the mind, is terrible. It is enough to make one never separate from a valuable spouse . . . When the fly had rumbled me a mile or two, rational and manly sensations took the place of tender and timid feebleness. I considered that I had left my wife and little daughter well. That I was going to London, whither so many Members of Parliament, lawyers, merchants, and others go and return in safety to their families. I saw nothing dangerous, nothing melancholy. I had taken leave of my wife last night, which had affected my spirits a good deal. She is of an anxious temper at all times; but being not yet fully recovered from child-birth, she was more anxious than usual.[20]

By the time he reached London any pangs of guilt had been pushed to the back of his mind and he actually congratulated himself on feeling less anxious for her than he had the previous year. And so the happiness and contentment in the marriage slowly drained away as Boswell continued to indulge himself at Margaret's expense. His excessive drinking, his melancholia and his whoring all became more pronounced, his temper deteriorated and old grievances about his father returned to the forefront of his mind. Even Margaret's patience wore thin, but he responded to reproaches with anger, cursing her and on one occasion throwing a candlestick in her direction, while on another he began smashing furniture, breaking a chair and a walking cane and throwing them into the fire. Painful remorse followed, but could not prevent further relapses, and Margaret gradually realised that while his love for her and their children was genuine, he was also bored and discontented with his life, including his marriage to her.[21]

There was a strong current of melancholia in Boswell's nature, as well as a vulnerability to addiction, which certainly contributed to his failures as a husband. Similarly, Lord William Russell complained of a lack of vitality and animal spirits which he blamed, not on his marriage or even his upbringing, but on a condition that he inherited from his mother, who was similarly afflicted, and which today might be labelled depression. In other cases it is plain that physical or mental illness destroyed the happiness of a marriage without either party behaving badly. John Pitt, 2nd Earl of Chatham, son of Pitt the Elder and brother of Pitt the Younger, made a happy, companionable marriage to Mary Townshend, daughter of Lord Sydney, another important political figure. Less than a year after the wedding Mary collapsed with severe rheumatic fever and was ill for more than twelve months, with her life in danger for some time. She experienced agonising pain in her hip and knee and was bedridden for eight months, and even in her recovery had to use an early form of a wheelchair. Eventually the symptoms disappeared and for the next twenty years she took an active part at court and in London society, supporting her husband's political career, although her only pregnancy ended in a miscarriage. Then, in 1806, she fell seriously ill again, with a 'delirious Fever', and remained 'in bed & delirious' for weeks. Her life did not appear to be in danger, but the doctors worried that her sanity might be at risk. Slowly she recovered but her mental state was extremely fragile. With the help of opiates and a strong sense of duty she accompanied her husband to social functions, but these imposed a strain which led to violence and '*horrid* language' in private which distressed everyone, Mary most of all. She told her sister that 'My cold is better, but I am *shocking horrible* in mind & Spirits &c. . . . Tell me I may be suddenly different.' She talked openly of suicide and may have made an attempt in October 1807. Her husband was unsure how to respond, although he remained kind and caring. Privately he admitted to her brother the toll it was taking: 'I am myself pretty well, but ye misery I have suffered the last fortnight or three weeks, has required all the fortitude I have left, to be able to bear up against.' The illness lasted three-and-a-half years, and while her recovery seemed like a miracle, Chatham feared a relapse and took care to conceal bad news from Mary and make 'everything appear to the best'.[22]

Lady Chatham remained relatively well for almost nine years, but in the spring of 1818 she suffered 'a severe bilious attack, attended with a good deal of fever' which left her 'uncomfortably low and nervous'. She never fully recovered. Chatham took good care of her and ensured that she was treated at home with the respect that she deserved, and never as an invalid, a problem or a 'poor Creature'; but the pressure and distress took its toll on his health, and one friend doubted how 'much longer [he could] support such a score of suffering'. Her consciousness of being a burden added a further layer of misery to them both, and again there was self-harm and the fear of an attempt at suicide. In the early months of 1821 her condition appeared to be improving slowly and in May she told her husband that she felt better than she had for several years. On the evening of 21 May she greeted an old friend of Chatham's who had come to dine, but did not join them, drinking a glass of barley water and brandy with laudanum and retired to bed. Her maid remained with her as she drifted to sleep and took some time to realise that she had stopped breathing. She was only fifty-eight and had probably died due to an inadvertent overdose of laudanum, although we cannot be sure. Chatham was grief-stricken, feeling bereft at the loss of someone he had known intimately for most of his life and who had helped shape it for almost forty years. Illness had made both husband and wife unhappy, despite their love for each other.[23]

Unhappy marriages took many forms and the unhappiness arose from a multitude of causes, although ill-matched personalities, habits and interests, and a lack of consideration and self-indulgence (most frequently on the part of the husband) were probably the most common. Whatever the cause, the unhappiness usually affected both spouses, although often not equally. Men were more easily able to pursue their interests away from home, to take a mistress and to lord it over their wives, and for some this was enough to give them a degree of happiness, even while their wife was miserable. It was much harder for women to enjoy themselves if their husband was unhappy, except through the excitement of an affair; while men who found living with their wife a trial usually ensured that their discontent was shared. All marriages contained some unhappiness, of course, arising from external events, from disagreements over important decisions, from the behaviour and remarks of the other spouse and even from self-sabotage: with some couples this unhappiness led to quarrels, with others withdrawal or sulking, but in a fundamentally happy marriage the couple overcame their differences and were reconciled. In less fortunate marriages the relationship gradually soured and the reconciliations became shallower and more transitory as the reservoir of affection and goodwill that existed at the outset slowly drained away. In other cases a single inci-dent, not always of great import, would snap bonds that were, perhaps unconsciously, already under strain. Once this stage was reached it was very difficult for the marriage to recover – too much trust had been lost and too much hurt suffered. Some couples would give up, others keep struggling to live together, but it was rare for the old harmony and mutual affection to be revived. Emily Eden was well aware of this problem and carefully avoided it in *The Semi-Attached Couple*. Relations between Lord and Lady Teviot were very unhappy, but they had not had time to settle into entrenched antipathy, so that the happy ending the novel inevitably reached was psychologically plausible, even if the plot twists that produce it are far-fetched. Unfortunately real couples did not have a benign author manipulating their lives to ensure that everything would come right in the end.

CHAPTER FIFTEEN

DOMESTIC VIOLENCE, ADULTERY, DIVORCE AND SEPARATION

IN THE EIGHTEENTH AND early nineteenth centuries a husband had the legal right to use violence against his wife in order to 'correct' her – perhaps the starkest manifestation of the way the law enshrined notions of male superiority. However, social attitudes were changing and such violence was becoming less acceptable, while the law was following suit, one step behind, with even conservative judges moving to restrict the amount of violence that was regarded as permissible and, more surprisingly, to accept the threat – not the reality – of violence as sufficient justification for a separation. It seems likely, although it cannot be proved, that these changes in attitude resulted in a reduction of the actual violence inflicted by husbands on their wives in this period, although many cases remained. There was already a perception that violence within a marriage was peculiarly associated with the lower classes of society: this was plainly unfounded – there were abusive husbands from all social strata – although the idea that such behaviour showed a lack of self-control unsuited to a gentleman may have helped make it less respectable.[1]

In most cases violence seems to have entered a marriage after some years, often accompanied by heavy drinking and a growing sense of disillusionment and boredom, with the wife or with life in general. However, a few husbands were abusive and violent from the outset. The adventurer Andrew Stoney Bowes, who married the widowed Countess of

Strathmore for her money, made his intentions plain almost immediately, issuing orders to the servants that any letter arriving addressed to his wife should first be taken to him. When Lady Strathmore called for a carriage to visit her greenhouses he refused to let her go and told her that she must never again order a carriage without his permission. When she spoke French to a guest at their first dinner party he sent her a message by a servant ordering her to speak English; and he refused to let her mother visit his wife and declared that he would never leave them alone together 'even for five minutes'. All this took place in the first weeks of marriage. The Reverend Samuel Markham later described Bowes as a man of 'a very savage and tormenting disposition', who 'put himself into the most violent passions upon the most frivolous occasions', while Lady Strathmore behaved towards him in 'a very obedient, dutiful manner, rather servile than otherwise'. Jesse Foot, who knew the family well, described the effect on Lady Strathmore of living with Bowes for a few years: she was 'wonderfully ALTERED and DEJECTED. She was pale and nervous, and her under-jaw constantly moved from side to side. If she said anything, she looked at Bowes first. If she was asked to drink a glass of wine, she took his intelligence before she answered.' Other witnesses gave details of Bowes's brutality: how he gave Lady Strathmore 'many violent blows on her face, head, and other parts of her body; he often kicked her and sometimes pinched her ears nearly through'; he threw a dish of hot potatoes at his wife and then made her eat them, throwing a glass of wine in her face 'to wash the potatoes off'; and he burned her face with a candle and thrust a quill into her tongue. Lady Strathmore endured this behaviour for some eight years before she escaped her tormentor, and even then her troubles were not completely over.[2]

Bowes appears to have sought absolute domination over his wife by his behaviour, or perhaps he just enjoyed cruelty. This seems to have been the norm for such men, but in a few cases the husband's motives were more calculated. John Patterson wanted to force his wife Mary to revoke a trust held in her name so that he could control her money. He threatened, 'I will horse whip you seven times a day if you don't chuse to do as I order and wish you'; and he locked her in her room, beat her with his fists and the furniture, hit her with a whip and at least twice threatened to shoot her with his pistol. An attempt at mediation failed, and he soon resumed his violence.[3]

More typical was John Shackleton who had eloped with a widow, Elizabeth Parker who was sixteen years older than him. The marriage appears to have been reasonably happy at first, at least there is little sign of serious discord in the first seven years, but then relations rapidly worsened, at the same time as Shackleton began drinking very heavily. According to Elizabeth, he was 'very Cross. Never pleas'd at what I say nor do.' He verbally abused her, was extremely rude and began to talk openly of wishing to separate or get away from her. 'He quite hates me, dos [sic] not like me. He behaves most cruelly to me. I had a most shocking night. Cry'd and fretted.' Worse was to come. It began when he threw some water over her, and it escalated from there. Next it was food, then he threw his wife out of her chair and broke a saucer and finally – some years after the abuse began – he began striking her directly, punching her in the face and even using a whip. Nor did this stop when Elizabeth was ill: 'he struck me violently many a time. Took the use out of my Arm, swell'd from my Shoulder to my wrist, the skin knock'd off at my elbow in great Misery and pain he afterwards got up & left my bed, went into another room pritty Matrimonial comforts god Bless and help me.'[4]

John's violence was not Elizabeth's only grievance. He consorted with low company and even invited his tenants, workmen and servants home to drink with him, bringing them into the parlour, which should have been Elizabeth's sanctum where politeness reigned. After the sheep-shearing in 1780, Elizabeth wrote in her diary that 'all drunk in the servants Hall and most Beastly so in the parlour. Great noise & reeking, tho' free from riots'. And, 'Atkinson wo'd come into parlour last night & sit with Mr S: all the shearers with the piper John Riley were most horridly drunk. A quantity they did drink. They all went about four this morning. What a nasty, drunken, beastly house . . . .' This was bad enough, but sharing a bed with him was worse than sharing a parlour: 'The gentleman came home near 12 at noon & Sans Ceremony went snoring to clean bed – where he farted and stunk like a Pole Cat.' 'Most exceedingly Beastly so to a degree never saw him worse – he had made water into the fire.' 'Mr S. was very sick & spew'd Abundantly. Sat in Tom Brindle's House upon the Long Settle before the fire & exposed himself as Publickly as he co'd . . . a very nasty, dirty, stinking creature.' '[H]e shits in bed with drinking so continualy.'[5]

Nelly Weeton reports similar behaviour by her employer Edward Pedder to his wife Mary and by her own husband, Aaron Stock, whom she married in 1814. In almost all these cases, the husband was intent on humiliating the wife and the violence was accompanied by highly sexualised verbal abuse, sometimes combined with accusations of infidelity. Alcohol loosened social restraints and gave the bully free rein, but most of these accounts also suggest that the men felt a degree of shame in their behaviour, sometimes, but not always, accompanied by short-lived remorse and resolutions to behave better in future.[6]

Women were unsure how best to respond to a violent husband. One school of thought was to avoid provoking trouble by absolute submission; the other that the only way of dealing with a bully was to stand up to him. Neither was particularly likely to work, and the dilemma is explored in Nelly Weeton's account of the Pedder's marriage, which is worth quoting at some length:

> What a tyrant he is to her! He seems to think that by lording it over two or three women, he increases his own consequence; and the more we submit, the worse he grows. Mrs. P. has often told me that she has been strongly advised never to let him abuse her without making resistance. I have often advised submission. She says she is told by those who have known him long, that the more a person submits to him, or seems afraid of him, the oftener he exerts the power he finds he has over them; and that when a strong resistance is made, when his violent passion meets with proportionate resentment or is treated with contempt, he in turn will become afraid of those he would oppress. Still, I advise *her* from pursuing such a conduct. I say it is a disgrace to the dignity of the female character for any woman to strive to become master in her husband's house, or to make her husband afraid of her. It is an equal disgrace to a man, so to submit. So she thinks too, provided a medium kind of conduct could be observed. But that is impossible; nothing will do but either the most abject slavery to his will, or the making him submit to hers. *He* knows

no medium between the tyrant and the slave. Acting according to the advice others have given her, Mrs. P. has at different times resented strongly his shamefully abusive language, and when she could no longer endure, has, two or three times, quitted his house and fled to her father's. Though I highly disapprove such conduct, I do not wonder at it. It is scarcely possible for human nature not to be maddened by the cruel language he makes use of. What a miserable house it is when such quarrels take place! And of late they have been very frequent.

I shall almost be a convert to Mrs. P.'s advisers and their opinions – that it will be more for the comfort of the whole household not to submit to all his humours – and yet I am very, very unwilling to either give, or take, such advice. Whenever Mr. P. is in one of his violent passions, I earnestly beg of Mrs. P. not to answer again, but to be quiet and as patient as she can. She has lately frequently endeavoured to do so; but what would please most men, seems to have no effect upon him. She trembles, she weeps, she submits – and he daily grows more and more tyrannical. He appears to be often visited by a strong compunction, though he makes no confession of the kind (he is too mean-spirited) and seems to think a ride in the curricle, or on horseback, will make atonement to his wife for his ill-treatment . . .[7]

Possibly there were marriages in which abuse was stopped either by submission or – rather more plausibly – by confrontation and the threat of retaliation. However, it seems likely that in most cases once a pattern of abuse was established no response from the wife would be effective, for the problem lay squarely with the husband, and having descended so low it was very difficult for him to sustain his fleeting resolutions to reform, especially when the abuse was tied up with excessive drinking.

Faced with a violent husband, wives might be driven to seek assistance from outside the home. They could appeal to the courts, as Nelly Weeton did, having her husband Aaron Stock bound over to the Quarter Sessions, charged with assault and having to enter sureties of his good behaviour in the meantime. (He retaliated by making similar allegations against her.)[8] However, it was more common, and generally more effective, for her to appeal to her family to intervene. This might take place in several escalating steps: first a quiet word of warning to the husband by either his brother- or father-in-law, possibly combined with the wife staying with her relatives or friends for a few days. Next a stronger remonstrance, possibly in conjunction with neighbours or family friends, to express the weight of local opinion. And finally intervention to facilitate a separation and to provide a temporary home for the wife while this was being negotiated. But this only worked if the wife had relatives, or occasionally friends, who were willing and able to intervene in this way. Mrs Pedder had been Mr Pedder's dairymaid, and while her father was a loving, decent man who saw all the difficulties of her position, he lacked the social and financial resources to confront her husband. Nelly Weeton's brother, who was an attorney and well placed to offer protection, instead betrayed her and sided with her husband, for unfathomable reasons of his own. Elizabeth Shackleton had offended her brother by eloping with her husband John, and although he might have responded to an appeal for assistance, she could not bring herself to admit her mistake and seek his assistance. And such interventions were also difficult if the husband was near the apex of society – a landed peer or even a senior diplomat such as Lord Malmesbury – men of this rank and standing would not take kindly to interference in their private affairs, even by their equals. Moreover, many abusive husbands were adept at appearing dotingly fond of their wife in public, which made any intervention much more difficult. Nonetheless, as we will see, many marriages, and not only those involving violence, did end in a formal separation, including Nelly Weeton's, although not Elizabeth Shackleton's or Mary Pedder's.[9]

A word should also be said about the wives who used violence against their husband. Such cases appear to have been extremely rare, but not unknown. It was believed, as we have already seen, that Lord Chancellor Erskine was attacked by his second wife, Sarah Buck, before they separated, although contemporaries might explain this aberrant behaviour by either her mental illness or her lower-class background. Joanne Bailey's study of more than six hundred incidents of domestic violence recorded in newspapers and court documents shows that 92 per cent of them were perpetrated by men, and there is no reason to doubt that that ratio would apply to domestic violence in the upper classes. One slight caveat is that it was even more humiliating for a husband to be the victim of assault than for a wife, and that men were probably even less likely to wish for it to become public knowledge. On the other hand, it was much easier for men to separate themselves from an abusive spouse than it was for women, so they were probably less likely to be the victims of a sustained period of violence. There is also the possibility of domestic violence perpetrated by other members of the household, most obviously by sons towards one or both their parents, but possibly even by servants towards their employers. However, this is speculative and was presumably rare. Overwhelmingly domestic violence was committed by men on their wives.[10]

The unequal treatment of husbands and wives by the law and by society as a whole is also starkly clear in regard to adultery. This was perceived as a far more serious offence when committed by a wife than by a husband: a husband could divorce his wife for committing adultery, whereas this did not constitute grounds for a wife divorcing her husband unless he compounded the offence with cruelty, or his adultery was with a close relative of his own or his wife. This distinction was justified with the argument that an unfaithful wife 'may introduce into the family circle a spurious offspring' – in other words, that the boy inheriting an estate or a title might not really be entitled to it. No less a moralist than Dr Johnson endorsed this argument with his customary confidence:

> Confusion of progeny constitutes the essence of the crime; and therefore a woman who breaks her marriage vows is much more criminal than a man who does it. A man, to be sure, is a criminal in the sight of GOD: but he does not do his wife a very material injury, if he does not insult her; if, for instance, from mere wantonness of appetite, he steals privately to her chambermaid. Sir, a wife ought not greatly to resent this. I would not receive home a daughter who had run away from her husband on that account.

Johnson went on to make matters worse by blaming the wife for her husband's infidelity and by making it her problem to solve: 'A wife should study to reclaim her husband by more attention to please him. Sir, a man will not, once in a hundred instances, leave his wife and go to a harlot, if his wife has not been negligent of pleasing.' Johnson was, of course, very conventional in his views, but it is surprising that his sturdy common sense and dislike of cant did not lead him to discover the obvious weaknesses of this argument. Any married person was likely to resent the infidelity of their spouse, regardless of gender or of the possibility of the infidelity producing progeny, let alone a child who might inherit anything, if, indeed, there was anything to inherit. Nor did he point out just how convenient and self-serving an argument it was, allowing married men as much sexual licence as they wished – with only a token acknowledgement of its immorality – while condemning wives who sought love outside marriage whatever their other circumstances.[11]

Johnson's views were, however, enormously influential – far more so than those of James Fordyce or any other author of works explicitly designed to teach morality and good conduct to young women. Jane Austen referred to him as her 'dear Dr Johnson', and, according to her brother, he was her favourite moral writer in prose as Cowper was in verse. In her own work she laid more emphasis on the immorality of adultery and the harm and misery it caused to those who committed it and their wider family, but she did not protest very vehemently at the double standard of society, simply acknowledging that 'In this world, the penalty is less equal than could be wished.' Still, Austen did not dismiss a husband's adultery as trivial, and in this she was part of a growing shift of attitudes in the second half of the eighteenth century. When Boswell published a second conversation, in which Johnson repeated his views, some ten years later, he commented (in his text, not face-to-face with his hero) that a husband's adultery 'must hurt a delicate attachment in which a mutual constancy is implied', and was keen to defend Johnson from any suggestion that he ever actually encouraged such immorality. Significantly, the first discussion occurred before Boswell's own marriage; by the time of the second he knew for himself the pain his own philandering had caused his wife, and also that Johnson's willingness to blame the wife for her husband's failings was nonsense, at least in his own case. Boswell was weak and self-indulgent, but he was no fool and he knew who to blame for his mistakes.[12]

There was a temptation to try to assess the wrong done by a husband's adultery according to external circumstances: that it was worse for him to have a long-term affair with a social equal than a casual lapse with a prostitute, and to criticise indiscretion as much as infidelity. Yet even here values quickly became muddled: it may have been convenient for a man to 'seduce' his wife's chambermaid, in Johnson's example, but surely most wives would have felt particularly hurt by adultery committed with one of her own servants in her own house? In fact such considerations seem to have been of secondary importance compared to the nature of the relationship between husband and wife, and the wife's expectations and attitudes. Even in the early 1770s Louisa Conolly was clear that she could not treat infidelity lightly, although she was apologetic, not righteous, in discussing this with her sister Sarah:

> I cannot undertake to answer that part of your letter at length, where you condemn me for saying that my heart would be broke by the inconstancy of my husband, because it would take up more time than I have at present at my disposal. But as shortly as I can, I will. In *primis*, I am *sure* that you are perfectly *right*, and recommend the only good and wise conduct, and the only one to bring back a husband, and it is certainly what I should try at. But I fear I could not do it. I own to you that I feel myself in the wrong, for I don't find in myself the least disposition towards making an allowance for my husband being a human creature, and like all other men. I have let myself go too far, expecting him to be all perfection in that *one* particular, and have allowed myself to place my greatest happiness in consequence of it. . . . I feel I am wrong. I know myself to be [of] a most jealous disposition, and my natural violence would add to it, so that I have always dreaded the least spark of it, for fear that it should lead me wrong . . . I don't know how it is, but I can never dwell a moment on the thought of losing my husband's love, without feeling it is the worst misfortune that can happen to me.[13]

Some women, such as Mrs Thrale's daughter, affected to dismiss their husband's adultery as a matter of no consequence, '*it is the Way* She says; & all those who understand *genteel Life* think lightly of such Matters', although one suspects that this was, at least in part, a façade to protect her pride. Some wives of officers in the army and navy who were absent for long periods on active service may have been resigned to their husbands being unfaithful while away, and this may even have extended to the wives of Members of Parliament, barristers and other men who had duties which called them from home for weeks or months at a time. And probably there were some unhappy marriages where the wife did not greatly resent her husband's infidelity if it meant that she no longer had to endure his unwelcome advances with the resulting risk of pregnancy or venereal disease. Yet even in these cases, the initial infidelity was probably a source of considerable pain, a blow to pride and either a threat to marital happiness or a confirmation that the marriage was unsuccessful. Few wives would have been genuinely indifferent to their husband's adultery.[14]

It is impossible to know how many husbands were unfaithful to their wives in this period; or, indeed, how many wives were unfaithful to their husbands, although it is reasonable to assume that infidelity was much rarer amongst wives than husbands. Many men and women had internalised social attitudes that laid much greater stress on female than male fidelity, so that, in general, there were greater psychological inhibitions to be overcome before a wife would commit adultery. Practical considerations added to this: men were out and about more than their wives, often travelling independently and without the attendance of servants; their clothes were less awkward to manage; there were large numbers of prostitutes ready to take their money; and unlike their wives, they did not need to be concerned at the possibility of a pregnancy that could not be explained by marital sex. Nonetheless it is highly likely that a number of married women had affairs without their husbands ever suspecting anything. Such affairs needed considerable discretion and often the assistance of a single, trusted servant (most obviously a lady's maid), or of a companion or friend, and the secret was less likely to be kept the longer the affair lasted. Equally, they were most likely to occur where couples lived relatively separate lives, and also when the wife travelled from home to stay with friends or relatives, or visit a spa or the seaside, and so was away from the scrutiny of her household staff and neighbours. Nor were these affairs always with men, as the diaries of Anne

Lister make clear. It is even possible that some married women may have felt fewer inhibitions having sex with another woman than with a man other than their husband.[15]

There were many other cases in which the husband either suspected or knew that his wife was having an affair, but turned a blind eye, or they quarrelled in private but decided not to take the matter further, maintaining the semblance of a united couple in public. This could take various forms: we have already seen how Sir James Erskine was reluctant to challenge his wife over his suspicions of her conduct, being intimidated by her temper and fearing that a confrontation would simply make things worse (see above, p. 245). Then there was Gerald Wellesley, brother of the Duke of Wellington, who was a clergyman who lived apart from his wife Emily but who would not move to divorce her, despite her flagrant adulteries, because his own conduct could not stand the scrutiny it would receive in the course of the proceedings. Finally, there were the well-publicised couples at the apex of society, such as the Duke and Duchess of Devonshire, or Lord and Lady Melbourne, where the wife's affairs were an open secret, but the couple either tacitly or explicitly agreed that it was in their best interests to avoid divorce proceedings and continued to live under the same roof and maintain their social and political position. Couples further down the social scale made similar compromises, where the husband chose to ignore evidence of his wife's infidelity and they continued to live together, although if the wife's conduct was too blatant she might be snubbed by local society. In many cases these compromises were probably the least bad choice for both husband and wife, but it is unlikely that either was very happy.[16]

Cases where either the husband was unwilling to tolerate his wife's infidelity or the wife was determined to break free of her husband to live with her lover most commonly led to a separation, without open scandal or divorce. The husband and wife would live apart, but they could not remarry. It was only a relatively small number of cases, mostly from the higher reaches of society, that went the extra step, incurring the expense and publicity of a formal divorce and a parliamentary bill enabling the husband and wife to remarry, and in almost all these cases the ground for divorce was the wife's adultery. These cases attracted a great deal of attention at the time and have left abundant detailed records, so that they loom disproportionately large in the historical record and even in the perceptions of contemporaries. They include cases where the wife committed adultery with a servant of the family (Clara Middleton's affair with her groom, John Rose); with the local curate (Emma Cecil and William Sneyd); with a protégé of her husband, the son of his friend and contemporary (Lady Cadogan and William Henry Cooper); with a family connection such as her sister's husband, whether the sister was still alive (Lady Louisa Erskine and General Wemyss), or after her death (Lady Rosebery and Sir Henry Mildmay); with a university friend of her husband (Lady Boringdon and Arthur Paget); or with a social equal and figure in the society in which she habitually moved (Lord Paget and Lady Charlotte Wellesley). Quite often a woman took a younger man for her lover: Lady Cadogan was forty-four when she began her affair with the twenty-eight-year-old William Henry Cooper; Clara Middleton was twenty-nine and John Rose only about twenty; the Duchess of Devonshire was seven years older than Charles Grey; and her sister, Lady Bessborough, eight years older than her lover, Granville Leveson Gower. And sometimes the man was notable for his good looks (John Rose and Granville Leveson Gower).[17]

They might make love in the family home when the husband was away (bedrooms, drawing rooms and dining rooms are all mentioned, with chairs pushed together sometimes), in the open air (Clara Middleton came in with the back of her dress dirty from lying on the grass), in a bathing house or the stables. Sometimes they appear to have had sex in a carriage, while Letitia Powlett and Lord Sackville had their assignation in the White Hart Inn, Winchester, although this did not go well for them, the landlord refusing a handsome bribe to keep quiet and informing her husband. (How many landlords pocketed the money and let the offence go undetected?) It might even occur in the cabin of a ship, as when Captain Pulteney Malcolm was detected sleeping with Selina Shee by her outraged – and very unpleasant – husband as they sailed home from India.[18]

In most of these cases the husband was slow to believe that his wife had been unfaithful. All the Middleton's servants were well aware that their mistress was sleeping with the groom whenever she could and was showering him with gifts, and they were deeply uneasy, disliking the immorality of the thing and fearing that it would lead to the break-up of the household with the loss of their jobs. Despite this fear they made repeated attempts to sound the alarm, usually alerting third parties, such as William Middleton's brother when he was visiting the family, but William refused to believe the accusation, or even to dismiss John Rose, arguing that this would imply that he did not trust his wife. Ironically, the final story that convinced him that the accusations were true was at least in part a fabrication, although the cumulative weight of evidence, and the fact that after they were separated Clara Middleton risked (and lost) everything by not keeping John Rose at a distance until the divorce proceedings had been concluded, leaves very little doubt of the affair. On other occasions the husband was only convinced that his wife was unfaithful when she left him for her lover, and there were no doubt times when the lovers had not actually consummated their relationship at that point. Adultery could take many forms, but for a sense of the impact it made, both on the principals and on those around them, it is better to explore a single case in some detail.[19]

On 25 July 1795, Lady Caroline Villiers, daughter of the 4th Earl of Jersey, married Lord Paget, eldest son and heir of the 3rd Earl of Uxbridge: she was twenty and he was twenty-seven years old, a dashing cavalry officer and friend of the Prince of Wales. According to her later testimony the marriage was very happy for nine years, and by early 1805 they had eight children. In early 1808 a series of musical parties were held at Uxbridge House by Paget's parents and among the guests were Lady Charlotte Wellesley and two of her sisters, the daughters of the Earl of Cadogan, who were old family friends of the Pagets. Lady Charlotte was the wife of Henry Wellesley, who was the younger brother of both the Marquess Wellesley and Sir Arthur Wellesley, the future Duke of Wellington. She had married Henry in 1803 (her sister Emily had already married his brother Gerald), and by the beginning of 1808 they had three children. On the formation of the Portland ministry in the spring of 1807 Henry Wellesley had accepted the position of Secretary to the Treasury, with particular responsibility for managing parliamentary business and maintaining the government's majority. It proved a difficult task for which his previous experience as a diplomat was not particularly helpful, and it seems that it left him preoccupied and probably bad tempered, and that Lady Charlotte felt neglected. Lady Charlotte was advised to take up riding for her health that spring, and Lord Paget provided her with a horse and attended to her, and their friendship soon ripened into something more. By July, when the parliamentary session was drawing to its close, Henry became aware that Lord Paget was paying his wife considerable attention and remonstrated with her. Partly because of this, but also because she was pregnant, the riding lessons ceased, and when parliament rose for the long break Henry and his family took a house on Putney Heath. It was almost certainly at this time, in the last months of 1808, that Charlotte gave birth to a son, Gerald Valerian Wellesley, whose paternity was later doubted. Henry believed that from then until February 1809 Charlotte had no communication with Lord Paget, but he was mistaken: the couple appear to have arranged several meetings and to have corresponded, despite Charlotte's pregnancy and Paget's absence on active service in Portugal and Spain for some of these months.[20]

Paget's wife, Lady Caroline, was well aware that her husband was being unfaithful, and as early as the beginning of 1808 had expressed her misery at her position to his brother Charles Paget, a distinguished naval officer. Charles and his brother Arthur were both very sympathetic to her. This was evidently not the first time that their brother's behaviour had given Caroline cause for complaint, and she had even talked of leaving him previously, for she had promised Arthur that she would not do so without first warning him. Charles was particularly anxious that she should 'not to fly for protection to any of her own family, but to ours', even though whoever received her would incur 'the direful wrath of Paget'. This he would willingly risk in doing 'justice to so amiable & wretched a creature as she is'. When Lord Paget was with the army in Spain she complained that his letters to her were 'like a newspaper . . . the *only* difference in any that I have had – is *dear Car* at the beginning & end. Now as I am *quite* sure that *very* different letters are sent by the same Post it makes me *now* feel as I ought to have done long ago.'[21]

Henry and Charlotte Wellesley returned to London from Putney in February 1809. Charlotte said that because there had been so many unpleasant rumours about her and Lord Paget the previous year she had resolved to stay at home and not venture much into society. Henry asked her what her feelings for Paget were, and she replied that he was nothing more than 'a common acquaintance & I believe he liked my society last year but I have no reason to believe that he thinks of me in any way that can be objectionable'. Henry responded that in that case she should not deprive herself of the pleasure of mixing in society, but should avoid riding-parties and be careful to treat Paget as nothing more than a common acquaintance. He expressed total confidence in her.[22]

However, over the next few weeks Charlotte and Paget saw a great deal of each other, walking together in Green Park, where on several occasions Charlotte dismissed the footman attending her, something that she had never done before. By early March events were moving inexorably to a crisis. Henry was ill, with a liver complaint, and Paget told his brother that his only hope was that Henry would die; at about the same time he discussed Caroline's future with her, noting her fondness for the unmarried Duke of Argyll, and hoping that this might provide a refuge for her. Charles Paget was shocked at this approach, writing to Arthur, 'This is the way, my dear fellow, he talks, and it is quite marvellous that on subjects so enormously dreadful he should be able to be so cool and deliberate.' Charles warned Caroline of what Paget was saying, and she assured him that while she was indeed on good terms with Argyll, nothing improper had ever taken place – something that Charles readily believed.[23]

Henry recovered from his illness and, on the evening of 5 March, had an argument with Charlotte, accusing her of conducting an improper correspondence with Paget. The next morning she left the house for her usual walk in the park, but soon dismissed the footman and hailed a hackney coach. Before she did so, she chanced upon Charles Arbuthnot, who was Henry's colleague and friend, in the street. When he approached her she would not speak to him and hurried away. He was alarmed by her manner and went straight to Henry, who worried that Charlotte might be planning to kill herself. She disappeared from sight, but that evening Henry received a letter from her announcing that she was safe but had left him and their children.[24]

The elopement had been in the wind for some days: Charlotte had even ordered some new clothes that were to be held by the dressmaker to be collected, but were mistakenly delivered to the house she had just left. She had taken refuge with Paget, who took her to an apartment belonging to his aide-de-camp Baron Tuyll, who moved into a hotel. Neither Paget nor Charlotte appear to have felt any joy at finally living together. He wrote to his brother Arthur, 'that event which we have long dreaded, has actually taken place. I pity you all. Pity us in return – we are in want of it.' And she wrote, in a letter to Charles Arbuthnot declining Henry's offer to have her back:

> degraded and unprincipled as I must appear in the eyes of everybody, believe me I am not lost to all Sense of Honor which would forbid my returning to a husband I have quitted, to children I have abandoned. Indeed, indeed, my Dear Mr Arbuthnot, if you knew all you would pity more than blame me. Could you tell all the resistance that has been made to this most criminal most atrocious attachment, could you know what are my Sufferings at this Moment you would feel for me. Henry has not deserved this of me. We have had some differences and he may perhaps have sometimes been a *little* too hard to me, but I can with truth assert & I wish you to publish it to the World that in essentials and indeed in trifling subjects, he has ever been *kind to me to the greatest Degree.*[25]

Paget's family were distressed and disapproved of the step he had taken. Lord Uxbridge, his father, wrote to Charlotte begging her to 'listen to the prayer of an aged & perhaps dying Father, and to restore my Son to his distracted Family', and backed this by a threat to stop Paget's allowance. All of his relatives rallied round Lady Caroline, doing what they could to comfort her and making it clear that they felt that Paget's behaviour was inexcusable. In private, his brothers and brothers-in-law were extraordinarily vituperative in their comments about Charlotte Wellesley and apocalyptic in their predictions of the consequences of the affair. One brother-in-law wrote, 'that stinking Pole Cat . . . Damn her! How Paget's stomach will heave in the course of six months, when she seizes him in her hot libidinous arms.' Another wished 'I could get some huge Paddy to satisfy her lust and outdo Paget.' And the normally sensible Charles Paget described her as 'that nefarious damned Hellhound' and 'the most wicked and profligate whore and liar that ever hell itself could or ever will produce'. What lay behind these remarks is not entirely clear, although it seems that they had heard some story, or stories, that made them believe that she was 'a most artful deceitful woman' independent of her connection to Paget – although what these stories were, and whether they had any foundation, is unclear. (There is no other evidence, or even suggestion, that she had previously been unfaithful to Henry, although there are hints that she had been a little wild before her marriage.) Nothing really explains the violence of their language, nor their fear that the affair would ruin Paget's career in the army. In fact it had little or no effect; the Prince of Wales and the Duke of York continued to favour him; he was employed in the Walcheren expedition in 1809 while the scandal was at its height; and he was given a choice command in 1815, even though this meant serving under Henry Wellesley's brother.[26]

Charlotte's brothers were almost equally upset by the affair, demanding that she abandon Paget and either return to Henry or seek refuge with them. Charlotte refused, and when her brother formally challenged Paget to a duel on 28 March, Paget would not fight, admitting that he was in the wrong, but saying that as he had so injured Charlotte he was determined to devote his life to alleviating her suffering (for her happiness was impossible). However, he accepted a second challenge two months later, and a duel was fought on Wimbledon Common on 30 May 1809, in which Paget fired wide and Henry Cadogan missed. By comparison Henry Wellesley was ill and depressed, feeling humiliated, and had no appetite for vengeance, even offering Charlotte his protection when Paget went on the Walcheren expedition at the end of July.[27]

Nonetheless Henry wanted a divorce and sued Paget for *criminal conversation*, the legal term for adultery. On 6 May his legal representatives called on Paget and Charlotte, by appointment, to see them together, and six days later the case was heard in the Sherriff's court where Paget made no defence, suffering judgment by default. Henry was awarded £20,000 in damages. The Consistory Court of the Bishop of London heard the divorce case in early June, and the final decree was granted on 7 July. A private bill dissolving the marriage and permitting the parties to marry again was passed by the House of Lords and became law on 22 February 1810, less than twelve months after Charlotte Wellesley left her husband.[28]

This still left Caroline and Paget married, and there were no grounds for him to divorce her, while adultery by the husband was insufficient grounds for a wife to seek divorce in England.[29] Lawyers provided the solution: Caroline would divorce Paget in Scotland, where a wife could obtain a divorce on the grounds of infidelity, and the divorce would be valid in England. Paget and Charlotte moved to Scotland and lived there under an assumed name for the requisite forty days, before visiting Edinburgh and being 'discovered' by Caroline's agents who obtained the necessary evidence of adultery, but took care not to recognise Charlotte, for Scottish law forbade the guilty parties to marry each other. All parties then perjured themselves by swearing that there had been no collusion, and the divorce was granted in October 1810; although there was considerable disquiet in Scotland at the obvious manipulation of their legal system, with suggestions being made that neither Caroline nor Paget's subsequent marriages would be valid, nothing ever came of this threat.[30]

Before the end of 1810 Paget married Charlotte, first in Scotland and then in England, after having some difficulty finding a clergyman willing to perform the service. In November 1810 Caroline married the Duke of Argyll, and by all accounts was extremely happy. Her mother commented, 'surely there is every reason to rejoice, and I am not too sanguine when I think she will be more comfortable than ever. I am out of patience with those who croak, and had more pleasure in pitying her than they have in seeing her happy.' Only Henry Wellesley was left forlorn, at least for some years, although he was kept busy in a new position as British ambassador to Spain, supporting his brother's work in the Peninsular War, and he may have found some comfort in the ladies of Cadiz. In February 1816 he married Lady Georgiana Cecil, daughter of the Marquess of Salisbury, a family who were old friends of the Wellesleys, and as far as we know this second marriage was happy.[31]

Paget's family took some time to be reconciled with him, but eventually softened, although they were never on easy terms with Charlotte. His children appear to have divided their time between their mother and father, and according to Lady Bessborough, 'they talk with filial tenderness of

Mama Argyll and Mama Paget'. Paget himself, despite all his fine talk, was not faithful to Charlotte and, if Mrs Arbuthnot can be believed, went on to seduce her sister – Gerald Wellesley's wife Emily – and made Charlotte tell the story to Gerald. He was not a nice man, not a nice man at all, but the Prince Regent gave him the Garter – the highest order of chivalry – and he was raised in the peerage to Marquess for his role at Waterloo, and even went on to serve as Lord Lieutenant of Ireland.[32]

The most striking thing about the whole affair, at least to modern eyes, is the intensity of the feelings it aroused and the anguish it caused, both for the principals and their families. Even at the height of their passion Charlotte and Paget appear to have been deeply unhappy and ran away together not in any spirit of joyous adventure but resigned to their doom, the victims of malevolent fate in the form of an uncontrollable – and frankly unwelcome – passion. The high-flown language and appeal for pity suggest a degree of exaggeration, perhaps even playing to the gallery, and it is possible that they may have relished portraying their position in the most melodramatic fashion, but even when this is stripped away, they were far from young lovers setting off for Gretna Green with a clear consciences and gleeful spirits. Both claimed to feel deeply the harm they were doing to their children. Paget told his brother that if he was to see his children he would feel so torn between his love for them and his sense of duty to Charlotte 'that he should return to his lodgings and put an end to [his] existence'. And Charlotte told Charles Arbuthnot, 'You know how much I love them, you are aware of their merits and what I must feel at having quitted them but I have the satisfaction, the inexpressible comfort of knowing they will be taken care of by their Father though their Mother has abandoned them. My dear little Henry and Charlotte, God bless you.' It is striking how both Charlotte and Paget bent over backwards to avoid any criticism of their respective spouses: the blame was theirs and theirs alone. Equally, both Caroline Paget and Henry Wellesley made clear that they would have their wayward spouse back and showed more sorrow than anger at the destruction of their marriages. On the other hand, there is some room to question if Henry Wellesley was really quite as blind to the affair in its early stages as he later claimed; whether he actually suspected or knew what was going on, at least by the middle of 1808 when he moved the family to Putney Heath, but preferred to turn a blind eye in the hope that it would all blow over and that an open scandal might be avoided. The general reaction to the affair in London society, at least among people who knew any of the parties even casually, contained far more shock and even horror than titillation, and Lady Harriet Cavendish drew a useful moral when she wrote to her bachelor brother, amidst all the details of the elopement, 'Pray, dearest Hartington, marry somebody you will like to stay with.'[33]

Divorce was rare in eighteenth- and early-nineteenth-century England: only just over one hundred cases were recorded between 1750 and 1799, although most of these cases were in the last third of the period, leading to much alarm among the self-appointed guardians of the public morals, and many earnest discussions in the press and popular debating clubs about falling standards and the way a dissolute aristocracy was leading the country to perdition. In fact even members of the *bon ton* had grave reservations about divorce, as Lady Bessborough explained in a letter to Granville Leveson Gower when he was keen on marrying a divorced Russian princess:

> to those who profess Religion (or affect to profess it, which comes to the same) such a Marriage must always be offensive, because it is in direct violation of a positive injunction. Withdraw the case from yourself and apply it to another person. In the way Girls are often married, hardly knowing their Husbands or what marriage is, how many there must be who would gladly separate, and still more gladly chuse again if they could do so without ruining their characters. . . . Parliament or a despotic Sovereign may waive the *legal* part of Marriage, but who can waive the Solemn vow taken at the Altar in the name of the God who made you, and which for *better* or for *worse* binds you till death dissolves it.[34]

Of course, Lady Bessborough may have had mixed motives in taking this line on this occasion, but it helps explain the intense discomfort and scandal with which divorce was viewed at the time.

The obvious collusion and perjury in the Paget divorce was not unusual. Lord Eldon, the Lord Chancellor, declared that 'nine out of every ten cases of adultery that came to the Courts . . . were founded on the most infamous collusion, and that, as the law stood, it was a farce and a mockery; most of the cases being previously settled in some room in the City; and that Juries were called to give exemplary damages, which damages were never paid, nor expected to be paid by the injured husband.' And the Duke of Clarence (the future King William IV) told the House of Lords that a husband who actually kept the damages he received from an action for *crim. con.* was generally considered 'not a very honourable man'. However, there appears to have been considerable exaggeration in these pronouncements. Henry Wellesley received and kept the £20,000 he was awarded in his action, and there were other cases where the wife's lover was imprisoned for debt because he could not pay the damages awarded against him.[35]

In a system that was so heavily stacked against women it is worth noting one legal quirk that counted in their favour. Until the divorce was granted, the husband was responsible for any debts his wife incurred, and this included the cost of legal counsel to defend her against his action for divorce. This meant that the wife who was opposed to a divorce could hire the best lawyers and instruct them to use every device to delay and obstruct his proceedings without regard to the cost, which in turn strengthened the argument for the couple to come to a mutually acceptable settlement.[36]

The financial position of divorced women seems to have varied considerably. If, like Caroline Paget, she was the innocent party, she would expect to receive her full jointure, that is, the income she would have received if her husband had died. She would not normally receive back the fortune she had brought into the marriage because that was, at least in theory, being used to generate her jointure and would ultimately provide for her younger children by the marriage, so this was not as unjust as it sounds. However, there may have been some partial exceptions or cases where a guilty husband provided for his wife over and above her jointure, perhaps by giving her a house. We do not know the financial details of Lady Paget's divorce, but Lord Paget told his brother in 1811 that it had cost him £10,000 and £1,000 a year, so she did not come empty-handed to her marriage to the Duke of Argyll.[37]

However, divorce usually only occurred when the wife had committed adultery and was regarded as the guilty party, whatever the behaviour of the husband. It was theoretically possible for a wife in this position to be left penniless, but this rarely ever happened, at least in this period. If the husband did not make adequate financial provision for his wife, parliament would insert its own clause into the divorce bill. It is said, as a rule of thumb, that the wife would not normally be granted less than her pin money, or more than her jointure, although it is not clear if this applied in all cases. Unfortunately, we do not know the financial terms on which Henry and Charlotte Wellesley parted. It is also likely that, as with jointures, some divorced wives had difficulty obtaining money to which they were legally entitled.[38]

The principal purpose of a parliamentary divorce was to enable the couple to remarry, although there were also cases – fortunately rare – in which the injured husband seems to have acted primarily from spite, wanting to humiliate his erring wife and subject her to as much scandal and obloquy as possible, with no thought of remarriage. Even where the wife was the innocent party, some people felt qualms about her remarriage. Betsey Fremantle (who was a Catholic) commented that Caroline Paget's marriage to the Duke of Argyll 'has something so revolting and extraordinary in it, that I cannot believe she ever can feel perfectly happy'. A 'guilty' woman, such as Charlotte Paget, might expect to be shunned by her new husband's family and by respectable society, at least for a time. What this meant in practice varied considerably: the divorced and remarried Lady Holland presided over one of the most famous political and literary circles in London, and very few men would scruple to accept an invitation to dine at Holland House on moral grounds, even though their wives would seldom give Lady Holland a reciprocal invitation. When Lord Paget (by then Marquess of Anglesey) served as Lord Lieutenant of Ireland, twenty years after his divorce and remarriage, the wife of his under-secretary refused to call on Lady Anglesey, but her scruples were not universally shared. General Dyott, a friend and neighbour of the Pagets in Staffordshire, noted in his diary at about the same time:

The strict moralist perhaps may not approve of taking my daughter to visit Lady Anglesey, but situated as I felt myself towards the noble

Marquis and the obligation I owed the family, added to the circumstance of her ladyship having called here to introduce her daughter to Eleanor, I naturally concluded I must either take Eleanor or give up my acquaintance altogether. Lady Anglesey's conduct cannot be justified. She has suffered for her misdeeds; they should not be visited on her children. And as Mrs Littleton, Lady Sophia Gresley, etc., had been to stay at Beaudesert, I did no longer hesitate in accompanying my daughter.[39]

Still, a woman in Lady Anglesey's position would be painfully aware of any snub and would probably avoid society where she was unsure how she would be received.

Divorce carried no such stigma for men and they continued to mix in society and pursue their profession without impediment and rarely attracted much opprobrium. It was the injured husband, not the man who had wronged him, who might retreat from society for a time to lick his wounds and try to forget that there was such a word as cuckold. William Middleton withdrew to a small hunting box and lived out his days in seclusion and, it may be supposed, misery and bitterness, but this was an extreme case, and most men were expected to get over their misfortune and show a brave face to the world. In 1816, the same year that Henry Wellesley married Lady Georgiana Cecil, he attended a dinner given by the Prince Regent at Carlton House at which Lord Anglesey was one of the other guests. The Prince apologised to Wellesley for the awkwardness, but Wellesley rose to the occasion and did not seem at all annoyed, while he told Castlereagh at about this time that he now considered Lord Anglesey as the best friend he had ever had in his life. Meanwhile relations between the Angleseys and the Argylls were civil, perhaps even cordial, and Caroline was always well disposed and friendly towards the wider Paget family.[40]

Not everyone could let go with grace. Richard Martin, MP, the great campaigner against cruelty to animals, wrote to the new husband of his ex-wife, 'Sir, I scorn to remind you of past events – the law has settled that question [by awarding Martin £10,000 in damages]. But, if ever I hear that you treat the lady who once had the honour to bear the name of Martin with anything but the strictest respect, you may be assured you shall answer [for] it to me.' Although this looks like an unwarranted intrusion into matters that no longer concerned him, it is possible that Martin's intentions were good and even that his intervention was helpful, for the former Mrs Martin's new husband 'was known to be a great savage, capable and likely to use her ill'. Still, it is unlikely that she welcomed his interference.[41]

There were also cases where the estranged couple could not detach themselves completely because parliament rejected the divorce bill. This was what happened to Letitia Powlett after her well-publicised affair with Lord Sackville in the White Hart Inn, Winchester. Colonel Powlett had won a case for *crim. con.* and been awarded £3,000 in damages but his bill divorcing his wife failed to pass the Lords, which suspected collusion between husband and wife. The couple therefore remained married, although they separated and lived apart. When the Colonel died sixteen years later (by which time he was a major-general), his widow married Thomas Lisle Follett of Lyme in Devon, a barrister of Lincoln's Inn and author of several works on Christianity and other weighty subjects. If nothing else, this shows that the loss of a lady's reputation was not quite as fatal as might be supposed, and that Jane Austen was perhaps being a little harsh in condemning Maria Rushworth to a life of obscurity and seclusion with only her Aunt Norris for company.[42]

＊

Divorces were rare, but separations were common, although we have no reliable evidence just how common. We do know that couples right across the social spectrum would agree to separate, and we have documented instances of the wife's maintenance ranging from £12 to £3,000 a year: the one suggesting a poor craftsman or labourer's wife; the other, a lady married to a wealthy member of the aristocracy or an unusually successful banker, merchant or industrialist. Prominent examples of men who were separated from their wives included the Prince of Wales, Lord Byron, Richard Marquess Wellesley and Lord Nelson. When Thomas Rowlandson produced a satirical print *The Four Seasons of Love* in 1814, the fourth scene, 'winter', showed the by now unhappy couple, listening with relief as a lawyer read out the terms of their separation. In other words, separation, not divorce, was seen as the natural conclusion of an unsuccessful marriage (see plate 7).[43]

When a couple separated they came to an agreement on terms: this would commonly be drawn up as a contract by an attorney: in some cases this might be approved by the Consistory court, while in others it might be a private agreement, perhaps not written at all. The most common arrangement, at least for couples in the upper levels of society, would include the husband's formal consent for his wife to live apart from him without his interference. He would pay her, or her trustees, an agreed allowance, which usually was related to the size of the jointure established in the marriage settlement, although depending on circumstances it might not be the full amount of the jointure. In return she, or her trustees, would indemnify him against any debts she incurred, and this left her free to buy and sell property and make contracts as if she was unmarried. Both parties might also agree not to take any further legal action over the marriage: the husband renouncing his right to sue for restitution of conjugal rights, and the wife renouncing her right to sue for cruelty or adultery. The agreement might also cover the children, and it was common, although not universal, for the husband to permit the younger children (up to about seven years old) to reside with the wife, while he would take responsibility for the older children, especially if they were boys. Occasionally a clause would be added making the wife's allowance conditional on her remaining chaste, but this was rare, and it was more common for both parties to accept that the other was free to form a fresh connection, although not to marry, and it was tacitly or explicitly agreed that any children the wife had after the separation would have no claim on the husband's estate.[44]

The legal status of these agreements was highly doubtful, and there are recorded cases of husbands flouting them after some years of separation and stripping their wife of all the possessions she had accumulated since leaving him, or forcibly taking the children away from her, in contravention of their agreement. However, these seem to have been most untypical. Agreements generally benefited both parties and were usually respected, while the most common problem was that of husbands failing to pay the maintenance they had promised. In most such cases legal enforcement was probably slower and less effective than the threat of publicity and shame, but here as so often the dice were heavily loaded against the wife.[45]

Couples were sometimes tempted to anticipate trouble and include the terms of any future separation in their marriage settlement: the eighteenth-century equivalent of a modern 'pre-nuptial agreement'. Walter Scott, himself a lawyer, had the villain of his novel *St Ronan's Well* propose such an agreement when he wished to marry Clara Mowbray and she was unwilling. The villain (the spurious Earl of Etherington) needed to marry her in order to inherit an estate, but he was happy to agree to a legal separation, which would take effect immediately after the wedding if she wished, in which he would renounce all claims to her society. The marriage would protect her from rumours about her past indiscretions and give her a respectable place in society, while he would get the estate he coveted. 'Such things happen every season, if not on the very marriage-day, yet before the honeymoon is over.' There is no doubt that he was exaggerating, and the courts eventually ruled such agreements invalid, but it is still significant that they were discussed, if seldom actually included in the settlement.[46]

Separations received less publicity than divorces and so, although they were much more common, there are fewer well-documented cases in the sources. Nonetheless there are some interesting examples which show how they could work. When Anne Stuart, daughter of the Earl of Bute, married Hugh Percy, heir of the Duke of Northumberland, their marriage settlement provided for a jointure of £1,600 should one or both of Hugh's parents survive him and £2,500 should both predecease him. When they agreed to separate in 1769 the maintenance agreement repeated these sums under the same conditions, adding only a stipulation that the payment would be made only 'so long as she should live in Great Britain.' In another case, a few years later, Lady Craven separated from her husband after alleged infidelities on both sides and moved to the Continent, taking with her their youngest child, Keppel Craven, then four years old. Her maintenance was set at £1,500 a year, although her continued affairs led her husband to prohibit their older children from corresponding with her. On his death in 1791 she promptly married the Margrave of Ansbach, with whom she had long been conducting an affair, and came back to England. She was not received at court, but was a prominent figure in London society and became a successful author and playwright, while her husband bred horses. Fanny Nelson was much more circumspect in her behaviour and took pains to make it known that she would welcome her erring husband home if he would return to her, while trying hard to remain on good terms with his family. She also had to consider the naval career of her son by her first marriage, Josiah Nisbet, which largely depended on Nelson's continued patronage. She negotiated these difficulties with some skill and emerged with her reputation unsullied and an income of £1,600, plus a further £200 from a legacy from her uncle.[47]

Much less generous was the behaviour of Lord Erne, Caroline Stuart Wortley's father. Lord and Lady Erne lived apart from the 1780s, although it is not clear whether there was any formal separation agreement. Lady Erne lived on the Continent for six years (1784–90) with her daughter, who was then only a child. In 1781 her mother, Lady Bristol, wrote, 'I dare not name Lord Erne as my bile has not enough subsided.' Lady Erne's father, the Earl Bishop (Earl of Bristol and Bishop of Derry), supplemented her income. He also approached her husband with a proposal that they each add £100 a year to her income, to which Lord Erne responded that 'when [she] was as good a Wife as [she] was a daughter he would listen to the proposal. I could have answered him by an *Inversion* of his Rule – but à quoi Bon.' However, relying on paternal support was not ideal, as a comment from her cousin, Mrs Dillon, makes clear: 'She is just at this moment in a most terrible situation. Her odious husband will settle so little on her that she must be dependent on her father, which is always an unpleasant thing.' When Lady Erne returned to England she lived a very retired life with her daughter at Christchurch, which combined a necessary economy with a good climate. She complained of her situation to her friend Lady Louisa Harvey: 'No, dearest Lady Louly, there is nothing for me whilst my penurious Tyrant thinks fit to keep me on this miserable pittance, but retirement and retirement in such an unfrequented spot as this, where (thanks again to your great kindness) we get constant exercise with very little cost, and where the shifts to which I am obliged are unobserved by others, and less felt by myself . . . .' Her position only improved with her daughter's marriage in 1799 – she got on well with her son-in-law, James Stuart Wortley – and when her sister, Lady Hawkesbury, later Lady Liverpool, secured a grace and favour apartment for her at Hampton Court.[48]

Lady Sebright also found her life difficult when she finally separated from her unpleasant and abusive husband. Mrs Calvert noted in February 1813 that Sir John 'has let his house in Curzon Street for four years, and lives at lodgings. Lady S. has got a small house in Baker Street. She has the six youngest daughters, he the two eldest. The son is at Westminster. He is a strange, good-for-nothing man.' And six months later she added, 'Poor Lady Sebright is here. She lives in a dismal place. Her health is wretched, and she really is the most forlorn looking creature I ever saw, and her children most miserably ugly. I feel great compassion for her in every particular. She seems in a most nervous and fidgety state.'[49]

Lady Erne and Lady Sebright may have been particularly unfortunate in their husbands, even by the standards of separated husbands, and we may hope that most separated wives went on to have rather happier and easier lives after leaving their marriage. Nonetheless many such women would have found it difficult to re-establish their lives, and much would have depended on the amount of support they received from their family and their financial position. It seems likely that their lifestyle would have had much in common with that of a widow, although without the possibility of remarriage. Bath and other spa towns and resorts were probably popular as residences, but this is speculation, for the whole subject has been neglected by historians and the available evidence to date is scanty. Nor is it clear how they were viewed by society: how much stigma attached to a woman who was separated from her husband compared to one who was divorced. On the whole it seems likely that a separated woman was not regarded with much prejudice so long as her current behaviour was discreet and there was nothing notorious in the circumstances of her separation, but even this conclusion is tentative at best.[50] What we can say with confidence, however, is that it was when a marriage went bad that the full weight of the social and legal bias against women and in favour of men was most starkly revealed.

CHAPTER SIXTEEN

WIDOWS AND WIDOWERS

MANY MARRIAGES IN THE eighteenth and early nineteenth centuries ended in the death of one partner while the other was still young or middle aged. Childbirth, tuberculosis, war, accidents and disease took a significant toll on men and women in the prime of life. Even in 1850 almost one in five marriages ended within ten years due to the death of a spouse. Women were four times more likely to die than their husbands in the first ten years of marriage, and twice as likely in the second decade of married life; thereafter husbands died at a greater rate, partly due to the fact that they tended to be older than their wives. This meant that widowers were commonly still quite young at the time of their bereavement, and widows rather older.[1]

These figures conceal a great emotional toll. Charles Arbuthnot was married twice, very happily, and bereaved twice, suffering intensely on both occasions. Harriet's death, in 1834, came unexpectedly when she was only forty. She had been taken ill with a stomach disorder at the end of July, but appeared to recover and was well enough to walk to a nearby farm, only to be seized by violent pains; she collapsed and died at six in the morning of Saturday 2 August, almost certainly of cholera. Charles, who was sixty-seven years old and had always assumed that he would predecease Harriet, was deeply shaken. Two months later he told his son (by his first marriage), 'I have had many dreadful nights – quite sleepless ones. . . . For many days I had scarcely an hour's sleep in 24 hours, & that sleep was produced by opiates.' Nonetheless he was determined 'to perform all the duties of life, feeling as I do that by performing them I shall best prepare for death, & for the Rest which I hope will follow death.' He felt 'weaned from the World', and that he had endured 'as much mental misery as I think I could suffer'. In December he wrote that 'Every hour of my life shows me more & more, what a blank is before me till I go into my grave.' Time gradually lessened the shock of Harriet's death, but Charles never fully recovered, although he lived on for another sixteen years, dividing his time between his adult children and the Duke of Wellington, a great friend of his and Harriet's, who gave him a London base at Apsley House. The two old men marked the anniversary of Harriet's death by dining alone together each year, and it was at Apsley House that Charles died on 18 August 1850 with his sons, a daughter-in-law and the Duke by his side.[2]

Lady Sarah Napier was equally affected by the death of her husband George in 1804 after twenty-three years of marriage:

I have lost him who made me like this world. It is now a dreary expanse, where I see thinly scattered a few beloved objects whose welfare and prosperity have still such strong hold on my heart as to keep it alive to whatever concerns them. But its *pleasant prospects* are all vanished! . . . While he lived I saw all objects through the medium of my own happiness. Even the joy occasioned by advantages falling to the share of any of my children was doubled because I shared it *with him* . . .[3]

Religion provided a comfort and solace for many people in a time of bereavement, but sometimes it was a struggle to accept that their loss was indeed the will of a merciful God. Anne Eliza Robbins lost her husband, a barrister, in 1814 when she was pregnant with her fifth child. Two days later she wrote to her niece:

The lord above only knows how extreme [my feelings] are and as it is *his* will to afflict me – so deeply he will I fervently hope restore my mind to some composure 'ere long. I ought to remember that through my *heavy* and *heart breaking* trial he *bears* me up and that I cannot better recommend myself to his favour than to submit with resignation and obedience to all his dispensations . . . Oh Sarah can you judge of my anguish or how agonizing my feelings must be when I reflect that my beloved husband is no more! It is like a frightful dream and requires more than human fortitude to bear it with proper composure. My poor dear children . . .[4]

Many people really did look forward to being reunited with their loved ones in heaven. Cassandra Austen was as grief-stricken as any spouse when Jane died in 1817, and she wrote to her niece Fanny that she liked to think of Jane as 'an inhabitant of Heaven. Oh! if I may one day be reunited to her there! — I know the time must come when my mind will be less engrossed by her idea, but I do not like to think of it. If I think of her less as on Earth, God grant that I may never cease to reflect on her as inhabiting Heaven & never cease my humble endeavours (when it shall please God) to join her there.'[5]

Not all widows and widowers felt this much. Jane Austen herself commented on her brother Henry, two months after his wife Eliza's death, 'Upon the whole his Spirits are very much recovered. – If I may so express myself, his Mind is not a Mind for affliction. He is too Busy, too active, too sanguine. – Sincerely as he was attached to poor Eliza moreover, & excellently as he behaved to her, he was always so used to be away from her at times, that her Loss is not felt as that of many a beloved Wife might be . . . .' Eliza's death was not unexpected, and where there had been a long and painful illness, the end might be – not welcomed exactly – but greeted with relief that the patient's suffering, and that of their loved ones, was finally at an end.[6]

In some unfortunate cases the death of a spouse might be a release from a deeply unhappy marriage, although it was still likely to trigger some complicated emotions. Nonetheless there are instances in which the surviving husband or wife of a couple who had long lived apart married very quickly after their spouse's death. Sir James Erskine was in the middle of divorcing his wife, Lady Louisa, when he died on 3 March 1825 at the age of fifty-two. For some years she had been living with Major-General Sir George Murray and they were now free to marry, which they did on 28 April, eight weeks to the day after Erskine's death.

Lady Hardy had never got on well with her husband Sir Thomas, and they spent a great deal apart, although they were never formally separated. Within a few weeks of his death in 1839 she had agreed to marry Charles Ellis, Lord Seaford, who had long been a close friend, but she insisted that they wait a full year before celebrating the wedding. Her second marriage was much happier than her first, although it only lasted five years before Seaford died suddenly, leaving her again a widow.[7]

The death of a husband might not only be a terrible emotional blow to his wife, it might also undermine her social and economic position. If he was a clergyman she would, at a stroke, lose the income from his position and the family home in a rectory or a vicarage, which she would soon have to vacate to make room for the new incumbent. The widows of men in other professions were little better off, except that their home was not usually tied to their husband's appointment. There was a regular system of pensions for the widows of officers in the army and navy, although it was far from generous: the widow of an army subaltern received only £36 a year, and the widow of a naval lieutenant or an army captain or major was entitled to £50 a year. A senior naval captain's widow would receive £90, while even the widow of an admiral or a lieutenant-general would only get a pension of £120 a year, all of which were very meagre sums if she did not have other sources of income. Naval widows in need could also apply to the officially funded Charity for Sea Officers' Widows, while their children (and those of army officers) might receive support from the Compassionate Fund, although again these were far from munificent. The family of an army officer would usually lose the value of his commission with his death, although if he died in action the Horse Guards might permit it to be sold and the proceeds given to his family. Much more generous grants might also be made, either by the government or by Lloyds Patriotic Fund, to officers who fell covered in glory in some illustrious action, but such cases were rare and did nothing for the family of the poor wretch who succumbed to dysentery or some tropical fever in a colonial garrison or during the Peninsular War. It was up to individual officers, just as it was up to lawyers, doctors and other professional gentlemen, to take their own measures to protect their wives and family in the event of misfortune. They might, for example, take out life insurance, possibly with the premiums being paid by income from the wife's fortune, but it is not clear whether this practice was widespread.[8]

In many cases extended family provided financial and practical support where it was needed. For example, when Jane Austen's father died, her mother was left with an income of approximately £210 a year from her capital: enough to save her from penury, but still a limited income which would compel a great reduction in her circumstances. Her sons, who were doing well, agreed to supplement this: James, Henry and Francis each contributed £50 a year, while Edward, who had inherited the Knight estate from distant relatives who had adopted him, gave his mother £100 together with the cottage in Chawton where she lived with her daughters. This gave her a comfortable income of £460 a year, more than many clergymen received or members of the other gentlemanly professions, and enabled her to live in much the same manner as she had when her husband was alive. She also had the assurance that if more money was needed it would be found for her. John Dashwood's failure to properly look after his stepmother is satirically condemned in *Sense and Sensibility*, and considerable social pressure might be brought to bear on wealthy relatives who neglected their responsibilities and left their poorer connections in need. Nonetheless not everyone had wealthy relatives, and Austen indicates the difficulties of such widows in her depiction of Mrs Bates and her daughter in *Emma*, whose circumstances were constrained and only likely to get worse (although Jane Fairfax's marriage to wealthy Frank Churchill would ensure that they were looked after in the end).[9]

More prosperous widows lived on their jointure, as established by their marriage settlement, which was sometimes increased by their husband's will. If their eldest son was unmarried they might, like Mrs Rushworth in *Mansfield Park*, keep house for him and help him select a suitable (or, in the case of Maria Bertram, an unsuitable) bride to take their place. When he married, or sometimes before, they might retire to a Dower House on the estate, or live nearby, or move further afield to Bath or some other spa or cathedral town. (London was too expensive for most widows, unless they had unmarried daughters to launch into the world, when means might be found, at least for a season or two.) Some widows were more adventurous. When Tysoe Saul Hancock died in 1775, his widow, Philadelphia, was left with one child, their daughter Eliza, and an income of about £600 a year. She felt that this was insufficient for her to continue living in London and instead moved to the Continent where she and her daughter lived for the next few years, undeterred by the lack of a gentleman to escort her.[10]

Widows had considerable independence and were often able to shape their lives to suit themselves with more freedom than at any other point in their lives. Where they lived, with whom and how they spent their time and money were all points that they were largely free to decide for themselves. Society did not expect them to renounce the pleasures of the world, so long as they observed some generally accepted restrictions in the first year of mourning, and so long as they remained chaste: their reputation and social position would struggle to surmount a sexual indiscretion or even rumours hinting at such impropriety. And while some widows remained grief-stricken and lonely for the rest of their lives, others made a fresh start, found new interests and pursuits and even had some fun along the way.[11]

When Sir John Shelley died at the age of eighty in 1852, Frances, Lady Shelley was sixty-five and still full of life. The following year she established her home, for part of the year, with her son, the Rev. Frederick Shelley, in his rectory in Cornwall, but she continued to lease a house in Fulham so as to spend some months in London each year. She grieved for Sir John, but 'the predominant feeling in my heart is one of thankfulness for the great blessings which have so completely softened the blow, and enabled me to realize that, though my great task is ended, my life is still of value to my children and to many kind friends . . . How much happier I feel . . . in the knowledge that I possess the love of all around me! I know not one who bears me any ill-will, or that I can remember to have injured . . . .' Even before she had properly established a pattern dividing her time between London and Cornwall, she was off to the Continent, travelling with her grandson Arthur and granddaughter Katty. They set off in August 1853 and travelled through Belgium, Germany, Switzerland and Italy, where they spent the winter, and then to France for the spring, before returning to England in June 1854, where she visited friends and did not return to Cornwall until September, delighted to be back in 'the true home of my heart and affections! Here

I breathe the atmosphere of love, where everything bears the impress of a truly Christian spirit, and where my dear son and his wife make all around them happy.' Subsequent trips included a return to France, a visit to Ireland and expeditions to the north of England and the Highlands of Scotland. In 1868 she gave up her house in London and, at the age of eighty-one, built herself a new house on the Isle of Wight which she called Maresfield Lodge. Queen Victoria invited her to dine at Osborne and frequently visited her. Her health began to fail at the beginning of 1873 and she died on 24 February at the age of eighty-five, a survivor of the long distant days of the Regency.[12]

Widowers were even less defined and constrained by their loss than widows. It affected them emotionally in much the same way and might lessen their domestic comfort, but it rarely damaged their financial or social position in the world. The 2nd Viscount Palmerston lamented the death of his first wife, Frances Poole, after less than two years of marriage, describing her as 'by far the most perfect [being] I have ever known . . . one who possessing worth, talents, temper and understanding superior to most persons of either sex, never during the whole of my connection with her spoke a word or did an act I could have wished to alter'. A few weeks after her death he set off on a tour of southern Wales with two friends to distract himself from her loss and the following year went on a tour of the Continent, but then he picked up the threads of his life: he remained in parliament, held office as a junior Lord of the Admiralty, and mixed a great deal in London society. He had affairs with several prominent courtesans and kept a succession of mistresses, for chastity was not expected of widowers. His marriage had not produced any surviving children who might suffer from the lack of a mother's care, which removed one impulse to remarry, and it was not until fourteen years later that a ripening friendship with Mary Mee led to his second marriage.[13]

＞◈＜

Second marriages were viewed with some ambivalence in eighteenth- and early-nineteenth-century Britain. Dr Johnson's quip that they represented 'the triumph of hope over experience' was a good line, but his more considered opinion was favourable, as Boswell records: 'When I censured a gentleman of my acquaintance for marrying a second time, as it shewed a disregard of his first wife, he said, "Not at all, Sir. On the contrary, were he not to marry again, it might be concluded that his first wife had given him a disgust to marriage; but by taking a second wife he pays the highest compliment to the first, by shewing that she made him so happy as a married man, that he wishes to be so a second time."' Mary Wollstonecraft agreed, condemning novelists who implied that true love could only be felt once, but still, there were probably many who shared Fanny Knight's youthful declaration that she was an 'inveterate enemy to second marriages, particularly if there is any family.' Not that this stopped her marrying a widower with six children some eleven years later.[14]

Widows might feel some reluctance to put themselves under the authority of a husband for a second time, as Elizabeth Montagu remarked to her fellow blue-stocking Elizabeth Carter in 1782:

When I was a wife I was obedient because it was my duty, and being married to a man of sense and integrity, obedience was not painful or irksome, in early youth a director perhaps is necessary if the sphere of action is extensive; but it seems to me that a new master and new lessons after ones opinions and habits were formed must be a little awkward, and with all due respect to the superior sex, I do not see how they can be necessary to a woman unless she were to defend her lands and tenements by sword or gun.[15]

Eliza de Feuillide struggled with the idea of giving up 'dear Liberty, and yet dearer flirtation' before she finally accepted Henry Austen, and in *Persuasion* Jane Austen wrote that Lady Russell did *not* end up marrying Sir Walter Elliot.

That Lady Russell, of steady age and character, and extremely well provided for, should have no thought of a second marriage, needs no apology to the public, which is rather apt to be unreasonably discontented when a woman *does* marry again, than when she does *not*; but Sir Walter's continuing singleness requires explanation. – Be it known then, that Sir Walter, like a good father, (having met with one or two private disappointments in very unreasonable applications) prided himself on remaining single for his dear daughter's sake.[16]

It was rarer for widows than for widowers to remarry, a fact which can be explained in several ways: that they were less willing to remarry, that widowers found it easier to secure a second spouse than widows or simply that they tended to be older at the time of their bereavement. Nonetheless second marriages were common. Lawrence Stone calculated that in the late eighteenth and early nineteenth century around 15 per cent of the gentry and aristocracy married more than once, roughly equal to the proportion that did not marry at all.[17] A more detailed study limited to peers yields an even higher proportion: 224 of the 826 peers who married in the eighteenth century went on to marry a second time, 36 married three times and Lord Harborough, like Richard Lovell Edgeworth, went through the ceremony four times.[18]

The motives behind second marriages varied widely. Sir Edward Knatchbull was prompted to think of marrying again by inheriting the family house and estate from his father. This large establishment, and the social position that went with it, required a mistress in a way which his more modest existing house did not: at least, this is the motive which he gave in his diary. Matthew Flinders Senior, the apothecary-surgeon in Lincolnshire, father of the famous explorer, was even more honest about his motives when his wife Susanna died in 1783, leaving him with five young children. 'My tears are plentifully shed each day, and when I regain my peace I cannot tell,' he wrote in his diary. 'My situation is truly deplorable and unhappy on my own account, and my comfit [sic] being gone, but doubly so on account of my 5 children, two very small and one at nurse.' He looked to his niece to manage his household in the short term, but within months was thinking of marrying again, on purely pragmatic grounds and not without a sense of guilt that it would seem that he had been quick to forget 'my late valuable partner & whom I shall regret to my latest hour', 'God knows I have yet many bitter hours on her account, and am not without some fears, that it will be impossible for me to be so happy as I have been, but what can I do?'[19]

However, this was far from a universal reaction. Jane Austen's brother Edward was left at the age of forty-one with eleven children under the age of sixteen, yet he did not marry again, and while his brothers Francis and Charles both took second wives, they did not do so until five or six years after their first wife's death. Only James Austen remarried fairly quickly, twenty months after the death of his wife Mary, and he had only one child from his first marriage, his daughter Anna. Possibly it was easier for a wealthy man like Edward Knight to employ efficient servants who would care for his children and make his household run smoothly than for an apothecary-surgeon like Matthew Flinders, but personality, the experience of their first marriage and whether or not they met someone who quickened their interest and who then responded to them were all probably more important.

Some men, such as Lord Harborough, mentioned above, remarried in search of a son and heir (in his case unsuccessfully), but the commoner motives for both men and women were surely loneliness and love. Lord Ilchester explained his decision to remarry by saying that:

he had been a happy man in that state before, and he hoped to be happy again; that he had endeavoured to act the part of a good parent to his dear children; and he had reason to believe that they in return would wish to see the evening of his days set in peace and comfort; that the daughters [sic] who was of most consequence to his domestic happiness was already settled; the elder might likewise leave him soon, and her stay became quite precarious; that the third, though a charming girl, was too young and too thoughtless to be his companion; and that he foresaw he should be desolate and solitary soon if he did not again enter the married state . . .[20]

Lord Ilchester was justifying his decision to the family governess, implicitly asking for her approval and forgiveness – for she had been greatly attached to his first wife – and also for her to use her influence to persuade his married daughter, Lady Mary Talbot, to give her approval to his marriage. Indeed, he had been willing to give up the scheme if his eldest daughter (who was unmarried) disapproved, and his intended bride, Miss Digby, made her acceptance conditional on the acquiescence of his two unmarried daughters. This sensitivity to the reaction of the children of a first marriage was not uncommon. When Harriet Fane accepted Charles Arbuthnot's proposal she was insistent that he not disrupt his children's lives on her account and leave it to her to win them over. Her confidence proved well founded: the children all soon came to love her and the family were close and affectionate for the rest of their lives.[21]

Maria Stanley's father, Lord Sheffield, married for a third time in January 1798, when he was sixty-two, a little over a year after she had married John Stanley. Maria, the daughter of his first wife, had greatly loved and admired her stepmother who had died in January 1797, and probably had some mixed feelings about her father's decision; however, she was well disposed towards her new stepmother and came to like her for her own sake when she got to know her. In March 1802 Lady Sheffield gave birth to a son, who would be his father's heir, displacing Maria from inheriting her father's title and estates. (His barony had been granted with a special remainder in favour of his daughters and their sons, if he died without a son of his own.) Maria reacted well to the news, telling her Aunt Serena, 'I hope like me you are well content now suspense and anxiety and doubt are at an end, and I am sure, like me, your first idea was pleasure that the dear lady had got over her business so well. . . . I think myself lucky to be out of the way of congratulations and condolences.' Her sister-in-law, Isa Stanley, wrote, 'Why would he not be a girl, instead of what Ralph Leycester calls "an unnecessary little boy"? But here he is, and all one can now say is, May you be happy with what cannot be intercepted! Nobody can suppose him very welcome to you, but all give you just credit for the manner in which you have expressed yourself on this trying occasion.' The fact that Maria herself had four daughters, but as yet no son, would not have made the news any easier to bear, but she was happily married to a wealthy landowner, and so in a good position to be gracious.[22]

William Cole, the Dean of Waterford, was quite open in writing to his brother Arthur (who was in India at the time), lamenting the possibility of their father's remarriage. 'You must by this time have heard of my poor dear Mother's death . . . My Father, as I expected, was much shocked at first, but having that easy kind of disposition it is now totally worn off. . . . God grant he may not think of marrying. That indeed would be a melancholy event for his family, who are already poor enough.' And even when there were no material interests at stake, the relatives of a deceased wife or husband might struggle to rejoice at the news that the survivor was to remarry. When Lord Liverpool announced his intention of remarrying after the death of his first wife, her sister, Elizabeth, Duchess of Devonshire, wrote to her other sister, Lady Erne, 'I did not expect his marriage would have been so soon declar'd. I am sure that we feel alike about it, and most sincerely do I wish him happy; but I should have liked a few more months to have pass'd . . . .'[23]

Relations in step-families, as in other families, could become very bad, especially where adult children felt threatened or displaced by the arrival of a step-parent. Lord John Russell warned his brother William to restrain his hostility to their stepmother the Duchess of Bedford, whom he acknowledged was 'a powerful, vindictive and unscrupulous enemy. . . . [but] it is very bad policy in us to quarrel with Woburn.' He worried that an open breach would simply make their father's life unhappy, and would actually increase the Duchess's influence and the risk that the Duke 'would hear less truth' and 'do more unjust things'. 'I have a great love & even reverence for my father which nothing will shake. . . . Whatever you do, pray do not abuse my father to the world.' This was bad enough, but it pales beside James Boswell's reaction to his father's second marriage, which went far beyond the boundaries of propriety and perhaps even of sanity. He wrote in his diary:

'Damn him. Curse him,' sounded somehow involuntarily in my ears perpetually. I was absolutely mad. I sent for worthy Grange [his friend], and was so furious and black-minded and uttered such horrid ideas that he could not help shedding tears, and even went so far as to say that if I talked so he would never see me again. I looked on my father's marrying again as the most ungrateful return to me for my having submitted so much to please him.

And he wrote to Margaret, 'What an infamous woman must she be who can impose on an old man worn out with business, and ruin the peace of a family!' and went on to describe his prospective stepmother as 'the legal prostitute of libidinous old age'. It was not a good beginning to the relationship, and not surprisingly the breach was never fully healed, although it is only fair to add that Boswell's relationship with his father had always been troubled.[24]

Fortunately such vehemence was unusual, and Edward Gibbon gives us what was probably a more typical response. He was in Switzerland when his father remarried, and he acknowledges that he received the news with displeasure and viewed his stepmother as 'a personal and domestic enemy' who had usurped his mother's bed.

> But the injustice was in my own fancy, and the imaginary monster was an amiable and deserving woman. I could not be mistaken in the first view of her understanding, her knowledge, and the elegant spirit of her conversation: her polite welcome, and her assiduous care to study and gratify my wishes announced at least that the surface would be smooth; and my suspicions of art and falsehood were gradually dispelled by the full discovery of her warm and exquisite sensibility. After some reserve on my side our minds associated in confidence and friendship, and as Mrs Gibbon had neither children nor the hopes of children, we more easily adopted the tender names and genuine characters of mother and of son.[25]

Nothing could guarantee the success of a second marriage, any more than a first, but the hostility of the children of the first marriage, even if they were independent adults who had left home, was a formidable obstacle. Tact and careful handling of the subject might reduce the risk of resentment, but it could not eliminate it, and some marriages that might have done well surely came to grief through such resentment. But second marriages could also prosper, bringing happiness and contentment to both parties until death again intervened, as Charles and Harriet Arbuthnot found.

CHAPTER SEVENTEEN

GROWING OLD TOGETHER

IN MANY MARRIAGES THE years passed with little change in the relationship between the couple. Both husband and wife were preoccupied with careers and children, the state of the crops and upsets among the servants, country sports, the latest fashions, politics and literature, while their relationship provided the context, a steady hum of pleasurable satisfaction or of discontent and disappointment. The calm might be broken by a storm: infidelity, financial disaster, illness or death, which would mark a sharp deterioration in the relationship, often permanent, sometimes only temporary. It was harder for a married couple to abruptly improve their relationship, although it might happen if one of the couple removed a thorn that had been alienating the other, or if their circumstances changed for the better, for example by inheriting money, while some couples gradually grew closer over the years, depending more not less on each other as they grew older.

The passage of years brought its own changes, which women commented on more frequently than men. In 1818 Frances Calvert wrote in her diary, 'Last Wednesday I became, Alas! a complete old woman – *fifty* years old. Well! The worst is now over. I always dreaded that age. Now all pretence to anything like youth is over. I hope I shall bear growing old with a better grace, and God grant I may grow better!' Another wife wrote to her husband after they had been married for twenty years, 'My dear friend, since I saw you I have lost my two front teeth and have suffered much in body and mind. I hope you will not think me *quite* a fright. I have so long experienced your attachment to me, I cannot suspect it to be capable of change from a loss of any *outward* advantage.' And when Hester, Lady Newdigate, was in London in 1790, having her portrait painted by Romney, she told her husband, Sir Roger, 'My picture is still too young & too handsome, but I fancy you will like it . . . .' The picture was not finished then, and two years later she added after another sitting, 'I fancy I call'd up very good looks to-day; where they came from I don't know, but my Picture is certainly much improv'd. All seem satisfy'd with it. I have reason to be so, for it is handsomer than ever I was in my life.' Being a widow and engrossed in writing her memoirs may have helped Lady Anne Barnard to defy the effects of time: 'I forget that I am 68 and if by chance I see myself in the glass looking very abominable, I do not care. When alone I am not above five and twenty.'[1]

Susan Pellew, Lady Exmouth, wrote to her husband the admiral when he was about to return from his command in the Mediterranean after three years' absence and, she hoped, retire for good, 'I flatter myself we shall meet about the same time three Years [since] we parted – neither of us I conclude much improved in appearance. Even Israel [her brother-in-law] will allow that a man does not improve after three score, and a woman, I will boldly affirm, is going fast down the hill . . . God bless you, dearest, take care of yourself, endure to the end and praise God for his mercies. Love your poor Old Wife and though we have lived little together in this world, let us not be separated in that which is to come. Your Own Affectionate, S.P.'[2]

Children grew up and left home, the boys generally departing to study or pursue careers, the girls to get married, and their absence could be painful. In 1801 Jane Austen's friend, Mrs Lefroy, wrote to her son Edward, who had been articled to an attorney on the Isle of Wight, 'This was the first morning in the course of 21 years that I ever arose at home without having my heart cheered by the sight of one at least of my children, & I cannot describe the melancholy sensations it occasioned . . .'. She began a letter-journal which she sent him every week or so, recording the news of home and maintaining some of the sense of closeness that she had felt when he lived at home. And Mrs Calvert felt bereft when her daughter Isabella was married to Sir James Stronge and left on her honey-moon: 'Though I was tired of the love-making, I miss Sir James and Isabella dreadfully. I feel to have nothing to do, and the house looks very, very dreary.' This, despite the fact that she still had many children at home and was heavily pregnant at the time![3] Emily Eden caught the feel-ings of the parents at this moment in her novel *The Semi-Attached Couple*. Lord and Lady Eskdale sat down to dinner tête-à-tête for the first time in ten years.

> Poor dear people, it fairly puzzled them. They were more attached to each other than many husbands and wives are after twenty-four years of married life; and they had been in the daily habit of taking a comfortable half-hour's talk in Lord Eskdale's library, uninterrupted by any of their children. But they had never contemplated the possi-bility of dining and passing the whole evening together, without a child to come in to dessert, or a daughter to look at and listen to. Then who was to make breakfast the next morning, and to answer notes, and to receive visitors? Lady Eskdale was quite posed. She actually ordered a riding-habit, and declared she would begin riding again with Lord Eskdale, who hated going out alone, and had always been accompanied by one of his children. Then she thought she could rub up music enough to play to him after dinner; but when the evening came she was fast asleep on the sofa, half dead with the fatigue of her morning ride, and she almost cried when a note was brought to her that required an answer – partly because, as she said and thought, she missed Helen so much, and partly because she was too indolent to sit up to write.
>
> 'I don't think I can ever exist in this way, Lord Eskdale,' she said. 'What is to be done? here is this note to be answered.'
>
> 'Give it to me, Jane; I will be your secretary.'[4]

In time, grandchildren might fill some of this gap, although accounts of the joys of being a grandparent are surprisingly sparse in the litera-ture. Sir Roger Newdigate wrote two charming letters to the newborn son of his heir (who was his cousin, not his son), but Maria, Lady Stanley, was far from enthusiastic at the prospect of having all nine of her eldest son's children to stay over Christmas, dreading the noise and turmoil they would bring, and her attitude does not seem untypical: if grand-children were a pleasure, it was one enjoyed most in moderation.[5]

Couples seldom thought of moving house as they grew older, unless, like Mr Austen, they retired from a profession and went to live in Bath or some other resort or seaside town where they would have the benefit of plenty of company and medical advice within easy reach. Widows, however, were often forced to look for a new home when their husband died. When Lord Stanley died in October 1850, Maria, then in her late seventies, at once began packing up and looking for a new home for her final years, moving out of the family home little more than a month after she was widowed. Her daughter-in-law, the new Lady Stanley, commented to her husband, 'They [Maria and her two unmarried daughters who accompanied her] do not take the pianoforte, nor indeed hardly anything, & your mother continually repeats, all she takes shall be returned at her death. She means to give the £100 left in the will to the poor, now, that we may not be obliged to give it. It is quite impossible for any person to have acted more kindly & generously than she has done, & her only feeling seems to be anxiety for you.' In fact Maria lived on for another thirteen years, dying in 1863 when she was ninety-two years old.[6]

There was a strong disinclination for the older generation to live with their married children. It was seen as natural for Maria Stanley to be accompanied by her two unmarried daughters, but it would have been exceptional if she, or they, had lived with her eldest son, his wife and their children. Mr Woodhouse was particularly lucky that Emma and Mr Knightley were willing to sacrifice their marital independence to preserve his comfort, but in general the world agreed with the Duchess of Portland who commented on Mary Delany's decision to move to Bath after her husband's death, 'I think it very proper Mrs Delany should have a house of her own'.[7]

But if retaining a home of your own brought independence from family, it also brought the possibility of increasing dependence on serv-ants, and while some elderly people were fortunate in having a loyal and devoted staff, others felt vulnerable, aware of their inability to maintain their authority or require servants to perform their duties to the standard they would have previously required, let alone dismiss those who fell short and engage replacements. In such cases family support – especially an unmarried daughter who could take over the management of the household – or, failing that, a paid companion, might be invaluable.[8]

People worried about their own health and that of their spouse and their children, just as they worried about their children's marriages and careers, and the state of the country, especially when the war with France was going badly or there were domestic upheavals. However, many also took stock and counted their blessings. In November 1801 Lord Palmerston spent some time at his property at Sheen, which he always associated with his first wife, Frances Poole, who had died more than thirty years previously. By his own account he indulged in a 'train of melancholy recollections and the mournful luxury of reviewing the affecting memorials of long departed worth, tenderness and attachment'. But at the same time he was aware of his good fortune in having made a second, equally happy marriage to Mary Mee, telling her that 'Nobody is so formed as you are to enter into these feelings', and that it was a 'relief' to discuss them with her. 'I cannot conceive why one is never to speak of what one has felt the most, and why the subjects that lie the deepest in one's heart and are the dearest to one's remembrance are to be eternally banished from one's lips.'[9]

Love in old age for most couples meant mutual affection, contentment, trust and shared interests and memories, but for some, passion still burnt bright. In August 1811 the seventy-year-old William Ogilvie wrote to his seventy-nine-year-old wife, Emily, Duchess of Leinster:

I last night after dinner received your letter of the 6th written as beautifully and with as steady a hand as the first letter I had the happiness of receiving from you about forty five years ago. How can I ever be sufficiently thankful to Providence for continuing the blessing of my life to me, and with a degree of health and strength that enable you to bear up against the infirmities of old age and to enjoy the different objects that attach you to life, or how can I ever be sufficiently grateful to you dearest Emily for the steadiness and warmth of your attachment to me. Be assured, my beloved Emily that I am thoroughly sensible of and properly grateful for the one and the other . . . I can truly assure you that from the first moment of our attachment to this instant you have been the first and reigning object of my thought and feeling and that you will continue to be so till the last hour of my life and that no other object has ever engaged my affections or interfered with my attachment to you.

They both defied old age, leading active lives, Ogilvie pursuing his interests in travel, building and investing, while Emily continued to dine out, visit her children and spend more than she felt she ought on plants at the nursery. In 1809, when she was seventy-eight, she sat for her portrait to Martin Archer Shee. 'It will not be what you were at 20 or 40,' Ogilvie wrote, 'but it will be the most beautiful woman of your age in the kingdom.'[10]

In 1795 Hester, Lady Newdigate, went to the seaside for the sake of her health, staying at Bognor Rocks, a small, new watering resort. She wrote, as she always had when away from home, every day to Sir Roger and with undiminished affection, which was evidently fully reciprocated. Commenting on a particularly fine moon one evening, she wrote, 'I pleas'd myself with thinking that our Eyes met in ye Moon last night. Indeed it was impossible to be otherwise unless you never look'd at it for Milly and I admired her & Jupiter & their reflection in ye Sea till we were almost blind . . . .' Unfortunately her health continued to deteriorate and in 1800 she made a last trip to the sea in the hope of regaining her strength, writing to Sir Roger from Margate:

You are a Dear Angel, I can read your thoughts in every line. It is all I wish & makes me doubly anxious to be enabled by a tollerable degree of returning health to reward you in some measure for all you have done & suffer'd for me. Did I not still entertain a Gleam of Hope that God in his great Mercy wd in his good time extend his Goodness so far I sh'd most earnestly pray him to take me to himself that I might no longer be a Bar to your happiness & that of all who Love me. But he has with numberless other Blessings given me a never failing hope & Confidence that I shall yet enjoy some years of Ease & of happiness with you at dear Arbury, & with this hope I ought with patience to endure ye Tryal however long it may be . . . .[11]

She returned home to Arbury, dying there on 30 September 1800 when she was sixty-three, and Sir Roger was eighty-one. A month after her death, Hester's sister, Nelly Mundy, sent him a copy of a hand-written morning prayer she had found in Hester's pocketbook. It was much worn and in places hard to read, but showed Hester's devotion and piety, and her gratitude for all the blessings she had received: 'the tenderest of Parents & the best & most affectionate of Husbands & kindest of friends, & throughout Life with a degree of happiness & prosperity so far surpassing the common lot of mortals & my own deserts, that my heart overflows with Gratitude unutterable . . .'

> Shower down thy heavenly Benediction upon my most Dearly beloved Husband, & if in thy Wisdom thou thinkest fit to deprive him of me, in whom, next to Thee, he looks for Support & Solace of his Old Age, do thou Gracious Lord grant him so great a supply of thy heavenly Comfort & consolation accompany'd with his good health, Chearful disposition & all other blessings that can make Life desirable to him, that the remainder of his days may pass as those already spent in that even peaceful tenor which only good men can experience.[12]

Sir Roger lived on for another six years, having his heir Francis Newdigate and his wife and son come to live with him at Arbury. In July 1806, when he was eighty-seven, Sir Roger wrote to a friend, 'I thank my good God my prayer is heard! I am unwell but have no particular complaint, but a general defailance, gradual decay, increasing weakness; but by His great mercy my road down hill is easy. I have only to look one way and to pray "Lord let Thy servant depart in peace . . ."'. He died a few months later.[13]

CONCLUSION

DESPITE THE IMMENSE POPULARITY of Jane Austen's novels today, the era in which she lived – the late eighteenth and early nineteenth centuries – does not have a reputation for happy marriages. Instead it is commonly associated with loose aristocratic morals and flamboyant affairs, epitomised by some of the most famous people of the time: Georgiana, Duchess of Devonshire, the Prince of Wales (later the Prince Regent and then George IV), Nelson, Wellington and Byron, none of whom are remembered for their fidelity or conjugal happiness. This impression existed at the time, created in part by a succession of much publicised cases of adultery and divorce among the leaders of society beginning in the late 1760s, reaching a crescendo in the 1790s and continuing well into the nineteenth century. These cases were given publicity both in the daily press and in journals such as the *Town and Country Magazine*, which relied on scandal as their main selling point, retelling old tales and inventing new ones when there was little genuine material to report. The behaviour of the young Prince of Wales and his brother the Duke of York in the 1780s, their wild living, numerous affairs, pursuit of actresses and close association with Charles James Fox and the Devonshire House Whigs reinforced the idea that the upper classes were hedonistic, irreligious and immoral. Self-appointed public moralists and popular debating societies frequently drew a contrast between the wicked aristocracy and the middle classes of society, who were presented as much more sober, industrious, respectable and virtuous; a view which was widely applauded even though there was little if any evidence to support it.[1]

Some reaction to this perceived spread of immorality was inevitable, and its beginnings may be dated to 1787 when George III issued a 'Royal Proclamation for the Encouragement of Piety and Virtue, and for Preventing and Punishing Vice, Profaneness and Immorality'. This was largely the work of William Wilberforce, who had recently experienced a spiritual epiphany and dedicated himself to the twin objects of reforming the morals of society (especially the upper classes) and abolishing the slave trade. Although the proclamation had little immediate effect, it marked the beginning of a sustained campaign which ultimately played a significant role in changing the mood of society, ensuring that a serious approach to religion, the observance of the sabbath and an earnest scrutiny of the morality of one's own behaviour – and that of others – ceased to be limited to a few eccentric religious enthusiasts. Like most reformers, however, Wilberforce and his fellow evangelicals exaggerated the problem they were seeking to solve, and their campaigning strengthened the idea that the British aristocracy was in dire need of salvation as it had strayed so far from the paths of righteousness.[2]

The French Revolution gave this movement added momentum. It was easy to believe that the immorality and extravagance of the French aristocracy had contributed to their downfall, and it was not a great step from that to suppose that the British upper classes needed to heed the warning. Some went further, seeing the loss of the American colonies and the many setbacks in the early years of the war with France as divine punishment for the country's iniquities, and feared that if repentance and improvement were too long delayed, God might withdraw his favour and Britain might be eclipsed just as the luxury and vice of Rome had led to the fall of her empire.[3]

Strangely the ultimate victory in the war did nothing to undermine this idea of the immorality of the upper classes. Indeed the Victorians delighted in drawing a contrast between their own cult of domesticity, represented by confident, indulged, bewhiskered gentlemen and adoring, simpering wives, presided over by the Queen herself, Prince Albert and their brood of children, and the licentious, raddled society of the Regency, epitomised by Lord Steyne, the aged, debauched roué in

Thackeray's *Vanity Fair*, who was based on the Prince's old crony Lord Hertford. Society was on a path of steady moral and material improvement, and the future looked bright. Echoes of this vision remain in the way we remember each era today, even though historians have shown that there was a great gulf between the Victorian ideal and the reality, and that many women throughout the nineteenth century ventured far and wide, both physically and intellectually, while for many others domesticity proved a straitjacket.[4]

Despite this contemporary view, the idea that the late eighteenth and early nineteenth centuries was a period of unusually loose morals and sexual freedom among the upper classes, or the country as a whole, rests on the flimsiest of foundations. Scandals in high society caught the eye, whereas those lower down the social scale did not, any more than the *Town and Country Magazine* would fill a column on the domestic virtues of a happily married lord and his lady. And even if all the stories in the *Town and Country* were entirely accurate – a foolhardy presumption – its profiles described only thirteen men a year, and not all of them belonged to the aristocracy. Similarly, while the rising numbers of actions for *crim. con.* made for entertaining reading, the historian Lawrence Stone calculated that only 79 out of approximately 2,050 men of title (peers, baronets and the holders of courtesy titles, including 'the honourable') were involved in *crim. con.* cases or parliamentary divorces in the sixty years from 1770 to 1830 whether as plaintiffs or as defendants. Of course, this was only a fraction of the cases of adultery that never went to court, but even so, as Stone concluded, it hardly justifies 'the idea of an indolent and degenerate aristocracy indulging in widespread adultery and wife-swapping'. This conclusion is supported by the discovery that of 2,143 men who served as Members of Parliament between 1790 and 1820 only 23 were divorced, while the number of divorce bills which passed through parliament reached its peak, not in the supposedly debauched 1790s, but in the 1840s, the first full decade of Victoria's reign. F.M.L. Thompson, a leading social historian, stated that:

> it is more than likely that there was nothing particularly remarkable about aristocratic morals and manners in the 30 or 40 years leading up to the outburst of reproval in the 1790s. Not only can one find

amazingly debauched and unpleasant aristocrats aplenty at any time since the Glorious Revolution, and before the Civil War as well, but also representatives of an entirely different stream of well-behaved, devout, faithful, and industrious aristocrats are not all that rare.[5]

More significantly, London high society, and indeed the aristocracy as a whole, represented only a thin layer of gaudy icing atop the rich cake of the upper classes, which included large numbers of independent country gentlemen and their families, together with many of those in the gentlemanly professions: clergymen, lawyers and officers in the army and navy. A simple dichotomy between aristocratic vice and bourgeois virtue was very satisfying to amateur orators in debating clubs, or to Victorian newspaper writers, but it has no room for Jane Austen, her family and the characters in her novels. Most couples of whatever class lived quietly together, some happily, some not, in a way that attracted little outside attention, neither saints nor desperate sinners.

The nature of marriage and the duties of husbands and wives were much discussed topics in Jane Austen's lifetime, partly because they are perennially popular subjects, and partly because all the talk of immorality, divorce and scandal made them appear topical. Newspapers, magazines, sermons and numerous books and pamphlets gave their readers advice and entertainment, although these works did not present a single, clear message, but rather a range of opinions, often more theoretical than practical. Some conservative writers continued to stress the importance of a wife's submission and obedience to her husband. As late as 1813 one author – unsurprisingly a man – instructed a female correspondent: 'By marrying you have committed yourself to the care of one whose province is government and direction: the duty on your part therefore is subjection and obedience . . . With this truth coincides experience; for the wife, as the weaker vessel, naturally cleaves to her husband, and expects from him both assistance and advice.' But such views were old-fashioned: during the second half of the eighteenth century the authors of conduct manuals generally changed their emphasis from husbands using their power overtly to control their wives, to husbands and wives securing each other's loyalty through trust and affection, a shift which was epitomised by the titles of two works: *The Art of*

Governing a Wife, published in 1747, and *The Art of Engaging the Affections of Wives to their Husbands*, which appeared in 1793.[6]

At the same time novels explored many aspects of courtship and marriage in a highly entertaining manner, and probably had a much greater influence on shaping assumptions and expectations about marriage than explicitly didactic works. These novels often had a young woman as their principal protagonist and were structured around a courtship plot, in which she overcomes mistakes and perils to find marriage and happiness with her true love. Tales like this had a great appeal for a new audience of literate, leisured young ladies, like Catherine Morland and Isabella Thorpe, who could get the books cheaply through circulating libraries. Many of these novels showed women in a wide variety of difficult and dangerous situations, including the amusing absurdities of the Gothic genre and Mary Brunton's *Self-Control*, where the heroine is kidnapped and taken to America by the villain, but manages to escape by faking her own death and shooting rapids tied to a canoe! The underlying message for some readers may have been that their future happiness depended on finding and marrying the right man, but for others it was that they should rely upon their own intelligence and judgement and not passively do as they were told. Fanny Price, the meekest and most dutiful of all Austen's heroines, defied Sir Thomas Bertram's wishes and refused to marry Henry Crawford, and the author makes clear that she was right to do so.

The plots of novels varied widely but some messages were commonplace if not universal. Mercenary marriages, or those made purely in order to secure social status or a family alliance, were unlikely to end well, and young women – and young men – were entitled to resist pressure from their parents to make such a match. It was too risky to marry without love: the emotional void might be filled by another attachment, which even if it did not lead to adultery, meant the great unhappiness of being bound to one person while loving another. It was also deeply unfair to the spouse, who was deprived of the chance of finding someone who would truly love them and who might well look for consolation elsewhere. Physical attraction was important: heroes and heroines were almost always good looking with a well-bred manner, but outright beauty, in either sex, could be a snare. Headlong passion was dangerous and a poor basis for a marriage: it would quickly burn itself out, leaving an incompatible couple tied together without anything in common. Hasty marriages in general were imprudent, although they might turn out well, and not all novelists resisted the appeal of love at first sight. A sufficient income was essential, and great disparities of wealth or social status were a potential problem, especially if the woman was in the superior position. It was also desirable that the man be older than the woman, or at least not more than marginally younger, while he might be as much as fifteen or even twenty years older (that is, roughly double her age) without making him ineligible, so long as he was in good health. Both his and her character and reputation were important: women should beware trying to reform a rake, and men should make sure that any shadow on their potential bride's reputation was indeed unmerited and the result of a misunderstanding. Finally, the couple should properly understand and respect each other and have similar views and values, especially about religion.

The connection between literature and life was complex: contemporaries commented that Austen's novels closely mirrored life, although she avoided some of its wilder and more dramatic extremes, while some other writers piled improbability upon improbability in order to create an action-packed adventure for their characters. But novels also influenced readers: as early as the 1760s, when the vogue for fiction was still in its early days, the moralist Dr Gregory worried that it might give young women unrealistic expectations, and that they would be disappointed by their husbands.

> Instead of meeting with sense, delicacy, tenderness, a lover, a friend, an equal companion, in a husband; you may be tired with insipidity and dullness; shocked with indelicacy, or mortified by indifference. You will find none to compassionate, or even understand your sufferings; for your husbands may not use you cruelly, and may give you as much money for your clothes, personal expence [sic], and domestic necessaries, as is suitable for their fortunes. The world would therefore look on you as unreasonable women, and that did not deserve to be happy, if you were not so.[7]

But men as well as women read novels, and some may have been encouraged by their reading to look for a wife who would be 'a friend, an equal companion' for them, and to make a corresponding effort themselves. Indeed it is quite clear, whether fiction was involved or not, that this was what men like John Stanley, James Stuart Wortley, Thomas Fremantle and Charles Arbuthnot sought and found in marriage.

Lawrence Stone believed that novels played a large part in causing a transformation in the nature of marriage in the eighteenth century, which saw romantic love and the ideal of a 'companionate marriage' overturn the old order in which marriages were made for the greater good of the wider family. Research by later historians has watered down this contrast: love had never been absent from the making of marriages; after all, the wedding service itself declared that one of the purposes of marriage was 'for the mutual society, help, and comfort, that the one ought to have of the other, both in prosperity and adversity'. Equally, prudential considerations never disappeared, although some couples chose to ignore them. Rather than a revolution there was a shift of emphasis, an adjustment in the weighting of priorities, with the personal preferences of the prospective couple gaining importance and the wishes of the parents and wider family retreating. Many parents had come to fear the responsibility they would incur if they took too active a part in encouraging a match, although they still valued the power of veto as a check upon folly and impetuosity, even while they knew that it might be overridden by a dash to Gretna Green.[8]

The implications of this shift of emphasis for the actual experience of marriage, rather than the selection of a partner through courtship, are less clear. There have always been some exceptionally happy marriages – the phrase 'Darby and Joan', used to describe a devoted couple, comes from a poem first published in 1735 – and some extremely unhappy marriages; but there is no way of determining whether the number of either increased or decreased in this period. Nor can we tell if the more common experience of couples who got along reasonably well on the whole, but not without periods of friction and some disenchantment, generally improved, remained about the same or got worse.

The law and social expectations continued to give women fewer rights than men, firmly subordinating them to their husbands, and these disadvantages were felt most keenly in bad marriages. It was difficult for a beaten and abused wife to escape her tormentor, let alone to divorce him. Even without violence or adultery, the wife in an unhappy marriage was much more constrained than her husband: it was harder for her to steer her own course within the marriage or to secure a separation on reasonable terms, especially if her own family were unable or unwilling to help her. Conversely, happy marriages were usually, although not always, founded on a basis of mutual respect and consideration that greatly lessened the impact of the legal subordination of women's rights and interests. Still, even the most considerate couples had internalised many attitudes about the role 'naturally' played by husbands and wives, which inevitably tended to favour men in most although not all respects. The particular circumstances of each marriage and the character of the individuals meant that every case was different, with the wife being the dominant figure in some marriages, but the cards were heavily stacked in favour of men.

The worst husbands were men like Andrew Stoney Bowes, who married their wives purely in order to acquire their wealth, and who abused and humiliated them from the outset of the marriage. Such extreme cases were rare, but there were many other marriages which began with goodwill and kind intentions, sometimes even with considerable love, only to descend into bullying and violence after some years. There were also many husbands who were unfaithful to their wives and – almost certainly a smaller number – of wives who were unfaithful to their husbands. This infidelity appears to range from the casual self-indulgence of Boswell's use of prostitutes, to passionate love affairs that the participants felt overwhelmed their ability to resist, such as that between Lord Paget and Charlotte Wellesley. Still, it is clear that such affairs seldom, if ever, arose in a vacuum: the lovers flirted and courted each other, piling up the kindling before the match was struck, sometimes deluding themselves until almost the last moment that their behaviour was quite innocent, and sometimes indulging in the pleasure of the chase without much, if any, compunction.

Many marriages were unsuccessful without ending in separation or a divorce. Some couples tolerated mutual infidelity and sought only to avoid an open scandal, while many wives and some husbands chose to look the other way, unsure how best to respond to their spouse's adultery. Society generally dismissed a husband's infidelities with a shrug, while it was also normally prepared to tolerate those of a wife, so long as her husband did not appear to object and there was no open breach. If forced to take a stand, it would judge women's behaviour harshly in the first instance, but might eventually forgive her if she married her lover, or even someone else. But infidelity was almost never a matter of genuine indifference, and the idea that appears in some modern accounts, that once an aristocratic lady had presented her lord with an heir, and perhaps a 'spare' as well, she was free to sleep with whomever she liked provided she was discreet, was not one that many couples in the late eighteenth or early nineteenth century would have recognised.

Marriages might falter and finally fail without any infidelity through differences of taste and temper. Sometimes this was a case of misjudgement: couples might be genuinely attracted to each other and marry, only to find that they really had little in common and that they could not find a way of living together that satisfied them both. Or one spouse – usually, but not always, the husband – might be extremely selfish, putting his needs and his pleasures first, and eventually exhausting his wife's patience and loyalty. Their character and outlook might prove incompatible so that they constantly grated on each other: one might enjoy teasing the other and cause serious hurt and offence unintentionally, but never learning from past experience; or they might be ill-matched in terms of intelligence and values. One might have friends or relatives whom the other never liked and came to detest; or be determined to pursue a style of living that the other tolerated for a time but which eventually caused insurmountable resentment. They might differ on how to bring up their children, or be made unhappy by too many or too few babies, or the demands of the husband's career, or by financial problems. There was no shortage of potential sources of friction in married life, and it took goodwill fuelled by love for these to be negotiated without damaging relations between wife and husband.

Some marriages succeeded despite considerable obstacles: Captain Fremantle and his wife Betsey spent most of the first year of their marriage on board his frigate, on active service in wartime, and this culminated in his being severely wounded, so that she had to combine nursing him with finding a home for them in England at a time when she was pregnant and far from family and friends. Yet these hardships may have had their advantages, for their marriage was a true partnership based on mutual respect and reliance: necessity had taught him that he could safely trust her judgement and courage, while it had given her the self-confidence to manage their family and financial affairs during the long periods of his absence on duty in later years.

Similarly, George and Joan Canning spent much time apart as she and their children lived in the Midlands to obtain specialist medical attention for their invalid eldest son, while he stayed in London pursuing his political career. However, it is clear from his correspondence that this separation was not one of mutual convenience, that they remained fiercely in love and that he consulted her on all important decisions about his career, listening carefully to her advice. The asymmetry in their positions when he first courted her was long forgotten, and they were united in their ambition for his success.

There were also some instances of apparently foolish marriages that nonetheless ended up succeeding, although not without heartache along the way. Matthew Flinders married Ann Chappelle even though he knew that the Admiralty was unlikely to allow her to accompany him on his voyage to Australia. An attempt to embark her without the Admiralty's knowledge ended in failure, with the result that he sailed without her only three months after their wedding. This made a separation of two or three years inevitable, but no one could have foreseen the circumstances that compelled him to put into Mauritius on his voyage home in 1803 or his detention by the French authorities there until 1810. Remarkably, their marriage, when they were reunited, proved very happy, although Matthew died on 19 July 1814, less than four years after his return to England.

It was circumstances, not differences in character, that made the Flinders' marriage risky; but when Frances Winckley tied her happiness to Sir John Shelley her family had good reason to think that she was being extremely unwise. She was nineteen and he was thirty-five, a confirmed gambler, rake and spendthrift whose motive in pursuing her (none too assiduously) seemed obvious: to obtain her fortune. She suffered greatly from his neglect of her and attention to others in the early years of their marriage, but in the end obtained his affection and became the dominant partner in the marriage. Sir John became very proud of his wife, and the marriage prospered, with each partner delighting in the success and happiness of the other. Still, it is unlikely that many marriages of this sort ended so happily, and the failure of James Boswell's marriage to his cousin Margaret Montgomerie, despite his intense happiness in its first years, is probably more typical; if anything, Boswell was better than most such men, having intelligence, a conscience and genuine love of Margaret which he never entirely lost, even in the midst of his self-indulgence at her expense.

Other marriages succeeded without having great obstacles to overcome. These successful marriages were each unique, but generally shared some unsurprising characteristics. The couple trusted each other on important matters and confided in each other when in difficulties or facing a serious decision. They often shared a sense of common purpose whether this was his career, if he had one; their children, if they had any; or their social life, in which either might make the running, but would normally appreciate the support and encouragement of the other. They would take care of the other's comfort, health and happiness, with generosity and thoughtfulness: for example, Anne Barnard's gift of £50 to her husband Andrew, specifically so that he could buy 'the best horse' in Cape Town when he arrived there, knowing that this would 'amuse you and keep you in health'.[9] They dealt with financial difficulties by pulling together, each making sacrifices and without reproaches, while husbands such as Thomas Fremantle and Charles Paget found no difficulty in acknowledging their wives' superiority at buying property or managing their finances as a whole.[10] They were kind and considerate to each other in the small exchanges of everyday life, adjusting their manner and language to suit their spouse, for some people enjoy the give and take of verbal jousting and a teasing manner, while others can be distressed by it. Equally, they took trouble to find a solution to small differences of habit and manner when they found that these threatened to become an irritation, each happy to suit the other more often than not and never to nurse the sacrifice as a grievance. They gave each other the freedom to pursue interests of their own, with wives accepting their husband's enthusiasm for sport or farming, for example, while husbands encouraged their wife if she was inclined to redecorate the house or establish a garden. And they handled relations with their in-laws with tact and delicacy if genuine enthusiasm was not possible.

In one of her early works Jane Austen wrote that 'Perfect felicity is not the property of mortals, and no one has a right to expect perfect uninterrupted happiness.'[11] Certainly few, if any, of the couples considered in this book led completely untroubled lives. The Palmerstons and the Arbuthnots, among others, faced serious financial problems; the Castlereaghs and the Cannings had to deal with professional setbacks that led not only to great disappointment but also to the loss of income that went with a loss of office or employment. Most naval and military officers and their wives, like Thomas and Betsey Fremantle, had to bear with separation and the anxiety it brought. Hester Newdigate's health was never robust, while Anne Barnard reluctantly let her beloved Andrew return to the Cape alone while she endeavoured to promote his career at home. Many parents endured the distress of losing children, while others struggled to reconcile themselves to not having children at all. Close family members might be ruined financially, commit adultery or be involved in a divorce, elope or suffer serious mental or physical illnesses; and these strains did not always arrive in a neat sequence, but might overlap placing both husband and wife under great pressure at the same time. Even the best marriages went through difficult periods, either because of some difference between the couple, or for some unconnected reason that drove a wedge between them, perhaps by making them less attentive to each other, or by souring their temper for a time, before they managed to restore their happiness.

Love and liking, enjoying each other's company and making them feel loved and important were at the heart of it. It might be the passionate, intense love of Emily and William Ogilvie or Lady Anne and Andrew Barnard, or it might be a calmer more everyday form of affection. We see it in the letters of Hester and Sir Roger Newdigate; of Palmerston and his two wives; of John and Mary Dickenson; of the Fremantles and the Arbuthnots, burning brightly through the years as they sailed through life together. It is not hard to imagine that Charles Arbuthnot would have felt, as Jane Austen supposed Mr Darcy felt, 'that mixture of Love, Pride & Delicacy', which meant that he would prize 'any Picture of her too much to like it should be exposed to the public eye'.[12]

DRAMATIS PERSONAE

Women are listed under the names in which they appear most commonly in the text. As a result some women appear under their maiden and some under their married names.

Arbuthnot, Charles (14 March 1767–18 August 1850, see plate 14) and Harriet (10 September 1793–2 August 1834, see plate 13). Charles Arbuthnot was a diplomat and politician, from a Scots gentry family but brought up by relatives in England. On 23 February 1799 he married Marcia Lisle, who died in Constantinople in 1806, leaving him a widower with four children. Harriet Fane was the daughter of Henry Fane (1739–1802), a younger brother of the Earl of Westmorland, who died when she was only eight. Charles and Harriet were married on 31 January 1814 when she was twenty and he was forty-six; and their marriage was very happy. She wrote one of the most important political diaries of the nineteenth century, covering the years 1820 to 1832, when she was close to the centre of conservative politics through her and her husband's friendship with the Duke of Wellington.

Austen, Jane (16 December 1775–18 July 1817), author. Her parents were George (1 May 1731–21 January 1805) and Cassandra (née Leigh, baptised 10 September 1739–18 January 1827), who married on 26 April

1764. The family lived at Steventon in Hampshire where Mr Austen was the rector until he retired in 1801 and they moved to Bath. After his death his widow and her two daughters (both unmarried) moved first to Southampton and then, in 1809, to Chawton, living in a cottage provided by their son and brother Edward. The Austens' children were:

James (13 February 1765–13 December 1819), a clergyman who succeeded to his father's living at Steventon.

George (26 August 1766–17 January 1838), epileptic from an early age and possibly deaf and dumb; he lived apart from the rest of the family.

Edward (7 October 1767–19 November 1852) was adopted by his wealthy cousins, inherited their estate and changed his name to Knight. He was the father of Jane's niece Fanny Knight (q.v.).

Henry (8 June 1771–12 March 1850), an officer in the militia, then an army agent and banker who went bankrupt in 1816 and became a clergyman. He married his cousin Eliza de Feuillide (q.v.) on 31 December 1797.

Cassandra (9 January 1773–22 March 1845) whose engagement to Tom Fowle was ended by his death in the West Indies in 1797, and who lived with her mother and sister for the rest of their lives.

Francis ('Frank') (23 April 1774–10 August 1865), a successful naval officer.

Jane (16 December 1775–18 July 1817).

Charles (23 June 1779–7 October 1852), naval officer. He married Fanny Palmer in Bermuda in 1807. She died in 1814, leaving him with four young children. In 1820 he married her sister Harriet and had another four children.

Barnard, Lady Anne (8 December 1750–6 May 1825) and Andrew (c. 1763–27 October 1807). She was Lady Anne Lindsay, eldest daughter of the Earl of Balcarres, and had many suitors and several lovers before her marriage on 31 October 1793. He was the impoverished son of the Bishop of Limerick. Anne used her influence with Henry Dundas to secure a position at Cape Colony for Andrew and they both lived there from 1797 to 1802, when Anne returned to England to seek preferment for Andrew, and he joined her in the following year. In 1807 he returned to the Cape alone and died there after a short illness. Their marriage was unusually close.

Bessborough, Harriet, Countess of (16 June 1761–11 November 1821), daughter of Lord and Lady Spencer and sister of Georgiana, Duchess of Devonshire. Her marriage on 27 November 1780 to Frederick Ponsonby, later 3rd Earl of Bessborough, was not close, and she had several love affairs, including a fifteen-year relationship with Granville Leveson Gower, a young diplomat and politician of considerable charm and exceptionally good looks. Her letters, particularly those to Leveson Gower, are remarkable for their freshness and spontaneity.

Boswell, James (29 October 1740–19 May 1795) and Margaret (1738–4 June 1789). James Boswell trained and worked as an advocate but gained lasting fame as a traveller, a biographer of his idol, Dr Johnson, and as a remarkable diarist. Margaret Montgomerie was his cousin, a close friend and confidante. They were married on 25 November 1769, and the marriage was extremely happy at first before gradually deteriorating. James's relationship with his father was always difficult and he reacted badly to the idea of his father remarrying.

Bowes, Andrew Stoney (19 January 1747–16 January 1810). Andrew Robinson Stoney was a half-pay lieutenant in the army, the younger son of a respectable Irish family, who married an heiress, Hannah Newton, and treated her badly. After her death he persuaded Mary, Countess of Strathmore, to marry him on the supposition that he was on his deathbed. (He changed his name to Bowes on his marriage, as required by her wealthy father's will.) He immediately recovered and subjected her to years of physical abuse before she finally escaped in 1785 and succeeded in divorcing him. He died in debtor's prison on 23 January 1810.

Bowes, Mary: see Strathmore, Mary Bowes.

Calvert, Frances (4 February 1767–22 February 1859), daughter and co-heiress of Edmond Sexten Pery, later Lord Pery, Speaker of the Irish House of Commons. On 9 January 1789 she married Nicolson Calvert (15 May 1764–13 April 1841), who was Member of Parliament for Hertfordshire for thirty-two years. They had eight children, four sons and four daughters.

Happily married and essentially conservative, her tart observations and sharp judgements enliven her diary, which was published as *An Irish Beauty of the Regency*.

Canning, George (11 April 1770–8 August 1827). One of the most brilliant and distrusted politicians of his age, Canning was a devoted follower of Pitt and a renowned Foreign Secretary, dying only four months after he had finally achieved his ambition of becoming prime minister. He married the wealthy and well-connected Joan Scott (15 March 1776– 14 March 1837) on 8 July 1800. After his death she was created Viscountess Canning of Kilbraham on 22 January 1828.

Capel, Lady Caroline (1773–9 July 1847), born Lady Caroline Paget, daughter of Henry Paget, 1st Earl of Uxbridge. Her siblings included Henry William Paget, who eloped with Charlotte Wellesley; Arthur Paget, who married Lady Boringdon after her divorce; Charles Paget, the naval officer; and Lady Louisa Erskine, who subsequently married George Murray.

On 2 April 1792 she married the Hon. John Capel (2 March 1769– 5 March 1819), second son of the Earl of Essex, whose gambling kept the family in debt and forced them to retire to Brussels in 1814. They had eleven children of whom the three eldest were Harriet Capel (1793– 1819), who suffered greatly with an infatuation with Baron Trip; Georgiana (1795–1835) and Maria (1797–1856) who were both in love with officers in Wellington's army who were too poor to marry them.

Castlereagh: see Stewart, Robert.

Eden, Emily (3 March 1797–5 August 1869), novelist. She was the daughter of William Eden, 1st Baron Auckland, a distinguished British diplomat, and she had a place in the Whig social and political world of the early nineteenth century. Her novel *The Semi-Attached Couple* was written in 1829 and reflected the attitudes of a slightly earlier era, although it was not published until 1860. She did not marry.

Edgeworth, Maria (1 January 1768–22 May 1849), novelist. The daughter of Richard Lovell Edgeworth, a noted Irish writer on education and other subjects. Her novels, including *Castle Rackrent*, brought her considerably greater acclaim and earnings than Austen received in her lifetime. In 1802 she declined an offer of marriage from a Swedish courtier, Abraham Niclas Clewberg-Edelcrantz, and remained unmarried. *Belinda*, published in 1801, was her second novel.

Erskine, Lieutenant-General Sir James (30 September 1772–3 March 1825), the younger son of a Scottish laird, married Lady Louisa Paget (1777–23 January 1842) on 5 March 1801 after a romantic courtship which succeeded, with the help of the Royal Family, in overcoming the opposition of her family. The marriage was not, however, successful and Sir James was on the point of divorcing her when he died. This enabled her to marry her lover Major-General Sir George Murray (6 February 1772–28 July 1846), with whom she had been living for several years, on 28 April 1825, just eight weeks after her husband's death.

Fane, Harriet (10 September 1793–2 August 1834): see Arbuthnot, Harriet.

Feuillide, Eliza de (22 December 1761–25 April 1813), Jane Austen's cousin and sister-in-law. Born Eliza Hancock, daughter of George Austen's sister Philadelphia and her husband Tysoe Saul Hancock, she was born in Calcutta but returned to England before her father's death in 1775. In 1781 she married Jean Capot de Feuillide, who was guillotined in Paris on 22 February 1794. They had one son, Hastings de Feuillide (1786–1801). On 31 December 1797 she married her cousin Henry Austen. They had no children.

Flinders, Matthew (16 March 1774–19 July 1814), naval officer and explorer. He was the son of an apothecary-surgeon, and distinguished himself for his ability as a navigator. In 1801 he was promoted to lieutenant and given command of a small ship, the *Investigator*, with orders to make a detailed exploration of the coast of Australia. On 17 April

1801, shortly before he was due to sail, he married Ann Chappelle (21 November 1772–10 November 1852),[1] hoping that she might accompany him. However, the Admiralty learnt of his marriage and forbade this, so that Ann was forced to remain home, living with her family. On his return voyage from Australia Flinders was forced to put into Mauritius where the French governor detained him until 1810, and so after a few weeks of marriage the couple were separated for more than nine years. After this, he remained at home, preparing his charts and the account of his voyages, which was published in 1814 as he lay dying. They had a daughter, Anne, who was born on 1 April 1812.

Fremantle, Betsey (19 April 1778[2]–2 November 1857), daughter of Richard Wynne (1744–98), who lived on the Continent from when Betsey was eight years old. She and her family were Catholics. In 1796 they were evacuated from Leghorn on a Royal Navy frigate HMS *Inconstant*, commanded by Captain Thomas Fremantle (20 November 1765–19 December 1819). After some months of hesitation, Fremantle proposed and the couple were married on 13 January 1797 at Naples. Fremantle was seriously wounded at Santa Cruz de Tenerife on 25 July 1797 and Betsey nursed him on the voyage home. They made their home in England, but when he had fully recovered from his wound Fremantle returned to sea and had a distinguished career as one of Nelson's ablest captains, including commanding the *Neptune* (98 guns) at Trafalgar. Much further service followed, so that he was separated from his beloved wife and children for extended periods until the end of the war. Fremantle came from a family with strong political ties to the Marquess of Buckingham and the Grenvilles. Both Betsey and her sister Eugenia kept revealing diaries.

Grenville, William, Lord (25 October 1759–12 January 1834), influential foreign secretary in his cousin William Pitt the Younger's wartime government in the 1790s and prime minister 1806–7. On 18 July 1792 he married Anne Pitt (10 September 1772–13 June 1864), daughter of Thomas Pitt, Lord Camelford. He was the brother of the Marquess of Buckingham and of Thomas Grenville, both political figures of some importance.

Hardy, Admiral Sir Thomas Masterman (5 April 1769–20 September 1839) rose from a humble background to be Nelson's flag captain at Trafalgar. He was then created a baronet and transferred to the North American station where he courted and, on 17 November 1807, married Lady Louisa Berkeley (*c.* 1788–2 November 1877), daughter of Admiral Sir George Berkeley, who commanded the station. Their marriage was not happy. Following her husband's death Lady Hardy married Charles Ellis, Lord Seaford, on 1 October 1840. Seaford died suddenly on 1 July 1845, and she remained a widow for the last thirty years of her life.

Holroyd, Maria: see Stanley, Maria Josepha.

Knight, Fanny (23 January 1793–24 December 1882), daughter of Edward Knight and niece of Jane Austen. Married a widower with six children, Sir Edward Knatchbull (20 December 1781–24 May 1849), on 24 October 1820 and they had nine further children.

Leinster, Emily, Duchess of (6 October 1731–27 March 1814), daughter of the 2nd Duke of Richmond and sister of Caroline (who married Henry Fox, 1st Lord Holland), Louisa (who married Thomas Conolly), Sarah (who married Charles Bunbury, was divorced and later married George Napier) and Charles, 3rd Duke of Richmond. Emily Lennox married William, Viscount Leinster, on 7 February 1747. He was created Duke of Leinster in 1761. They had a large family. He died on 19 November 1773. She then, in 1774, married William Ogilvie (1740–18 November 1832), the humbly born tutor of her children who had become her lover before her husband's death, a marriage which proved enduringly happy, and which produced further children.

Lindsay, Lady Anne (8 December 1750–6 May 1825), eldest daughter of James, 5th Earl of Balcarres and his wife Anne (née Dalrymple). Despite her lack of fortune she was very popular in society and was accused of being a coquette for refusing many offers of marriage before she finally married Andrew Barnard on 31 October 1793. See under Barnard for their life together.

Lister, Anne (3 April 1791–22 September 1840), daughter of a younger son, she ended up inheriting her unmarried uncle's estate following the deaths of her brothers. She had a succession of love affairs with other women, which she recorded in considerable detail in coded passages of her voluminous diary, before forming a union with Ann Walker (1803–54) which lasted until her death. She travelled extensively and adventurously, dying after a short illness in Georgia in the Caucasus.

Lloyd, Martha (1765–24 January 1843) and Mary (1771–3 August 1843). Family friends of the Austens. Mary married James Austen on 17 January 1797, and after her mother's death the unmarried Martha lived at Chawton with Mrs Austen, Cassandra and Jane. On 24 July 1828 Martha married Francis Austen.

Lyttelton, William and Sarah: see Spencer, Lady Sarah.

Middleton, William (1762–1847) was a substantial Catholic landowner in Yorkshire who married Clara Grace (1762–1833) in 1782. For some years their marriage appeared happy, and they had a number of children. Then, in 1791 or 1792, she fell in love with John Rose (*c*. 1771–?), a newly appointed groom, and began an affair which ultimately led to her divorce in 1796. Neither William nor Clara remarried.

Newdigate, Sir Roger (20 May 1719–23 November 1806)[3] was a long-serving Member of Parliament for Oxford University. In 1743 he married Sophia Conyers, who died in 1774. On 3 June 1776 he married Hester Mundy (*c*. 1737–30 September 1800). Her letters to him when they were apart reveal a deeply loving marriage marked by mutual confidence.

Ogilvie, William: see Leinster, Emily.

Paget, Henry William, Lord (later Earl of Uxbridge, later Marquess of Anglesey) (17 May 1768–29 April 1854 , see plate 15), eldest son and heir of Henry, 1st Lord Uxbridge; brother of Lady Caroline Capel (q.v.), Lady Louisa Erskine (q.v.), Arthur Paget who married Lady Boringdon after her divorce and Charles Paget, the naval officer. On 25 July 1795 he married Lady Caroline Villiers (16 December 1774–16 June 1835, see plate 16), daughter of the 4th Earl of Jersey. They had three sons and five daughters. His affair with Lady Charlotte Wellesley (11 July 1781–8 July 1853) led his wife to divorce him in Scotland in October 1810. She then married George Campbell, 6th Duke of Argyll (22 September 1768–22 October 1839) on 29 November 1810. Paget married Charlotte Wellesley in November 1810. Paget was a distinguished cavalry officer who served as second-in-command to Wellington in the Waterloo campaign and was made a Knight of the Garter. He also served as Lord Lieutenant of Ireland, 1828–9, 1830–33.

Palmerston, Henry Temple, 2nd Viscount (4 December 1739–16 April 1802), Irish peer and member of the British House of Commons for forty years. On 6 October 1767 he married Frances Poole (1733–1 June 1769); they had no surviving children. He remained a widower for almost fourteen years, having a number of mistresses in this time. He married for a second time on 7 January 1783[4] to Mary Mee (1754–20 January 1805), the daughter of a City merchant. They had five children of whom the eldest, the 3rd Viscount, became the famous nineteenth-century Foreign Secretary and prime minister. Both Palmerston's marriages appear to have been very happy.

Russell, Lord (George) William, (8 May 1790–16 July 1846), the second son of the 6th Duke of Bedford by his first wife, brother of Lord John Russell, who was prime minister 1846–52 and 1865–6. After serving in the army on Wellington's staff in the Peninsula, he married, on 21 June 1817, Elizabeth (Bessy) Rawdon (2 October 1793–10 August 1874)[5] a niece of Lord Moira (later the Marquess of Hastings). They had four children, but the marriage was troubled, and in 1835 he began an affair which led to them living largely, but not completely, apart.

Shelley, Frances, Lady (1787–24 February 1873). Born Frances Winckley. Her parents' marriage was unhappy, and after her father's death in 1793 her mother married again, even more unhappily, to Major Barrington.

Lady Frances was a wealthy heiress and was much courted on being introduced into London society, but fell in love with Sir John Shelley (3 March 1772–28 March 1852), a man whose gambling had seriously impaired his fortune. They were married on 4 June 1807 and, after some difficulties in the early years, became very happy together.

Spencer, Lady Sarah (29 July 1787–13 April 1870 , see plate 12), daughter of John, 2nd Earl Spencer, a Whig politician who served as First Lord of the Admiralty in Pitt's government in the 1790s. She was the niece of Georgiana, Duchess of Devonshire, and Harriet, Lady Bessborough. On 3 March 1813 she married William Lyttelton (3 April 1782–30 April 1837, see plate 11), a younger son of Lord Lyttelton, who succeeded to the title in 1828. A few months after they were married they went on an extended tour of Sweden and Russia. They went on to have five children. After her husband's early death she became a lady-in-waiting to Queen Victoria and then, in 1842, Governess to the Royal Children, retiring in 1850. Unfortunately she destroyed all her letters to her husband before she died, so that the record, which is very revealing of her feelings up to her marriage, then largely runs dry.

Stanley, Maria Josepha (3 January 1771–1 November 1863, see plate 10). Born Maria Holroyd, she was the daughter of the 1st Earl Sheffield (1735–1821) and his first wife, Abigail (1746–93). Sheffield was a noted intellectual and the friend and patron of Edward Gibbon. Strong willed and highly intelligent, Maria was encouraged to read and explore ideas, although her struggle to master her temper was not always successful. On 11 October 1796 she married John Thomas Stanley (26 November 1766–23 October 1850, see plate 9), who was both a Member of Parliament and a member of the Royal Society. Their marriage was very happy, even if Maria was sometimes bored with life in the country.

Stewart, Robert (18 June 1769–12 August 1822). From 1796 to 1821 he was known as Lord Castlereagh; he succeeded his father as 2nd Marquess Londonderry in 1821. As a young man of great promise he courted Lady Amelia (Emily) Hobart (20 February 1772–12 February 1829), daughter of the 2nd Earl of Buckinghamshire, and they were married on 9 June

1794. Their marriage was extremely close; they had no children. Castlereagh went on to be a major figure in British politics and one of Britain's most famous and successful foreign secretaries, helping to secure the peace of Europe in the years after the defeat of Napoleon. He killed himself, having suffered a mental breakdown which was probably either caused or made worse by the stress of many years in high office.

Strathmore, Mary Bowes, Countess of (24 February 1749–28 April 1800), the only child and heiress of George Bowes, a wealthy land and coal owner in County Durham who died in 1760. On 24 February 1767 she married John Lyon, 9th Earl of Strathmore, on her eighteenth birthday. Their marriage was not happy. He died at sea, en route to Lisbon, on 7 March 1776. She then intended to marry her lover, George Grey, but instead was tricked into marrying Andrew Robinson Stoney (who changed his name to Andrew Stoney Bowes). He treated her very badly, subjecting her to years of physical abuse, before she escaped in 1785 and succeeded in divorcing him and regaining control of her property. Her final years were tranquil and when she died, at the age of only fifty-one, she was buried in Westminster Abbey.

Stuart Wortley, Caroline (5 March 1779–23 April 1856). Born Lady Caroline Creighton, she was the daughter of Lord Erne and his second wife, Mary, the daughter of Frederick Hervey, Bishop of Derry and Earl of Bristol (1730–1803). Her parents separated when she was still young and she lived with her mother, much of the time on the Continent. Her mother's sisters were Lady Elizabeth Foster, later Duchess of Devonshire, and Louisa, wife of Lord Hawkesbury, later Liverpool, the prime minister 1812–27. On 30 March 1799 she married James (Zac) Stuart Wortley (6 October 1776–19 December 1845), an officer in the army until he retired in 1801 and an influential Member of Parliament from 1802 to 1826, when he was created Lord Wharncliffe. His grandfather was Lord Bute, the prime minister, and his grandmother was Lady Mary Wortley Montagu. No details survive of their courtship.

Weeton, Nelly (25 December 1776–12 June 1849), governess and diarist. She grew up in considerable poverty and supported herself by teaching.

From late 1809 until early 1811 she worked as governess and companion in the household of Edward Pedder, where she witnessed his drinking and violence towards his wife. In September 1814 she married Aaron Stock (24 January 1776–27 December 1828), a struggling manufacturer in Wigan who was a widower with two daughters. They had a daughter, but he treated Nelly badly, including using physical violence, and in early 1822 the couple separated. In 1826 Stock's business failed and he was declared bankrupt; and in May 1828 he was declared insane and admitted to Lancaster Lunatic Asylum where he died that December. This reunited Nelly Stock with her daughter and gave them some financial security. Her letters and diary give great insight into the lives of people – not just single women – living on limited incomes (less than £100 a year) while endeavouring to maintain some claim to gentility.

Wellesley, Henry (20 January 1773–27 April 1847), youngest son of the 1st Earl of Mornington and brother of Arthur, Duke of Wellington, and Richard, Marquess Wellesley. Served as an army officer, diplomat and politician. On 20 September 1803 he married Lady Charlotte Cadogan (11 July 1781–8 July 1853), daughter of 1st Earl Cadogan. He divorced her in 1810 after she left him for Lord Paget. He married for a second time, on 27 February 1816, Lady Georgiana Cecil (20 March 1786–18 January 1860), daughter of the Marquess of Salisbury. In 1828 he was created Lord Cowley.

Wellington, Arthur Wesley, then Wellesley, Duke of (c. 1 May 1769–14 September 1852). Younger son of the 1st Earl of Mornington and brother of Richard, Marquess Wellesley. In his youth the family surname was spelt Wesley; the change was made by his eldest brother, with Arthur following suit in 1798. As a young army officer with limited means and prospects he twice proposed to Kitty Pakenham (? January 1772–24 April 1831) in 1792 and 1794 and, although she was willing, he was rejected by her family as unsuitable. He then went to India where he made fame and fortune in the capture of Seringapatam (1799) and the war against the Marathas (1803–4). He returned to England and proposed again, without meeting Kitty. She accepted and they were married on 10 April 1806. They had two sons in 1807 and 1808, but the marriage was not happy and they lived much apart, even when he was not serving overseas. Despite his numerous infidelities, she appears to have remained devoted to him and there was never any question of them separating, let alone a divorce. He took an active part in British politics and public life, as an influential cabinet minister, prime minister and commander-in-chief, up until his death in 1852.

Winckley, Frances: see Shelley, Frances, Lady.

Wynne, Betsey: see Fremantle, Betsey.

Wynne, Eugenia (1780[6]–2 January 1853),[7] diarist. She was the daughter of Richard Wynne (1744–98) and the sister of Betsey Fremantle (q.v.) and, like her, was brought up mostly on the Continent and was a Catholic. On 22 July 1806 she married Robert Campbell (*c.* 1771[8]–14 December 1814), the son of Walter Campbell, 9th Laird of Skipness, after a troubled courtship. Robert Campbell's brother was married to a sister of the 6th Duke of Argyll. He had trained as a lawyer but hoped for diplomatic employment. The marriage was happy, but was cut short by his early death.

ENDNOTES

PREFACE

1. Jane Austen to her sister Cassandra Austen, London, 24 May 1813, *Jane Austen's Letters*, no. 85, pp. 220–2.

1 MEETING

1. Mrs Cawley moved with her three charges from Oxford to Southampton before they fell ill. Corley, 'Jane Austen's Schooldays', pp. 14–24, *passim*. See also Austen-Leigh, *Jane Austen: A Family Record*, pp. 44–49, 53–56.
2. Shelley, *Diary of Frances, Lady Shelley*, vol. 1, p. 6; see also Austen, *Mansfield Park*, vol. 1, ch. 2, pp. 18–19, cf. vol. 3, ch. 17, pp. 463–4, on the education of Maria and Julia Bertram and its deficiencies.
3. Sarah Spencer to her brother Robert Spencer, 4 February 1810, *Correspondence of Sarah Spencer, Lady Lyttelton*, pp. 93–4.
4. Fanny Knight to Miss Chapman, 18 October 1811, Kent Archives, U951/C108/11. I am grateful to Elizabeth Finn and Lara Joffe of the Kent Archives for supplying me with a copy of this letter. The part describing the dresses is quoted in Wilson, *Almost Another Sister*, p. 39, with minor variations: the most significant being that in my reading the hairdresser came 'from Town' whereas Wilson reads it as saying that the hairdresser was 'for Four'. Either interpretation of the handwriting is plausible. See also ibid., pp. 31–9, for other details in this paragraph. Seventeen or eighteen was a common age for girls to 'come out'; Lydia Bennet at fifteen was unusually young to be out. Austen, *Pride and Prejudice*, vol. 1, ch. 9, p. 45.
5. Wilson, *Almost Another Sister*, p. 80. For descriptions of presentation at court see *Correspondence of Sarah Spencer, Lady Lyttelton*, pp. 2–3; Calvert, *Irish Beauty of the Regency*, pp. 151–2 and Stanley, *Early Married Life of Maria Josepha, Lady Stanley*, pp. 398–400.

6. Austen, *Mansfield Park*, vol. 1, ch. 5, pp. 48–51 (which includes a fascinating discussion led by Tom Bertram about the difficulty young men sometimes encountered in discovering whether or not a young woman was out or not), and, for the ball in Fanny's honour, vol. 2, chs 7–10, pp. 249–81 (pp. 275–6 for Fanny's cousins' unfulfilled wish for a ball at home). For an example of a young lady being ambiguously placed, attending a ball and mixing in society before being considered fully 'out', see Fanny Knight's sister Louisa in 1817: Hillan, *May, Lou and Cass*, pp. 47–53.

7. Austen, *Mansfield Park*, vol. 2, chs 9 and 10, pp. 266, 273–81.

8. Ibid., vol. 2, chs 6 and 7, pp. 233, 249.

9. For the difficulties young men faced in getting established in a career and gaining their financial independence see Muir, *Gentlemen of Uncertain Fortune*, *passim*.

10. Scott, *St Ronan's Well*, ch. 2, p. 18; Rainier's letter is printed in Parkinson, *War in the Eastern Seas*, pp. 432–6.

11. Fremantle's letters quoted in Hounslow, *Nelson's Right Hand Man*, pp. 34–5; *The Times*, 2 August 1791, cited in Muir, *Wellington: The Path to Victory*, p. 18.

12. See Jones, *Jane Austen and Marriage*, p. 44, for examples of such local marriages in Austen's circle of friends and family.

13. Austen-Leigh, *Jane Austen: A Family Record*, pp. 85–87; Austen, *Northanger Abbey*, vol. 1, ch. 7, p. 50.

14. Austen, *Northanger Abbey*, vol. 1, ch. 3, p. 30; Calvert, *Irish Beauty of the Regency*, n.d. 1816, pp. 270–1.

15. Both Byng and Fox-Strangways, quoted in Schutte, *Women, Rank and Marriage*, p. 98.

16. Wollstonecraft, quoted in Vickery, *Gentleman's Daughter*, p. 269.

17. Lamb's verse quoted in Thompson, *English Landed Society in the Nineteenth Century*, p. 18.

18. *The Lady's Monthly Museum*, quoted in Stone, *Family, Sex and Marriage*, p. 381.

19. Fremantle (ed.), *Wynne Diaries*, vol. 2, pp. 142–5. This ball was held in Elba, but it is unlikely that Eugenia's emotions and anxieties would have been any different if it had taken place in England. See also Austen, *Pride and Prejudice*, vol. 1, ch. 3, p. 12, where Catherine and Lydia Bennet are said to be young enough to be happy at a ball so long as they had a partner for each dance.

20. Sarah Spencer to her brother Robert Spencer, 'Saturday', [May 1808], *Correspondence of Sarah Spencer, Lady Lyttelton*, p. 13.

21. Austen, *Persuasion*, vol. 1, ch. 1, pp. 6–7. For another fictional example see Lady Penelope Pennyfeather in Scott, *St Ronan's Well*, ch. 6, p. 61.

22. Austen-Leigh, *Jane Austen: A Family Record*, pp. 121–2; Frances Poole, quoted in Connell, *Portrait of a Whig Peer*, p. 80; see also the examples of Esther Acklom and Lady Anne Lindsay discussed below, pp. 62–4.

23. On the importance of lack of money as an obstacle to marriage see Blacker, *War without Pity*, 15 July 1802, p. 123. Lack of money, and the family opposition that it caused, delayed the marriage of John Constable, the artist, to Maria Bicknell for seven years, until after he turned forty: see Gayford, *Constable in Love*, *passim*. On the position of spinsters and bachelors see below, chapter 8.

24. Calvert, *An Irish Beauty of the Regency*, 31 January 1822, p. 361; Shelley, *Diary of Frances, Lady Shelley*, vol. 1, pp. 18–21.

25. Schutte, *Women, Rank and Marriage*, pp. 15–16, 196; Heather Carroll, 'The Making and Breaking of Wedlock: Visualising Jane, Duchess of Gordon *After* Marriage', in

DiPlacidi and Leydecker (eds), *After Marriage in the Long Eighteenth Century*, pp. 129–56; George and Stephens, *Catalogue of Political and Personal Satires Preserved in the Department of Prints and Drawings in the British Museum*, vol. 7, no. 9084, p. 387; for the circumstances leading to Colonel Lennox's marriage to Lady Charlotte Gordon see Probert, *Marriage Law and Practice in the Long Eighteenth Century*, p. 89n. Edgeworth, *Belinda*, ch. 1, p. 14, ch. 2, pp. 22–4. See also Mary Russell Mitford's comments on the match-making endeavours of an acquaintance quoted in Jones, *Jane Austen and Marriage*, p. 52.

26. The 1776 marriage of Lord and Lady Stormont (later the Earl and Countess of Mansfield) appears to have been presented to the bride by her father as a *fait accompli*; see Aspinall-Oglander, *Freshly Remembered: The Story of Thomas Graham*, pp. 13–15. Surprisingly this marriage appears to have been successful. For other examples see Malcomson, *Pursuit of the Heiress*, pp. 8, 118, 127, but, as Malcomson points out, such instances were rare then, and became almost unknown later.

27. Lady Caroline Capel to her mother Lady Uxbridge, March 1815, in Anglesey (ed.), *The Capel Letters*, pp. 88–9.

28. Edgeworth, *Belinda*, chs 24, 25 and 29, pp. 309–11, 328, 410–12; Philadelphia Walter to her brother James Walter, 19 September 1787, in Le Faye, *Jane Austen's 'Outlandish Cousin'*, p. 80.

29. Calvert, *Irish Beauty of the Regency*, p. 22; Austen, *Pride and Prejudice*, vol. 3, ch. 8, p. 312; for examples of enduring happy marriages of passion see below, pp. 176–8 and 183 (Andrew and Anne Barnard, and Emily, Duchess of Leinster and William Ogilvie).

30. Addison, *The Spectator*, quoted in Staves, *Married Women's Separate Property*, pp. 223–4; Matthew Flinders to Ann Flinders, 30 June 1807, in Flinders, *Matthew Flinders: Personal Letters from an Extraordinary Life*, p. 182; French and Rothery, *Man's Estate*, pp. 193–4, on what men expected from marriage.

31. Lord William Russell to his brother Lord John Russell, 7 November [October?] [1829], Lord John Russell to his sister-in-law Lady William Russell, 12 February 1828, in Blakiston, *Lord William Russell and His Wife*, pp. 200, 153; Frances Poole, quoted in Connell, *Portrait of a Whig Peer*, p. 81; see also Vickery, *Gentleman's Daughter*, p. 39.

2 ATTRACTION

1. Hyde, *The Rise of Castlereagh*, pp. 115–17 (including 'fine, comely' quotation); Bew, *Castlereagh*, pp. 72–5 (including both quotations from Stewart) and *passim*. Strictly speaking Camden was Stewart's step-grandfather: the father of his stepmother, but they were close. For the date of the wedding see Hyde, op. cit., p. 117; Bew's statement that it was 9 July 1794 appears to be a slip of the pen.

2. Maria Josepha Holroyd to her aunt Serena Holroyd, 23 October 1795, [Stanley], *Girlhood of Maria Josepha Holroyd*, pp. 338–9.

3. Maria Josepha Holroyd to her aunt Serena Holroyd, 11 November 1795, [Stanley], *Girlhood of Maria Josepha Holroyd*, pp. 346–7.

4. Maria Josepha Holroyd to Miss Ann Firth, 17 May 1796, [Stanley], *Girlhood of Maria Josepha Holroyd*, p. 384.

5. Ibid., pp. 384–5, and p. 104 for his service in the Cheshire Militia.

6. Davidson, *Dress in the Age of Jane Austen*, pp. 52–3.

7. Ibid., pp. 52–3, 151–2.

8. Calvert, *Irish Beauty of the Regency*, May 1809, p. 177, see also pp. 82–3. When the Prince propositioned Lady Bessborough in late 1809 she was annoyed not least by the realisation that she had reached an age where she appealed to him in that way; *Lord Granville Leveson Gower: Private Correspondence*, vol. 2, p. 349.

9. Austen, *Northanger Abbey*, vol. 1, ch. 1, p. 15.

10. Scott, *St Ronan's Well*, ch. 4, p. 42.

11. Austen, *Mansfield Park*, vol. 1, ch. 5, pp. 44–5; Smith, *Wellington and the Arbuthnots*, p. 42; Austen, *Northanger Abbey*, vol. 1, ch. 10, p. 74; Davidson, *Dress in the Age of Jane Austen*, p. 41.

12. Austen, *Northanger Abbey*, vol. 1, ch. 3, p. 25.

13. Ibid., vol. 2, ch. 1, p. 131 and vol. 2, ch. 15, p. 243.

14. Edgeworth, *Belinda*, ch. 17, p. 209; Serena Holroyd to her niece Maria, 25 October 1795, [Stanley], *Girlhood of Maria Josepha Holroyd*, p. 340.

15. Austen, *Pride and Prejudice*, vol. 1, ch. 6, pp. 21–2.

16. Shelley, *Diary of Frances, Lady Shelley*, vol. 1, pp. 23–4.

17. Austen, *Northanger Abbey*, vol. 1, ch. 3, p. 30 and vol. 2, ch. 15, pp. 244–6; cf. Malcomson, *Pursuit of the Heiress*, pp. 132–3.

18. Austen, *Persuasion*, vol. 2, ch. 4, p. 148.

19. Austen, *Pride and Prejudice*, vol. 2, ch. 10, p. 183; Cannon, *Aristocratic Century*, p. 82.

20. Schutte, *Women, Rank, and Marriage*, pp. 6, 13, 21–2, 27, 35, 71–2. For an example of the ridicule attracted by an excessive concern for birth over achievements see Austen's depiction of Sir Walter Elliot in *Persuasion*, vol. 1, ch. 3, p. 19 and *passim*.

21. Austen, *Persuasion*, vol. 1, ch. 4, pp. 26–30; Kindred, *Jane Austen's Transatlantic Sister*, pp. 90–1, 95, 115.

22. Southam, *Jane Austen and the Navy*, p. 138; Burnham and McGuigan, *The British Army against Napoleon*, pp. 173–4.

23. Edward Knight's income from Clery, *Jane Austen: The Banker's Sister*, p. 220; Austen, *Pride and Prejudice*, vol. 1, ch. 3, p. 10; Muir, *Gentlemen of Uncertain Fortune*, pp. 26–8; Creevey to Miss Ord, 13 September 1821, in *Creevey Papers*, p. 374 (for Lambton's remark); Thorne, *History of Parliament*, vol. 1, pp. 288–9.

24. Lady Massereene, quoted in Malcomson, *Pursuit of the Heiress*, p. 128; Mrs Jackson to her son George Jackson, 8 March 1812, in Jackson, *The Bath Archives*, vol. 1, pp. 337–8.

25. Connell, *Portrait of a Whig Peer*, pp. 72–6; Taylor, *Defiance*, p. 193; Calvert, *Irish Beauty of the Regency*, pp. 103, 108–9 and 240; Emily Eden to Lady Buckinghamshire, December 1814, in Eden, *Miss Eden's Letters*, p. 5. Mrs Calvert believed that 'General Carr' was 'a dozen years younger than herself', p. 240.

26. For Esther Acklom see Calvert, *Irish Beauty of the Regency*, p. 72; for Picton see Stanhope, *Notes of Conversations with the Duke of Wellington*, 17 November 1847, p. 323. According to Stone, *The Family Sex and Marriage*, p. 49 (graph 4), the average age of young ladies getting married for the first time rose in the late eighteenth and early nineteenth centuries from about twenty-one to about twenty-three, while for men it remained about twenty-six or twenty-seven. See also Barclay, *Love, Intimacy and Power*, pp. 19–21; Holloway, *Game of Love*, p. 12; and Jalland, *Women, Marriage and Politics, 1860–1914*, pp. 79–84. The median age of first marriage of officers who rose to command a brigade in Wellington's army in the Peninsula or Waterloo was thirty-one: calculation based on information in McGuigan and Burnham, *Wellington's Brigade Commanders*, *passim*. Curiously, the average age of women

marrying for the first time in Britain in 1971 was twenty-two, and men twenty-four, although both these figures had risen by eight years in 2012. Langhamer, *The English in Love*, pp. 171, 211.

27. Austen, *Mansfield Park*, vol. 3, ch. 1, p. 317; Johnson, *The History of Rasselas, Prince of Abyssinia*, vol. 2, ch. 4, p. 80.

28. Austen, *Pride and Prejudice*, vol. 2, ch. 9, p. 179 and vol. 3, ch. 19, p. 385; Calvert, *Irish Beauty of the Regency*, p. 166.

29. Schutte, *Women, Rank and Marriage*, pp. 130–1; Phegley, *Courtship and Marriage in Victorian England*, pp. 160–2; for Charles Austen see Austen-Leigh, *Jane Austen: A Family Record*, pp. 237–8; for Edgeworth and other examples see Probert, *Marriage Law and Practice in the Long Eighteenth Century*, p. 277+n.

30. Eliza de Feuillide to Warren Hastings, 26 December 1797, in Le Faye, *Jane Austen's 'Outlandish Cousin'*, p. 151; see also Lord John Russell to his brother Lord William Russell, 8 May [1829] in Blakiston, *Lord William Russell and His Wife*, p. 190.

31. In other words, that her husband, the Duke, was not Louisa's father; both these examples from Malcomson, *Pursuit of the Heiress*, pp. 129–30.

32. Edgeworth, *Belinda*, ch. 29, pp. 410–12; Shelley, *Diary of Frances, Lady Shelley*, vol. 1, p. 20; and diary of Harriet Wynne, 9 June 1806, *Wynne Diaries*, vol. 3, p. 277.

33. Austen, *Pride and Prejudice*, vol. 2, ch. 18, p. 231 and vol. 3, ch. 4, pp. 278–9; Mrs Delaney quoted in Vickery, *Behind Closed Doors*, p. 139; for more on illegitimate children see below, pp. 124–5.

34. Jones, quoted in Collins, *Jane Austen and the Clergy*, p. 132; on the subject more generally see Barclay, *Love, Intimacy and Power*, pp. 22–3 and Jalland, *Women, Marriage and Politics, 1860–1914*, pp. 87–90. For an instance of religious differences preventing a marriage see *Wynne Diaries*, vol. 3, p. 313; and for a more typical response, regarding it as a slight disadvantage, see George Spencer to Capt. F. Spencer, 12 May 1821, *Correspondence of Sarah Spencer Lady Lyttelton*, pp. 234–5.

3 COURTSHIP

1. Kindred, *Jane Austen's Transatlantic Sister*, p. 46, tells the story which also appears in a slightly different form in Mellors, *Men of Nottingham and Nottinghamshire*, pp. 42–3, but I have been unable to discover the original source, and the story does not appear in Anson's biography of Warren or in any of the contemporary obituaries and biographical notices of Sir John or Lady Warren that I have seen.

2. Austen-Leigh, *Jane Austen: A Family Record*, pp. 71–2; Austen, *Persuasion*, vol. 1, ch. 10, p. 92.

3. Austen, *Pride and Prejudice*, vol. 1, chs 13, 15 and 22, pp. 63, 70–1, 121; Jones, *Jane Austen and Marriage*, p. 16, however, makes it eleven days between Mr Collins's arrival on a Monday and his departure on a Saturday.

4. Sarah Spencer to her brother Robert Spencer, 16 April 1809, *Correspondence of Sarah Spencer, Lady Lyttelton*, pp. 67–8. According to Lady Sarah, Miss Brown was the daughter of a deceased army officer, Captain Brown, who had left his widow and daughter to live on the income from £5,000, or about £250 a year. This was the same fortune as Mrs Bennet would have had to support herself and five daughters in the event of Mr Bennet's death.

5. 'Marry in haste, repent at leisure' is said to have been coined in William Congreve's play *The Batchelour* (1693) and was certainly in general use by the late eighteenth

century. *Lady's Magazine* for March 1811, quoted in Jones, *Jane Austen and Marriage*, p. 15; Austen, *Emma*, vol. 3, ch. 7, p. 372. See Matthews, 'Love at First Sight: The Velocity of Victorian Heterosexuality', *passim*, for a discussion of how attitudes to the idea of love at first sight changed over the course of the nineteenth century.

6. Murray to his sister Augusta, 13 March 1803, quoted in Harding-Edgar, *Next to Wellington*, p. 69. Captain Wentworth in *Persuasion* was intent on marriage and was 'actually looking round, ready to fall in love with all the speed which a clear head and quick taste could allow' (Austen, *Persuasion*, vol. 1, ch. 7, p. 61).

7. Shelley, *Diary of Frances, Lady Shelley*, vol. 1, p. 23; Austen, *Pride and Prejudice*, vol. 1, ch. 18, p. 102.

8. Austen, *Northanger Abbey*, vol. 1, ch. 9, *passim* (her drive with John Thorpe), and ch. 13, p. 104 (Mr Allen); vol. 2, ch. 5, pp. 156–7 (being driven by Henry Tilney); Dr Johnson, in Boswell's *Life of Johnson*, vol. 2, p. 124 (19 September 1777).

9. Harriet Fane's account, written a few months later in a letter to Charles Arbuthnot, quoted in *Correspondence of Charles Arbuthnot*, pp. x–xi and Smith, *Wellington and the Arbuthnots*, pp. 27–8.

10. Sarah Spencer to her brother Robert Spencer, 7 July 1812, *Correspondence of Sarah Spencer, Lady Lyttelton*, pp. 133–4.

11. Sarah Spencer to her grandmother Countess Spencer, 29 August 1812, *Correspondence of Sarah Spencer, Lady Lyttelton*, p. 135.

12. Quoted in Vickery, *Gentleman's Daughter*, p. 40.

13. Harriet, Lady Granville to Lady Harrowby, 4 May 1824, *Letters of Harriet, Countess Granville*, vol. 1, pp. 289–90. Lady Granville was considering the young man as a potential suitor for her daughter or her friend's daughter.

14. Mary, Lady Palmerston, 6 March 1795, quoted in Connell, *Portrait of a Whig Peer*, pp. 310–11.

15. Austen, *Pride and Prejudice*, vol. 3, ch. 17, p. 376.

16. Scott, *St Ronan's Well*, ch. 6, pp. 62–5; Edgeworth, *Belinda*, ch. 3, p. 35.

17. Austen, *Northanger Abbey*, vol. 1, ch. 14, pp. 110–11. See also Lady Mary Wortley Montagu to her daughter, Lady Bute, 28 January 1753, in *The Letters and Works of Lady Mary Wortley Montagu*, vol. 2, pp. 226–8; and Edgeworth, *Belinda*, ch. 9, p. 101.

18. Nelly Weeton to her brother Tom, 15 November 1809, in *Miss Weeton's Journal*, vol. 1, p. 198; Lady Salisbury's diary for 2 April 1835 in Oman (ed.), *The Gascoyne Heiress*, p. 163. However, when Anne Lindsay's father was dying in 1768, when she was seventeen he urged her to continue her studying in order to improve her chances of making a good marriage; Taylor, *Defiance*, p. 25.

19. Jane Austen to her sister Cassandra, 23–24 September, 11–12 October 1813 and 9 March 1814, *Jane Austen's Letters*, nos 89, 91 and 99, pp. 235, 242–3, 272; Le Faye, 'Fanny Knight's Diaries: Jane Austen through her Niece's Eyes', pp. 16, 18.

20. Fanny Knight's diary for 7 February, 6 March and 21 June 1814, quoted in Wilson, *Almost Another Sister*, p. 54.

21. Jane Austen to Fanny Knight, 18–20 November 1814, *Jane Austen's Letters*, no. 109, pp. 291–4.

22. Le Faye, *Jane Austen's Letters*, p. 562; Wilson, 'What happened to "Mr J. P."?', pp. 315–17; Wilson, *Almost Another Sister*, p. 154+n6.

23. Jane Austen to Fanny Knight, 18–20 November 1814, *Jane Austen's Letters*, no. 109, pp. 291–4.

24. Jane Austen to Fanny Knight, 30 November 1814, *Jane Austen's Letters*, no. 114, pp. 298–9.
25. Jane Austen to Fanny Knight, 20–21 February and 20–23 March 1817, *Jane Austen's Letters*, nos 151 and 153, pp. 344–5, 347.

4 HESITATION AND HEARTBREAK

1. Capt. Thomas Fremantle to his brother William, 13 July 1796, in Parry, *The Admirals Fremantle*, pp. 41–2.
2. Capt. Thomas Fremantle to his brother William, 10 December 1796, in Parry, *The Admirals Fremantle*, pp. 45–6; Fremantle's journal, 31 December 1796, in the one-volume edition of *The Wynne Diaries*, pp. 259–60.
3. Capt. Thomas Fremantle to his brother William, 13 July 1796, in Parry, *The Admirals Fremantle*, pp. 41–2. One reason for doubting that money was the sole reason for Fremantle's hesitation was that Betsey was not without a fortune of her own: when she married, her father settled £5,000 on her immediately, with a further £10,000 to follow at his death, and Fremantle was aware of this as early as 20 October 1796: see his journal entry of that date in the one-volume edition of *The Wynne Diaries*, p. 258.
4. Canning to Granville Leveson Gower, 22 August 1799, *Lord Granville Leveson Gower: Private Correspondence*, vol. 1, pp. 250–5.
5. Canning to Lady S. Ryder, quoted in Marshall, *The Rise of George Canning*, p. 203.
6. Canning to Lady S. Ryder, quoted in Marshall, *The Rise of George Canning*, pp. 204–8; Canning to Granville Leveson Gower, 22 August 1799, *Lord Granville Leveson Gower: Private Correspondence*, vol. 1, pp. 250–5; Hinde, *George Canning*, p. 73.
7. Canning to Granville Leveson Gower, 22 August 1799, *Lord Granville Leveson Gower: Private Correspondence*, vol. 1, pp. 250–5.
8. Canning to the Leighs, 26 August and 2 September 1799, quoted in Hinde, *George Canning*, p. 74; Canning to his wife Joan, quoted in Marshall, *The Rise of George Canning*, pp. 210–11.
9. Muir, *Wellington: The Path to Victory*, pp. 27–8; Wilson, *A Soldier's Wife*, pp. 10–15; for a further discussion of the difficulties of interpreting the surviving evidence see Muir, www.lifeofwellington.co.uk, ch. 3.
10. Eliza de Feuillide to her cousin Philadelphia Walter, 1 August 1791 and 13 December 1796, in Le Faye, *Jane Austen's 'Outlandish Cousin'*, pp. 103, 132.
11. Austen, *Mansfield Park*, vol. 1, ch. 4, p. 43, see also vol. 3, ch. 5, p. 363, where Mary again calls Henry a flirt.
12. Shelley, *Diary of Frances, Lady Shelley*, vol. 1, pp. 26–9.
13. Stirling, *The Letter-Bag of Lady Elizabeth Spencer-Stanhope compiled from the Cannon Hall Papers*, vol. 1, p. 194.
14. Calvert, *Irish Beauty of the Regency*, quotes on pp. 90, 134 and 207; see also pp. 72, 77, 83 and 92 for Mrs Calvert's relations with Miss Acklom, and pp. 188, 192 and 207 for Miss Acklom's engagement with Mr Madocks. Francis Jackson to George Jackson, 30 December 1810, in Jackson, *The Bath Archives*, vol. 1, pp. 187–8 for General Tilson, and George Jackson to his mother, 28 March 1814, for the effect on 'Maddox' of the breaking of the engagement, Jackson, *The Bath Archives*, vol. 2, pp. 418–19.

15. Taylor, *Defiance*, pp. 48–50 (Kames) and 64.
16. A woman who changed her mind soon after accepting a proposal, as both Frances Winckley and Jane Austen did, would seldom be criticised. But one who did so repeatedly, or after the engagement had lasted some time, or when she came into money, might be abused as a jilt (the word was current at the time).
17. Austen, *Persuasion*, vol. 2, ch. 11, p. 242; Gaskell, *Cranford*, ch. 9, p. 161; see also Scott, *St Ronan's Well*, ch. 2, p. 28.
18. Lady Caroline Capel to her mother Lady Uxbridge, Brussels, February 1815, in Anglesey (ed.), *The Capel Letters*, p. 86.
19. Maria Capel to her grandmother Lady Uxbridge, Brussels, 1 March 1815; Lady Caroline Capel to her mother Lady Uxbridge, Brussels, March 1815, in Anglesey (ed.), *The Capel Letters*, pp. 87–9.
20. Lady Caroline Capel to her mother Lady Uxbridge, Brussels, June 1815, in Anglesey (ed.), *The Capel Letters*, pp. 103, 237.
21. Harriet Capel to Baron Trip, 24 December 1814, in Anglesey (ed.), *The Capel Letters*, pp. 188–9. Trip's name is more properly given as Jonkheer Otto Ernst Gelder Trip van Zoudtlant.
22. Harriet Capel to Baron Trip, n.d. [March ? 1815], in Anglesey (ed.), *The Capel Letters*, pp. 190–1.
23. Ibid., pp. 191–2.
24. Ibid., pp. 193–4.
25. Lady Caroline Capel to her mother Lady Uxbridge, Brussels, 19 April and ? May 1815, in Anglesey (ed.), *The Capel Letters*, pp. 197–200; Lt-Col. John Fremantle to his uncle William Fremantle, Brussels, 21 April 1815, in Glover, *Wellington's Voice*, p. 203 (on the duel and its cause).
26. Harriet Capel to Baron Trip, 24 June 1815, in Anglesey (ed.), *The Capel Letters*, p. 205.
27. Harriet Capel to Baron Trip, n.d. [June 1815], in Anglesey (ed.), *The Capel Letters*, pp. 202–3.
28. Harriet Capel to Baron Trip, n.d. [June 1815]; Lady Caroline Capel to her mother Lady Uxbridge, 4 September and 9 November 1815, in Anglesey (ed.), *The Capel Letters*, pp. 207–9.
29. Harriet Capel to Baron Trip, 1 January 1816; Lady Caroline Capel to her mother Lady Uxbridge, ? February and June 1816; Harriet Capel to her grandmother Lady Uxbridge, 1 October 1815, in Anglesey (ed.), *The Capel Letters*, pp. 210–14.
30. Lady Caroline Capel to her mother Lady Uxbridge, 18 November 1816; Harriet Capel to her grandmother Lady Uxbridge, Brussels, December 1816, in Anglesey (ed.), *The Capel Letters*, pp. 215–18, 241 for details of Trip's suicide.
31. Anglesey (ed.), *The Capel Letters*, p. 221; *Gentleman's Magazine*, vol. 104, pt 2, November 1833, p. 467. For an example of almost equal suffering see the account of Lady Anne Lindsay's love affair with William Windham, in Taylor, *Defiance*, pp. 123–4, 154–61, 165–7 and especially pp. 173–86.

5 PROPOSALS, ENGAGEMENTS AND MARRIAGE SETTLEMENTS

1. Austen, *Mansfield Park*, vol. 2, ch. 8, p. 255.
2. Maria Josepha Holroyd to her aunt Serena Holroyd, 5 May 1796, [Stanley], *Girlhood of Maria Josepha Holroyd*, pp. 375–6; Reiter, *The Late Lord*, pp. 17–18, and for further

details, Reiter, '"Likely to get frampy": In which the 2nd Lord Chatham has trouble getting his act together', blogpost dated 11 November 2014, https://thelatelord.com/2014/11/11/likely-to-get-frampy-in-which-the-2nd-lord-chatham-has-trouble-getting-his-act-together/.

3. Jones, *Jane Austen and Marriage*, p. 25 (bended knee), p. 71 (rings); Austen, *Pride and Prejudice*, vol. 1, ch. 19, pp. 104–5; Austen, *Emma*, vol. 1, ch. 15, pp. 129–30.

4. Austen, *Mansfield Park*, vol. 3, ch. 13, pp. 422–3. See below, p. 103 for Sir Arthur Wellesley's written proposal to Kitty Pakenham; Knatchbull-Hugessen, *Kentish Family*, p. 166, for Sir Edward Knatchbull's letter proposing to Fanny Knight; and Ziegler, *Melbourne*, p. 45, for William Lamb's letter to Lady Caroline Ponsonby.

5. Austen, *Emma*, vol. 1, ch. 15, pp. 129–33 and ch. 16, pp. 135–6; Austen, *Pride and Prejudice*, vol. 1, ch. 19, pp. 104–9.

6. Eugenia Wynne's journal, 27 July–9 August 1805, *Wynne Diaries*, vol. 3, pp. 179–181.

7. Austen, *Pride and Prejudice*, vol. 1, ch. 21, p. 115 (Mr Collins) and vol. 3, ch. 16, pp. 366–70 (Mr Darcy). On the risk of suicide see Holloway, *The Game of Love*, pp. 133–7, which cites a number of real, as well as fictional, instances. The immense success of Goethe's *The Sorrows of Young Werther* had made a whole generation or two conscious that disappointment in love might lead to suicide, and we have already seen how Baron Trip's suicide was attributed to money worries and unrequited love (see above, ch. 4, p. 70). For Wellington see Muir, *Wellington: The Path to Victory*, pp. 27–8, 172–5.

8. Austen-Leigh, *Jane Austen: A Family Record*, pp. 121–2; Shelley, *Diary of Frances, Lady Shelley*, vol. 1, pp. 27–8.

9. Edgeworth, *Memoirs of Richard Lovell Edgeworth*, pp. 87–8.

10. Eugenia Wynne's journal, 30 April 1806, *Wynne Diaries*, vol. 3, p. 255.

11. Eugenia Wynne's journal, 1 May 1806, *Wynne Diaries*, vol. 3, p. 255.

12. Eugenia Wynne's journal, 6, 8 and 11 May 1806, *Wynne Diaries*, vol. 3, pp. 258–9, 262–3.

13. Mrs Calvert's journal, 23 June 1811, in Calvert, *Irish Beauty of the Regency*, p. 178; Austen, *Northanger Abbey*, vol. 2, ch. 16, p. 249; for instances of young men being sent abroad see Holloway, *Game of Love*, pp. 80ff; Gore, *Nelson's Hardy and His Wife*, p. 152; Austen, *Pride and Prejudice*, vol. 1, ch. 20, pp. 110–12; Taylor, *Defiance*, pp. 23–4.

14. Austen, *Persuasion*, vol. 2, ch. 12, p. 248; Vickery, *Gentleman's Daughter*, p. 52, on susceptibility of fathers.

15. Gash, *Lord Liverpool*, pp. 31–2. Young Jenkinson went on to become, as Lord Liverpool, the longest-serving and arguably the most successful prime minister of the nineteenth century. For another example of royal intervention in favour of young lovers see Harding-Edgar, *Next to Wellington*, p. 304.

16. Sarah Spencer to her brother Robert Spencer, 13 January 1813, *Correspondence of Sarah Spencer, Lady Lyttelton*, pp. 137–8. My thanks to Elaine Chalus, who identifies 'Clifford' as Augustus Clifford, the illegitimate son of the Duke of Devonshire and Lady Elizabeth Foster who, although not a blood relation of the Spencers, was treated as if he was Lady Sarah's cousin.

17. Sarah Spencer to her brother Robert Spencer, 10 February 1813, *Correspondence of Sarah Spencer, Lady Lyttelton*, pp. 138–9.

18. Maria Holroyd to her aunt Serena Holroyd, 5 May 1796, to Anne Frith, ? May 1796 and 23 June 1796, [Stanley], *Girlhood of Maria Josepha Holroyd*, pp. 375–6, 376–7, 391.

19. Jones, *Jane Austen and Marriage*, pp. 57–8; Calvert, *Irish Beauty of the Regency*, 23 July 1810, p. 167.

20. Calvert, *Irish Beauty of the Regency*, n.d. *c*. end of August 1810, p. 167; Sarah Spencer to her brother Robert Spencer, 28 April 1812, *Correspondence of Sarah Spencer, Lady Lyttelton*, p. 132. To be fair to Mrs Calvert, she was in the advanced stages of pregnancy when she made this remark.

21. References to kissing and cuddling: Frances Winckley quoted above, p. XXX (this chapter, p. 5); Canning to his wife Joan, quoted in Marshall, *The Rise of George Canning*, pp. 210–11; Vickery, *Behind Closed Doors*, pp. 99–100 (Joshiah Wedgwood and Elizabeth Allen). The *Lady's Magazine* is quoted in Stone, *Family, Sex and Marriage*, p. 504. On the attitudes in novels of the period see Tompkins, *The Popular Novel in England, 1770–1800*, pp. 152–4 (the male novelist was Robert Bage, ibid., p. 154n). For Lady Anne Lindsay see Taylor, *Defiance*, p. 196, cf. pp. 84–5, 183. For Harriet Spencer see Soames, *The Profligate Duke*, pp. 177–81; Schutte, *Women, Rank and Marriage*, pp. 102–3 and *Journal of Mrs Arbuthnot*, vol. 1, pp. 12–13, 9 April 1820.

22. Shelley, *Diary of Frances, Lady Shelley*, vol. 1, p. 32. On press announcements of engagements see Cannon, *Aristocratic Century*, p. 73 where it is stated that the size of the lady's fortune was regularly included in announcements in the *Gentleman's Magazine* in the eighteenth century. However, there is no trace of this in the issues for April and May 1808, for either engagements or marriages.

23. Robert Garrett to Charlotte Bentinck, 20 June and 1 August 1813, in White, 'A Subaltern in the Peninsular War', pp. 17, 20; and Holloway, *Game of Love*, pp. 57 and 90 for the last two quotations. For more details of Garrett's letters see Gibson, 'General Garrett 1791–1869', pp. 126–35 and Holloway, op cit., p. 51.

24. Hester Mundy, quoted in Newdigate-Newdegate, *The Cheverels of Cheverel Manor*, pp. 5–6; Fane, quoted in Smith, *Wellington and the Arbuthnots*, p. 28.

25. Robert Garrett: Holloway, *Game of Love*, pp. 69, 98; Gash, *Mr Secretary Peel*, p. 260; Maria Holroyd to Miss Ann Firth, 30 May 1796, [Stanley], *Girlhood of Maria Josepha Holroyd*, p. 389; miniatures and hair, Holloway, op cit., pp. 72–8, 81–4, and also Jones, *Jane Austen and Marriage*, pp. 71–2.

26. Jane Austen to Fanny Knight, 30 November 1814, *Jane Austen's Letters*, no. 114, pp. 298–9; Austen, *Persuasion*, vol. 2, ch. 11, p. 231.

27. *Wynne Diaries*, vol. 3, pp. 254–91, quotation from Eugenia's journal for 25 May 1806, p. 268; for Captain Fremantle's impatience see pp. 286, 294.

28. Eden, *Semi-Attached Couple*, ch. 2, p. 14; Maria Holroyd to Miss Ann Firth, 17 and 30 May, 11 September and 7 October 1796, [Stanley], *Girlhood of Maria Josepha Holroyd*, pp. 384, 389, 392, 393.

29. Lady Uxbridge to her son Arthur Paget, 17 April 1805, in Paget, *The Paget Brothers*, p. 31. For the breakdown of Esther Acklom's engagement see Calvert, *Irish Beauty of the Regency*, pp. 177–82; and for Anne Lindsay's see Taylor, *Defiance*, pp. 49–52.

30. Barclay, *Love, Intimacy and Power*, pp. 82–3, 95 (disinterest particularly disadvantaged women); Staves, *Married Women's Separate Property*, p. 205; see also Connell, *Portrait of a Whig Peer*, pp. 381–2, where Lady Palmerston confessed ignorance of the details of her own settlement, and Jalland, *Women, Marriage and Politics, 1860–1914*, p. 63, for good evidence from a later period.

31. Smith, *Wellington and the Arbuthnots*, pp. 33–4.

32. Staves, *Married Women's Separate Property*, pp. 60, 201–2 (variety in settlements); pp. 27–8, 98, 116 ('dower rights'); p. 133 (pin money); Malcomson, *Pursuit of the*

Heiress, pp. 11, 27–8 (entails and restrictions), pp. 20–1 ('dower rights'), pp. 27–8 (size of jointures).

33. Malcomson, *Pursuit of the Heiress*, pp. 30–2, 123–7.
34. Staves, *Married Women's Separate Property*, pp. 96, 114–15, 203–4; Malcomson, *Pursuit of the Heiress*, pp. 9–12, 30, 33, 38–9; Jalland, *Women, Marriage and Politics, 1860–1914*, pp. 59–60. See Virgin, *Sydney Smith*, pp. 58–60, for one father's extreme reaction when he was denied access to his daughter-in-law's capital. The whole issue of the use of trustees and the sequestration of the capital of marriage settlements remains obscure, with different authorities taking contradictory positions as almost self-evident, while their concentration on large estates and eldest sons distracts from the more common situation of younger sons and their small fortunes.
35. Austen, *Persuasion*, vol. 2, ch. 10, p. 218, for the burden of having two daughters marry at once; Barclay, *Love, Intimacy and Power*, pp. 81–2 (on financial contributions being used to offset lack of social standing); Bailey, *Unquiet Lives*, p. 90 and Staves, *Married Women's Separate Property*, p. 60, for the use of marriage settlements across the upper and middle classes.
36. Le Faye, *A Chronology of Jane Austen*, p. 27; Tomalin, *Jane Austen*, p. 297; Wilson, *A Soldier's Wife*, pp. 75–6; Reiter, 'The Second Earl of Chatham's marriage settlement, Bromley Archives, 1080/3/1/1/26', blogpost dated 15 July 2013, https://thelatelord.com/2013/07/15/the-second-earl-of-chathams-marriage-settlement/. For the inheritance of the Bennet girls see Austen, *Pride and Prejudice*, vol. 3, ch. 8, p. 308.

6 WEDDINGS AND HONEYMOONS

1. Jones, *Jane Austen and Marriage*, pp. 61, 63, 82–3 (quoting Caroline Austen); Austen, *Emma*, vol. 3, ch. 19, p. 484.
2. Canon law: Probert, *Marriage Law and Practice in the Long Eighteenth Century*, pp. 1–3, 222–4, 232; Jones, *Jane Austen and Marriage*, p. 84. Catholics: Eugenia Wynne's diary for 22 July 1806, *Wynne Diaries*, vol. 3, p. 291; see also ibid., vol. 2, p. 151 and vol. 3, p. 322, for her sisters' weddings, which followed the same pattern. Mr Austen: Cass, 'In Defence of George Austen', pp. 59, 61. St George's: Jones, *Jane Austen and Marriage*, p. 84.
3. Special licences: Probert, *Marriage Law and Practice in the Long Eighteenth Century*, pp. 232–3; Canning's wedding: Hinde, *George Canning*, p. 78; Harriet Cavendish's wedding: Gleeson, *An Aristocratic Affair*, p. 418; Virgin, *Sydney Smith*, p. 41.
4. Maria Holroyd to Miss Ann Firth, Sheffield Place, 23 June 1796, [Stanley], *Girlhood of Maria Josepha Holroyd*, pp. 391–2; the Duke of Bedford to his son Lord William Russell, 22 May 1817, in Blakiston, *Lord William Russell and His Wife*, p. 36; Calvert, *Irish Beauty of the Regency*, p. 171n.
5. The Duke of Bedford to his son Lord William Russell, 22 May 1817, in Blakiston, *Lord William Russell and His Wife*, pp. 35–7.
6. Lady Spencer to Lady Harriet Spencer, [1780], in Bessborough and Aspinall (eds), *Lady Bessborough and Her Family Circle*, pp. 33–6.
7. Mary Le Couteur to Harriet Janvrin, 1817, in Stevens, *Victorian Voices*, p. 62.
8. Bessborough (ed.), *Georgiana: Extracts from the Correspondence of Georgiana, Duchess of Devonshire*, p. 238n; Huxley, *Lady Elizabeth and the Grosvenors*, p. 1; the *Lady's Magazine*, quoted in Stuart, *The Daughters of George III*, p. 30; Eliza de Feuillide to her cousin Philadelphia Walter, London, 3 May 1797, in Le Faye, *Jane Austen's*

'*Outlandish Cousin*', p. 137; Austen, *Sense and Sensibility*, vol. 2, ch. 10, p. 215. See also Lady Caroline Capel to her mother Lady Uxbridge, Brussels, March 1816, in Anglesey (ed.), *The Capel Letters*, p. 158, for another example of a bride's trousseau being put on display.

9. Davidson, *Dress in the Age of Jane Austen*, pp. 105–7, 157; Jones, *Jane Austen and Marriage*, pp. 62–4, 68–9; Le Faye, *Chronology of Jane Austen*, p. 27 (for Mrs Austen); Porter, *A Governess in the Age of Jane Austen*, pp. 154–5.

10. Davidson, *Dress in the Age of Jane Austen*, p. 107; Jones, *Jane Austen and Marriage*, p. 70.

11. Canning quoted in Hinde, *George Canning*, p. 78; Wilberforce diary, Bodleian MS Wilberforce c.34, ff 138–9 – I am grateful to John Coffey of the Wilberforce Diaries Project for supplying this quotation; Jones, *Jane Austen and Marriage*, p. 79 (Marianne Clayton); Bess Canning to her mother Mehitabel Canning, 1 September 1798, quoted in Hunt, *Mehitabel Canning*, pp. 148–50.

12. Bess Canning to her mother Mehitabel Canning, 1 September 1798, quoted in Hunt, *Mehitabel Canning*, pp. 148–50; Fox-Strangways: Porter, *A Governess in the Age of Jane Austen*, pp. 154–5; Maria Josepha Holroyd to Miss Ann Firth, 17 October 1796, [Stanley], *Girlhood of Maria Josepha Holroyd*, p. 398. See also Elizabeth Montagu's comments, quoted in Rizzo, *Companions without Vows*, p. 4.

13. Jones, *Jane Austen and Marriage*, pp. 76–7; Harness, in Duncan-Jones, *Trusty and Well Beloved*, p. 29; Sweetman, *Raglan: From the Peninsula to the Crimea*, pp. 65–6, quotes several slightly different versions of the story. The curious point is that it was Somerset's *right* arm that was amputated: evidently he had worn the ring on that hand. Flinders, *Letters to Ann*, p. 113.

14. Mrs Pole-Carew to a friend, 5 March 1813, in *Correspondence of Sarah Spencer, Lady Lyttelton*, pp. 139–41. There is a problem in the times given in this account, and it is possible that the first line has been mistranscribed and that they left London at ten not two o'clock, in which case everything would fall into place.

15. Jones, *Jane Austen and Marriage*, p. 81 (Caroline Lybbe Powys); Porter, *A Governess in the Age of Jane Austen*, pp. 154–5 (Fox-Strangways); Festing, *John Hookham Frere and His Friends*, p. 31 (Canning); Austen, *Mansfield Park*, vol. 2, ch. 3, p. 203.

16. Caroline Austen and Mary Russell Mitford, both quoted in Jones, *Jane Austen and Marriage*, pp. 85–6; Bess Canning to her mother Mehitabel Canning, 1 September 1798, quoted in Hunt, *Mehitabel Canning*, pp. 148–50.

17. For an example of a couple moving straight into the marital home see Duncan-Jones, *Trusty and Well Beloved*, pp. 30–1; and for one of a couple in lodgings see Glover, *An Eloquent Soldier*, pp. 9–10. Betsey Fremantle's journal in Fremantle, *Wynne Diaries*, vol. 2, pp. 163ff; for Captain Palmer see journal of Graham Moore in Wareham, *Frigate Commander*, pp. 8–10; and for Flinders see Flinders, *Letters to Ann*, pp. 24–33.

18. Muir, *Wellington: The Path to Victory*, pp. 173–5, 181–2; Wilson, *A Soldier's Wife*, pp. 76–81.

19. Jones, *Jane Austen and Marriage*, p. 93; Bew, *Castlereagh*, p. 75; Austen, *Mansfield Park*, vol. 2, ch. 3, pp. 203–4.

20. Jones, *Jane Austen and Marriage*, p. 94, which includes the quotation from Caroline Scott's novel *A Marriage in High Life* (1828).

21. Calvert, *Irish Beauty of the Regency*, p. 6.

22. Eden, *Semi-Attached Couple*, ch. 9, pp. 41–2 (on the tone of letters from newly married brides); Julia Peel's letter to her mother quoted in Gash, *Mr Secretary Peel*, p. 261; Queen Victoria's journal quoted in Phegley, *Courtship and Marriage in Victorian England*, pp. 3–4; Davidson, *Dress in the Age of Jane Austen*, p. 72 (quoting Maria Edgeworth on Miss Brownlow's chemises); cf. Gleeson, *An Aristocratic Affair*, p. 286, for a letter from Lady Bessborough about her daughter Caroline's wedding night which refers to an alternative view.
23. Selwyn, quoted in Cannon, *Aristocratic Century*, p. 73; Mrs Arbuthnot in Smith, *Wellington and the Arbuthnots*, p. 132; and, more generally, see Jones, *Jane Austen and Marriage*, pp. 97–8.
24. Eugenia Campbell's diary for 24 July 1806, *Wynne Diaries*, vol. 3, p. 295.
25. Maria Stanley to her aunt Serena Holroyd, 14 October 1796, Stanley, *Early Married Life of Maria Josepha, Lady Stanley*, p. 109.
26. Sarah Lyttelton to her parents Lord and Lady Spencer, Stockholm, 16 August 1813, *Correspondence of Sarah Spencer, Lady Lyttelton*, p. 154.
27. Eugenia Campbell's diary for 22 August 1806, *Wynne Diaries*, vol. 3, p. 297.
28. Betsey Fremantle's diary for 22–24 January, 1, 8, 9 and 10–11 February 1797, *Wynne Diaries*, vol. 2, pp. 163, 166–7.

7 ELOPEMENTS, ABDUCTIONS, MISTRESSES AND *MÉSALLIANCES*

1. Rowlandson, *Fillial Affection, or a Trip to Gretna Green*; see George and Stephens, *Catalogue of Political and Personal Satires Preserved in the Department of Prints and Drawings in the British Museum*, vol. 6, no. 6861, p. 261.
2. Cockayne, *Complete Peerage*, vol. 12, pt 2, p. 577; Elliott, *Gretna Green Memoirs*, pp. 17–18.
3. Elliott, *Gretna Green Memoirs*, pp. 29–33.
4. Schutte, *Women, Rank and Marriage*, p. 238.
5. Perceval to Dudley Ryder, n.d. [August 1790], quoted in Gray, *Spencer Perceval*, p. 10.
6. Aspinall, 'The Old House of Commons and its Members', pt 7, p. 290; Elliott, *Gretna Green Memoirs*, pp. 19–20; *Oxford Dictionary of National Biography* (*ODNB*); Cockayne, *Complete Peerage*, vol. 5, p. 108n; Farington, *Diary*, vol. 8, p. 268; Thorne, *History of Parliament*, vol. 3, p. 713; Stone, *Road to Divorce*, pp. 276–7.
7. Elliott, *Gretna Green Memoirs*, p. 63; Calvert, *Irish Beauty of the Regency*, 4 March 1805, p. 37. Couples continued to elope to Gretna Green until as late as 1939, when the law changed, although the minimum age had been raised to sixteen and a requirement of a short period of residence had been added. Langhamer, *The English in Love*, p. 172.
8. Elliott, *Gretna Green Memoirs*, pp. 18–19.
9. Twiss, *The Public and Private Life of Lord Chancellor Eldon*, vol. 1, p. 77.
10. Rowlandson, *Reconciliation or the Return from Scotland*, 1785 (not in BM Catalogue but available online from many websites, including https://www.nga.gov/collection/art-object-page.31006.html); Wilson, *Almost Another Sister*, pp. 93–6.
11. For an excellent account of the whole affair see Ashby and Jones, *The Shrigley Abduction*, *passim*.
12. Clifford, 'The Bristol Elopement: Clementina Clerke and Richard Vining Perry', blogpost dated 13 August 2013, https://www.naomiclifford.com/the-bristol-elopement/.

13. *Leeds Intelligencer*, 24 September 1771, quoted in Clifford, 'Newspaper Reports of Elopements and Abductions [1770–73]'; and Clifford, 'Grady v Richards, 1828: Rare Prosecution of the Bride and Her Family', blogpost dated 23 September 2013, both at www.naomiclifford.com

14. For Irish abductions see Malcomson, *Pursuit of the Heiress*, pp. 62–5, 141; Wilson, *Women, Marriage and Property*, pp. 24–8; and Clifford, 'The Abduction Club', blogpost dated 16 October 2013, https://www.naomiclifford.com/abduction-club/.

15. Austen, *Pride and Prejudice*, vol. 3, ch. 10, pp. 322–3 (Lydia's lack of shame); ch. 5, p. 282 (Mr Gardiner's view); ch. 6, p. 298 (Wickham's debts); ch. 7, pp. 302–3 and ch. 10, p. 324 (terms of settlement).

16. Gibson, '"I am not on the Footing of Kept Women": Extra-marital Love in Eighteenth-century England', *Cultural and Social History: The Journal of the Social History Society*, vol. 17, no. 3 (2020), pp. 2–3, rightly chides historians for neglecting love as a motive in extra-marital affairs.

17. Soames, *The Profligate Duke*, pp. 153–4; this was the same Marquess of Blandford who seduced Harriet Spencer a few years later, as mentioned above, chapter 5, p. 83. For other instances of fake marriages see Hostettler and Braby, *Sir William Garrow*, p. 151; Augustus Hare, *The Story of My Life*, vol. 2, p. 178; and, with the curious twist that the sham marriage proved valid, Costley-White, *Mary Cole, Countess of Berkeley*, p. 37.

18. Soames, *The Profligate Duke*, pp. 154–6.

19. Malcomson, *Pursuit of the Heiress*, pp. 169–70. Conyngham subsequently instructed his lawyer to provide an annuity of £40 to Bulstrode on his decease.

20. Martin, *Life of James Boswell*, pp. 236–9: the quotations coming from Boswell's letters and journal, as quoted by Martin.

21. Gibson, '"I am not on the Footing of Kept Women": Extra-marital Love in Eighteenth-century England', pp. 355, 358–64.

22. Ibid., pp. 355–6, 362, 365–7. A charcoal study for the painting is in the British Museum, number 1967,1014.121.18. For more on Lady Tyrconnel and her affair with Lord Strathmore see Arnold, *The Unhappy Countess*, pp. 157–61.

23. Tomalin, *Mrs Jordan's Profession*, pp. 240–57, 288–90, 293–9.

24. Wilson, *The Memoirs of Harriette Wilson*, passim; Connell, *Portrait of a Whig Peer*, p. 128. Another peer, 'Lord B.', arranged for his mistress to marry his butler, for whom he procured a 'genteel place' in the customs service. However, the late butler soon died and his widow soon after became the mistress of a son of Lord North. Stone, *Family, Sex and Marriage*, p. 531.

25. Connell, *Portrait of a Whig Peer*, pp. 334–40.

26. Niall, *Georgiana*, pp. 5–7, 9–10; Chamberlain, *Lord Aberdeen*, pp. 18, 25 (for Aberdeen's income see Muir, *Gentlemen of Uncertain Fortune*, pp. 1–3); Stone, *Family, Sex and Marriage*, pp. 533–4 (for Lord Pembroke's son); Beresford, *Marshal William Carr Beresford*, pp. 1–2, 258–9.

27. Edgeworth, *Belinda*, ch. 11, p. 135 and ch. 24, p. 297.

28. Jane Austen to Cassandra, 8–9 January 1801, *Jane Austen's Letters*, no. 30, p. 74; Austen, *Mansfield Park*, vol. 1, ch. 4, p. 41; Soames, *The Profligate Duke*, pp. 191–8, 209–13. For an instance of adult children accepting the marriage of their father to a long-standing mistress of obscure birth see the case of Lord Delaval (1728–1808) in Gibson, '"I am not on the Footing of Kept Women": Extra-marital Love in Eighteenth-century England', p. 10.

29. Austen, *Emma*, vol. 3, ch. 11, p. 413; Austen, *Persuasion*, vol. 2, ch. 9, p. 202.

30. Jane Austen to her sister Cassandra, 20 November 1808, *Jane Austen's Letters*, no. 61, p. 160.
31. Stanhope's letter, quoted in Newman, *The Stanhopes of Chevening*, pp. 188–9; Lady Lucy's letter and other details in the paragraph from Jacqueline Reiter, '"A dirty Apothecary": The Elopement of Lady Lucy Stanhope and Thomas Taylor', blog-post dated 28 June 2019, https://thelatelord.com/tag/charles-3rd-earl-stanhope/, citing Lady Lucy Stanhope to Mary, Countess of Chatham, n.d., National Army Museum, Combermere Mss 8408-114.
32. Reiter, '"A dirty Apothecary"'; Newman, *The Stanhopes of Chevening*, pp. 188–9; Gillray, *Democratic Levelling*, published 4 March 1796, no. 8787, in George and Stephens, *Catalogue of Political and Personal Satires Preserved in the Department of Prints and Drawings in the British Museum*, vol. 7, p. 242.
33. Horace Walpole to Lord Hertford, 1 November 1764, *The Yale Edition of Horace Walpole's Correspondence*, vol. 38, pp. 456–7.
34. Anon., 'Singular Mésalliance', pp. 270–1 (this was based on an article in the *Literary Souvenir* for 1831, a memoir of Sarah Curran who married Henry Sturgeon). See also Smith, *Whig Principles and Party Politics*, pp. 4, 26, 113; Parliament, *Parliamentary Debates*, vol. 135 (1854), cols 385–6; Schutte, *Women, Rank and Marriage*, p. 149; and for Henry Sturgeon see John Hussey, '"Let no man lay to Wellington's charge the suicides of these two men": The Problems of Reminiscence and the Failings of Old Age', pp. 98–109; and Garwood, 'The Royal Staff Corps', pp. 81–96.
35. Tillyard, *Aristocrats*, pp. 245–51, 298–303, 308–22 (quotation from Mrs Delany on pp. 317–18); see also Malcomson, *Pursuit of the Heiress*, p. 41. For more on this marriage see below, pp. 176–77, 183, 303–4.
36. *ODNB* entries for Elizabeth Farren and Louisa Brunton; Creevey's Journal, 11 November 1809, in *The Creevey Papers*, p. 112.
37. Harriet, Duchess of St Albans to Sir Walter Scott, 16 July 1827, quoted in *Journal of Sir Walter Scott*, vol. 1, p. 414, entry for 30 June 1827.
38. Creevey, *The Creevey Papers*, 30 September 1835, p. 656. Byng was a well-known figure in society and had been an officer in the army and then a clerk in the Foreign Office, who had escorted the Hawaiian King Kamehameha II on his visit to London in 1824, and served as Gentleman Usher of the Privy Chamber. He later became an advocate of sanitary reform in London.
39. Weeton, *Miss Weeton's Journal of a Governess*, vol. 1, pp. 218–21, 239, 256–7, 310–11; Weeton, *Miss Weeton Governess and Traveller*, edited by Alan Roby, pp. 395–9 (Appendix on Edward Pedder and his family by Alex Hayes).

8 SPINSTERS AND BACHELORS: THE ALTERNATIVE TO MARRIAGE

1. Figures from Stone, *Family, Sex and Marriage*, graphs 2 and 3, pp. 45 and 47; Stone and Stone, *An Open Elite?*, Table 3.2 (unpaginated appendix); Cannon, *Aristocratic Century*, p. 82; and Schutte, *Women, Rank and Marriage*, pp. 50, 53 and 205n. Census figures only become useful in this context later in the nineteenth century.
2. Gregory, quoted in Lincoln, *Naval Wives and Mistresses*, p. 26; Weeton, *Miss Weeton's Journal of a Governess*, vol. 1, p. 178 (17 July 1809); Gaskell, 'The Last Generation in England', p. 160. See also Sbaraini, '"Those that Prefer the Ripe Mellow Fruit to Any Other": Rethinking Depictions of Middle-aged Women's Sexuality in England, 1700–1800', p. 168.

3. Jane Austen to Fanny Knight, Chawton, 20–23 March 1817, *Jane Austen's Letters*, no. 153, p. 347; Austen, *Emma*, vol. 1, ch. 10, p. 85; Austen, *The Watsons*, p. 23; see also Wilson, *Women, Marriage and Property*, p. 110, for a modern historian's support for this view.

4. Marishall, *A Series of Letters*, vol. 3, pp. 114–15, quoted in Copeland, 'What's a Competence? Jane Austen, her Sister Novelists and the 5%'s', p. 163; for the decision not to marry see above, p. 14.

5. Jane to Cassandra Austen, 24 and 29 January 1813, *Jane Austen's Letters*, nos 78 and 79, pp. 206–9, 209–11 and 418; Austen-Leigh, *Jane Austen: A Family Record*, p. 242; see also Austen's letter of 9 December 1808 (*Letters*, no. 62, p. 163) in which she felt as happy at thirty-three as when she was eighteen: this before the family had moved to Chawton and she had resumed her writing.

6. Cassandra Austen to Philadelphia Whitaker, January 1832, quoted in Lane, *Jane Austen's Family: Through Five Generations*, pp. 218–19; Austen-Leigh, *Jane Austen: A Family Record*, p. 240; *Jane Austen's Letters*, p. 546 for identification of who was staying with Cassandra at the time she wrote.

7. Cassandra Austen to Philadelphia Whitaker, February 1833, quoted in Lane, *Jane Austen's Family: Through Five Generations*, pp. 219–20.

8. Austen-Leigh, *Jane Austen: A Family Record*, p. 241; John White, quoted in Tucker, *A Goodly Heritage*, p. 164.

9. Dr Gregory, see above n2; for Cassandra Austen's capital see Jones, Looser and Sabor 'Cassandra Austen's last years and wishes', p. 45; and, for the context of Mrs Leigh Perrot's gift, Le Faye *A Chronology of Jane Austen and Her Family*, pp. 646–7. Mahony *Wealth or Poverty*, pp.121–2 for the number of women investors and advice literature, and Froide 'Old Maids: The Lifestyle of Single Women in Early Modern England', p. 97, for women's investments. See also Weeton, *Miss Weeton's Journal of a Governess*, vol 1, pp. 138–9, for an example of a spinster investing in mortgages in search of a higher return on her capital.

10. Rizzo, *Companions without Vows*, pp. 30–5, is interesting if over-stated on the financial difficulties facing elite spinsters. This paragraph benefits from many helpful comments on Twitter in response to a query of mine dated 11 May 2021. The responses from Elaine Chalus and Jacqueline Reiter were especially useful.

11. Gaskell, 'The Last Generation in England', *passim*, and Gaskell, *Cranford*, *passim*.

12. Anne Lister's Aunt Anne's life is glimpsed through her niece's journal and correspondence: see Steidele, *Gentleman Jack*, pp. 32–5, 64–8, 85 and 90–8. After her brother's death the elder Anne Lister spent five years in Paris, ibid., p. 179. Gill, *William Wordsworth: A Life*, pp. 202–5, 211; for Charles and Mary Lamb see Burton, *A Double Life: A Biography of Charles and Mary Lamb*, *passim*. For an example of an unmarried niece who kept house for her bachelor uncle see Nancy Woodforde and her uncle James Woodforde, details of their life being recorded in the journals they both kept and which have been published as *The Diary of a Country Parson* and in *Woodforde Papers and Diaries*.

13. Nelly Weeton to Mrs Sudlow, n.d., *Miss Weeton's Journal*, vol. 2, pp. 68–9, see also ibid., vol. 1, pp. 200–323 and vol. 2, pp. 10–118 and Porter, *A Governess in the Age of Jane Austen*, *passim*, for their experiences as governesses.

14. Austen, *Emma*, vol. 1, ch. 3, p. 22, and vol. 1, ch. 4, pp. 28–9 (Mrs Goddard's school); Faderman, *Scotch Verdict*, pp. 28–9, 60, 142–3, 170 (the Edinburgh school and Miss Pirie and Miss Woods' school); Weeton, *Miss Weeton's Journal of a Governess*,

vol. 1, pp. 71–2; Austen, *The Watsons*, pp. 24–5. See also Stone, *Family, Sex and Marriage*, p. 517, for Arthur Young's daughter sharing a bed at a fashionable London school in 1797.

15. Jane to Cassandra Austen, 21 April 1805, *Letters*, no, 44, p. 107; Anne Platt quoted in Vickery, *Behind Closed Doors*, p. 193; Porter, *A Governess in the Age of Jane Austen*, pp. 172–4, 187–8, 192, 202. On the role of companions in general see Rizzo, *Companions without Vows, passim*, where she argues that companions filled a similar role to that of a wife (pp. 1–3) and provides many detailed case studies of the relations between a companion and her employer.

16. Porter, *A Governess in the Age of Jane Austen*, pp. 30, 346–7; Austen, *Emma*, vol. 1, ch. 7, pp. 55–6; Wilson, *Almost Another Sister*, pp. 92, 98.

17. Nelly Weeton to Miss Chorley, 1 April 1808, and to Miss Winkley, 11 May 1810, *Miss Weeton's Journal of a Governess*, vol. 1, pp. 76–8, 261–2; see also Maria Porter's ambivalent reflections about marriage in Looser, *Sister Novelists*, pp. 309–10.

18. Serena Holroyd to her niece Maria Josepha Stanley, n.d. 1817, Stanley, *Early Married Life*, p. 405; Porter, *A Governess in the Age of Jane Austen*, p. 117; Froide, 'Old Maids: The Lifestyle of Single Women in Early Modern England', pp. 90, 94–7, 102.

19. Scott, *St Ronan's Well*, ch. 16, pp. 181–9.

20. Clerk, in the *ODNB*, and in Paterson, *Kay's Edinburgh Portraits*, vol. 2, pp. 265–8.

21. Dr Johnson, in *Boswell's Life of Johnson*, vol. 1, p. 677 (*c.* 25 March 1776); Emily Cowper quoted in Bourne, *Palmerston*, p. 186; Georgiana Capel to her grandmother Lady Uxbridge, Brussels, 10 August 1815, Anglesey (ed.), *The Capel Letters*, p. 139.

22. Metcalfe, 'To Let or For Lease: "Small, but Genteel" Lodgings for Bachelors in and about the Late Georgian Town', p. 13 (including the quotations from Gibbon); see also Vickery, *Behind Closed Doors*, pp. 57–61.

23. Figures on MPs from Thorne *History of Parliament*, vol. 1, p. 279. Of the 54 British officers who commanded brigades (but not larger formations) under Wellington in the Peninsula and Low Countries, ten never married; only two of these died below the age of forty and they were both over 35: calculations based on McGuigan & Burnham *Wellington's Brigade Commanders passim*. For a different but complementary perspective on the status of bachelors see Carter 'Brothers in Arms?', p. 39.

24. Amy Harris's important study *Being Single in Georgian England* only appeared after this book was completed.

25. Cocks, 'Secrets, Crimes and Diseases, 1800–1914' in Cook et al. (eds), *A Gay History of Britain*, pp. 108, 115–18.

25. This presumption may be overturned by the discovery of fresh evidence in the same way that the discovery of Anne Lister's diaries has transformed our understanding of the possibilities for lesbian relationships at the time – on which see below.

26. Burg, *Boys at Sea, passim*; Pietsch, *The Real Jim Hawkins*, pp. 128–33.

27. Contemporary sources for these incidents have been collected and made available online by Rictor Norton at http://rictornorton.co.uk/vere.htm and http://rictornorton.co.uk/clogher1.htm, together with additional material from later research. See also Cocks 'Secrets, Crimes and Diseases' in Cook et al. (eds), *A Gay*

History of Britain, pp. 109–11; *ODNB* entry for Jocelyn in *ODNB*; and George and Stephens, *Catalogue of Political and Personal Satires Preserved in the Department of Prints and Drawings in the British Museum*, vol. 10, nos 14,377, 14,378 and 14,391, pp. 298–9, 306–7.

28. For Tomlinson see O'Keefe, 'A Natural Passion?', pp. 181–90; for Bentham see Crompton, *Byron and Greek Love*, pp. 26–31, 38–53, 252–83; and for effeminate men in women's trades and the reaction to them see Trumbach 'Modern Sodomy: the Origins of Homosexuality' in Cook et al. (eds), *A Gay History of Britain*, p. 98 (quoting Mary Hays and Priscilla Wakefield).

29. Aspinall, 'The Old House of Commons and its Members', pt 7, p. 293; Thorne, *History of Parliament*, vol. 5, pp. 420–2. For another instance see http://rictor-norton.co.uk/eighteen/1820kept.htm

30. Trumbach, 'Modern Sodomy: The Origins of Homosexuality' in Cook et al. (eds), *A Gay History of Britain*, pp. 104–5 (for Riddle); Bew, *Castlereagh*, pp. 540–4, 550–5.

31. On Deskford see Taylor, *Defiance*, pp. 24, 26, 33 and Thane, 'Love against All Rules: The Scottish Nobleman and the Private Secretary', *passim*; on Bennet see Aspinall 'The Old House of Commons and its Members', pt 4, pp. 445–6; for other exiles see Crompton, *Byron and Greek Love*, pp. 308–9; and for Sackville see Mackesy, *The Coward of Minden*, pp. 254–7.

32. Steidele, *Gentleman Jack*, *passim* and pp. 1–3, 6, 14–15, 42–4. Lister's diaries for the period 1816 to 1826 have been published as: *The Secret Diaries of Miss Anne Lister* and *The Secret Diaries of Miss Anne Lister: No Priest but Love 1824–1826*, both volumes edited by Helena Whitbread. For the continuing transcription of Lister's diaries see https://wyascatablogue.wordpress.com/exhibitions/anne-lister/anne-lister-diary-transcription-project/. Imposing the modern category of 'lesbian' on Lister, or anyone else from this time, raises many questions, and we cannot know how she would identify if given the choice; however, the record of her life provides us with much evidence of the position of women who had sex with other women in this period.

33. Steidele, *Gentleman Jack*, pp. 6–18, 27.

34. Ibid., pp. 32, 34–6, 38, 46–7.

35. Ibid., pp. 86, 143, 105, 129–30, 72, 108.

36. Ibid., pp. 89–90, 206–8 and *passim*; for examples of her later diaries see entries from 1839 at https://verycivil.blogspot.com/search?updated-max=2021-05-15T14:03:00Z&max-results=7

37. Steidele, *Gentleman Jack*, pp. 45–6, 64, 74–6, 84–5, 88–9, 108–11, 158, 204.

38. *ODNB* entry for Lady (Charlotte) Eleanor Butler; and Mavor, *The Ladies of Llangollen*, *passim*.

39. Faderman, *Scotch Verdict*, pp. 262–3 (literature); 220, 228–9, 259 (Scottish judges). George and Stephens, *Catalogue of Political and Personal Satires Preserved in the Department of Prints and Drawings in the British Museum*, vol. 10, nos 14,074–5, p. 167 (prints). Hitchcock, *English Sexualities*, pp. 44–9, 100 (changing views of female sexuality). While court cases involving male homosexuals were widely reported, the Scottish Court of Session went to extraordinary lengths to ensure that the evidence given in the libel case involving Miss Pirie and Miss Woods (which turned on whether they had had sex together) should be kept from the public. Faderman, *Scotch Verdict*, pp. 78–9, 258.

9 EARLY MARRIED LIFE

1. Calvert, *Irish Beauty of the Regency* (memoirs), pp. 6–7; Lady Charlotte Bury, quoted in Smith, *Wellington and the Arbuthnots*, p. 36; Martin, *Life of James Boswell*, pp. 265–6.
2. Newdigate-Newdegate, *The Cheverels of Cheverel Manor*, pp. 7–8.
3. Ibid., pp. 9, 12.
4. Lady Caroline Stuart Wortley to her mother Lady Erne, Warfield Grove, 19 July [1799], Grosvenor, *First Lady Wharncliffe*, vol. 1, pp. 42–3.
5. Lady Caroline Stuart Wortley to her mother Lady Erne, Grosvenor Square, n.d., 16, 21 and 29 October 1799, Grosvenor, *First Lady Wharncliffe*, vol. 1, pp. 45–50.
6. Lady Caroline Stuart Wortley to her mother Lady Erne, Warfield Grove, 29 October [17]99, Grosvenor, *First Lady Wharncliffe*, vol. 1, pp. 49–50.
7. Maria Stanley to her sister Louisa, [Newcastle], ? January 1797, Stanley, *Early Married Life*, p. 116.
8. Maria Stanley to her aunt Serena Holroyd and her sister Louisa, 4 August 1797 and ? January 1797, in Stanley, *Early Married Life*, pp. 134–5 and 115.
9. Maria Stanley to her sister Louisa, Blyth, 2 September 1797, Stanley, *Early Married Life*, p. 139.
10. Major John Stanley to Captain William Clinton, Alderley, 21 November 1797, and Lord Sheffield to his sister Serena Holroyd, Alderley Park, 11 December 1797, Stanley, *Early Married Life*, pp. 147–8.
11. Shelley, *Diary of Frances, Lady Shelley*, vol. 1, pp. 37–8.
12. Ibid., vol. 1, pp. 32–3.
13. Ibid., vol. 1, pp. 33–4, 39. Lady Shelley spells 'Haggerston', 'Haggerstone'.
14. Huxley, *Lady Elizabeth and the Grosvenors*, pp. 33–6. See also Gleeson, *An Aristocratic Affair*, p. 31, for another newly married aristocratic couple who lived with the groom's family in the early days of their marriage (in this case Harriet Spencer and Viscount Duncannon with his widowed father, Lord Bessborough).
15. Betsey Fremantle's journal, 28 February and 30 April 1797, in *Wynne Diaries*, vol. 2, pp. 170, 176; Capt. Thomas Fremantle to his brother William, 2 March 1797, in Parry, *Admirals Fremantle*, p. 47.
16. Quotations from Betsey Fremantle's journal, 3, 24 and 25 July 1797, in *Wynne Diaries*, vol. 2, pp. 183, 185–6, see also pp. 183–96 for Thomas Fremantle's slow recovery and Betsey's experiences.
17. Gore, *Nelson's Hardy and His Wife*, pp. 40–1.
18. Copeland, '*Persuasion*: The Jane Austen Consumer's Guide', p. 115–16; Austen-Leigh, *Jane Austen: A Family Record*, p. 67; see also Vickery, *Behind Closed Doors*, p. 16.
19. Austen, *Mansfield Park*, vol. 2, ch. 3, pp. 202–3; Isa Stanley to her sister-in-law Maria, n.d., Stanley, *Early Married Life*, pp. 127–8.
20. Maria Stanley to her sister Louisa Clinton and her aunt Serena Holroyd, n.d. and 21 March 1798, Stanley, *Early Married Life*, pp. 147, 157.
21. Louisa, Lady Hopetoun to her father, Godfrey, Lord Macdonald, 14 May 1827, in Stewart, *Family Tapestry*, pp. 84–6.
22. Chapone, *Letters on the Improvement of the Mind*, ch. 7, p. 80; Vickery, *Gentleman's Daughter*, pp. 129–32; Smith, *Wellington and the Arbuthnots*, pp. 30–2.
23. Eden, *Semi-Attached Couple*, ch. 29, pp. 137–8, 142–3 and ch. 32, pp. 153; Lord William Russell to his mother-in-law Mrs Rawdon, 17 [July 1817], Blakiston, *Lord William Russell and His Wife*, p. 38; Harriet Lady Granville to her sister Lady G. Morpeth, Paris, August 1817, *Letters of Harriet Lady Granville*, vol. 1, pp. 126–7.

24. Jenkins, *Jane Austen*, p. 43.
25. Aspinall-Oglander, *Freshly Remembered: The Story of Thomas Graham*, pp. 7–8.
26. Muir, *Wellington: The Path to Victory*, p. 222; Wilson, *A Soldier's Wife*, p. 107; *Wynne Diaries*, vol. 3, pp. 286, 294 (and see p. 86); Blakiston, *Lord William Russell and His Wife*, pp. 46, 65–6, 113–14, 118, 120 and 124–5; Stanley, *Early Married Life*, pp. 208, 298. See also Martin, *Life of James Boswell*, p. 267, for another example of a marriage exacerbating existing tensions in a family.
27. Austen, *Persuasion*, vol. 1, ch. 6, pp. 44–6.

10 'MY LOVE...'

1. Maria Stanley to her aunt Serena Holroyd, 25 March 1797, Stanley, *Early Married Life*, p. 124; Scott, *St Ronan's Well*, ch. 32, p. 389; Eden, *Semi-Attached Couple*, ch. 13, p. 56 – Eden changes 'foibles' to 'trifles' in the second line of the quotation and omits two lines of the original: see the full text of More's 'Sensibility: A Poetical Epistle to the Hon. Mrs Boscawen', in Wu (ed.), *Romanticism: An Anthology*, pp. 59–68, lines 307–12. See also Wilson, *Almost Another Sister*, pp. 73–4.
2. Ferrier, *Marriage*, ch. 3, p. 40; Duncan-Jones, *Trusty and Well Beloved*, p. 22; Vickery, *Behind Closed Doors*, p. 120; Davidson, *Dress in the Age of Jane Austen*, p. 91.
3. Jupp, *Lord Grenville*, pp. 294–5.
4. Ibid., p. 294; James Stuart Wortley to his wife Caroline, 1 January 1811, Grosvenor *First Lady Wharncliffe*, vol. 1, p. 173; William Harness to his wife Elizabeth, Guernsey, 14 March 1794, in Duncan-Jones, *Trusty and Well Beloved*, pp. 43–4; see also Williamson, *British Masculinity in the* Gentleman's Magazine, pp. 167–8, for other open expressions of love from husbands to their wives.
5. George Canning to his wife Joan, 20 September 1809, printed in *Later Correspondence of George III*, vol. 5, pp. 368n–70n.
6. Mary Dickenson to John Dickenson, 20 October 1785, in Anson and Anson, *Mary Hamilton*, p. 284; Emily, Duchess of Leinster, quoted in Tillyard, *Aristocrats*, pp. 321–2; Anne Barnard, in Taylor, *Defiance*, p. 275.
7. John Dickenson to Mary Dickenson, n.d., in Anson and Anson, *Mary Hamilton*, pp. 330–2; William Ogilvie, quoted in Tillyard, *Aristocrats*, p. 321.
8. Quoted in Bew, *Castlereagh*, p. 168.
9. Newdigate-Newdegate, *The Cheverels of Cheverel Manor*, p. 81; Taylor, *Defiance*, pp. 292–3.
10. Major-General William Pringle to his wife Harriet, Lisbon, 20 May 1812, in Thompson, 'Peninsular War Letters of Lieutenant-General Sir William Henry Pringle', p. 35.
11. Connell, *Portrait of a Whig Peer*, p. 169; Betsey Fremantle's diary, 26 October 1806, and Fremantle to Betsey, 26 March 1811, *Wynne Diaries*, vol. 3, pp. 304, 331.
12. Smith, *Wellington and the Arbuthnots*, pp. 38–9, 160.
13. Quoted in Anson and Anson, *Mary Hamilton*, pp. 149–50.
14. Calvert, *Irish Beauty of the Regency*, 20 July 1808, p. 107; Retter and Sinclair, *Letters to Ann*, pp. 115–16; Maria Josepha Stanley to her aunt Serena Holroyd, 20 January 1803, Stanley, *Early Married Life*, p. 250.
15. Williamson, *British Masculinity in the* Gentleman's Magazine, *1731–1815*, p. 168.
16. On the Wedgwoods see Vickery, *Behind Closed Doors*, p. 99; Caroline Stuart Wortley to her mother Lady Erne, 31 July and 3 August 1803, James Stuart Wortley to his

wife Caroline, n.d. [August and September 1804], Grosvenor, *First Lady Wharncliffe,* vol. 1, pp. 92, 93, 103 and 105.

17. Nelly Weeton to Miss Bolton, 27 August 1808, *Miss Weeton's Journal of a Governess,* vol. 1, pp. 104; Gittings and Manton, *Dorothy Wordsworth,* p. 141.

18. Rebow, quoted in Vickery, *Behind Closed Doors,* p. 97; Tillyard, *Aristocrats,* p. 321, quoted above, pp. 176–7; Taylor, *Defiance,* pp. 196–8. For a further discussion of sex and contraception see below, pp. 231–3.

11 GETTING ALONG

1. Eugenia Wynne's diary, 9 June 1806, *Wynne Diaries,* vol. 3, pp. 277–8; Eliza Austen to her cousin Philadelphia Walter, 16 February 1798, in Le Faye, *Jane Austen's 'Outlandish Cousin',* pp. 152–3.

2. Wilson, *Almost Another Sister,* pp. 72–5; Austen, *Mansfield Park,* vol. 3, ch. 6, p. 370; Eden, *Semi-Attached Couple,* ch. 1, p. 9.

3. Barclay, *Love, Intimacy and Power,* pp. 128, 136.

4. On the issue of wives paying lip-service to their husband's authority see Vickery, *Gentleman's Daughter,* pp. 84–5; Lady Spencer: Sarah Spencer to her brother Robert Spencer, 19 October 1809, *Correspondence of Sarah Spencer, Lady Lyttelton,* p. 84; see also Chalus, *Elite Women in English Political Life,* pp. 21–3; General Conway, Vickery, *Behind Closed Doors,* pp. 131–2, quoting Horace Walpole's *Correspondence,* vol. 37, p. 566; for Lord and Lady Holland see Mitchell, *Holland House,* especially, pp. 30–2, Rogers, *Tabletalk of Samuel Rogers,* pp. 216–19, and diary of George Jackson, 18 April 1809, Jackson, *Diaries and Letters of George Jackson,* vol. 2, pp. 424–5.

5. Edgeworth, *Belinda,* ch. 3, p. 35; Lady William Russell to Lord Lynedoch, [24 February 1826], and Lord William Russell to his wife, 2 August 1828, in Blakiston, *Lord William Russell and His Wife,* pp. 136–7, 168–9.

6. Louisa Clinton to her sister Maria Stanley, 18 March 1801, Stanley, *Early Married Life,* p. 214; Captain Fremantle to his wife Betsey, 11 April 1804, cf. his letter to her of 22 June 1805, *Wynne Diaries,* vol. 3, pp. 112, 174, and see below for other examples of his praise.

7. Maria Stanley to her aunt Serena Holroyd, 25 March 1797, Stanley, *Early Married Life,* p. 124; Eden, *Semi-Attached Couple,* ch. 12, p. 54.

8. Congreve, quoted in Vickery, *Behind Closed Doors,* p. 204; Edgeworth, *Belinda,* ch. 14, p. 162; Calvert, *Irish Beauty of the Regency,* April 1809, pp. 131–2.

9. Chapone, *Letters on the Improvement of the Mind,* pp. 75–6.

10. Captain Fremantle to his wife Betsey, 17 and 21 March 1801 and 21 December 1805, *Wynne Diaries,* vol. 3, pp. 31–5, 236–7. Similarly, Lady Exmouth, wife of Admiral Sir Edward Pellew, Lord Exmouth, bought and sold houses when her husband was at sea, Taylor, *Commander,* p. 230.

11. Captain Charles Paget RN to his brother Arthur, 11 [November] 1814, Paget, *The Paget Brothers,* p. 267; the Duke of Bedford to Lady William Russell, 26 September [1828], in Blakiston, *Lord William Russell and His Wife,* p. 171; Mary Dickenson to her father-in-law John Dickenson snr, 12 December 1789, Anson and Anson, *Mary Hamilton,* p. 297: this letter was written after more than four years of marriage. See also Martinovich, *The Sea is My Element,* p. 127, for Pulteney Malcolm's confidence in his wife Clementina on money (and other) matters.

12. For John Harwood see *Jane Austen's Letters*, ed. Le Faye, p. 532; for Colonel Jervoise, Vickery, *Behind Closed Doors*, pp. 110–11.
13. Mary, Lady Palmerston to her husband, 11 November 1796, in Connell, *Portrait of a Whig Peer*, p. 349.
14. Connell, *Portrait of a Whig Peer*, pp. 349–50, 381–4.
15. Calvert, *Irish Beauty of the Regency*, n.d. [March 1810], p. 155.
16. Lady Caroline Capel to her mother Lady Uxbridge, October 1816, in Anglesey (ed.), *The Capel Letters*, p. 179.
17. George Murray to Anthony Murray, 20 January 1831, in Harding-Edgar, *Next to Wellington: General Sir George Murray*, p. 343.
18. Letters quoted from Smith, *Wellington and the Arbuthnots*, pp. 101–2; see also *Letters of King George IV*, vol. 1, pp. 44ff and *Correspondence of Charles Arbuthnot*, pp. 62ff, for the King's role in assisting them.
19. Edgeworth, *Belinda*, ch. 3, p. 38; Barclay, *Love, Intimacy and Power*, p. 155; Lady William Russell to Lord Lynedoch, [24 February 1826], in Blakiston, *Lord William Russell and His Wife*, pp. 136–7.
20. Newdigate-Newdegate, *The Cheverels of Cheverel Manor*, pp. 39–40, 46–7. While the cutlery evidently cost less than the 50 guineas he sent, it was still a much more significant purchase than it would be today.
21. Shelley, *Diary of Frances, Lady Shelley*, vol. 1, p. 36; for an instance of the wife definitely retaining control of her portion after her marriage see Wilson, *Women, Marriage and Property*, p. 53.
22. Sherwood, *The Life of Mrs Sherwood*, pp. 237, 241.
23. For the Fremantles see *Wynne Diaries*, *passim*; Lady Caroline Stuart Wortley to her mother Lady Erne, n.d. [May 1800], Grosvenor, *First Lady Wharncliffe*, vol. 1, p. 55; Barclay, *Love, Intimacy and Power*, pp. 22–3.
24. Eden, *Semi-Attached Couple*, ch. 14, p. 62, and ch. 24, pp. 107–8; Eden, *Miss Eden's Letters*, *passim*.
25. Smith, *Wellington and the Arbuthnots*, *passim*; Arbuthnot, *Journal of Mrs Arbuthnot, 1820–1832*, *passim*; Chalus, *Elite Women in English Political Life, c.1754–1790*, is the definitive study of the subject for this slightly earlier period; see especially p. 85 for another example where a wife's political views differed strongly from those of her husband. Calvert, *Irish Beauty in the Regency*, p. 76.
26. Caroline Stuart Wortley to her mother Lady Erne, Camelford, 3 November 1806, Grosvenor, *First Lady Wharncliffe*, vol. 1, pp. 130–1. For a vivid description of women's role in canvassing and eagerness about an election see Eden, *Semi-Attached Couple*, chs 36–8, pp. 173–91. For women's roles in elections see Chalus, *Elite Women in English Political Life*, pp. 157–221 and Malcomson, *Pursuit of the Heiress*, p. 137.
27. A great many of George Canning's letters to his wife Joan are quoted at length in the notes to *Later Correspondence of George III*; see also Hinde, *George Canning*; and Temperley, 'Joan Canning on Her Husband's Policy and Ideas', *passim*. For Palmerston's correspondence with his wife on politics see Connell, *Portrait of a Whig Peer*, pp. 182ff, 212, 448 and 451.
28. Betsey Fremantle's diary, 29 and 30 July, 2 August 1798, *Wynne Diaries*, vol. 3, pp. 1–2; James Stuart Wortley to his mother-in-law Lady Erne, [July 1800], and Caroline Stuart Wortley to her mother Lady Erne, Brook Street, London, 11 July 1818, Grosvenor, *First Lady Wharncliffe*, vol. 1, pp. 57–8, 256.
29. Smith, *Wellington and the Arbuthnots*, pp. 37–8.

30. Caroline Stuart Wortley to her mother Lady Erne, n.d. [c. October 1806], Grosvenor, *First Lady Wharncliffe*, vol. 1, p. 128; Smith, *Wellington and the Arbuthnots*, p. 38.

31. Calvert, *Irish Beauty of the Regency*, ? January 1815, p. 241, and 1 January 1816, p. 259; Maria Stanley to her aunt Serena Holroyd, Alderley Park, 6 October and 2 November 1800, Stanley, *Early Married Life*, pp. 207, 208.

32. The Tate's holdings can be seen online and are mostly preliminary sketches and drawings from a notebook or a portfolio.

33. Chapone, quoted in Vickery, *Behind Closed Doors*, p. 244; Lady Caroline Stuart Wortley to her mother Lady Erne, n.d. [May 1800], Grosvenor, *First Lady Wharncliffe*, vol. 1, p. 55; Maria Stanley to her sister Louisa Clinton, 7 February 1806, and to her daughter Louisa Stanley, 6 December 1816, Stanley, *Early Married Life*, pp. 285 and 394.

34. Caroline Stuart Wortley to her mother Lady Erne, Thoresby, n.d. [November 1811], Grosvenor, *First Lady Wharncliffe*, vol. 1, p. 180; Smith, *Wellington and the Arbuthnots*, p. 117; Gore, *Nelson's Hardy and His Wife*, p. 57; Tysoe Saul Hancock to his wife Philadelphia Hancock, Calcutta, 22 June 1773, Le Faye, *Jane Austen's 'Outlandish Cousin'*, pp. 33–4; see also Chalus, *Elite Women in English Political Life*, pp. 174n, 202–3.

35. Caroline Stuart Wortley to her mother Lady Erne, Wortley Hall, 1 September 1803, Grosvenor, *First Lady Wharncliffe*, vol. 1, p. 99; Shelley, *Diary of Frances, Lady Shelley*, vol. 1, p. 13; Austen *Mansfield Park*, vol. 1, ch. 12, p. 115.

36. Maria Stanley to her aunt Serena Holroyd, London, 1 June, 19 July 1799, Stanley, *Early Married Life*, pp. 180–2.

37. Maria Stanley to her sister Louisa, [Privy Gardens], ? January, 3 and 22 May 1809, and to her sister-in-law Kitty Stanley, 23 May 1812, Stanley, *Early Married Life*, pp. 309, 316, 317, 334.

38. For an alternative and interesting interpretation of the ingredients that made for a happy marriage in this period see Vickery, *Gentleman's Daughter*, pp. 72, 83.

12 CAREERS

1. Collins, *Jane Austen and the Clergy*, ch. 8, pp. 121–41, gives a good account of the position of the parson's wife.

2. For careers open to gentlemen see Muir, *Gentlemen of Uncertain Fortune*, *passim*; for more on the position of wives of army and navy officers see below, pp. 213–23.

3. Austen, *Mansfield Park*, vol. 1, ch. 2, pp. 19–20; see also Shapard chronology in *The Annotated Mansfield Park*, pp. 855–6, for two years; Austen, *Emma*, vol. 1, ch. 12, pp. 99–100, for Mr Knightley's commitments; for an example of the wife of a Member of Parliament deciding whether to come up to London with her husband or stay in the country when parliament was sitting see Connell, *Portrait of a Whig Peer*, pp. 169, 191.

4. Horn, *British Diplomatic Service*, p. 40, for Lady Torrington; Taylor, *Defiance*, pp. 203–5, for Lady Anne Barnard; *Wynne Diaries*, vol. 3, pp. 38, 44–5, for Betsey Fremantle; Lincoln, *Naval Wives and Mistresses*, pp. 101, 112–13, for Fanny Nelson; *ODNB* entry for Mary Buckland; letter from George Canning, quoted in *Later Correspondence of George III*, vol. 3, p. 379n; Maria Stanley to her aunt Serena Holroyd, 6 October 1800, *Early Married Life*, p. 207; and Chalus, *Elite Women in*

English Political Life, pp. 131–2, discusses women seeking patronage to advance their husband's career.

5. Lincoln, *Naval Wives and Mistresses*, p. 57, for Lady Spencer; Lady Hawkesbury to her sister Lady Erne, n.d. [April 1807], Grosvenor, *First Lady Wharncliffe*, vol. 1, p. 136; Blakiston, *Lord William Russell and His Wife*, pp. 200–1, 208–9, 213, 229.

6. Nelson to Frances Nisbet before they were married, quoted in Knight, *The Pursuit of Victory*, p. 97; Broke to his wife Sarah, *Shannon* off Halifax, 11 December 1812, quoted in Gill, *Naval Families*, p. 15; King, *Richard Bourke*, p. 45; Sir A. Wellesley to Bourke, 18 and 21 June 1809, Wellington, *Dispatches*, vol. 3, pp. 305–6, 310–11; Torrens to Bourke, 25 April 1812, WO 3/602, pp. 43–4.

7. Jenny Rodney, quoted in Lincoln, *Naval Wives and Mistresses*, p. 15; Louisa to Philip Broke, 24 June 1813, quoted in Gill, *Naval Families*, p. 40; Captain Charles Paget RN to his brother Arthur Paget, *Revenge*, 16 November 1809, Paget, *The Paget Brothers*, p. 123.

8. Retter and Sinclair (eds), *Letters to Ann*, p. 40; Matthew Flinders to Ann Flinders, Spithead, 5 July 1801, and Port Jackson, 25 June 1803, Flinders, *Matthew Flinders: Personal Letters*, pp. 74–5, 99–101; see also Gill, *Naval Families*, pp. 39–40.

9. Maria Stanley to her aunt Serena Holroyd and her sister Louisa, 8 September, 22 October and ? December 1797, *Early Married Life*, pp. 140–5, 150. James Stuart Wortley similarly quit the army a couple of years after his marriage.

10. Lady Louisa Erksine to her mother the Countess of Uxbridge, 18 March 1804, Paget, *The Paget Brothers*, pp. 19–20.

11. Sherwood, *Life of Mrs Sherwood*, p. 249.

12. Ibid., p. 252. It was eleven years before Mrs Sherwood returned to England.

13. Susanna Middleton, quoted in Lincoln, *Naval Wives and Mistresses*, p. 125 (see also Gill, *Naval Families*, pp. 147–53, for more on Middleton); Sherwood, *Life of Mrs Sherwood*, pp. 254, 259.

14. Autobiographical fragment by Charles Arbuthnot, printed in Arbuthnot, *Memories of the Arbuthnots of Kincardshire and Aberdeenshire*, p. 435; see also ibid., pp. 189, 231–2 and Smith, *Wellington and the Arbuthnots*, pp. 19–23. Smith states that Charles and Marcia had a total of four children, but Arbuthnot (pp. 231–2) gives biographical details of five, so I have assumed that this is correct and the figure of four a mere slip not a deliberate correction.

15. Lady Burghersh's letters home describing her experiences are published as Burghersh, *The Letters of Lady Burghersh ... from Germany and France during the Campaign of 1813–14*; the Duchess of Wellington's letter is quoted in Wilson, *A Soldier's Wife*, p. 158.

16. See Kindred, *Jane Austen's Transatlantic Sister*, p. 33, for the biannual move from Bermuda to Halifax and back; Gore, *Nelson's Hardy and His Wife*, pp. 40–1; Henegan, *Seven Years Campaigning in the Peninsula and the Netherlands*, vol. 1, ch. 29, pp. 149 (condemns morals of the British community in Lisbon); Brett-James, *Life in Wellington's Army*, pp. 273–6; memorial tablet quoted in Bromley and Bromley, *Wellington's Men Remembered*, vol. 1, p. 229. The Dalbiacs had no children at the time that Susanna accompanied her husband in the field.

17. Betsey Fremantle's diary, 21 August 1800, and Harriet Wynne's diary, 13 July 1803, *Wynne Diaries*, vol. 3, pp. 13–14, 20, 84; Elizabeth Bass and Anna Walker, quoted in Gill, *Naval Families*, pp. 150–1, 175; Matthew Flinders, *Letters to Ann*, p. 36; see also Gill, *Naval Families, passim*; Lincoln, *Naval Wives and Mistresses*, pp. 65–71; Smallwood, 'Shore Wives', pp. 22–4, 28–32; and Chalus, '"My Dearest Tussy": Coping with

Separation in the Napoleonic Wars' and 'The Loneliness of Leadership' for further discussion of the effects of separation and anxiety on the marriages of naval officers serving abroad during this period.

18. Fremantle to Betsey, 17 and 23 May, and 14 June 1805, *Wynne Diaries*, vol. 3, pp. 168, 170, 172–3.
19. Philip to Louisa Broke, 29 July and 24 June 1810, quoted in Gill, *Naval Families*, pp. 43–4.
20. Matthew to Ann Flinders, *Letters to Ann*, pp. 42–4; Thomas to Betsey Fremantle, 12 September 1804, *Wynne Diaries*, vol. 3, pp. 135–6. See also the letters of another naval officer, Edward Codrington, to his wife Jane in Bourchier, *Memoir of the Life of Admiral Sir Edward Codrington*, vol. 1, pp. 44, 46, 84 and 104, for similar sentiments.
21. Chalus, '"My Dearest Tussy": Coping with Separation in the Napoleonic Wars', p. 52 (numbering letters); Lincoln, *Naval Wives and Mistresses*, p. 68 (code); Thomas to Betsey Fremantle, 6 July and 6 December 1805, *Wynne Diaries*, vol. 3, pp. 182–3, 234; Gill, *Naval Families*, p. 20 (George Bass); p. 21 (Broke beginning a new letter); pp. 23–4 (not burning letters); Flinders, *Letters to Ann*, p. 37.
22. Lincoln, *Naval Wives and Mistresses*, pp. 104–5 (Collingwood); Betsey Fremantle's journal, 2 November 1804, *Wynne Diaries*, vol. 3, p. 142.
23. Francis Austen's letter in Hubback and Hubback, *Jane Austen's Sailor Brothers*, pp. 148–61; see also Southam, *Jane Austen and the Navy*, pp. 98–100, and Muir, *Gentlemen of Uncertain Fortune*, pp. 227–9; Southam, op. cit., p. 71, for different causes of naval mortality; Lincoln, *Naval Wives and Mistresses*, pp. 104–5 (Collingwood); Thomas to Betsey Fremantle, 5 April 1801, *Wynne Diaries*, vol. 3, pp. 44–5.
24. Betsey Fremantle's diary, 7 November 1805, *Wynne Diaries*, vol. 3, pp. 216–17.
25. Muir, *Gentlemen of Uncertain Fortune*, *passim*, for an account of the difficulties and limited rewards of the different professions open to gentlemen; Austen, *Persuasion*, vol. 2, ch. 12, p. 252.

13 CHILDREN

1. Stone and Stone, *An Open Elite?*, pp. 99–100, for proportion of childless marriages; Clery, *Jane Austen: The Banker's Sister*, pp. 87–8, 132–3, for the marriage of Henry and Eliza Austen.
2. Taylor, *Defiance*, pp. 229, 280–1.
3. Both quotes from Vickery, *Gentleman's Daughter*, p. 97.
4. Lady Sheffield to Maria Stanley, 14 November 1801; Maria Stanley to her sister Louisa, ? April 1807, *Early Married Life*, pp. 225, 291.
5. Mitchell, *Lord Melbourne*, p. 62 (Caroline Lamb); Anna Walker, quoted in Gill, *Naval Families*, p. 154; Lady William Russell to Lady Holland, n.d. [*c.* August 1823], Blakiston, *Lord William Russell and His Wife*, pp. 106–7, see also pp. 115 and 123 for her recovery.
6. Lord William Russell to his mother-in-law, Mrs Rawdon n.d. [1819], Blakiston, *Lord William Russell and His Wife*, pp. 44–5; Calvert, *Irish Beauty of the Regency*, 16 August 1805 and 9 January 1806, pp. 50, 59.
7. Betsey Fremantle's journal, 11 March 1798, *Wynne Diaries*, vol. 2, p. 203; mother's letter, quoted in Vickery, *Gentleman's Daughter*, p. 104; Fanny Knight, quoted in Wilson, *Almost Another Sister*, pp. 101–2.
8. Vickery, *Gentleman's Daughter*, pp. 97–8 and Lewis, ''Tis a Misfortune to Be a Great Ladie', pp. 28, 31–2 (statistics); Austen-Leigh, *Jane Austen: A Family Record*,

pp. 150, 194, 239; Calvert, *Irish Beauty of the Regency*, 23 February, 8–12 June 1818, pp. 310, 319–20.

9. Yet Granville Leveson Gower was with his wife Harriet when she was in labour: see Gleeson, *An Aristocratic Affair*, p. 329.

10. Serena Holroyd to Maria Stanley, 13 November 1801, *Early Married Life*, pp. 225–6; Connell, *Portrait of a Whig Peer*, pp. 191, 195, 206, see also p. 156. See also Calvert, 'A more Careful Tender Nurse Cannot Be than My Dear Husband', *passim*, for an interesting expansion of the role some men played in childbirth.

11. Betsey Fremantle's journal, 13–31 March 1798, *Wynne Diaries*, vol. 2, pp. 203–4.

12. Maria Josepha Stanley to aunt Serena Holroyd and her sister Louisa, 4 and 9 August 1797, *Early Married Life*, pp. 134–6.

13. Pamela, Lady Campbell (née Fitzgerald) to Emily Eden, 20 June 1824, *Miss Eden's Letters*, p. 84.

14. Austen, *Northanger Abbey*, vol. 1, ch. 1, p. 13; Anglesey (ed.), *The Capel Letters*, p. 228 (Lady Uxbridge).

15. Tysoe Saul Hancock to his wife Philadelphia Hancock, Calcutta, 9 August 1773, Le Faye, *Jane Austen's 'Outlandish Cousin'*, p. 34; Austen, *Sanditon*, ch. 2, pp. 370, 373–4, cf. Miss Weeton to Mrs Dodson, 18 August 1812, *Miss Weeton's Journal*, vol. 2, p. 61.

16. Stone, *Family, Sex and Marriage*, pp. 398, 417, 422–4, 537; Hitchcock, *English Sexualities*, pp. 52–4; Jones, *Jane Austen and Marriage*, pp. 162–9; Arnold, *The Unhappy Countess*, pp. 42, 47: Lady Strathmore was a widow at the time of these pregnancies.

17. Eugenia Wynne's diary, 5 March 1806, *Wynne Diaries*, vol. 3, p. 251; Lady Caroline Capel to her mother Lady Uxbridge, Brussels, 1 November 1814, Anglesey (ed.), *The Capel Letters*, p. 74; Greville, *Memoirs*, 23 January 1850, vol. 6, p. 195, who says that Emily had an affair with Lord Alvanley both before and after her marriage. The question is not discussed in John Sweetman's biography of Somerset: *Raglan: From the Peninsula to the Crimea*.

18. Jane Austen to Fanny Knight, 20–21 February 1817, *Jane Austen's Letters*, no. 151, p. 344; Tillyard, *Aristocrats*, pp. 327–9.

19. Calvert, *Irish Beauty of the Regency* (memoirs), p. 7; Lady William Russell to Lady Holland, [Spa, 14 July 1821]; Lord William Russell to Lady Holland, Schlangenbad, 18 August [1821], and same to same, Florence, 27 June [1822], quoted in Blakiston, *Lord William Russell and His Wife*, pp. 52, 55–6, 65–6; Caroline Stuart Wortley to her mother Lady Erne, 15 August 1801 and 30 July 1803, and James Stuart Wortley to his wife Caroline, n.d. [late August or early September 1804], Grosvenor, *First Lady Wharncliffe*, vol. 1, pp. 65, 91–2, 105.

20. Huxley, *Lady Elizabeth and the Grosvenors*, pp. 25–30.

21. Anglesey (ed.), *The Capel Letters*, pp. 34–5, 129–30; Duke of Bedford to Lady William Russell, 8 December [1828], Blakiston, *Lord William Russell and His Wife*, p. 174; Betsey Fremantle's diary, 27 December 1811 and Thomas to Betsey Fremantle, 1 October 1805, *Wynne Diaries*, vol. 3, pp. 210, 350; see also Vickery, *Gentleman's Daughter*, pp. 105, 289.

22. Calvert, *Irish Beauty of the Regency*, pp. 54–5, 269, 272. Compare this with Duncan-Jones, *Trusty and Well Beloved*, p. 90, where William and Elizabeth Harness feel obliged to adopt an unwelcome suggestion for the name of their daughter from Elizabeth's great-aunt.

23. Vickery, *Gentleman's Daughter*, pp. 110–17; Gill, *Naval Families*, pp. 50–1.

24. Caroline Stuart Wortley to her mother Lady Erne, 9 August 1807, Grosvenor, *First Lady Wharncliffe*, vol. 1, p. 141; Kitty, Lady Wellington, quoted in Wilson, *A*

Soldier's Wife, p. 148; Thomas to Betsey Fremantle, 5 November 1803, *Wynne Diaries*, vol. 3, pp. 95–6; Maria Stanley to Louisa Clinton, 5 April 1808, *Early Married Life*, p. 300; Chalus, '"My Dearest Tussy": Coping with Separation in the Napoleonic Wars', pp. 53–4 (this passage is not in the printed edition of the *Wynne Diaries*).

25. George to Joan Canning, 20 September 1809, quoted in *Later Correspondence of George III*, vol. 5, p. 369n; Betsey to Thomas Fremantle in Chalus, '"My Dearest Tussy": Coping with Separation in the Napoleonic Wars', pp. 58–9 (this passage is not in the printed edition of the *Wynne Diaries*).

26. Betsey to Thomas Fremantle in Chalus, '"My Dearest Tussy": Coping with Separation in the Napoleonic Wars', p. 53 (this passage is not in the printed edition of the *Wynne Diaries*).

27. Shelley, *Diary of Lady Shelley*, vol. 1, pp. 1–3 (her parents), vol. 2, p. 312 (on the Duchess of Wellington); Longford, *Wellington: Pillar of State*, p. 82, quotations from Wellington's sons' letters to their mother.

28. Austen, *Northanger Abbey*, vol. 1, ch. 1, pp. 14–15 and ch. 14, pp. 109–10; Maria Stanley to her aunt Serena Holroyd, 2 November 1800, 25 January 1801, and to her sister Louisa Clinton, ? May 1803, *Early Married Life*, pp. 208, 212, 255.

29. Maria Stanley to her aunt Serena Holroyd, 6 November 1803, *Early Married Life*, p. 264; Thompson, *English Landed Society in the Nineteenth Century*, p. 84.

30. Lady Palmerston's journal, 10 November 1800, in Connell, *Portrait of a Whig Peer*, p. 431; Dr Spencer Madan to his son Spencer Madan, 16 September and 26 December 1814, in Madan, *Spencer and Waterloo*, pp. 16–17, 72–3.

31. Betsey to Thomas Fremantle, 29 December 1810, quoted in Chalus, '"My Dearest Tussy": Coping with Separation in the Napoleonic Wars', p. 58 (passage not printed in *Wynne Diaries*); for differing discussions of the issue of 'wife or mother' see Vickery, *Gentleman's Daughter*, pp. 90–91, and Stone, *Family, Sex and Marriage*, p. 397.

14 UNHAPPY MARRIAGES

1. Eden, *Semi-Attached Couple, passim*.
2. Arnold, *The Unhappy Countess*, pp. 25–35 (quotation on p. 27); see also Moore, *Wedlock*, pp. 41–3, 64–5, 75–92.
3. Harding-Edgar, *Next to Wellington*, pp. 304–5. Wemyss was married to Erskine's sister Frances. According to Malcomson's survey of Irish divorces in the eighteenth century love matches were at least as likely to fail as those made under duress: Malcomson, *Pursuit of an Heiress*, p. 153.
4. Eugenia Wynne's diary, 18 and 19 December 1796, *The Wynne Diaries*, vol. 2, pp. 141–2. Eugenia was sixteen when she wrote these entries.
5. Austen, *Mansfield Park*, vol. 1, ch. 11, p. 111; Austen, *Emma*, vol. 1, ch. 11, pp. 92–3; Austen, *Sense and Sensibility*, vol. 1, ch. 20, p. 112.
6. Vickery, *Gentleman's Daughter*, pp. 9, 218–21; Vickery, *Behind Closed Doors*, p. 198; Gaskell, *Cranford*, chs 1, 12 and 16, pp. 13, 212–13, 287.
7. Eliza Chute, quoted in Jones, *Jane Austen and Marriage*, p. 151; Admiral Young, quoted in Lincoln, *Naval Wives and Mistresses*, p. 25; see also Stone, *Road to Divorce*, p. 266, for the contemporary view that neglectful husbands were frequently to blame for their wife's adultery.
8. Taylor, *Defiance*, pp. 55–6 (see also pp. 37, 40–4 for background).

9. Lady Bessborough to Granville Leveson Gower, 1 March 1805, *Lord Granville Leveson Gower: Private Correspondence*, n.d., vol. 2, p. 34; Calvert, *Irish Beauty of the Regency*, p. 21; *Journal of Mrs Arbuthnot*, 8 October 1825, vol. 1, pp. 416–17; see also Shelley, *Diary of Frances, Lady Shelley*, vol. 1, p. 33.
10. Vickery, *Behind Closed Doors*, pp. 198–200.
11. Shelley, *Diary of Frances, Lady Shelley*, vol. 1, p. 14; Eden, *Semi-Attached Couple*, ch. 18, p. 80 and ch. 19, pp. 82–3.
12. Arnold, *The Unhappy Countess*, pp. 49–50; Moore, *Wedlock*, pp. 44–63; Calvert, *Irish Beauty of the Regency*, 10 October 1808 and 8 February 1813, pp. 112, 196.
13. Weeton, *Miss Weeton's Journal of a Governess*, vol. 1, pp. 18–19.
14. Stone, *Broken Lives*, pp. 162–247 (quotation on p. 170).
15. Grosvenor, *Lady Wharncliffe and Her Family*, n.d. [1811], vol. 1, pp. 83–4; Anglesey (ed.), *The Capel Letters*, pp. 71–6, 125–6, 130–1, 161; Madan, *Spencer and Waterloo*, pp. 12–13, 23–4, 40–1, 61–3; Paget, *The Paget Brothers*, pp. 40, 217; Calvert, *Irish Beauty of the Regency*, p. 171; Brynn, *Crown & Castle*, p. 31; Somerville and Ross, *An Incorruptible Irishman*, p. 186; *Lord Granville Leveson Gower: Private Correspondence*, vol. 2, p. 333; Bagot, *George Canning and His Friends*, vol. 2, pp. 77–8.
16. Bourne, *Palmerston*, p. 182.
17. Blakiston, *Lord William Russell and His Wife*, pp. 216–18: the original entries are in a sort of phonetic code, the passages quoted are from Blakiston's decoded version and only amount to part of most entries.
18. Ibid., *passim* and pp. 168–9 ('brutality'), pp. 336ff (affair).
19. Martin, *A Life of James Boswell*, pp. 265–71, 275–9 (quotations on pp. 277, 278).
20. Ibid., pp. 288–90 (quote on p. 290).
21. Ibid., pp. 290, 331–3, 342–4, 350–1, 364–5.
22. Blakiston, *Lord William Russell and His Wife*, p. 324; Reiter, *The Late Lord Chatham*, pp. 20–1, 85, 90–2; see also Reiter, 'The Invisible Countess', *passim*. See Malcomson, *Pursuit of the Heiress*, pp. 137–8, for another instance of mental illness ruining an otherwise very happy marriage.
23. Reiter, *The Late Lord Chatham*, pp. 176–8, 181–2.

15 DOMESTIC VIOLENCE, ADULTERY, DIVORCE AND SEPARATION

1. Bailey, *Unquiet Lives*, pp. 110–11, 118, 122–4; Barclay, *Love, Intimacy and Power*, pp. 47–8, 185–6; Stone, *Family, Sex and Marriage*, p. 326; Stone, *Road to Divorce*, pp. 203–5; for an example of the belief that such violence belonged to the lower classes see Eugenia Wynne's diary for 29 November 1796, *Wynne Diaries*, vol. 2, p. 135.
2. Arnold, *The Unhappy Countess*, pp. 74, 85, 89–90, 98, 101; for another instance of a husband whose abuse began in the first days of the marriage see the account of the marriage of John and Caroline Mytton in Stone, *Road to Divorce*, pp. 200–1.
3. Barclay, *Love, Intimacy and Power*, pp. 186–7.
4. Vickery, *Gentleman's Daughter*, pp. 73–5.
5. Ibid., pp. 215–16.
6. Weeton, *Miss Weeton's Journal of a Governess*, vol. 1, pp. 221–3, 256–60, 267–8, 276–81, 301, 315–17 and vol. 2, pp. 131–47, 154–69, 176–89; Barclay, *Love, Intimacy and Power*, p. 191.
7. Weeton, *Miss Weeton's Journal of a Governess*, April/May 1810, vol. 1, pp. 259–60.

8. Ibid., vol. 2, p. 178.
9. Bailey, *Unquiet Lives*, pp. 32–45; Barclay, *Love, Intimacy and Power*, p. 181; Weeton, *Miss Weeton's Journal of a Governess*, vol. 1, pp. 301, 310–11 and vol. 2, pp. 159ff, especially, pp. 172, 180–1 (her brother's betrayal); Vickery, *Gentleman's Daughter*, p. 76; for Malmesbury see above, p. 251 and Bourne, *Palmerston*, p. 182.
10. For Lady Erskine's violence see Thorne, *History of Parliament*, vol. 3, p. 713, and above, p. 112; Bailey, *Unquiet Lives*, pp. 110–11.
11. Boswell, *Life of Johnson*, vol. 1, p. 372 (1768); Martha Bailey, 'The Marriage Law of Jane Austen's World', p. 11, quoting a parliamentary debate from 31 July 1857 on the Divorce and Matrimonial Causes Bill (wrongly cited as *Hansard*, vol. 167 when it should be vol. 147, col. 880).
12. Jane Austen to her sister Cassandra, 8–9 February 1807, *Jane Austen's Letters*, no. 50, p. 126; Austen-Leigh, *Jane Austen: A Family Record*, p. 54; Austen, *Mansfield Park*, vol. 3, ch. 17, p. 468; but cf. her sympathy for the Princess of Wales: Jane Austen to Martha Lloyd, 16 February 1813, *Jane Austen's Letters*, no. 82, p. 217; Boswell, *Life of Johnson*, vol. 2, p. 305 (1779); Martin, *Life of Boswell*, pp. 289, 332–3, 364. See also Andrew, '"Adultery à-la-mode": Privilege, the Law and Attitudes to Adultery 1770–1809'; and Bailey, *Unquiet Lives*, pp. 143–9, for discussion of changing attitudes towards male adultery.
13. Quoted in Tillyard, *Aristocrats*, pp. 401–2.
14. Mrs Thrale's daughter in Thrale, *Thraliana: The Diary of Hester Lynch Thrale*, vol. 2, 11 October 1796, p. 967. For examples of the husband's adultery leading to him catching venereal disease, which he then risked passing on to his wife, see Stone, *Family, Sex and Marriage*, pp. 599–600; Steidele, *Gentleman Jack*, p. 83; and Martin, *A Life of James Boswell*, p. 289. On some evidence of naval officers having affairs when serving far from home see Taylor's biography of Sir Edward Pellew, *Commander*, p. 226.
15. Stone, *Road to Divorce*, pp. 222, 267–70; Steidele, *Gentleman Jack*, pp. 73–4, 141–3, for examples of Lister's affairs with married women.
16. Harding-Edgar, *Next to Wellington*, p. 304 (Sir James Erskine); Severn, *Architects of Empire*, p. 391 and Arbuthnot, *Journal of Mrs Arbuthnot*, 8 May 1820, vol. 1, pp. 16–17 (Gerald Wellesley's marriage). George Elers mentions a case (with disapproval) where a husband accepted a sum of money from his wife's lover to turn a blind eye: Elers, *Memoirs of George Elers*, p. 50; and Mrs Calvert mentions that Lady Clare's behaviour had been 'very far from correct' but that as her husband had chosen 'to be blind, she continued to be received in Company'. Calvert, *Irish Beauty of the Regency*, 7 May 1805, pp. 42–3; Steidele, *Gentleman Jack*, pp. 150–2 – Charles Lawton came to accept his wife's adulterous affair with Anne Lister; but his wife, Mariana, was angry at evidence of his adultery.
17. Stone, *Broken Lives*, pp. 162–247 (Middleton) and pp. 270–9 (Cadogan); Malcomson, *Pursuit of the Heiress*, pp. 142–3 (Cecil); Harding-Edgar, *Next to Wellington*, p. 304 (Erskine); Aspinall, 'The Old House of Commons and its Members', pt 7, pp. 286–7; and Ward, *Letters to 'Ivy'*, pp. 270–2 (Rosebery); Viveash, 'Lady Morley and the "Baron so Bold"', p. 54 (Boringdon).
18. Stone, *Broken Lives*, p. 190 (Middleton); Mahony, 'What Became of Mrs Powlett?', p. 57; Proceedings in the Court of Common Pleas, 5 December 1803, as reported in *The Sporting Magazine or Monthly Calendar*, vol. 23 (December 1803), pp. 125–7; Martinovich, *The Sea is My Element*, pp. 80–3, 128.

19. Stone, *Broken Lives*, pp. 162–247, especially pp. 189, 212, 228–30.
20. Anglesey, *One-Leg*, pp. 53, 62, 89–90. A mystery surrounds the date on which Gerald Wellesley was born: see ibid., pp. 353–4, but Miss Berry – reported by Lady Harriet Cavendish to her brother the Marquess of Hartington, 16 March 1809, *Hary-O: The Letters of Lady Harriet Cavendish*, pp. 311–12 – implies October or November 1808.
21. Anglesey, *One-Leg*, pp. 90–1.
22. Ibid., pp. 91.
23. Ibid., pp. 91–2.
24. Ibid., pp. 93–4.
25. Ibid., pp. 94–6.
26. Ibid., pp. 93, 96–7, 99–101, 354–5. Henry's mother strongly disapproved of the marriage at the time: Anne, Countess of Mornington, to her son Lord Wellesley, 3 February 1804, *The Diary and Correspondence of Henry Wellesley*, pp. 14–15.
27. Anglesey, *One-Leg*, pp. 100–4, 109.
28. Ibid., p. 103; Plomer, *Lord Paget's Letters and Trial in the Affair of Lady Charlotte Wellesley*, *passim*, gives the speeches of the counsel and the evidence of the witnesses in the *crim. con.* case. According to Stone, *Road to Divorce*, p. 235, by the 1790s most cases of *crim. con.* were uncontested.
29. There was only one instance of a wife securing a parliamentary divorce from her husband in England before 1831, the case of Jane Addison in 1801, and she succeeded only because her husband had committed adultery with her sister, which was regarded as incest. For more on Addison's divorce see Alison Daniell, '"Too many restrictions could not be thrown in the way of divorce": Attitudes to Women's Petitions for Divorce by Act of Parliament, 1801–1831', blogpost dated June 2022, https://thehistoryofparliament.files.wordpress.com/2022/06/alison-daniell-too-many-restrictions.pdf
30. Anglesey, *One-Leg*, pp. 110–11; *Lord Granville Leveson Gower: Private Correspondence*, vol. 2, p. 366.
31. Anglesey, *One-Leg*, pp. 110–11.
32. Ibid., p. 112; *Lord Granville Leveson Gower: Private Correspondence*, vol. 2, p. 428 (Lady Bessborough); *Journal of Mrs Arbuthnot*, 8 May 1820, vol. 1, pp. 16–17; Severn, *Architects of Empire*, p. 391 (evidence supporting most of Mrs Arbuthnot's story).
33. Anglesey, *One-Leg*, pp. 95–6, 98, 100–3. Charlotte appears to have lived with Henry for a time even *after* they were divorced, when Paget was serving at Walcheren, while on Paget's return he lived for some time in the same house as Caroline. The motives and circumstances for these arrangements are unclear and are puzzling: ibid., p. 109. Lady Harriet Cavendish to her brother the Marquess of Hartington, 8 March 1809, *Hary-O: The Letters of Lady Harriet Cavendish*, pp. 307–8.
34. Lady Bessborough to Granville Leveson Gower, 13 February 1807, *Lord Granville Leveson Gower: Private Correspondence*, vol. 2, pp. 241–2; Wolfram, 'Divorce in England', p. 157, for the number of divorces; and Andrew, '"Adultery à-la-mode": Privilege, the Law and Attitudes to Adultery 1770–1809', *passim* and especially pp. 17–19, for public debate and moral outrage.
35. Eldon was quoted in the House of Commons by Dr Phillimore, in Parliament, *Hansard's Parliamentary Debates*, n.s., vol. 24 (3 June 1830), col. 1264; Duke of Clarence, quoted in Stone, *Road to Divorce*, p. 286 – see, more generally, ibid.,

pp. 286–8, 329ff; Bailey, 'The Marriage Law of Jane Austen's World', pp. 10–11; and Stone, *Broken Lives*, pp. 24, 159, cf. pp. 234, 246, 277–8. For Henry Wellesley keeping the money – or at least not returning it to Paget – see Anglesey, *One-Leg*, p. 109, and Paget, *The Paget Brothers*, p. 225. In January 1806, Henry Caulfield was arrested for debt on the petition of George Chambers, who had been awarded £2,120 damages against him in a *crim. con.* case, and Caulfield was imprisoned until he died in 1808. Chambers also refused to divorce his wife, presumably to prevent her marrying Caulfield; see Looser, *Sister Novelists*, p. 199. Stone, *Road to Divorce*, pp. 284–5, also gives several examples of lovers who fled Britain because they were unable to pay the high damages awarded against them; clearly they had no expectation that the husband would secretly return the money.

36. Stone, *Broken Lives*, pp. 224, 246, 266; cf. Stone, *Road to Divorce*, pp. 187, 190, which says that the husband was only liable for certain types of legal costs incurred by his wife.

37. Anglesey, *One-Leg*, p. 109.

38. Stone, *Broken Lives*, pp. 266–7, 278; Malcomson, *Pursuit of the Heiress*, pp. 43–4.

39. *Dyott's Diary*, 23 November 1829, vol. 2, pp. 65–6; Anglesey, *One-Leg*, p. 356; Betsey Fremantle diary, 18 September 1811, *Wynne Diaries*, vol. 3, p. 341; Stone, *Broken Lives*, p. 233, for a vindictive husband pursuing a divorce even though he would not remarry because he was a Catholic. Yet Mrs Calvert, who was quite prim, showed no discomfort in meeting Lady Holland at Cassiobury, Lord Essex's house, Calvert, *Irish Beauty of the Regency*, n.d. 1816, pp. 269–70.

40. Stone, *Broken Lives*, p. 246; Anglesey, *One-Leg*, p. 355; Paget, *The Paget Brothers*, pp. 172–3; Harding-Edgar, *Next to Wellington*, p. 306.

41. Malcomson, *Pursuit of the Heiress*, p. 150.

42. Mahony, 'What Became of Mrs Powlett?', pp. 56–9, cf. Austen, *Jane Austen's Letters*, no. 153, p. 137, and Stone, *Road to Divorce*, p. 236; Austen, *Mansfield Park*, vol. 3 ch. 17, p. 465. The presumption that the Powletts separated has been confirmed by Rachel Bynoth, who is working on the Canning family correspondence, in a reply on Twitter dated 17 September 2021. On the wider question of how society treated divorced women who had then married their lover see Stone, *Road to Divorce*, pp. 342–4, where he admits uncertainty and describes the question as 'intractable'.

43. Staves, *Married Women's Separate Property*, pp. 162–3, 170, 192; Rowlandson, 'The Four Seasons of Love', George and Stephens, *Catalogue of Political and Personal Satires Preserved in the Department of Prints and Drawings in the British Museum*, vol. 9, no. 12, pp. 407, 480–1.

44. Staves, *Married Women's Separate Property*, pp. 163–4; Stone, *Broken Lives*, pp. 19–21; Stone, *Road to Divorce*, pp. 153–4.

45. Staves, *Married Women's Separate Property*, p. 192 and pp. 7, 162–95 for the legal status of private separation agreements in general; also Stone, *Broken Lives*, pp. 19–21.

46. Scott, *St Ronan's Well*, ch. 29, p. 341; Staves, *Married Women's Separate Property*, p. 146.

47. Staves, *Married Women's Separate Property*, pp. 173–4 (Lady Bute); Lanfersieck and Looser, 'Austen's *Sense and Sensibility* and Lord Craven', p. 379 (Lady Craven); Knight, *Pursuit of Victory*, pp. 657, 659, 791n; Lincoln, *Naval Wives and Mistresses*, pp. 118–19. It would be interesting to know if all these maintenance agreements were honoured.

48. Grosvenor, *First Lady Wharncliffe*, vol. 1, pp. 9 (Mrs Dillon), pp. 11–12 (Lord and Lady Bristol), pp. 20, 30 (Lady Erne to Lady Louisa Hervey), pp. 61–2, 84–5, 176, 279, 312.

49. Calvert, *Irish Beauty of the Regency*, 8 February and 28 September 1813, pp. 196, 210. For another example of a wife's suffering following a separation see Weeton, *Diary of a Governess*, vol. 2, pp. 180–5, 189–92, 216–17.

50. It is worth noting that in Scott's *St Ronan's Well*, ch. 29, p. 341 (see above, p. 283), the Earl of Etherington suggests that Clara Mowbray's social position would be secured by marriage and immediate separation, which would hardly be the case if there was a stigma attaching to the position of a separated wife; although it is probably not fair to rest too much weight on a literary plot device in a novel whose plausibility is not especially notable. For a contrary example see French and Rothery, *Man's Estate*, p. 204.

16 WIDOWS AND WIDOWERS

1. Stone and Stone, *An Open Elite?*, pp. 94–5 and Table 3.5 (unpaginated appendix); Phegley, *Courtship and Marriage in Victorian England*, p. 157. The high number of wives dying in the first ten years of marriage is only partly explained by childbirth. It is possible that their traditional role in nursing sick members of their families, and the consequent risk of catching tuberculosis or another infectious disease, accounts for most of the rest of the excess.

2. Smith, *Wellington and the Arbuthnots*, pp. 152–4, 158. It is often said that after Harriet's death Charles went to live with Wellington at Apsley House, but this is not quite true: he stayed there often and for quite long periods, but also spent a great deal of time with his children, including at Woodford.

3. Quoted in Tillyard, *Aristocrats*, p. 404.

4. Quoted in Vickery, *Gentleman's Daughter*, pp. 88–9.

5. Cassandra Austen to Fanny Knight, 29 July 1817, *Jane Austen's Letters*, pp. 363–4.

6. Jane Austen to Francis Austen, 3 July 1813, *Jane Austen's Letters*, no. 86, p. 224.

7. Harding-Edgar, *Next to Wellington*, p. 314 (Murray); Gore, *Nelson's Hardy and His Wife*, pp. 207–8, 210, 229–30.

8. Collins, *Jane Austen and the Clergy*, p. 128; private information from Nicholas Blake in October 2021 for pensions for naval officers, see also Smallwood, 'Shore Wives', pp. 72–82; and Lincoln, *Naval Wives and Mistresses*, pp. 44–7; Burnham and McGuigan, *The British Army against Napoleon*, pp. 179–81; Haythornthwaite, *Armies of Wellington*, p. 40. For an example of the use of life insurance in a settlement see Wilson, *Women, Marriage and Property*, p. 52; Charles Arbuthnot, above p. 89 and, much later and fictional, but interesting as it is presented being nothing unusual, Trollope, *Framley Parsonage*, ch. 1, p. 4.

9. For Mrs Austen's finances see Austen-Leigh, *Jane Austen: A Family Record*, pp. 130–1, 135–6; Tomalin, *Jane Austen*, pp. 188, 254, 333. These arrangements changed several times over the years in response to circumstances such as Henry's bankruptcy, but Mrs Austen's financial position remained fairly secure. Austen, *Sense and Sensibility*, especially vol. 1, ch. 2, pp. 8–13; Austen, *Emma*, vol. 1, ch. 3, p. 21 and vol. 3, ch. 7, p. 375.

10. Le Faye, *Jane Austen's 'Outlandish Cousin'*, p. 40; Austen, *Jane Austen's Letters*, p. 485.

11. Vickery, *Behind Closed Doors*, p. 220.

12. Shelley, *Diary of Frances, Lady Shelley*, vol. 2, pp. 319–21, 379–84, 387, 399, 403, 409–12.
13. Connell, *Portrait of a Whig Peer*, pp. 94, 96–8, 100, 107–11, 128.
14. Boswell, *Life of Johnson*, vol. 1, p. 421 (1770), p. 384 (30 September 1769); Wollestonecraft, quoted in Jones, *Jane Austen and Marriage*, p. 40; Knight, quoted in Knatchbull-Hugessen, *Kentish Family*, p. 166. Fanny Knight's opinion probably reflected a fear that her father might remarry.
15. Quoted in Rizzo, *Companions without Vows*, p. 4.
16. Eliza de Feuillide to Philadelphia Walter, 13 December 1796, Le Faye, *Jane Austen's 'Outlandish Cousin'*, p. 132; Austen, *Persuasion*, vol. 1, ch. 1, p. 5.
17. Stone, *Family, Sex and Marriage*, p. 45, graph 2. Stone and Stone, *An Open Elite?*, Table 3.2 (unpaginated appendix), state that 13 per cent of all marriages in the gentry group they survey were remarriages and 16 per cent of those men who married once married a second time. Cannon's figures equate to 27 per cent of peers married more than once. Of the 2,143 MPs who served in the Commons between 1790 and 1820, 367 married more than once, or 17 per cent; Thorne, *History of Parliament*, vol. 1, pp. 279–80.
18. Cannon, *Aristocratic Century*, pp. 83–4.
19. Knatchbull, quoted in Wilson, *Almost Another Sister*, p. 90; Flinders, quoted in Vickery, *Behind Closed Doors*, pp. 50–51, see also p. 128.
20. Agnes Porter to Lady Mary Talbot, 11 September 1794, Porter, *A Governess in the Age of Jane Austen*, p. 148.
21. Ibid.; Smith, *Wellington and the Arbuthnots*, p. 30 – see above, p. 169.
22. Maria Josepha Stanley to her aunt Serena Holroyd, ? March 1802; Isa Stanley to her sister-in-law Maria Stanley, 23 March 1802, Stanley, *Early Married Life*, pp. 231–2.
23. William to Arthur Cole, 20 October 1802, *Memoirs of Sir Lowry Cole*, p. 27; Elizabeth, Duchess of Devonshire to her sister Lady Erne, n.d., Grosvenor, *First Lady Wharncliffe*, vol. 1, pp. 310–11.
24. Lord John Russell to his brother Lord William Russell, n.d. and 20 August [1824], Blakiston, *Lord William Russell and His Wife*, pp. 118, 120; Boswell, quoted in Martin, *Life of Boswell*, pp. 254–5.
25. Gibbon, *Memoirs*, p. 109.

17 GROWING OLD TOGETHER

1. Calvert, *An Irish Beauty of the Regency*, 8 February 1818, p. 307; Malcomson, *Pursuit of the Heiress*, p. 141, quoting the Duchess of Leinster to her husband, the 2nd Duke, in 1795; Newdigate-Newdegate, *The Cheverels of Cheverel Manor*, pp. 100–3; Taylor, *Defiance*, p. 323.
2. Quoted in Taylor, *Commander*, p. 232.
3. Anne Lefroy to Edward Lefroy, 29 May 1801, *Letters of Mrs Lefroy*, p. 30; Calvert, *Irish Beauty of the Regency*, 8 February 1818, p. 168.
4. Eden, *Semi-Attached Couple*, pp. 42–3.
5. Newdigate-Newdegate, *The Cheverels of Cheverel Manor*, pp. 142–4; [Stanley, Maria J.], *The Ladies of Alderley*, p. 86, see also p. 40. Serena Holroyd also sent a letter to her newborn godchild and great-niece, Stanley, *Early Married Life of Maria Josepha, Lady Stanley*, pp. 136–7. See Ottaway, *The Decline of Life*, pp. 155–64 for a discussion of the role of grandchildren in the lives of grandparents.

6. [Stanley, Maria J.], *The Ladies of Alderley*, pp. 244, 248–9.
7. Ottaway, 'The Old Woman's Home in Eighteenth-century England', pp. 113–14, 117, 121 (Duchess of Portland quoted on p. 113); Vickery, *Behind Closed Doors*, pp. 6–7; Austen, *Emma*, vol. 3, ch. 15, pp. 448–50, ch. 17, pp. 466–8 and ch. 19, pp. 483–4. And yet, as we have seen, it was not uncommon to expect a newly married couple to live for a time with the groom's parents: see above, p. 164.
8. Vickery, *Gentleman's Daughter*, pp. 135, 141–4.
9. Connell, *Portrait of a Whig Peer*, pp. 450–1.
10. Tillyard, *Aristocrats*, p. 416. Tillyard gives the artist's name as *William* Archer Shee; however, this is probably a slip of the pen.
11. Newdigate-Newdegate, *The Cheverels of Cheverel Manor*, pp. 167, 211–12.
12. Ibid., pp. 213–17.
13. Ibid., pp. 222–6; Namier and Brooke, *History of Parliament, 1760–90*, vol. 3, p. 199.

CONCLUSION

1. Andrew, '"Adultery à-la-mode": Privilege, the Law and Attitudes to Adultery 1770–1809', pp. 7–14; McCreery, 'Keeping up with the *Bon Ton*: The *Tête-à-Tête* Series in the *Town and Country Magazine*', in Barker and Chalus (eds), *Gender in Eighteenth-century England: Roles, Representations and Responsibilities*, pp. 207–29, especially, pp. 208–13; Binhammer, 'Sex Panic of the 1790s', pp. 415–16, 427–8.
2. Roberts, *Making English Morals*, pp. 17–58; Jaeger, *Before Victoria*, pp. 5–11, 14–15.
3. Binhammer, 'Sex Panic of the 1790s', pp. 417–18, 430; Roberts, *Making English Morals*, pp. 58, 68.
4. Of course, this was only one of many strands in the complicated way in which Victorians viewed their own society, and that of the late eighteenth and early nineteenth centuries. For example, disapproval of upper-class immorality did not diminish their patriotic pride in the victories against France.
5. McCreery, 'Keeping up with the *Bon Ton*', p. 208; Stone, *Road to Divorce*, pp. 258–9 and Table 9.2, p. 430; Stone, *Family, Sex and Marriage*, pp. 531–2; Thorne, *History of Parliament*, vol. 1, p. 280; Thompson, *Gentrification and the Enterprise Culture*, pp. 26–7, see also p. 32.
6. Giles, quoted in Barclay, *Love, Intimacy and Power*, p. 53; Fielding, 'The Indissoluble Knot?', pp. 179–82.
7. Gregory, quoted in Jones, *Jane Austen and Marriage*, p. 145; for contemporary comments on Austen's verisimilitude see Le Faye, *Jane Austen: The World of her Novels*, pp. 153, 221, 251 and the bibliographical essay below, p. 371.
8. Stone, *Family, Sex and Marriage*, pp. 7–8, 273, 298–304 and, for the role of novels, pp. 283–4; Stone and Stone, *An Open Elite?*, pp. 98–9; Vickery, *Gentleman's Daughter*, pp. 40–4; Vickery, *Behind Closed Doors*, pp. 89–90; Malcomson, *Pursuit of the Heiress*, pp. 112–20; Holloway, *The Game of Love*, pp. 9–10; Jalland, *Women, Marriage and Politics, 1860–1914*, p. 46; on parents' fear of responsibility see Malcomson, *Pursuit of the Heiress*, p. 118 and Lady Caroline Capel quoted above, p. 16, from Anglesey (ed.), *The Capel Letters*, pp. 88–9.
9. Quoted above, p. 178, from Taylor, *Defiance*, pp. 292–3.
10. See above, pp. 190–1.
11. Austen, 'A Collection of Letters', in *Volume the Second*, in Austen, *Minor Works*, p. 161.

12. Jane Austen to her sister Cassandra Austen, 24 May 1813, *Jane Austen's Letters*, no. 85, pp. 220–2, quoted above in the Preface.

DRAMATIS PERSONAE

1. Her memorial stone and other sources say 10 February, but this is corrected to 10 November, 'from family sources', in Retter and Sinclair, *Letters to Ann*, p. 133.
2. Chalus, '"My Dearest Tussy": Coping with Separation in the Napoleonic Wars', p. 48 and *ODNB* entry give 1778, whereas the editor of the published diaries says 1779, despite the text of the diaries consistently implying 1778. On 19 April 1796 Betsey wrote in her diary: 'This is my birthday. I am eighteen years old. It does not please me much I shall soon be an *old lady* I declare', *Wynne Diaries*, vol. 2, p. 84.
3. Date from Namier and Brooke, *History of Parliament 1760–90*, vol. 3, p. 199; Newdigate-Newdegate, *The Cheverels*, says 25 November.
4. According to Brian Connell, *Portrait of a Whig Peer*, p. 143; Thorne, *The History of Parliament*, vol. 5, p. 347 and the *Complete Peerage* both say 5 January 1783.
5. Blakiston, *Lord William Russell and His Wife*, does not appear to give this date, which I have only from thepeerage.com
6. This date is from the *Wynne Diaries*.
7. This date was found online and may not be reliable.
8. His father married in 1768 according to *Wynne Diaries*, vol. 3, p. 405, and he had an older brother. See also Thorne, *History of Parliament*, vol. 3, p. 374, for entry for his older brother John.

BIBLIOGRAPHICAL ESSAY

1. Stone, *Family, Sex and Marriage*, p. 287.
2. Le Faye, *Jane Austen: The World of her Novels*, p. 153 (Mrs Guiton); p. 251 (Lady Vernon and Anne Romilly); p. 221 (*The British Critic*). The full text of the *British Critic*'s review is printed in *Jane Austen: The Critical Heritage*, edited by B.C. Southam, pp. 79–84.

BIBLIOGRAPHICAL ESSAY

It was almost fifty years ago that Lawrence Stone published *The Family, Sex and Marriage in England, 1500–1800*, a seminal work that helped establish the history of the family as a legitimate subject of study in the universities, and attracted a broad readership beyond. Stone went on to publish three further volumes of relevance to this period: *The Road to Divorce: England 1530–1987* (1990); *Broken Lives: Separation and Divorce in England, 1660–1837* (1993 – a volume of case studies); and, with Jeanne C. Fawtier Stone, *An Open Elite? England, 1540–1880* (1984). These works have many virtues that have stood the test of time: they contain a vast amount of useful data; their chronological breadth and ambition gave the subject great vitality; and Stone's writing was generally accessible, especially in the later volumes. However, some aspects of his work now feel very dated, especially his imitation of the social sciences in *The Family, Sex and Marriage*, and some of the assumptions and attitudes he displays, for example when he attributes the failure of the marriage of Arthur and Lucy Annesley to her unreasonable jealousy of her husband's infidelities, rather than placing any of the blame on the husband for his actions.[1] The range of the work also produced some sloppiness in argument and unduly rough handling of the evidence, as when he claimed that the generous damages awarded in *crim. con.* cases in the 1790s encouraged more husbands to sue and also that collusion was so widespread that these damages were almost never actually paid: a reasonable case can be made for either proposition, but not both (Stone, *Road to Divorce*, pp. 276, 284, 286–7).

Subsequent, more detailed research has challenged the broad interpretive frame in which Stone presented his evidence. No serious scholar would now accept without modification his arguments about the rise of companionate marriages and the transformation of the nature of courtship. At the same time, the field has been enormously enriched and fresh dimensions added by historians such as Amanda Vickery, A.P.W. Malcomson, Katie Barclay and Sally Holloway. Vickery's studies, *The Gentleman's Daughter: Women's Lives in Georgian England* and *Behind Closed Doors: At Home in Georgian England*, give a vivid picture of domestic life with a particular focus on the north of England and a class a shade or two below Jane Austen's. A.P.W. Malcomson's *The Pursuit of the Heiress: Aristocratic Marriage in Ireland, 1740–1840* provides a wide-ranging and entertaining account of courtship and marriage choices among the aristocracy in Ireland, which has done much to inform my own work. Katie Barclay's *Love, Intimacy and Power: Marriage and Patriarchy in Scotland, 1650–1850* is a sophisticated and carefully argued examination of the subject, with particularly interesting things to say about how the increased emphasis on romantic love affected the power balance within marriages. And Sally Holloway's book *The Game of Love in Georgian England: Courtship, Emotions, and Material Culture*, and her article on adulterous correspondence give detailed attention to previously neglected topics, including love letters and gifts, the language used by lovers and breach-of-promise suits.

Other important scholarly works that set the scene include Elaine Chalus's *Elite Women in English Political Life*, which neatly undercuts simplistic arguments about the relegation of women to a private, domestic sphere; Joanne Bailey's *Unquiet Lives: Marriage and Marriage Breakdown in England, 1660–1800*, a well-written and thoroughly researched account that ranges across all social classes using court records as its primary source of evidence; and Tim Hitchcock's *English Sexualities*, which is a useful introduction that concentrates on the mass of the population rather than the upper classes. Pat Jalland's *Women, Marriage and Politics, 1860–1914* obviously relates to a later period, but her approach opened up the subject to me when I first read it many years ago. It is still immensely readable and thought-provoking, and it can now be supplemented with Jennifer Phegley's *Courtship and Marriage in Victorian England*. Kimberly Schutte's *Women, Rank and Marriage in the British Aristocracy, 1485–2000* is a significant monograph based on solid statistical analysis, examining the men who married the daughters of aristocratic families. Marriage settlements and laws relating to marriage, two subjects that produce more than their share of misunderstanding, are admirably handled in *Married Women's Separate Property in England* by Susan Staves and *Marriage Law and Practice in the Long Eighteenth Century* by Rebecca Probert; while Deborah Wilson's *Women, Marriage and Property in Wealthy Landed Families in Ireland, 1750–1850* supplements both Staves' work and that of Malcomson, mentioned above. Unfortunately Amy Harris's welcome study of a neglected subject *Being Single in Georgian England* (Oxford University Press, 2023) only appeared after my book was completed.

The history of masculinity has attracted attention in recent years, in particular from Henry French and Mark Rothery, writing together. Their monograph *Men's Estate: Landed Gentry Masculinities, c.1600–c.1900* covers a wide sweep, with a particular emphasis on the formation and reproduction of masculine values. They have also edited *Making Men*, a useful collection of primary source material well suited to students. Gillian Williamson's study of the portrayal of, and attitudes towards, masculinity in the *Gentleman's Magazine* adds some interesting and surprising dimensions to the subject. Michael Fielding's unpublished thesis 'The Indissoluble Knot?' looks at the role played by men in both courtship and marriage and includes some good material from unpublished letters and diaries in different archives. Two articles by Louise Carter on 'Scarlet Fever' and 'Brothers in Arms' examine the position of officers in the army through the lens of the study of masculinity, while the family life of naval officers and the position of naval wives are usefully explored in the work of Ellen Gill and Margarette Lincoln, and in two fascinating articles by Elaine Chalus: '"My Dearest Tussy"', which draws on unpublished Fremantle correspondence, and 'The Loneliness of Leadership'.

The insecure position of a mistress is illuminated in Kate Gibson's excellent article '"I am not on the footing of a Kept Woman"', while Ella Sbraini's article '"Those that Prefer the Ripe Mellow Fruit"' draws on a wide range of evidence to show that 'middle-aged' women (defined here as those between thirty and fifty years old) were commonly regarded as sexually appealing. Eamonn O'Keeffe's '"A Natural Passion?"' convincingly questions whether attitudes towards male homosexuality were as dogmatic and uniform as has frequently been assumed; while Jen Manion uncovers a handful of examples of 'female husbands', showing that there have always been individuals who rejected the gender to which they were assigned at birth. Nicholas Rogers in 'Money, Marriage and Mobility' looks at intermarriage between members of the gentry and successful London businessmen in the mid-eighteenth century, discovering that there were reservations on both sides. Articles by Helen Metcalfe on the lodgings procured by bachelors, Sybil Wolfram on divorce, Amy Froide on the position of single women and four fine articles by Leanne Calvert on middle-class marriages in Ulster in this period are all richly rewarding.

There are a number of biographies of individuals or studies of couples that concentrate primarily on their private lives, and these are often a fruitful source of material, quoting so extensively from their private papers as to straddle the distinction between a primary and secondary source. Georgiana Blakiston's *Lord William Russell and His Wife* is a good example, although the story it tells is both sad and rather depressing. Stephen Taylor's *Defiance: The Life and Choices of Lady Anne Barnard* and Stella Tillyard's *Aristocrats: Caroline, Emily, Louisa and Sarah Lennox, 1740–1832* are both immensely entertaining and full of good material. Mary Soames's *The Profligate Duke: George Spencer-Churchill, fifth Duke of Marlborough and his Duchess* and Peter Martin's life of James Boswell are also enjoyable and useful. The unhappy marriages of Mary Bowes, Countess of Strathmore, have been recounted by both Ralph Arnold and Wendy Moore and provide useful examples of two types of unhappy marriages, the second much worse than the first.

Devoney Looser's *Sister Novelists* should be mentioned here, although it only appeared after my book was substantially finished. It contains a wealth of fascinating material on the romantic and emotional lives of Jane and Maria Porter, two novelists who achieved greater fame in their lifetime than Jane Austen and who, like her, never married but, unlike Austen, left a full and revealing correspondence about their private lives. If this had been available before I began writing, I am sure that I would have frequently drawn on it to illustrate the dilemmas of women in love and the obstacles that prevented courtships prospering.

Other biographies often contain good material about their subject's private life, even if this is overshadowed by their other claims to fame. Biographies of Canning and Castlereagh, especially the studies of their youth by Dorothy Marshall and H. Montgomery Hyde, but supplemented by lives by John Bew and Wendy Hinde, are very useful for giving insight into their courtship and their married life. Peter Jupp's *Lord Grenville* admirably shows the softer private side of the austere and reserved public man; while Jacqueline Reiter tells the story of the 2nd Lord Chatham's marriage and his wife's struggle with mental illness with great skill and compassion. *One-Leg: The Life and Letters of Henry William Paget, First Marquess of Anglesey* by the Marquess of Anglesey is invaluable on the elopement of Lord Paget with Charlotte Wellesley, although the author is a little too forgiving of his ancestor's failings in the aftermath of the affair. And Tom Wareham's life of Graham Moore, the naval officer, brother of General Sir John Moore, has a fascinating and painful account of an unrequited love affair that I left out of my study with great reluctance.

The courtship and marriage of Charles and Harriet Arbuthnot are described in E.A. Smith's joint biography, supplemented by material in the Camden Society edition of his correspondence, her published journal, the family history, and glimpses of them in the correspondence of their contemporaries. For many public figures such as these the *History of Parliament* volumes, together with the *Oxford Dictionary of National Biography*, *The Complete Peerage* and other reference works, provide an immensely useful skeleton of biographical facts: basic but essential points such as dates of birth, maiden names, dates of weddings and numbers of children, which help to reduce the risk of mistaking one Lord X or Lady Y for their namesake of another generation.

Jane Austen and her family have attracted some excellent historical research, all the more valuable for their being, in all respects but one, such an ordinary, undistinguished family. The starting point for biographical information remains *Jane Austen: A Family Record*, by William and Richard Arthur Austen-Leigh, revised and supplemented by Deirdre Le Faye; and Austen's letters, edited with a wonderfully rich biographical index again by Le Faye. Other biographies include Elizabeth Jenkins' influential but now dated *Jane Austen*, and *Jane Austen: A Life* by Claire Tomalin, while Le Faye's *Chronology of Jane Austen and her Family* is an extraordinary, if rather unwieldy, accumulation of meticulous data. There are useful histories of the family by Maggie Lane and George Holbert Tucker. Emma Clery's *Jane Austen: The Banker's Sister* provides a much-needed biography of the mercurial Henry Austen. Brian Southam's *Jane Austen and the Navy* is a fine study, with much on her naval brothers, Francis and Charles, which supersedes the old and now very dated volume by the Hubbacks. Sheila Johnson Kindred recounts the story of Charles's first marriage in *Jane Austen's Transatlantic Sister: The Life and Letters of Fanny Palmer Austen*; while it is Deirdre Le Faye again who gives us a 'life and letters' of Eliza de Feuillide (*Jane Austen's 'Outlandish Cousin'*) who married Henry Austen. There are a number of sources for Fanny Knight, Jane Austen's niece, including the wonderful letters Austen wrote to her when Fanny was struggling to sort out her feelings for John Plumptre. *Almost Another Sister: The Story of Fanny Knight* by Margaret Wilson has some snippets of useful information, while Knight's diary has been carefully edited and published by, inevitably, Deirdre Le Faye. Knight's unpublished correspondence is held by the Kent Archive Service, who kindly provided me with a copy of a letter partially quoted by Wilson, describing her coming out; while some details of her married life can be found in Knatchbull-Hugessen's *Kentish Family*. The interesting story of her sisters' lives has been well told by Sophia Hillan in *May, Lou and Cass: Jane Austen's Nieces in Ireland*.

There have also been some excellent works that use Jane Austen and her family to look at aspects of the social history of the time, including Hilary Davidson's exemplary *Dress in the Age of Jane Austen*, Stephen Mahony's *Wealth or Poverty: Jane Austen's Novels Explored* and Irene Collins's *Jane Austen and the Clergy*. *Jane Austen and Marriage* by Hazel Jones addresses the same subject as this book, and, although our approaches are rather different and we sometimes disagree in our conclusions, I can recommend it as an excellent and entertaining introduction to the subject, which frequently prompted me to think harder about my own ideas.

There is such an abundance of published primary source material that it is impossible to read it all, but the works that I have found most useful include Mrs Calvert's diary with some recollections, published as *An Irish Beauty of the Regency*; the correspondence of Caroline Stuart Wortley in *The First Lady Wharncliffe and Her Family*; *The Diary of Lady Shelley*; and Brian Connell's *Portrait of a Whig Peer compiled from the Papers of the Second Viscount Palmerston*. Maria Stanley (née Holroyd)'s delightful correspondence has been published as *The Girlhood of Maria Josepha Holroyd* and *The Early Married Life of Maria Josepha, Lady Stanley*. A later volume of her correspondence with her daughter-in-law, *The Ladies of Alderley*, edited by Nancy Mitford, while interesting, does neither woman justice, for they did not bring out the best in each other. The three volumes of *The Wynne Diaries* contain a substantial selection from the diaries and correspondence of Betsey and Eugenia Wynne, continuing after Betsey's marriage to Captain Fremantle. The editing of these volumes leaves much to be desired, including in the choice of material to be published, but the inherent interest of the story and the distinctive voices of the two sisters, nonetheless, emerge clearly. A single-volume abridgement is valuable for adding material from Fremantle's diary not included in the three-volume edition, while several important letters from him are printed in Parry's *The Admirals Fremantle*. A biography of Fremantle by E.J. Hounslow puts his private life into its professional context, as well as giving interesting information about his escapades before he met Betsey. Elaine Chalus has written a number of articles about Betsey Fremantle, of which the most useful for my study was '"My Dearest Tussy"' which includes some wonderful unpublished material from her letters describing life at home when he was at sea on active service. These articles whet the appetite for the full-length study on which Chalus is working.

A good parallel to the Fremantles is provided by the correspondence of another naval officer, Edward Codrington, with his wife Jane, published by their daughter, Lady Bourchier, in her *Memoir* of her father. Other primary sources of particular note include the *Correspondence of Sarah Spencer, Lady Lyttelton*; *The Cheverels of Cheverel Manor* (Hester and Sir Roger Newdigate) by Lady Newdigate-Newdegate; *The Capel Letters* (which includes Harriet Capel's disastrous infatuation with Baron Trip), edited by the Marquess of Anglesey; and *The Paget Brothers*. Many of Lady Bessborough's inimitable letters are published in *Lord Granville Leveson Gower (First Earl Granville): Private Correspondence* and in *Lady Bessborough and her Family Circle*. There is also an entertaining biography of her by Janet Gleeson, *An Aristocratic Affair*.

Anne Lister's diaries shed light not just on the position of lesbians in early-nineteenth-century England, but also on the lives of the gentry in northern England: a full biography will probably have to wait until all the diaries have been transcribed, but *Gentleman Jack* by Angela Steidele serves very well in the interim. Two contrasting diaries by governesses, by Agnes Porter and Nelly Weeton, reveal much about the position of women whose claims to gentility were fragile, but extend well beyond this: for example, Nelly Weeton is a particularly rich source about domestic violence, while Agnes Porter has some remarkable material describing the diffidence of a noble widower announcing his intention to remarry and hoping for the approval of his daughters' governess and of his already married daughter. *Trusty and Well Beloved: The Letters home of William Harness, an Officer of George the Third* edited by Caroline Duncan-Jones tells a sad but evocative story of a long engagement, a happy marriage and a parting brought about by war and the demands of a career. It is a rich source that I would have liked to have quoted more.

Novels reveal much about contemporary attitudes that is often taken for granted in other sources. Walter Scott generally set his novels in the past, but *St Ronan's Well* is a contemporary watering-place comedy, and, while it lacks the subtlety of Austen's work and is certainly not Scott's finest, it is still amusing and revealing. Maria Edgeworth's *Belinda* has much that is relevant, especially its depiction of an unhappy marriage and the heroine's contemplation of a marriage of esteem and affection but not love. Emily Eden's *The Semi-Attached Couple* shows how quickly selfish love could turn to disappointment and estrangement, although, of course, everything is happily resolved in the end. Susan Ferrier's *Marriage* has aged less well and may have been old-fashioned even when it was published in 1819, although there are still some interesting touches. And *Cranford*, based on Elizabeth Gaskell's recollections of the lives of an older generation in her youth, remains a delight to anyone not intent on reading for plot, while her non-fiction article 'The Last Generation in England' is a useful supplement to it.

Nonetheless it is to Austen's novels that we turn to see her world most clearly: the world of the gentry and the gentlemanly professions, living in rural, southern England. Contemporaries commented on the authenticity of her portrayal, not always as a compliment. Mrs Guiton thought *Emma* 'too natural to be interesting', while Lady Vernon half-heartedly recommended *Mansfield Park*, 'It is not much of a novel, more the history of a family party in the country, very natural, the characters well drawn.' Anne Romilly complained that *Mansfield Park* lacked any 'elevation of virtue, something beyond nature', but acknowledged that it was 'true to life'. And in 1818, after Austen's death, an anonymous reviewer in *The British Critic* commented, in a generally favourable article, that 'In imagination, of all kinds, she appears to have been extremely deficient.' The article continued:

> her characters, her incidents, her sentiments, are obviously all drawn exclusively from experience. The sentiments which she puts into the mouths of her actors, are the sentiments, which we are every day in the habit of hearing. . . . Her heroes and heroines, make love and are married, just as her readers make love, and were or will be, married; no unexpected ill fortune occurs to prevent, nor any unexpected good fortune to bring about the events on which her novels hinge. She seems to be describing such people as meet together every night, in every respectable house in London; and to relate such incidents as have probably happened, one time or other, to half the families in the United Kingdom . . . and the sentiments which she places in their mouths, the little phrases which she makes them use, strike so familiarly upon our memory as soon as we hear them repeated, that we instantly recognize among some of our acquaintance, the sort of persons she intends to signify, as accurately as if we had heard their voices.[2]

It is strange and rather wonderful that novels which eschewed dramatic plots and exotic settings that were only modestly successful in their own day and which told relatively simple, plausible stories, albeit with unmatched irony and wit, should not only survive to be read with pleasure by millions today, but should also inspire such a range of adaptations, continuations and retellings that they shape our view of the whole era. For us, though not for her contemporaries, it has become the Age of Jane Austen.

BIBLIOGRAPHY

MANUSCRIPTS

Fanny Knight to Miss Chapman, 18 October 1811, Kent Archives, U951/C108/11.

Torrens to Bourke, 25 April 1812, The National Archives, WO 3/602, pp. 43–4.

Wilberforce diary, Bodleian MS Wilberforce c.34, ff 138–9 – quotation courtesy of John Coffey of the Wilberforce Diaries Project.

PRIVATE INFORMATION

Concerning Cassandra Austen's bank account at the time of her death: Pamela Hunter of Hoare's Bank, 22 July 2022.

Concerning Lord Chatham's marriage settlement: Dr Jacqueline Reiter, 14 September 2020.

Concerning naval pensions: Nicholas Blake, 26 October 2021.

Concerning the separation of Lieutenant-Colonel Powlett and his wife Letitia: Rachel Bynoth, 17 September 2021.

ONLINE RESOURCES

Dictionary of Canadian Biography, online edition.

'Manuscript of the Month', February 2013, 'Customer Ledger showing Jane Austen's Account, 1816–17': https://www.hoaresbank.co.uk/sites/default/files/styles/Documents/Feb%2013%20-%20Jane%20Austen.pdf

Muir, Rory, lifeofwellington.co.uk – online supplement and commentary to *Wellington: The Path to Victory* and *Wellington: Waterloo and the Fortunes of Peace*.

Norton, Rictor (ed.), *Homosexuality in Nineteenth-century England: A Sourcebook* (updated 1 November 2020): http://rictornorton.co.uk/eighteen/nineteen.htm and especially http://rictornorton.co.uk/vere.htm; http://rictornorton.co.uk/clogher1.htm; http://rictornorton.co.uk/eighteen/1822news.htm; http://rictornorton.co.uk/eighteen/1820kept.htm

The Oxford Dictionary of National Biography.

Transcriptions of some of Anne Lister's later diary entries at: https://verycivil.blog-spot.com/search?updated-max=2021-05-15T14:03:00Z&max-results=7

www.gretnagreen.com/david-and-simon-lang

BOOKS AND ARTICLES

Adeane, Jane H. (ed.): see under Stanley.

Andrew, Donna T., '"Adultery à-la-mode": Privilege, the Law and Attitudes to Adultery 1770–1809', *History*, vol. 82, no. 265 (Jan. 1997), pp. 5–23.

Anglesey, Marquess of (ed.), *The Capel Letters: Being the Correspondence of Lady Caroline Capel and her Daughters with the Dowager Countess of Uxbridge from Brussels and Switzerland, 1814–1817* (London, Jonathan Cape, 1955).

—— *One-Leg: The Life and Letters of Henry William Paget, First Marquess of Anglesey, K.G. (1768–1854)* (London, Jonathan Cape, 1962).

Anon., 'Singular Mésalliance', *Chambers's Edinburgh Journal*, n.s., vol. 14, no. 356 (26 October 1850), pp. 270–1.

Anson, Elizabeth and Florence Anson, *Mary Hamilton afterwards Mrs John Dickenson at Court and at Home: From Letters and Diaries 1756 to 1816* (London, John Murray, 1925).

Anson, Captain Walter Vernon, *The Life of Admiral Sir John Borlase Warren* (Privately printed, 1914).

Arbuthnot, Charles, *The Correspondence of Charles Arbuthnot*, ed. by A. Aspinall. Camden 3rd series, vol. 55 (London, Royal Historical Society, 1941).

Arbuthnot, Harriet, *The Journal of Mrs Arbuthnot, 1820–1832*, 2 vols (London, Macmillan, 1950).

Arbuthnot, P.S.-M., *Memories of the Arbuthnots of Kincardineshire and Aberdeenshire* (London, George Allen & Unwin, 1920) (includes a short autobiographical memoir by Charles Arbuthnot printed as an appendix).

Arnold, Ralph, *The Unhappy Countess and Her Grandson John Bowes* (London, Constable, 1957).

Ashby, Abby and Audrey Jones, *The Shrigley Abduction: A Tale of Anguish, Deceit and Violation of the Domestic Hearth* (Stroud, Sutton, 2003).

Aspinall, A., 'The Old House of Commons and its Members', *Parliamentary Affairs*, vol. 14 (1960–61), pp. 13–25, 162–77, 291–311, 435–50, vol. 15 (1961–62), pp. 15–38, 171–77, 284–93, 424–449.

Aspinall-Oglander, Cecil, *Freshly Remembered: The Story of Thomas Graham, Lord Lynedoch* (London, Hogarth Press, 1956).

Austen, Cassandra, 'Her will and codicil to her will', *Jane Austen Society Collected Reports*, vol. 2 (1966–75), pp. 103–6, with further note by William Jarvis in vol. 3, pp. 179–81.

Austen, Jane, *The Watsons* (London, Leonard Parsons, 1923).

—— *Emma*, ed. by R.W. Chapman (Oxford, Clarendon Press, 1926).

—— *Mansfield Park*, ed. by R.W. Chapman (Oxford, Clarendon Press, 1926).

—— *Northanger Abbey*, ed. by R.W. Chapman (Oxford, Clarendon Press, 1926).

—— *Persuasion*, ed. by R.W. Chapman (Oxford, Clarendon Press, 1926).

—— *Pride and Prejudice*, ed. by R.W. Chapman (Oxford, Clarendon Press, 1926).

—— *Sense and Sensibility*, ed. by R.W. Chapman (Oxford, Clarendon Press, 1926).

—— *Catharine, or the Bower* in *Minor Works*, ed. by R.W. Chapman (Oxford University Press, 1954).

—— *Lady Susan* in *Minor Works*, ed. by R.W. Chapman (Oxford University Press, 1954).

—— *Sanditon* in *Minor Works*, ed. by R.W. Chapman (Oxford University Press, 1954).

—— *Volume the Second* in *Minor Works*, ed. by R.W. Chapman (Oxford University Press, 1954).

—— *Jane Austen's Letters*, ed. by Deirdre Le Faye (4th edn, Oxford University Press, 2011).

—— Also the editions of Jane Austen's novels annotated and ed. by David Shapard (Anchor Books, 2010–17).

Austen-Leigh, W., R.A. Austen-Leigh and Deirdre Le Faye, *Jane Austen: A Family Record* (London, British Library, 1989).

Bagot, Josceline (ed.), *George Canning and His Friends*, 2 vols (London, John Murray, 1909).

Bailey, Joanne, 'Favoured or Oppressed? Married Women, Property and "Coverture" in England, 1660–1800', *Continuity and Change*, vol. 17, no. 3 (2002), pp. 351–72.

—— *Unquiet Lives: Marriage and Marriage Breakdown in England, 1660–1800* (Cambridge University Press, 2003).

Bailey, Martha, 'The Marriage Law of Jane Austen's World', *Persuasions On-Line*, vol. 36, no. 1 (Winter 2015).

Barclay, Katie, 'Negotiating Patriarchy: The Marriage of Anna Potts and Sir Archibald Grant of Monymusk, 1731–1744', *Journal of Scottish Historical Studies*, vol. 28, no. 2 (2008), pp. 83–101.

—— *Love, Intimacy and Power: Marriage and Patriarchy in Scotland, 1650–1850* (Manchester University Press, 2011).

—— 'Love and Other Emotions', in *The Routledge History of Women in Early Modern Europe*, ed. by Amanda L. Capern (New York, Routledge, 2019), pp. 77–96.

—— 'Mobile Emotions: Bigamy and Community in Scotland, 1660–1830', in *Courtship, Marriage and Marriage Breakdown: Approaches from the History of Emotion*, ed. by Katie Barclay, Jeffrey Meek and Andrea Thomson (New York, Routledge, 2019), pp. 66–80.

Beauman, Francesca, *Shapely Ankle Preferr'd: A History of the Lonely Hearts Advertisement* (London, Vintage, 2012).

Beckett, John, *The Rise and Fall of the Grenvilles* (Manchester University Press, 1994).

Bell, Alan, *Sydney Smith* (Oxford, Clarendon Press, 1980).

Beresford, Marcus de la Poer, *Marshal William Carr Beresford* (Newbridge, Irish Academic Press, 2019).

Bessborough, Earl of (ed.), *Georgiana: Extracts from the Correspondence of Georgiana, Duchess of Devonshire* (London, John Murray, 1955).

Bessborough, Earl of and A. Aspinall (eds), *Lady Bessborough and Her Family Circle* (London, John Murray, 1941).

Bew, John, *Castlereagh: Enlightenment, War and Tyranny* (London, Quercus, 2011).

Binhammer, Katherine, 'The Sex Panic of the 1790s', *Journal of the History of Sexuality*, vol. 6, no. 3 (Jan. 1996), pp. 409–34.

Blacker, Valentine, *War without Pity in the South Indian Peninsula 1798–1813: The Letter Book of Lieutenant-Colonel Valentine Blacker*, ed. by David Howell (Warwick, Helion, 2018).

Blakiston, Georgiana, *Lord William Russell and His Wife, 1815–1846* (London, John Murray, 1972).

Boswell, James, *The Life of Samuel Johnson, L.L.D*, 2 vols (Oxford University Press, 1922).

Botelho, Lynn and Pat Thane (eds), *Women and Ageing in British Society since 1500* (Harlow, Longman, 2001).

Bourchier, Lady, *Memoir of the Life of Admiral Sir Edward Codrington*, 2 vols (London, Longmans, Green & Co., 1873).

Bourne, Kenneth, *Palmerston: The Early Years, 1784–1841* (London, Allen Lane, 1982).

Bowman, Peter James, 'A Real-Life Jane Austen Heroine and her Naval Hero', *Trafalgar Chronicle*, n.s., vol. 3 (2018), pp. 13–23.

Brett-James, Antony, *Life in Wellington's Army* (London, George Allen & Unwin, 1972).

Bromley, Janet and David, *Wellington's Men Remembered: A Register of Memorials to Soldiers Who Served in the Peninsular War and at Waterloo 1808–1815*, 2 vols (Barnsley, Praetorian Press, 2012).

Brynn, Edward, *Crown & Castle. British Rule in Ireland, 1800–1830* (Toronto, Macmillan of Canada, 1978).

Burg, B.R., *Boys at Sea: Sodomy, Indecency and Courts Martial in Nelson's Navy* (Basingstoke, Palgrave Macmillan, 2007).

Burghersh, Priscilla, Lady, *The Letters of Lady Burghersh . . . from Germany and France during the Campaign of 1813–14*, ed. by her niece Lady Rose Weigall (London, John Murray, 1893).

—— *Correspondence of Lady Burghersh with the Duke of Wellington* (London, John Murray, 1903).

Burnham, Robert and Ron McGuigan, *The British Army against Napoleon* (Barnsley, Frontline, 2010).

Burton, Sarah, *A Double Life: A Biography of Charles and Mary Lamb* (London, Penguin, 2004).

Butler, Iris, *The Eldest Brother: The Marquess Wellesley, the Duke of Wellington's Eldest Brother* (London, Hodder & Stoughton, 1973).

Calvert, Frances, *An Irish Beauty of the Regency, compiled from "Mes Souvenirs", the unpublished journals of the Hon. Mrs Calvert, 1789–1822*, ed. by Mrs Warrenne Blake (London, John Lane, 1911).

Calvert, Frances: see also Richardson.

Calvert, Leanne, ' "A more Careful Tender Nurse Cannot Be than My Dear Husband": Reassessing the Role of Men in Pregnancy and Childbirth in Ulster, 1780–1838', *Journal of Family History*, vol. 42, no. 1 (2017), pp. 22–36.

—— ' "Do not forget your bit wife": Love, Marriage and the Negotiation of Patriarchy in Irish Presbyterian Marriages, c.1780–1850', *Women's History Review*, vol. 26, no. 3 (2017), pp. 433–54.

—— ' "He came to her bed pretending courtship": Sex, Courtship and the Making of Marriage in Ulster, 1750–1844', *Irish Historical Studies*, vol. 42, no. 162 (2018), pp. 244–64.

—— ' "to recover his reputation among the people of God": Sex, Religion and the Double Standard in Presbyterian Ireland, c.1700–1838', *Gender & History* (June 2022), pp. 1–18.

Cannon, John, *Aristocratic Century: The Peerage in Eighteenth-century England* (Cambridge University Press, 1984).

Carter, Louise, 'Scarlet Fever: Female Enthusiasm for Men in Uniform, 1780–1815', in *Britain's Soldiers: Rethinking War and Society, 1715–1815*, ed. by Kevin Linch and Matthew McCormack (Liverpool University Press, 2014), pp. 155–79.

—— 'Brothers in Arms? Martial Masculinities and Family Feeling in Old Soldiers' Memoirs, 1793–1815', in *Martial Masculinities: Experiencing and Imagining the Military in the Long Nineteenth Century*, ed. by Michael Brown et al. (Manchester University Press, 2019), pp. 35–57.

Cass, Jocelyn Creigh, 'In Defence of George Austen', *Persuasions On-Line*, no. 16 (1994), pp. 55–62.

Cavendish, Lady Harriet, *Hary-O: The Letters of Lady Harriet Cavendish, 1796–1809*, ed. by Sir George Leveson Gower and Iris Palmer (London, John Murray, 1940).

Chalus, Elaine, *Elite Women in English Political Life, c. 1754–1790* (Oxford, Clarendon Press, 2005).

—— '"My Dearest Tussy": Coping with Separation in the Napoleonic Wars (the Fremantle Papers, 1800–1814)', in *A New Naval History*, ed. by Quintin Colville and James Davey (Manchester University Press, 2018), ch 2.

—— 'The Loneliness of Leadership: Royal Naval Officers in the Revolutionary and Napoleonic Wars', in *The Routledge History of Loneliness*, ed. by Katie Barclay, Elaine Chalus and Deborah Simonton (forthcoming).

Chamberlain, Muriel E., *Lord Aberdeen: A Political Biography* (London and New York, Longman, 1983).

Chapone, Hester, *Letters on the Improvement of the Mind: Addressed to a Lady* (London, J. Walker et al., 1808).

Clammer, David, 'Women All at Sea: Soldiers' Wives aboard Naval Transports during the Napoleonic War', *Trafalgar Chronicle*, n.s., vol. 3 (2018), pp. 55–66.

—— *Ladies, Wives and Women: British Army Wives in the Revolutionary and Napoleonic Wars, 1793–1815* (Warwick, Helion, 2022).

Clery, E.J., *Jane Austen: The Banker's Sister* (London, Biteback, 2017).

Clifford, Naomi, 'The Bristol Elopement: Clementina Clerke and Richard Vining Perry', blogpost dated 13 August 2013, https://www.naomiclifford.com/the-bristol-elopement/

—— 'Newspaper Reports of Elopements and Abductions [1770–73]', blogpost n.d., www.naomiclifford.com

—— 'Grady v Richards, 1828: Rare Prosecution of the Bride and her Family', blogpost dated 23 September 2013, www.naomiclifford.com

—— 'The Abduction Club', blogpost dated 16 October 2013, https://www.naomiclifford.com/abduction-club/

[Cockayne, G.E.], *The Complete Peerage of England, Scotland, Ireland, Great Britain and the United Kingdom*, new and enlarged edn, 13 vols in 14 (London, St Catherine Press, 1910–59).

Cocks, H.G., 'Secrets, Crimes and Diseases, 1800–1914', in *A Gay History of Britain*, ed. by Matt Cook et al.

Cole, G.L., *Memoirs of Sir Lowry Cole*, ed. by Maud Lowry Cole and Stephen Gwynn (London, Macmillan, 1934).

Collins, Irene, *Jane Austen and the Clergy* (London and New York, Hambledon and London, 2002).

Connell, Brian, *Portrait of a Whig Peer compiled from the papers of the Second Viscount Palmerston, 1739–1802* (London, Andre Deutsch, 1957).

Cook, Matt, et al. (eds), *A Gay History of Britain: Love and Sex between Men Since the Middle Ages* (Oxford, Greenwood, 2007).

Copeland, Edward, 'What's a Competence? Jane Austen, her Sister Novelists and the 5%'s', *Modern Language Studies*, vol. 9, no. 3 (Autumn 1979), pp. 161–8.

—— '*Persuasion*: The Jane Austen Consumer's Guide', *Persuasions*, no. 15 (1993), pp. 111–23.

Corley, T.A.B., 'Jane Austen's Schooldays', *Jane Austen Society Collected Reports, 1996–2000*, pp. 14–24.

Costley-White, Hope, *Mary Cole, Countess of Berkeley: A Biography* (London, George G. Harrap & Co., 1961).

Creevey, Thomas, *The Creevey Papers*, ed. by Sir Herbert Maxwell (London, John Murray, 1923).

Crompton, Louis, *Byron and Greek Love: Homophobia in 19th-century England* (Berkeley, University of California Press, 1985).

Daniell, Alison, ' "Too many restrictions could not be thrown in the way of divorce": Attitudes to Women's Petitions for Divorce by Act of Parliament, 1801–1831', blogpost dated June 2022, https://thehistoryofparliament.files.wordpress.com/2022/06/alison-daniell-too-many-restrictions.pdf

Darwin, Emma, *Emma Darwin: A Century of Family Letters, 1792–1896*, ed. by Henrietta Litchfield, 2 vols (London, John Murray, 1915).

Davidson, Hilary, *Dress in the Age of Jane Austen: Regency Fashion* (New Haven and London, Yale University Press, 2019).

DiPlacidi, Jenny and Karl Leydecker, *After Marriage in the Long Eighteenth Century: Literature, Law and Society* (Cham, Palgrave Macmillan, 2018).

Duncan-Jones, Caroline M., *Trusty and Well Beloved: The Letters Home of William Harness an Officer of George III*, ed. by Caroline M. Duncan-Jones (London, SPCK, 1957).

Dyott, William, *Dyott's Diary, 1781–1845: A Selection from the Journal of William Dyott, Sometime General in the British Army and Aide-De-Camp to His Majesty King George III*, ed. by Reginald W. Jeffery, 2 vols (London, Constable, 1907).

Eden, Emily, *Miss Eden's Letters*, ed. by Violet Dickinson (London, Macmillan, 1919).

—— *The Semi-attached Couple* (London, Folio Society, 1955).

Edgeworth, Maria, *Belinda* (Oxford University Press, 2020).

Edgeworth, Richard Lovell and Maria Edgeworth, *Memoirs of Richard Lovell Edgeworth Esq., 'begun by himself and concluded by his daughter Maria Edgeworth'*, 3rd edn (London, Richard Bentley, 1844).

Elers, George, *Memoirs of George Elers, Captain in the 12th Regiment of Foot (1777–1842)* (New York, Appleton, 1903).

Elliott, Robert, *The Gretna Green Memoirs* (London, Gretna Green Parson, 1842).

Eustace, Nicole, ' "The Cornerstone of a Copious Work": Love and Power in Eighteenth-century Courtship', *Journal of Social History*, vol. 34, no. 3 (Spring 2001), pp. 517–46.

Faderman, Lillian, *Scotch Verdict: Miss Pirie and Miss Woods v. Dame Cumming Gordon* (London, Quartet Books, 1985).

Farington, Joseph, *The Farington Diary*, ed. by James Grieg, 8 vols (London, Hutchinson, 1922–8).

Ferrier, Susan, *Marriage* (London, Nelson, n.d. [*c.* 1953]; first published 1818).

Festing, Gabrielle, *John Hookham Frere and His Friends* (London, James Nisbet, 1899).

Fielding, Michael John, 'The Indissoluble Knot? Public and Private Representations of Men and Marriage, 1770–1830' (PhD thesis, University of Exeter, 2012).

Fisher, D.R., *The History of Parliament: The Commons, 1820–1832*, 7 vols (Cambridge University Press for the History of Parliament Trust, 2009).

Flinders, Matthew, *Matthew Flinders: Personal Letters from an Extraordinary Life*, ed. by Paul Brunton (Sydney, Hordern House, 2002).

Flinders: see Retter.

Fremantle: see Wynne (also Hounslow, Parry and Glover).

French, Henry and Mark Rothery, ' "Upon your entry into the World": Masculine Values and the Threshold of Adulthood among Landed Elites in England, 1600–1800', *Social History*, vol. 33, no. 4 (Nov. 2008), pp. 402–22.

——— *Man's Estate: Landed Gentry Masculinities, c.1600–c.1900* (Oxford University Press, 2012).

Froide, Amy M., 'Old Maids: The Lifecycle of Single Women in Early Modern England', in *Women and Ageing in British Society since 1500*, ed. by Lynn Botelho and Pat Thane (Harlow, Longman, 2001), pp. 89–110.

Furneaux, Robin, *William Wilberforce* (London, Hamish Hamilton, 1974).

Garwood, Lt-Col. F.S., 'The Royal Staff Corps', *Royal Engineers Journal*, vol. 57 (1943), pp. 81–96.

Gash, Norman, *Mr Secretary Peel: The Life of Sir Robert Peel to 1830* (London, Longmans, 1961).

——— *Lord Liverpool* (London, Weidenfeld and Nicolson, 1984).

Gaskell, Elizabeth, *Cranford* (London, Macmillan, 1924).

——— 'The Last Generation in England', in the Oxford World's Classics 2011 edn of *Cranford*, pp. 159–65, ed. by Elizabeth Porges Watson (Oxford University Press, 2011), originally published in *Sartain's Union Magazine* (1849).

Gayford, Martin, *Constable in Love: Love, Landscape, Money and the Making of a Great Painter* (London, Fig Tree, 2009).

Gentleman's Magazine, vol. 104, pt 2 (November 1833) (obituary of David Okeden Parry-Okeden).

George III, *The Later Correspondence of George III*, ed. by A. Aspinall, 5 vols (Cambridge University Press, 1962–70).

George IV, *The Letters of King George IV 1812–1830*, ed. by A. Aspinall, 3 vols (Cambridge University Press, 1938).

George, Mary Dorothy and Frederick George Stephens, *Catalogue of Political and Personal Satires Preserved in the Department of Prints and Drawings in the British Museum*, 11 vols (London, British Museum Publications, 1978; first published 1870–1954).

Gibbon, Edward, *Memoirs of My Life*, ed. by Betty Radice (Harmondsworth, Penguin, 1984).

Gibson, D.C. 'General Garrett, 1791–1869', *Archaelogia Cantiana*, vol. 81 (1966), pp. 126–35.

Gibson, Kate, '"I am not on the Footing of Kept Women": Extra-marital Love in Eighteenth-century England', *Cultural and Social History: The Journal of the Social History Society*, vol. 17, no. 3 (2020), pp. 355–73.

Gill, Ellen, *Naval Families, War and Duty in Britain, 1740–1820* (Woodbridge, Boydell Press, 2016).

Gill, Stephen, *William Wordsworth: A Life* (Oxford, Clarendon Press, 1989).

Gittings, Robert and Jo Manton, *Dorothy Wordsworth* (Oxford, Clarendon Press, 1985).

Gleeson, Janet, *An Aristocratic Affair: The Life of Georgiana's Sister, Harriet Spencer, Countess of Bessborough* (London, Bantam, 2007).

Glover, Gareth (ed.), *An Eloquent Soldier: The Peninsular War Journals of Lieutenant Charles Crowe of the Inniskillings, 1812–1814* (Barnsley, Frontline, 2011).

——— (ed.), *Wellington's Voice: The Candid Letters of Lieutenant Colonel John Fremantle, Coldstream Guards, 1808–1837* (Barnsley, Frontline, 2012).

Gore, John, *Nelson's Hardy and His Wife* (London, John Murray, 1935).

Gower: see Leveson Gower.

Granville: see Leveson Gower.

Granville, Harriet, Lady, *Letters of Harriet, Countess Granville, 1810–1845*, 2 vols (London, Longmans, Green & Co., 1894).

Greenwood, Adrian (ed.), *Through Spain with Wellington: The Letters of Lieutenant Peter Le Mesurier of the 'Fighting Ninth'* (Stroud, Amberley, 2016).

Greville, Charles C.F., *The Greville Memoirs 1814–1860*, ed. by Lytton Strachey and Roger Fulford, 8 vols (London, Macmillan, 1938).

Grosvenor, Caroline, *The First Lady Wharncliffe and Her Family (1779–1856)*, by her grandchildren Caroline Grosvenor and the late Charles Beilby, Lord Stuart of Wortley, 2 vols (London, William Heinemann, 1927).

Harding-Edgar, John, *Next to Wellington: General Sir George Murray* (Warwick, Helion, 2018).

Hare, Augustus, *The Story of My Life*, 6 vols (London, George Allen, 1896–1901).

[Hayley, William], *A Philosophical, Historical, and Moral Essay on Old Maids by a Friend to the Sisterhood*, 3 vols, 3rd edn (London, Cadell, 1793).

Haythornthwaite, Philip J., *The Armies of Wellington* (London, Arms and Armour, 1994).

Heathcote, Ralph, *Ralph Heathcote Letters of a Young Diplomatist and Soldier during the Time of Napoleon* (London, John Lane: The Bodley Head, 1907).

Henegan, Sir Richard D., *Seven Years Campaigning in the Peninsula and the Netherlands, 1808–1815*, 2 vols (Stroud, Nonsuch, 2005; first published 1846).

Hibbert, Christopher, *Queen Victoria: A Personal History* (London, HarperCollins, 2000).

Hillan, Sophia, *May, Lou & Cass: Jane Austen's Nieces in Ireland* (Belfast, Blackstaff Press, 2011).

Hinde, Wendy, *George Canning* (London, Collins, 1973).

—— *Castlereagh* (London, Collins, 1981).

Hitchcock, Tim, *English Sexualities, 1700–1800* (Basingstoke, Macmillan, 1997).

Holloway, Sally, '"You know I am all on fire": Writing the Adulterous Affair in England, c.1740–1830', *Historical Research*, vol. 89, no. 244 (May 2016), pp. 317–39.

—— *The Game of Love in Georgian England: Courtship, Emotions, and Material Culture* (Oxford University Press, 2019).

Holroyd, Maria J.: see Stanley.

Horn, D.B., *The British Diplomatic Service, 1689–1789* (Oxford, Clarendon Press, 1961).

Hostettler, John and Richard Braby, *Sir William Garrow: His Life, Times and Fight for Justice* (Hook, Waterside Press, 2010).

Hounslow, E.J., *Nelson's Right Hand Man: The Life and Times of Vice Admiral Sir Thomas Fremantle* (Stroud, The History Press, 2016).

Howell, David W., *Patriarchs and Parasites: The Gentry in South-West Wales in the Eighteenth Century* (Cardiff, University of Wales Press, 1986).

Hubback, J.H. and Edith Hubback, *Jane Austen's Sailor Brothers* (London, John Lane, 1906).

Hunt, Giles (ed.), *Mehitabel Canning: A Redoubtable Woman – Family Letters*, ed. by Giles Hunt (Royston, Rooster, 2001).

Hunter, Archie, *Wellington's Scapegoat: The Tragedy of Lieutenant-Colonel Charles Bevan* (Barnsley, Leo Cooper, 2003).

Hurren, Elizabeth and Steve King, 'Courtship at the Coroner's Court', *Social History*, vol. 40, no. 2 (2015), pp. 185–207.

Hussey, John, '"Let no man lay to Wellington's charge the suicides of these two men": The Problems of Reminiscence and the Failings of Old Age', *Journal of the Society for Army Historical Research*, vol. 80 (2002), pp. 98–109.

Huxley, Gervas, *Lady Elizabeth and the Grosvenors: Life in a Whig Family, 1822–1839* (London, Oxford University Press, 1965).

BIBLIOGRAPHY

Hyde, H.M., *The Rise of Castlereagh* (London, Macmillan, 1933).

Jackson, George, *The Diaries and Letters of Sir George Jackson*, ed. by Lady Jackson, 2 vols (London, Richard Bentley, 1872).

—— *The Bath Archives: A Further Selection from the Diaries and Letters of Sir George Jackson, K.C.H. from 1809 to 1816*, ed. by Lady Jackson, 2 vols (London, Richard Bentley, 1873).

Jaeger, Muriel, *Before Victoria* (London, Chatto & Windus, 1956; subtitle given on dust jacket but not title page: *Changing Standards & Behaviour, 1787–1837*).

Jalland, Pat, *Women, Marriage and Politics, 1860–1914* (Oxford, Clarendon Press, 1986).

—— *Death in the Victorian Family* (Oxford University Press, 1996).

Jenkins, Elizabeth, *Jane Austen* (London, Cardinal, 1973; first published 1938).

Johansson, Sheila Ryan, 'Sex and Death in Victorian England: An Examination of Age- and Sex-specific Death Rates, 1840–1910', in *A Widening Sphere. Changing Roles of Victorian Women*, ed. by Martha Vicinus (London, Methuen, 1980), pp. 163–81.

Johnson, Samuel, *The History of Rasselas, Prince of Abyssinia* (Leipzig, Regner, 1846; first published 1759).

Jones, Hazel, *Jane Austen and Marriage* (London, Continuum, 2009).

Jones, John Avery, Devoney Looser and Peter Sabor, 'Cassandra Austen's Last Years and Wishes, with New Documents and Transcriptions' *Jane Austen Society Report* 2022, pp. 33–55.

Jupp, Peter, *Lord Grenville, 1759–1834* (Oxford, Clarendon Press, 1985).

Khan, Mirza Abul Hassan, *A Persian at the Court of King George 1809–1810*, ed. by Margaret Cloake (London, Barrie & Jenkins, 1988).

Kindred, Sheila Johnson, *Jane Austen's Transatlantic Sister: The Life and Letters of Fanny Palmer Austen* (Montreal and Kingston, McGill-Queen's University Press, 2017).

King, Hazel, *Richard Bourke* (Melbourne, Oxford University Press, 1971).

Knatchbull-Hugessen, Sir Hughe, *Kentish Family* (London, Methuen, 1960).

Knight, Roger, *The Pursuit of Victory: The Life and Achievement of Horatio Nelson* (London, Allen Lane, 2005).

Lane, Maggie, *Jane Austen's Family: Through Five Generations* (London, Robert Hale, 1984).

Lanfersieck, Lindsey and Devoney Looser, 'Austen's *Sense and Sensibility* and Lord Craven', *Notes and Queries*, vol. 56, no. 3 (Sept. 2009), pp. 376–81.

Langhamer, Claire, *The English in Love: The Intimate History of an Emotional Revolution* (Oxford, Oxford University Press, 2013).

Le Faye, Deirdre, 'Fanny Knight's Diaries: Jane Austen through her Niece's Eyes', Jane Austen Society of North America, *Persuasions*, Occasional Papers no. 2 (1986).

—— *Jane Austen: The World of Her Novels* (London, Frances Lincoln, 2002).

—— *Jane Austen's 'Outlandish Cousin': The Life and Letters of Eliza de Feuillide* (London, British Library, 2002).

—— '"Three or Four Families": Suggestions for New Directions in Biographical Research', *Persuasions On-line*, vol. 30, no. 2 (Spring 2010).

—— *A Chronology of Jane Austen and Her Family, 1600–2000*, rev. edn (Cambridge University Press, 2013).

—— 'Jane Austen: Her Biographies and Biographers – or, "Conversations minutely repeated"', *Sensibilities*, no. 58 (June 2019), pp. 10–31.

Lefroy, Anne, *The Letters of Mrs Lefroy: Jane Austen's Beloved Friend*, ed. by Helen Lefroy and Gavin Turner (Winchester, The Jane Austen Society, 2007).

Leveson Gower, Lord Granville, *Lord Granville Leveson Gower (First Earl Granville): Private Correspondence 1781–1821*, ed. by Castalla Countess Granville, 2 vols (London, John Murray, 1917).

Lewis, Judith, ' "'Tis a Misfortune to be a Great Ladie": Maternal Mortality in the British Aristocracy, 1558–1959', *Journal of British Studies*, vol. 37, no. 1 (Jan. 1998), pp. 26–53.

Lincoln, Margarette, *Naval Wives and Mistresses* (London, National Maritime Museum, 2007).

Lister, Anne, *The Secret Diaries of Miss Anne Lister*, ed. by Helena Whitbread (London, Virago, 2010).

—— *The Secret Diaries of Miss Anne Lister: No Priest But Love 1824–1826*, ed. by Helena Whitbread (London, Virago, 2020).

Longford, Elizabeth, *Wellington: Pillar of State* (London, Weidenfeld & Nicolson, 1972).

Looser, Devoney, *Sister Novelists: The Trailblazing Porter Sisters, Who Paved the Way for Austen and the Brontës* (New York, Bloomsbury, 2022).

McCreery, Cindy, 'Keeping Up with the *Bon Ton*: The *Tête-à-Tête* Series in the *Town and Country Magazine*', in *Gender in Eighteenth-century England: Roles, Representations and Responsibilities*, ed. by Hannah Barker and Elaine Chalus (London and New York, Longman, 1997), pp. 207–29.

McGuigan, Ron and Robert Burnham, *Wellington's Brigade Commanders: Peninsula and Waterloo* (Barnsley, Pen & Sword Military, 2017).

Mackesy, Piers, *The Coward of Minden: The Affair of Lord George Sackville* (London, Allen Lane, 1979).

Madan, Spencer, *Spencer and Waterloo: The Letters of Spencer Madan, 1814–1816*, ed. by Beatrice Madan (London, Literary Services, 1970).

Maguire, W.A., *Living Like a Lord: The Second Marquis of Donegall, 1769–1844* (Belfast, Appletree Press and Ulster Society for Historical Studies, 1984).

Mahony, Stephen, *Wealth or Poverty: Jane Austen's Novels Explored* (London, Robert Hale, 2015).

—— 'What Became of Mrs. Powlett?', *Jane Austen Society Report* (2019), pp. 56–9.

Malcomson, A.P.W., *The Pursuit of the Heiress: Aristocratic Marriage in Ireland, 1740–1840* (Belfast, Ulster Historical Foundation, 2006).

Manion, Jen, *Female Husbands: A Trans History* (Cambridge University Press, 2020).

Marshall, Dorothy, *The Rise of George Canning* (London, Longmans, Green, 1938).

Martin, Peter, *A Life of James Boswell* (London, Weidenfeld & Nicolson, 1999).

Martinovich, Paul, *The Sea is My Element: The Eventful Life of Admiral Sir Pulteney Malcolm 1768–1838* (Warwick, Helion, 2021).

Matthews, Christopher, 'Love at First Sight: The Velocity of Victorian Heterosexuality', *Victorian Studies*, vol. 46, no. 3 (Spring 2004), pp. 425–54.

Mavor, Elizabeth, *The Ladies of Llangollen: A Study in Romantic Friendship* (Harmondsworth, Penguin, 1976).

Mellors, Robert, *Men of Nottingham and Nottinghamshire* (Nottingham, J. & H. Bell 1924).

Metcalfe, Helen, 'To Let or For Lease: "Small, but Genteel" Lodgings for Bachelors in and about the Late Georgian Town', *Journal for Eighteenth-century Studies*, vol. 44, no. 1 (2021), pp. 3–19.

Mitchell, L.G., *Lord Melbourne 1779–1848* (Oxford University Press, 1997).

Mitchell, Leslie, *Holland House* (London, Duckworth, 1980).

Montagu, Lady Mary Wortley, *The Letters and Works of Lady Mary Wortley Montagu* ed. by her great grandson Lord Wharncliffe, 2 vols (London, Henry Bohn, 1861).

Moore, Graham: see Wareham.

Moore, Wendy, *Wedlock* (London, Weidenfeld & Nicolson, 2009).

More, Hannah, 'Sensibility: A Poetical Epistle to the Hon. Mrs Boscawen', in *Romanticism: An Anthology*, ed. by Duncan Wu (4th edn, Malden, MA, Wiley-Blackwell, 2012).

Muir, Rory, *Wellington: The Path to Victory, 1769–1814* (New Haven and London, Yale University Press, 2013).

—— *Wellington: Waterloo and the Fortunes of Peace, 1814–1852* (New Haven and London, Yale University Press, 2015).

—— *Gentlemen of Uncertain Fortune: How Younger Sons Made Their Way in Jane Austen's England* (New Haven and London, Yale University Press, 2019).

Namier, Sir Lewis and John Brooke, *The History of Parliament: The House of Commons 1754–1790*, 3 vols (London, Her Majesty's Stationery Office for the History of Parliament Trust, 1964).

Newdigate-Newdegate, Lady, *The Cheverels of Cheverel Manor* (London, Longmans, Green & Co., 1898) .

Newman, Aubrey, *The Stanhopes of Chevening: A Family Biography* (London, Macmillan, 1969).

Niall, Brenda, *Georgiana: A Biography of Georgiana McCrae, Painter, Diarist, Pioneer* (Melbourne University Press, 1994).

Noel-Smith, Heather and Lorna M. Campbell '"I shall be anxious to know": Lives of the *Indefatigable* Women', *Trafalgar Chronicle*, n.s., vol. 3 (2008), pp. 44–54.

O'Keefe, Eamonn, ' "A Natural Passion?" The 1810 Reflections of a Yorkshire Farmer on Homosexuality', *Historical Research*, vol. 94, no. 263 (February 2021), pp. 181–90.

Oman, Carola, *The Gascoyne Heiress: The Life and Diaries of Frances Mary Gascoyne-Cecil, 1802–39* (London, Hodder & Stoughton, 1968).

Orrok, John, *The Letters of Captain John Orrok*, ed. by Alison McBrayne (Leicester, Matador, 2008).

Ottaway, Susannah, 'The Old Woman's Home in Eighteenth-century England', in *Women and Ageing in British Society since 1500*, ed. by Lynn Botelho and Pat Thane (Harlow, Longman, 2001), pp. 111–38.

—— *The Decline of Life: Old Age in Eighteenth-century England* (Cambridge University Press, 2004).

Outhwaite, R.B., *Scandal in the Church: Dr Edward Drax Free, 1764–1843* (London and Rio Grande, The Hambledon Press, 1997).

Paget, Arthur, *The Paget Brothers, 1790–1840*, ed. by Lord Hylton (London, John Murray, 1918).

Parkinson, C. Northcote, *War in the Eastern Seas, 1793–1815* (London, George Allen & Unwin, 1954).

Parliamentary Debates, n.s., vol. 24, April–June 1830 (London, Hansard, 1830).

Parliamentary Debates, n.s., vol. 135, 1854 (London, Hansard, 1854).

Parry, Ann, *The Admirals Fremantle 1788–1920* (London, Chatto & Windus, 1971).

Paterson, James, *Kay's Edinburgh Portraits: A Series of Anecdotal Biographies Chiefly of Scotchmen*, 2 vols, ed. by James Maidment (London, Hamilton, Adams & Co., 1885).

Payne, Reider, *War and Diplomacy in the Napoleonic Era: Sir Charles Stewart, Castlereagh and the Balance of Power in Europe* (London, Bloomsbury Academic, 2019).

Phegley, Jennifer, *Courtship and Marriage in Victorian England* (Santa Barbara, Praeger, 2012).

Pietsch, Roland, *The Real Jim Hawkins: Ships' Boys in the Georgian Navy* (Barnsley, Seaforth, 2010).

Plomer, J., *Lord Paget's Letters and Trial in the Affair of Lady Charlotte Wellesley: in which is included the Eloquent Speech of Mr Dallas* (London, Purday & Son, 1809; reprinted in *The Making of Modern Law: Trials, 1600–1926*, Gale).

Porter, Agnes, *A Governess in the Age of Jane Austen: The Journals and Letters of Agnes Porter*, ed. by Joanna Martin (London and Rio Grande, The Hambledon Press, 1998).

Probert, Rebecca, *Marriage Law and Practice in the Long Eighteenth Century: A Reassessment* (Cambridge University Press, 2009).

Proceedings in the Court of Common Pleas, 5 Dec. 1803, as reported in *The Sporting Magazine or Monthly Calendar*, vol. 23 (Dec. 1803), pp. 125–7.

Pückler-Muskau, Prince, *A Regency Visitor: The English Tour of Prince Pückler-Muskau described in his letters, 1826–1828*, trans. by Sarah Austin, ed. and with introduction by E.M. Butler (London, Collins, 1957).

Reiter, Jacqueline, 'The Second Earl of Chatham's marriage settlement', Bromley Archives, 1080/3/1/1/26', blogpost dated 15 July 2013, https://thelatelord. com/2013/07/15/the-second-earl-of-chathams-marriage-settlement/

—— '"Likely to get frampy": In which the 2nd Lord Chatham has trouble getting his act together', blogpost dated 11 November 2014, https://thelatelord. com/2014/11/11/likely-to-get-frampy-in-which-the-2nd-lord-chatham-has-trouble-getting-his-act-together/, accessed 10 July 2019.

—— *The Late Lord: The Life of John Pitt, 2nd Earl of Chatham* (Barnsley, Pen & Sword History, 2017).

—— 'Invisibility and Disability in High Politics, 1783–1810: The Case of Mary Elizabeth Pitt, Countess of Chatham', unpublished conference paper for 'Passionate Politicians: Parliament, Print and Theatre in the Age of Sheridan and Austen' (15 March 2018).

—— '"A dirty Apothecary": The Elopement of Lady Lucy Stanhope and Thomas Taylor', blogpost dated 28 June 2019, https://thelatelord.com/tag/charles-3rd-earl-stanhope/

—— 'The Invisible Countess', *History Today*, vol. 68, no. 7 (July 2018), pp. 52–5.

Retford, Kate, *The Art of Domestic Life: Family Portraiture in Eighteenth-century England* (New Haven and London, Yale University Press for the Paul Mellon Centre, 2006).

Retter, Catharine and Shirley Sinclair, *Letters to Ann: The Love Story of Matthew Flinders and Ann Chappelle* (Sydney, Angus & Robertson, 1999).

Richardson, Ethel M., *Next Door Neighbours (at 9 and 10 Grafton Street, W.)* [includes extracts from Mrs Calvert's later diaries] (London, Hutchinson, n.d. [*c.* 1926]).

Rizzo, Betty, *Companions without Vows: Relationships among Eighteenth-century British Women* (Athens and London, University of Georgia Press, 1994).

Roberts, M.J.D., *Making English Morals: Voluntary Association and Moral Reform in England, 1787–1886* (Cambridge University Press, 2004).

Rodger, N.A.M., *The Wooden World: An Anatomy of the Georgian Navy* (London, Collins, 1986).

Rogers, Nicholas, 'Money, Marriage, Mobility: The Big Bourgeoisie of Hanoverian London', *Journal of Family History*, vol. 24, no. 1 (1999), pp. 19–34.

Rogers, Samuel, *Reminiscences and Table-talk of Samuel Rogers . . .*, ed. by G.H. Powell (London, Brimley Johnson, 1903).

Rothery, Mark and Henry French (eds), *Making Men: The Formation of Elite Male Identities in England, c.1660–1900. A Sourcebook* (Basingstoke, Palgrave Macmillan, 2012).

Sbaraini, Ella '"Those that Prefer the Ripe Mellow Fruit to Any Other": Rethinking Depictions of Middle-aged Women's Sexuality in England, 1700–1800', *Cultural and Social History*, vol. 12, no. 2 (2020), pp. 165–87.

Schutte, Kimberly, *Women, Rank and Marriage in the British Aristocracy, 1485–2000* (Basingstoke, Palgrave Macmillan, 2014).

Scott, Sir Walter, 'The Surgeon's Daughter', in *Chronicles of the Canongate*, first series (Oxford University Press, 1912; first published 1827).

—— *St Ronan's Well* (Oxford University Press, 1912).

—— *The Journal of Sir Walter Scott from the Original Manuscript at Abbotsford*, 2 vols (New York, Burt Franklin, 1970; first published 1890).

Severn, John, *Architects of Empire: The Duke of Wellington and His Brothers* (Norman, University of Oklahoma Press, 2007).

Shelley, Frances, *The Diary of Frances Lady Shelley, 1787–1873*, ed. by Richard Edgcumbe, 2 vols (New York, Charles Scribner's Sons, 1913).

Sherwood, Mary Martha, *The Life of Mrs Sherwood, chiefly autobiographical . . .*, ed. by her daughter Sophia Kelly (London, Darton and Co., 1857).

Smallwood, Amy Lynn, 'Shore Wives: The Lives of British Naval Officers' Wives and Widows, 1750–1815' (MA thesis, Wright State University, 2008).

Smith, E.A., *Whig Principles and Party Politics: Earl Fitzwilliam and the Whig Party* (Manchester University Press, 1975).

—— *Wellington and the Arbuthnots: A Triangular Friendship* (Stroud, Alan Sutton, 1994).

Soames, Mary, *The Profligate Duke: George Spencer-Churchill, fifth Duke of Marlborough and his Duchess* (London, Collins, 1987).

Somerville, E.O. and Martin Ross, *An Incorruptible Irishman . . . Chief Justice Charles Kendal Bushe and his wife Nancy Crampton . . . 1767–1843* (London, Ivor Nicholson & Watson, 1932).

Southam, Brian, *Jane Austen: The Critical Heritage* (London, Routledge & Kegan Paul, 1968).

—— *Jane Austen and the Navy* (Greenwich, National Maritime Museum, 2005).

Spencer, Sarah, *Correspondence of Sarah Spencer Lady Lyttelton 1787–1870*, ed. by Mrs Hugh Wyndham (London, John Murray, 1912).

Stanhope, Philip Henry, 5th Earl, *Notes of Conversations with the Duke of Wellington, 1831–1851* (London, John Murray, 1888).

Stanley, Rev. Edward, *Before and After Waterloo: The Letters of Edward Stanley*, ed. by Jane H. Adeane and Maud Grenfell (London, T. Fisher Unwin, 1907).

[Stanley, Maria J.], *The Girlhood of Maria Josepha Holroyd [Lady Stanley of Alderley] Recorded in letters of a Hundred Years Ago: From 1776 to 1796*, ed. by Jane H. Adeane (London, Longmans, Green & Co., 1897).

—— *The Early Married Life of Maria Josepha, Lady Stanley, with extracts from Sir John Stanley's 'Præterita'*, ed. by Jane H. Adeane (London, Longmans, Green & Co., 1900).

—— *The Ladies of Alderley being the Letters between Maria Josepha Lady Stanley of Alderley and her Daughter-in-Law Henrietta Maria Stanley during the Years 1841–1850*, ed. by Nancy Mitford (London, Hamish Hamilton, 1967).

Staves, Susan, *Married Women's Separate Property in England, 1660–1833* (Cambridge, MA, Harvard University Press, 1990).

—— 'Resentment or Resignation? Dividing the Spoils among Daughters and Younger Sons', in *Early Modern Conceptions of Property*, ed. by John Brewer and Susan Staves (London and New York, Routledge, 1995), pp. 194–218.

Steidele, Angela, *Gentleman Jack – A Biography of Anne Lister: Regency Landowner, Seducer & Secret Diarist* (London, Serpent's Tail, 2019).

Stevens, Joan, *Victorian Voices: An Introduction to the Papers of Sir John Le Couteur* (St Helier, La Société Jersiaise, 1969).

Stewart, Averil, *Family Tapestry* (London, John Murray, 1961).

Stirling, A.M.W., *The Letter-Bag of Lady Elizabeth Spencer-Stanhope compiled from the Cannon Hall Papers, 1806–1873*, 2 vols (London, John Lane, 1913).

Stone, Jeanne C. Fawtier, 'The Calvert Diaries', *Princeton University Library Chronicle*, vol. 47, no. 3 (Spring 1986), pp. 317–51.

Stone, Lawrence, *The Family, Sex and Marriage in England, 1500–1800* (London, Weidenfeld & Nicolson, 1979).

—— *Road to Divorce: England 1530–1987* (Oxford University Press, 1990).

—— *Broken Lives: Separation and Divorce in England 1660–1837* (Oxford University Press, 1993).

Stone, Lawrence and Jeanne C. Fawtier Stone, *An Open Elite? England, 1540–1880* (Oxford, Clarendon Press, 1984).

Stott, Anne, *Hannah More: The First Victorian* (Oxford University Press, 2003).

Stuart, Dorothy Margaret, *The Daughters of George III* (London, Macmillan, 1939).

Stuart Wortley: see Grosvenor.

Sweetman, John, *Raglan: From the Peninsula to the Crimea* (London, Arms and Armour, 1993).

Taylor, Stephen, *Commander: The Life and Exploits of Britain's Greatest Frigate Captain* [Sir Edward Pellew] (New York and London, W.W. Norton, 2012).

—— *Defiance: The Life and Choices of Lady Anne Barnard* (London, Faber & Faber, 2016).

Temperley, Harold, 'Joan Canning on Her Husband's Policy and Ideas', *English Historical Review*, vol. 45 (July 1930), pp. 409–26.

Thane, Anna M., 'Love against All Rules: The Scottish Nobleman and the Private Secretary', https://regency-explorer.net/love-against-all-rules/.

Thompson, F.M.L., *English Landed Society in the Nineteenth Century* (London, Routledge & Kegan Paul, 1963).

—— *Gentrification and the Enterprise Culture: Britain 1780–1980* (Oxford University Press, 2001).

Thompson, Paul, 'Peninsular War Letters of Lieutenant-General Sir William Henry Pringle, 1812, 1813, 1814', *Journal of the Society for Army Historical Research*, vol. 100, no. 400 (Spring 2022), pp. 32–49.

Thorne, R.G., *The History of Parliament: The Commons, 1790–1820*, 5 vols (Secker & Warburg for the History of Parliament Trust, 1986).

Thrale, Hester, *Thraliana: The Diary of Hester Lynch Thrale (Later Mrs Piozzi) 1776–1809*, ed. by Katharine C. Balderston, 2 vols (Oxford, Clarendon Press, 1942).

Tillyard, Stella, *Aristocrats: Caroline, Emily, Louisa and Sarah Lennox, 1740–1832* (London, Chatto & Windus, 1994).

Todd, Janet, 'Jane Austen and the Professional Wife', in *Repossessing the Romantic Past*, ed. by Heather Glen and Paul Hamilton (Cambridge University Press, 2006), pp. 203–25.

Tomalin, Claire, *Mrs Jordan's Profession* (London, Viking, 1994).

—— *Jane Austen: A Life* (London, Viking, 1997).

Tompkins, J.M.S., *The Popular Novel in England, 1770–1800* (London, Methuen, 1961, first published 1932).

Treitel, Prof. G.H., 'Legal Puzzles in Jane Austen's Works', *Jane Austen Society Report* (1986).

Trollope, Anthony, *Framley Parsonage* (London, Zodiac Press, n.d.; first published 1860).

Trumbach, Rudolf, 'Modern Sodomy: The Origins of Homosexuality, 1700–1800', in *A Gay History of Britain*, ed. by Matt Cook et al.

Tucker, George Holbert, *A Goodly Heritage: A History of Jane Austen's Family* (Manchester, Carcanet, 1983).

Twiss, Horace, *The Public and Private Life of Lord Chancellor Eldon*, 3 vols (London, John Murray, 1844).

Vickery, Amanda, *The Gentleman's Daughter: Women's Lives in Georgian England* (New Haven and London, Yale University Press, 1998).

—— *Behind Closed Doors: At Home in Georgian England* (New Haven and London, Yale University Press, 2009).

—— 'No Happy Ending? At Home with Miss Bates in Georgian England', *Persuasions*, no. 37 (2015), pp. 134–51.

Virgin, Peter, *Sydney Smith* (London, HarperCollins, 1994).

Viveash, Chris, 'Lady Morley and the "Baron so Bold"', *Persuasions*, no. 14 (1992), pp. 53–7.

Walpole, Horace, *The Yale Editions of Horace Walpole's Correspondence*, ed. by W.S. Lewis, vol. 38 (New Haven, Yale University Press, 1974).

Ward, J.W., *Letters to 'Ivy' from the first Earl of Dudley*, ed. by S.H. Romilly (London, Longmans, Green & Co., 1905).

Wareham, Tom, *Frigate Commander* [Graham Moore] (Barnsley, Pen & Sword Maritime, 2004).

—— *Frigate Commander – A Supplement* (privately published by the author, n.d.).

Wasson, Ellis Archer, *Whig Renaissance: Lord Althorp and the Whig Party 1782–1845* (New York and London, Garland, 1987).

Weeton, Nelly, *Miss Weeton's Journal of a Governess*, ed. by Edward Hall, 2 vols (Newton Abbot, David & Charles, 1969; first published 1936).

—— *Miss Weeton: Governess and Traveller*, ed. by Alan Roby (Wigan Archives, 2016).

Wellesley, Henry, *The Diary and Correspondence of Henry Wellesley, First Lord Cowley, 1790–1846*, ed F.A. Wellesley (London, Hutchinson, n.d. [1930]).

Wellington, Arthur, Duke of, *The Dispatches of Field Marshal the Duke of Wellington* ed. by John Gurwood, 8 vols (London, Parker, Furnivall and Parker, 1844).

Wheatley, Edmund, *The Wheatley Diary: A Journal and Sketch-book kept during the Peninsular War and the Waterloo Campaign*, ed. by Christopher Hibbert (London, Longmans, 1964).

White, A.S., 'A Subaltern in the Peninsular War: The letters of Lieutenant Robert Garrett, 1811–1813', *Journal of the Society for Army Historical Research*, vol. 13, no. 49 (Spring 1934), pp. 3–22.

Williamson, Gillian, *British Masculinity in the* Gentleman's Magazine, *1731 to 1815* (Basingstoke, Palgrave Macmillan, 2016).

Wilson, Deborah, *Women, Marriage and Property in Wealthy Landed Families in Ireland, 1750–1850* (Manchester University Press, 2008).

Wilson, Frances, *The Courtesan's Revenge: Harriette Wilson, the Woman who Blackmailed the King* (London, Faber & Faber, 2003).

Wilson, Harriette, *The Memoirs of Harriette Wilson, written by herself*, 2 vols (London, Eveleigh Nash, 1909).

Wilson, Joan, *A Soldier's Wife: Wellington's Marriage* (London, Weidenfeld & Nicolson, 1987).

Wilson, Margaret, 'What happened to "Mr J.P."?', *Jane Austen Society Collected Reports*, vol. 4, pp. 315–17.

—— *Almost Another Sister: The Story of Fanny Knight, Jane Austen's Favourite Niece* (Maidstone, George Mann Books, 1998).

Wolfram, Sybil, 'Divorce in England, 1700–1857', *Oxford Journal of Legal Studies*, vol. 5, no. 2 (1985), pp. 155–86.

Woodforde, James, *The Diary of a Country Parson: The Reverend James Woodforde 1758–1802*, ed. by John Beresford, 5 vols (London, Oxford University Press, 1924–31).

—— *Woodforde Papers and Diaries*, ed. by Dorothy Heighes Woodforde (London, Peter Davies, 1932).

Wynne, E. and E. Wynne, *The Wynne Diaries*, ed. by Anne Fremantle, 3 vols (Oxford University Press, 1935–40).

—— *The Wynne Diaries*, ed. by Anne Freemantle (one-volume edition of selections, but with an additional chapter of Thomas Fremantle's diary), introduction by Christopher Hibbert (Oxford University Press, 1982).

Ziegler, Philip, *Melbourne: A Biography of William Lamb, 2nd Viscount Melbourne* (London, Collins, 1976).

INDEX

INDEX